MITRE AND SCEPTRE

OTHER BOOKS BY CARL BRIDENBAUGH

CITIES IN THE WILDERNESS:
The First Century of Urban Life in America, 1625–1742

CITIES IN REVOLT:
Urban Life in America, 1743–1776

PETER HARRISON, FIRST AMERICAN ARCHITECT

THE COLONIAL CRAFTSMAN

SEAT OF EMPIRE:
The Political Role of Eighteenth-Century Williamsburg

MYTHS AND REALITIES:
Societies of the Colonial South

REBELS AND GENTLEMEN:
Philadelphia in the Age of Franklin (co-author)

GENTLEMAN'S PROGRESS:
Dr. Alexander Hamilton's Itinerarium, 1744 (edited, with an Introduction)

An Attempt to land a Bishop in America

MITRE AND SCEPTRE

Transatlantic Faiths, Ideas, Personalities, and Politics

1689-1775

CARL BRIDENBAUGH

NEW YORK *Oxford University Press* MCMLXII

TO

THE MEMORY OF

CHARLES H. BRIDENBAUGH

1870–1952

PRINTED IN THE UNITED STATES OF AMERICA

Preface

Sixty years ago, the late Arthur Lyon Cross published *The Anglican Episcopate and the American Colonies.* Based upon intensive research and distinguished for its cautious judgments, this study immediately became the standard authority on the subject. In *The Anglican Episcopate,* Professor Cross concerned himself with the history of an abortive institution and with a detailed analysis of the pamphlet literature for and against American bishops. His treatment was judicious and thorough, and I commend it to those readers who wish to read more on the topic than I offer in the pages that follow. *Mitre and Sceptre* is meant to supplement rather than to replace Mr. Cross's fine book and to deal with matters he did not investigate.

Certain developments in the discipline of history since 1902 explain why there is a need to re-examine all aspects of the episcopacy question. The application of the approaches of social and intellectual history to the history of institutions places the entire subject in a new and different light. In addition, the publication of the writings of Samuel Johnson, first president of King's College, and the availability at Yale of the significant manuscript correspondence of Ezra Stiles and William Livingston, together with the minutes of the Dissenting Deputies at Dr. Williams's Library in London, now enable us to describe the backstage maneuvers of individuals and organizations, which were unknown to Arthur Cross. Finally, our modern absorption with the role of public opinion leads us back to the eighteenth-century newspaper press that so profoundly influenced the whole controversy.

Every year the revolution in research eases the historian's labors by means of photostat, microfilm, Xerox, and half a dozen other kinds of reproductions of the materials he needs, distant though the originals may be. But none of the wonders of technology can ever replace the exhilarating freemasonry of international scholarship practiced by devoted librarians, archivists, and one's own colleagues. It has been my good fortune to be able to call upon a host of these scholars in England and the United States, and it is now my privilege to record my deep gratitude for their helpfulness and courtesy.

Through the good offices of my friend Dr. J. R. Pole of University College, London, I received every aid from Dr. Williams's Library, Gordon Square, London. The librarian, Roger Thomas, not only supplied me with reproductions of important manuscripts but gave my second chapter a highly critical reading which measurably improved its accuracy.

Successive research assistants when I was at the University of California helped me in numerous capacities, and I came to think of David Corkran, Dr. William Hanna, Martin Lodge, and Richard Simmons more as colleagues than as students. Also at Berkeley, Mrs. F. C. Uridge and her assistants of the Inter-Library Loan Department of the University Library procured for me many books that I needed. Through the kindness of Vice Chancellor James D. Hart, Dean Lincoln Constance, and President Clark Kerr, financial assistance for travel and materials was made available. Professor and Mrs. Bryce Lyon assisted me in many ways, and their offer of a loan for more than a year of an excellent microfilm reader was indeed a boon.

In the United States the librarians and custodians of records at the great universities and historical societies lightened my burdens, as always, and told me about items I would otherwise have missed. At Yale, Miss Marjorie Wynne steered me through the maze of the Stiles Papers, which are not as yet fully catalogued; my former students Frederick B. Goff and Jeannette D. Black of the Library of Congress and the John Carter Brown Library lavishly gave me their usual intelligent help; Miss E. Marie Becker of the New York Historical Society went out of her way, and on her own time, to send me much-needed data; while at the Massachusetts Historical Society, Dr. Malcolm Freiberg saved another scholar and me from unnecessary duplication of research.

For many kinds of assistance, always generously rendered, I also wish to thank Dr. Lester J. Cappon of Williamsburg, Professor Wesley F. Craven of Princeton, Wendell Garrett of Boston, Professor Brooke Hindle of New York, Dr. Guy S. Klett of Philadelphia, Professor Harold Kirker of Cambridge, Professor Lawrence H. Leder of Brandeis University, Dr. Robert McColley of Urbana, Professor Edmund S. Morgan of New Haven, Donald H. Mugridge of Washington, Dr. Edward M. Riley of Colonial Williamsburg, Inc., Stephen T. Riley of Boston, Professor Caroline Robbins of Bryn Mawr, Clifford K. Shipton of Shirley, Milton H. Thomas of Princeton, and Juliet Walchan of the New York State Library, Albany.

The impulse to complete this study came when Dr. John E. Pomfret invited me to assemble some of the material I had been casually collecting over a period of years in a paper which I read to a conference at the Henry E. Huntington Library in 1957. That it now appears as a full-length book is due to the immeasurable contribution of Roberta Herriott Bridenbaugh, who joined me in making the acquaintance of the intense and often eccentric worthies who people these pages.

Carl Bridenbaugh

The John Carter Brown Library
Providence
July 1962

Table of Contents

List of Illustrations

While a frightened bishop ascends the shrouds, praying with clasped hands: *Lord, now lettest thou thy Servant depart in peace,* two irate bully-boys push *The Hillsborough* away from a Boston quay with a boat hook. On deck beside a coach are its wheels, an episcopal crook, and mitre. Ashore a turbulent "mob" is assembling: one man flourishes a flag with a liberty cap and motto: *Liberty & Freedom of Conscience;* two others wave copies of *Locke* and *Sydney on Government;* a third throws *Calvin's Works* at the prelate; a sober Quaker holds a copy of *Barclay's Apology;* and a bystander shouts: *No Lords Spiritual or Temporal in New England.* In the foreground a monkey is about to throw a cap at the bishop. Near it lies a paper marked: *Shall they be obliged to maintain Bishops that cannot maintain themselves.* The engraving is taken from the *Political Register* (London: Volume V, September, 1769, facing p. 119), where it was meant to illustrate a severe review of Bishop Secker's letter to Horatio Walpole (1769). Courtesy of the John Carter Brown Library.

Photograph supplied by the kindness of Wendell Garrett, author of *Apthorp House, 1760–1960* (Cambridge, Mass., 1960).

Courtesy of the John Carter Brown Library.

Introduction

We live in an increasingly secular society. Religiosity in our day (if not actual church-going) declines apace; whereas our fore-fathers of the eighteenth century considered piety, religious observance, even theology, as part of their daily existence. Such a profound shift in the Anglo-American outlook upon the universe has inevitably affected the writing of history, for the most important as well as difficult problem confronting the historian is that of re-constructing a reasonably accurate image of what a given period of the past was like; the more modern we are, the more strenuously we must exercise our historical imaginations when we write. We ask very few questions of religion today, and they are seldom imagina-tive. This neglect is unfortunate because no understanding of the eighteenth century is possible if we unconsciously omit, or con-sciously jam out, the religious theme just because our own milieu is secular. The era of the Enlightenment was far more an Age of Faith (and Emotion) than an Age of Reason.

II

The purpose of this work is to discover what Englishmen and Americans thought about the relation of church to state, where they acquired their opinions, what they did with and about these ideas, and, finally, how their outlook and actions affected the long course of history. People, therefore, are our subject: people individually and in groups grappling with ecclesiastical problems in the course of everyday life, for in England's American colonies the most en-during and absorbing public question from 1689 to 1776 was re-ligion.

The eighteenth was the first century during which public opinion exerted a primary influence on the destinies of nations and peoples; and in the American colonies it attained even greater power than in the Mother Country. We must, therefore, look long and carefully at the Anglicans and Dissenters of that century, and make an effort to assess their state of mind and to recapture the sense of the immediacy and the great excitement that leap out at the reader from the foxed and faded letters, newspapers, pamphlets, and books dealing with the religious concerns of this earlier age. The atmosphere was highly charged with passions, historical grievances, suspicions, fears, bitternesses, hatreds. Alternately, the participants were hopeful or fearful, seldom apathetic. This we must grasp. If we can succeed in delineating human nature working at its highest and lowest levels, and often at many stages in between, we ought to approach much nearer to the truth than if we merely think of our task as the sterile one of striking some kind of an Olympian balance among the issues or between the parties. If we know how people felt, we ought to be better able to understand why they acted as they did. In any event, we should concern ourselves more with what happened than with what we may conceive was right; in a revolutionary situation it is fruitless to emphasize legality.

The perspective gained from taking the long view is one of the primary values of history. It is a grave mistake to look for the roots of the religious causes of the American Revolution no farther back than 1763, or 1755, for it is clear that they extend well beyond 1700 into the previous century. The year 1689 will serve as a good starting point for our survey of the problem of church and state in the first British Empire. Only thus can one properly envisage the cumulative effect on the unconscious cerebration of several generations of Englishmen and colonials of the great debate over mitre and sceptre in the pulpit and the press.

Power and *place* were the stakes for which Episcopalians contended throughout this ecclesiastical struggle. They fought for them in two grand theaters: in Europe (Tiny Old England chiefly) and in Vast New America. The drama was a transatlantic one with several acts and many scenes. It poses a difficult literary problem of organization, which, even if not wholly solved, does place the actors before the backdrop of International Protestantism where their contemporaries recognized that they belonged. Thus, we hope to have escaped most of the perils of retrospective nationalism.

This contest was, in truth, far more than the customary religious strife; it was a *Kulturkampf* between the dissenting bodies — already well entrenched in New England, everywhere in the colonies numerically superior, fortunate in the possession of a strong, usable tradition — and the Church of England — few in numbers, new, aspiring, and contriving. The Anglicans aimed at nothing less than the complete reordering of American Society. Looking down upon the Nonconformists as mere republican boors, the Anglicans, in turn, were called High-Church men and Jacobites. The Anglicans had, of course, good and sufficient reasons for wanting to complete Episcopal organization in the colonies; on the other side, the Dissenters acted chiefly from fear, fear of eventually losing the religious liberties their forefathers had won for them.

The contest over an American episcopate went on for decades, calling forth men's best and their worst; and the prediction that the arrival of bishops would mean violence was made seriously. The Anglicans had managed their campaigns badly and suffered from the curse of Puritan history; John Adams could never overlook their "sacerdotal impudence." No amount of clerical double talk ever disabused the Dissenters of their suspicions of the motives of the Churchmen. Men of the cloth on both sides resorted to base and un-Christian conduct for good ends: intrigue, misrepresentation, outright lying, character assassination. One reads, in the sources of this seemingly endless debate, very little about the work of the Lord but much about the operation of human nature in divines and laymen alike. Above all, one glimpses clearly the force of personalities in the shaping of events, of men doing as well as thinking.

As we shuttle back and forth across the Atlantic, we should realize that we are tracing the marshaling of these two contenders and their clashes in a great struggle for power which ceased only with American independence. For eighty-five years church and state was the greatest and most familiar issue before the colonial public. Religion had always been very real, immediate, and dear to the colonists. Their very clamor, if we may tamper with Edmund Burke's fine phrase, reflected the dissonance of dissent. The truth of this is not lost upon us if we approach this era by coming up to it from the deeply pious seventeenth century, rather than by glancing backward from the impious twentieth. Viewed thus, we shall see that the essential ingredient of the nascent American sense of nationality was, for better or worse as time would tell, the belief in an American version of religious liberty, one which bore fruit in the first series of state constitutions of 1776 to 1783. And we shall also see that the epoch-making mental change that we call the American Revolution occurred in a religious atmosphere. It is indeed high time that we repossess the important historical truth that religion was a fundamental cause of the American Revolution.[1]

1. After this volume was completed, Douglass Adair and John A. Schutz brought out the first edition of Peter Oliver's *Origin & Progress of the American Rebellion* (San Marino, Calif., 1961). This highly important Tory history had lain in manuscript since it was written in 1781! In a communication of 1 October 1961, Mr. Adair drew my attention to the startling parallels between Judge Oliver's account of the Revolution in Massachusetts and that of John Adams as set forth in his celebrated letters to Jedidiah Morse, William Tudor, and Benjamin Rush. Both writers date its beginning from 1761, both introduce the same cast of characters, both choose the same catalogue of events, which they view as crucial features of the growing crisis, and both look upon the arousing of "Mr. *Otis's* black Regiment, the *dissenting* Clergy," [pp. 41–45] as the key to the great agitator's conquest of public opinion. Though one cannot get from Oliver *why* it was so easy to recruit the Congregational ministers for the opposition to Governors Bernard and Hutchinson, or any real understanding of the motives of the two sides, this agreement about the role of the preachers in the American Revolution by two diametrically opposed participants stands in striking contrast to the tendency of modern historians to omit any consideration of the significance of religion at all.

PART ONE

ECCLESIASTICAL IMPERIALISM, 1689–1760

I

The Christian Union

*The right of conscience and private judgment is unalienable; and it is
truly the interest of all mankind to unite themselves into one body, for
the liberty, free exercise, and unmolested enjoyment of this right, especially in religion. . . . God be thanked we are not embarrassed
with subscriptions and oaths to uninspired rules for defining truth, in
this land of liberty, where the* SCRIPTURES *are professedly our only*
RULE. . . . *And being possessed of the precious jewel of religious
liberty, a jewel of inestimable worth, let us prize it highly, and esteem
it too dear to be parted with on any terms; lest we be again entangled
with that yoke of bondage which our fathers could not, would not, and
God grant we may never submit to bear. . . . You are very sensible
that there is a formal attempt on the chastity and order of our churches,
which is vigilantly to be guarded against, at present, till our churches
grow into one . . . large, pure, defensible body. . . . Our cause is
one, and a cause not in decline, not in disrepute, but in honor and a
most flourishing prosperity. Let us be cemented together by forebearance,
fellowship, union. . . . Let the grand errand into America never be
forgotten.*[1]

A mere handful of ministers in an obscure Rhode Island village
heard these stirring words, which were published over a year later
in September, 1761, at Boston for a larger audience by the famous
"patriot printers," Edes and Gill, under the title: *A Discourse on
the Christian Union: The Substance of which was delivered Before
the Reverend Convention of the Congregational Clergy in the Colony of Rhode-Island; Assembled at Bristol, April 23, 1760. By Ezra*

1. Ezra Stiles, *A Discourse on the Christian Union* (Boston, 1761), 28, 30, 96,
102, 126.

Stiles, A. M. Pastor of the Second Congregational Church in New-port.[2]

That eighteenth-century Bostonians could ever bring themselves to concede that any religious good might come out of Rhode Island may seem astonishing, but such was the case nevertheless. The Reverend Charles Chauncy, looking after the details of publication, gave the work to Edes and Gill rather than to Richard Draper, the provincial printer, because the former agreed to print three hundred copies "on good paper" for the author at seventy-five dollars instead of eighty, and to deliver them within three months. Dr. Chauncy read and corrected the proofs with care and made plans to send "the supernumerary 200 ones" to Connecticut, "for I know of no other work that is, in my opinion, so well adapted to serve that Colony in its proper circumstances. . . ." He expressed great enthusiasm for the *Christian Union* in a letter to the young author: "I doubt not, this your first, publication will be of great service to the Churches, as it reflects honor on you, and will propagate thro the Country that good reputation, you have justly merited."[3]

The reception accorded Stiles's piece surpassed all expectations. In October, 1761, Dr. Chauncy was reporting to Newport that no copies had gone off to Connecticut, because "the Printers have so good a sale of you here." In the following March, the Reverend Francis Alison, Vice Provost of the College of Philadelphia, wrote: "I am exceedingly pleased with your ingenious performance relating to the New English churches; it shews great Industry, great candor and good Judgment, and has been greatly admired by some of the best Judges of such matters in this place; two copies I sent home to Ireland to give some importance to my own Correspondence. . . ." Four years later the author noted, "I was at Boston when Edes and Gill told me they printed between Seven and Eight Hundred Copies of my Sermon, sold them and had none left — and said they made more by it than was ever made in Boston by one

2. Edes and Gill allowed one-third of a column for the advertisement of the *Christian Union* in their *Boston Gazette,* Sept. 7, 14, 1761.

3. Chauncy to Stiles, June 15, July 21, Aug. 3, 1761, Ezra Stiles Papers (Yale University Library). This very important collection is only partly arranged at present; therefore I cite the letters by date only; Franklin B. Dexter, ed., *Extracts from the Itineraries and other Miscellanies of Ezra Stiles, D.D., L.L.D., 1754–1794* (New Haven, 1916), 439-40.

Sermon, and would readily now print an Edition if any body would engage 200 Copies." [4]

What was the purpose of Stiles's sermon? What did he have to say in this best-selling discourse consisting of one hundred twenty-eight pages of text and eleven of appendix? What was there about the *Christian Union* that caused a transatlantic ecclesiastical sensation? What was all the excitement about, anyway?

II

Ezra Stiles took for his text Philippians III, 16: "Nevertheless, whereto we have already attained, let us walk by the same Rule, let us mind the same Thing." Employing the rigidly logical sermon structure devised by the great Puritan preachers of the seventeenth century and so familiar to New England listeners and readers, he opened his discourse with "the necessary illustration of the text," in which he pictured the chaotic situation prevailing among the early Christian churches and St. Paul's recommended principle of union. Then the minister proceeded to what he had principally in view, "the application of it to us, my brethren, of the *congregational* denomination, as well in New-England in general, as the particular district of this colony." [5]

The Congregational churches of New England had just passed through two decades of revivalism and shattering ecclesiastical strife. Congregations had split into "Old Lights" and "New Lights"; the latter often tended to affiliate with either the aggressive Church of England or with the evangelical Baptists. By 1760 the fever of the Great Awakening had run its course; tempers also had subsided. General Wolfe's decisive victory at Quebec the previous year had forecast the end of the greatest of the colonial wars. To the Newport minister, ecclesiastical quite as much as civil peace seemed the order of the day, and he, a tolerant, moderate, and patriotic Old Light, would proffer the olive branch.

He argued with great tact that among Congregationalists of all opinions there existed a wide area of agreement on the fundamen-

4. Chauncy to Stiles, Oct. 6, 1761; Francis Alison to Stiles, June 2, 1761, Mar. 24, 1762, Stiles Papers; Stiles, *Itineraries*, 440n.

5. *Christian Union*, 3–8.

tals of Christianity and church polity, a common ground which they also shared with Protestant churches throughout the world: Protestants exhibit a striking consensus about the "being and character of God," universal depravity, the doctrine of the atonement, the operations of the Holy Spirit, that "he that believes shall be saved," the need to recommend a life of practical religion, the efficacy of prayer, the resurrection of the dead, baptism, the Lord's Supper, and, perhaps most important, the inspiration of the Scriptures.[6]

Where church and society meet, the Reverend Mr. Stiles pointedly remarked, we Congregationalists are of one mind in our opposition to powerful church councils and official interpretations of religion. No person, no civil or ecclesiastical authority, may interfere with the right of private judgment in matters religious, which is a natural right. All mankind must unite to defend this natural right, which the individual never yielded in the civil compact. "Not all the difference of sentiment, not all erroneous opinions that have yet been started, afford just umbrage for its extinction, abridgement or embarrassment." Man-made tests and definitions of heresy are absolutely unacceptable to all of us. Proof of this may be found in the failure of the article of consensus at Geneva. "All that can be advanced for public human tests among protestants, can be and has been advanced with equal force for those of the romanists; for it is not so much the real truth or error contained in these texts and formularies that is contested, as the authority by which they were imposed, which is only human, and therefore not obligatory on conscience." [7]

Anglicans, Baptists, and Presbyterians can agree with us Congregationalists on all of these points, Mr. Stiles sturdily maintained. They can accept also the sufficiency and validity of presbyterian ordination of ministers: the Apostles practiced it and so did the primitive Christians. In justice to the Episcopalians, he conceded quickly and candidly that the distinction between presbyters and bishops began early in the Christian church. Episcopacy is antique, to be sure, but there is no scriptural warrant for it. At the time of

6. Stiles followed Jonathan Edwards on original sin, and in his psychology accepted the idea of the *tabula rasa* mind of "the great Mr. Locke." *Christian Union*, 9, 11, 12, 14–28.

7. *Christian Union*, 28, 29, 30.

the Reformation, presbyterianism would have prevailed in England, "but for the *dignities* and *revenue*." The truth is, that "pure and uncorrupted antiquity is on the side of ordination by co-equal presbyters." Stiles supported this assertion by a careful exposition of the practices in the Protestant churches of Scotland, the North of Ireland, Holland, Germany, Switzerland — and even the method of ordination of Lutheran superintendents in Germany, Denmark, and Sweden. He thought that, exclusive of the Lutherans, twice as many Protestants employed presbyterian ordination as used the episcopal: "tho' strictly speaking, the whole protestant world except the Church of England, agree in the validity of presbyterian ordination." And yet, though the decision by numbers be overwhelmingly on our side, Scripture alone should determine the truth — as it does.[8]

Departing from his argument for union at this point, Mr. Stiles takes the opportunity to score heavily against the Church of England. He would not for a moment interfere with any "protestant sect"; all he is attempting by this recital of history is to teach the rising generation in New England the principles of conduct and self-defense. "We desire to live in peace and harmony with all — nor do we attempt to proselite from any communion. We desire only equal protestant liberty. And even our episcopal brethren must confess that we treat them with much greater lenity, charity, and christian benevolence than they treat our congregational brethren in England. And in general the declamations on the superior excellency and purity of the church established in south Britain, necessitates us to adduce the equal excellency and purity of that established in north Britain, with which we have the happiness so nearly to agree. And as the parliamentary establishments of neither of these extend to the british American provinces, so every sect have a right to vindicate their peculiar forms." [9]

Turning to the pressing topic of church polity, Mr. Stiles raised his sights far beyond New England, and even the British Isles, to include International Protestantism, much in the same fashion that he had earlier in the *Discourse* appealed from English law to the

8. *Christian Union*, 30, 34, 36.

9. *Christian Union*, 36–7.

law of nature. "Churches can then alone be said to be *perfectly free,* when each congregation has an *unlimited, absolute,* and *self-determining* power in the choice of their officers: — such as british freemen enjoy and exercise uncontroulably in the choice of a representative or member of assembly." The congregational form of polity is the safest form of guarantee of "this fundamental principle of *universal liberty,*" because by it every church enjoys the sole power of regulating its own affairs. Appealing to tradition, the preacher reminded his audience that "Our fathers would not suffer a sister church, or body of sister churches, to lord it over one another, or hold a negative upon one another's elections and pastoral investitures." Though himself an Old Light and strongly averse to all forms of religious enthusiasm, Stiles here declared himself to be against certain ecclesiastical laws of Connecticut claimed by "heretical" seceding New-Light groups to stand in the way of self-determination.[10]

Members of other faiths, Stiles continued, are admitted to communion with the Congregationalists, who desire to hold Christian fellowship not with New Englanders alone but with the reforming churches of Scotland, Ireland, Holland, and the other parts of Europe. Ministerial conventions, such as the one to which he was preaching, met annually at Boston; their role was "advisory only," they had no power at all, nor did the consociations of ministers in Connecticut. Concluding this subject, he pointed out the significant fact that since the revival of learning among the laity, the reading of the vernacular translations of the Scriptures had rendered "common christians good judges of pastoral qualifications," with the consequence that New Englanders insist upon a pious and learned ministry. He proudly declared his colleagues to be as well adapted to elucidate piety and virtue "as any body of pastors in the protestant world." [11]

III

From this discussion of the elements of doctrine and polity, about which there was very general agreement in the churches, Ezra

10. *Christian Union,* 37, 43.

11. *Christian Union,* 43, 44, 48–50.

Stiles moved on to some things on which there were some real or supposed differences of opinions: these do not need to obstruct the general harmony recommended by St. Paul; they may be lessened by mutually honorable concessions. Without question a principal source of friction is the "unhappy excesses" that have occurred since the Great Awakening of 1740. "In the public mistaken zeal, religion was made to consist in extravagancies and indecencies, which were not according to the faith once delivered. Multitudes were seriously, soberly and solemnly out of their wits. . . . Sober reason gave way to enthusiasm. . . . Besides this, the standing ministry were aspersed, and represented under abusive suspicions of being unconverted, legalists, arminians. And they were thus publicly and indecently vilified, so it was taught as a duty to forsake their ministrations, and form into separate assemblies." Now, in 1760, the churches have in some measure cooled off, though traces of enthusiasm linger on and take new forms. Nevertheless, one hundred and fifty new Congregational churches, not founded upon separation, have been established because of the natural increase of population during the past two decades of religious confusion and uproar. Time is on the side of union.[12]

Almost too blithely, it seems, the minister minimized the serious theological issues separating strict Calvinists from Arminians. "Some perhaps entertain sentiments really different in these important subjects. Their conviction however is not to be laboured by the coercion of civil or ecclesiastical punishment [as in Connecticut and Massachusetts], but by the gentle force of persuasion and truth — not by appeals to the tenets of parties and great men; not by an appeal to the positions of Arminians or Calvin; but by an appeal to the inspired writings." The *Bible* will guide us all.[13]

More formidable by far are the existing differences over the nature of ecclesiastical councils and the authority and powers of particular churches. Here Stiles displays his vast critical knowledge of church history as he analyzes at length the development of the early churches of New England in proving "what is well known," that the first ministers and churches were partly presbyterian, partly congregational, both independent. In his view, the whole religious

12. *Christian Union,* 50.

13. *Christian Union,* 51–4.

establishment of New England was congregational, except in Rhode
Island, where the law provided for "universal protestant liberty, but
without annexing parochial privileges to any sect." This meant that
councils or consociations could have no authority over individual
churches: "As to what authority *any* councils have *jure divino,*
or by *divine right,* I shall not enlarge upon in *this age of liberty
and Light.* . . . Coercive uniformity is neither necessary in politics
nor religion." [14]

IV

Ezra Stiles showed himself to be an American *philosophe* and the
prophet of religious manifest destiny in his third and most exciting set of arguments for Congregational union. Let him speak
for himself:

Providence has planted the british America with a variety of sects,
which will unavoidably become a mutual balance upon one another.
Their temporary collisions, like the action of acids and alcalies after
a short ebullition, will subside in harmony and union, not by the destruction of either, but in the friendly cohabitation of all. An antecedent
fermentation may take place, as it has done in the philosophic world,
but generous inquiry and liberal disquisition will issue all in this. Re-
splendent and all-pervading TRUTH will terminate the whole in universal harmony. All surreptitious efforts and attempts on the public
liberty will unavoidably excite the public vigilance of the sects, till the
terms of general union be defined and honorably adjusted. The notion
of erecting the polity of either sect into universal dominion to the
destruction of the rest, is but an airy vision — may serve to influence a
temporary enthusiasm — but can never succede — all the present sects
will subsist and increase into distinct respectable bodies, continuing
their distinctions for a long time yet to come in full life and vigor. Indeed mutual oppression will more and more subside from their mutual
balance of one another. Union may subsist on these distinctions,
coalescence only on the sameness of public sentiment, which can again
be effected in the Christian world only by the gentle, but almighty
power of truth. It has been effected in past ages, but can never be effected again on the former measures — so great an alteration is made

14. *Christian Union,* 48 (italics mine), 57, 83, 85, 92, 95.

among mankind by science and letters. The sects cannot destroy one another, all attempts this way will be fruitless. . . . Nothing however will content us but actual experiment — this experiment will be made in one century, and then perhaps we shall be satisfied.[15]

To determine accurately which denomination is most favorable to religious liberty, Stiles offers a detailed survey of the religious establishments in the continental colonies. In Pennsylvania, the Jersies, and Rhode Island, there are no Dissenters; all faiths enjoy the same common immunities. "But the happy policy of establishing one sect without infringing on the essential rights of others is peculiar to the three New England provinces, where *congregationalism* is the establishment," and in Massachusetts and Connecticut, "it is said to be confirmed by the royal assent." [16]

Where denominations are equally established, "there is properly no toleration, all partaking in the benefit of the establishment." The New England arrangement calls for taxing all inhabitants for the support of religion, but exempting members of all other bodies from contributing to the Congregational ministers. The Episcopalians pay taxes, but they all go to the support of their own clergy. With evident relish, Stiles emphasized that in Virginia and Maryland the Anglicans did not confer such a privilege on the numerous Presbyterians there. Congregationalism was as friendly — "I will not say more so" — to the public liberty, religious and civil, as any other sect; and it did not in the least interfere with the liberty and essential rights of members of other faiths. Moreover, he insisted: "Our peculiar forms do not prevent *our distinguished loyalty,* for we may boldly say his majesty has not a body of more loyal and well affected subjects in his dominions." [17]

The *Discourse* reveals that its author was an early proponent of religious voluntarism. Support of the ministers of any sect, including his own, from provincial taxes was distasteful to Ezra Stiles, but he justified the Congregational establishments of New Hampshire, Massachusetts, and Connecticut largely on the grounds

15. *Christian Union,* 97–8.

16. *Christian Union,* 99.

17. *Christian Union,* 98, 100; and for the religious establishments of each colony, 98–9.

of their results. Instruction in Christianity and the public observance of religion, he believed, were performed as well there as anywhere in the world. Likewise, the practice and knowledge of Christian precepts were unequaled outside of New England. With particular pride he stressed the fact that "the numerous body of our denomination may be justly distinguished for the popular acquaintance with the sacred writings, and knowledge both of the histories and great doctrines of revelation." This being the case, the brethren must realize that the only certain defense of "the chastity and order of our churches" against the attacks of the Anglican missionaries, of which we are all so acutely aware, is union now! [18]

Great confidence in the future came to the preacher as he contemplated the flourishing state of the five hundred and thirty existing Congregational churches. And by extension, this faith applied to all British America. Using carefully made calculations, he demonstrated that the number of organized churches in New England had doubled every thirty years since the Great Migration of the 1630's, almost keeping pace with the natural increase of colonial population, which, according to his friend Dr. Benjamin Franklin, doubled every twenty-five years. Estimating the population of New England to be half a million in 1760, he projected population and sectarian increases for the next century:

A.D.	EPISCOPALIANS	FRIENDS	BAPTISTS	CONGREGATIONALISTS
1760	12,600	16,000	22,000	440,000
1785	23,200	32,000	44,000	880,000
1810	46,400	64,000	88,000	1,760,000
1835	92,800	128,000	176,000	3,520,000
1860	185,600	256,000	352,000	7 MILLIONS

Time and the birth rate would work for the Congregationalists without any future accessions of immigrants from Europe.[19]

18. *Christian Union*, 98, 101.

19. Concerning Stiles's population estimates, the Reverend Francis Alison wrote in July, 1761: "I am perfectly of your Opinion with respect to the Increase of the Inhabitants of our Colonies, and I doubt not but the Number of Presbyterians and Congregationalists (which I also look on as the same) will be as great in another Centurie in America as in all the British Dominions beside. . . ." It is worth noting that Stiles inclined to think that the colonial population doubled every

In the light of such predictions, the future obligation of the Congregationalists is to diffuse a love of liberty among the anticipated inhabitants with zeal and caution. To do this, the minister warns, we must not merely walk in harmony with each other, but we must teach our children to pursue and cherish the great treasure of religious liberty. It is particularly vital to inculcate in those who leave the already settled communities to found new towns in the upper Connecticut River valley and the hill country of northern New England the necessity of founding new churches promptly and of calling learned ministers to them. Such a future expansion as he contemplated would provide unprecedented encouragement to New England schools and colleges, whose goal would be to supply a trained ministry. Himself a modest speculator in undeveloped lands, Ezra Stiles knew well the formula for promoting westward expansion that would become the American standard: "Free and absolute tenure of *land* and unburdened property," as well as *"liberty in religion."* [20]

Above all, every effort must be made to endear the memory of the worthy and venerable founders of New England in the minds of those to come. "We should often relate to our posterity the history of the wonderful providences of God in the settlement of this country; and remark the growth of our churches, and engage them by all the honorable motives of christianity to steadfastness in the faith once delivered to the saints, and in the liberty wherewith the Gospel made us free. . . . Let the grand errand into America never be forgotten." History — myth — as always, was to serve the cause of religion.[21]

In the "wise and happy junction" of the Old-Side Synod of Philadelphia with the New-Side Synod of New York in 1758, whose object was to form one body of more than one hundred

---

twenty as compared with Franklin's every twenty-five years. Alison to Stiles, July 10, 1761; Stiles to Alison, Aug. 16, 1761, Stiles Papers; *Christian Union*, 102–9, 112–13, 114 (population table), 117n, 121n; Benjamin Franklin, "Observations Concerning the Increase of Mankind and Peopling of Countries" (written 1751, published 1755), in Jared Sparks, *The Works of Benjamin Franklin* (Boston, 1836), II, 319.

20. *Christian Union*, 114–15, 116, 121n.

21. *Christian Union*, 116.

Presbyterian pastors and their churches in the Middle Colonies, Maryland, and Virginia, the minister found an additional and potent incentive to union. Besides, the two denominations, Presbyterian and Congregationalist, had much in common. Stiles also felt that the Congregational churches should co-operate with such sister bodies as the Dutch Reformed and the French Protestants.[22]

Finally, Stiles capped his discourse with what most clergymen of the time would have considered the canonical reason. Union will enable a great number of present New Englanders and untold numbers to come to live the Christian life: "How good and pleasant it is for brethren to dwell together in unity." Appended to the sermon when it was printed were ten pages listing the churches of New England in 1760: Congregational, Baptist, Episcopal, and the meetings of the Society of Friends, with the names of their ministers. The total for the Congregational churches, including Presbyterians, was Massachusetts 306, Connecticut 170, New Hampshire 43, Rhode Island 11; in all, 530. Allowing for fifteen churches without ministers, or otherwise not meeting, he pointed out that there had been an increase of 108 over the 407 churches listed by Dr. William Douglass in 1749 — or 19 per cent.[23]

v

By almost any criterion — choice of subject, content, forcefulness of argument, mood, literary style, effectiveness of appeal — the *Christian Union* was one of the most remarkable sermons ever preached in colonial America. It is notable not so much for its originality — and it had some — as for its enunciation of certain new and revolutionary ideas which were about to become part of the conscious thinking of many leading New Englanders and colonials in general, lay as well as ecclesiastical. Ezra Stiles was an

22. *Christian Union*, 117n, 118n.

23. William Allen, Chief Justice of Pennsylvania and leading Presbyterian layman of the colonies, told the Reverend Jonathan Mayhew of Boston that "I perused, with pleasure, Mr. Stiles's Discourse . . . his account of the state and number of the congregational churches, truly surprises me, as it much exceeds my expectations." Mayhew Papers (Boston University), Apr. 2, 1761, No. 66; *Christian Union*, 124, Appendix, 129–39.

exegete and a synthesizer rather than an innovator. His *Discourse* dealt not with theology or piety but with currently debated, practical, and pressing questions of ecclesiastical power in which both religious and political, or secular, considerations were involved.

The author of the *Christian Union* could not have had better credentials. A graduate of Yale College in the class of 1744, holder of an honorary master's degree from Harvard (1754), a member of the New Haven bar, and the librarian of the famous Redwood Library of Newport, Ezra Stiles had every attribute of the learned man. His great scholarship stemmed from the mastery of many languages, omnivorous reading, an insatiable curiosity, and a catholicity of mind. Besides possessing an eminently moderate and urbane manner, Stiles lived in Newport, a stronghold of Anglicans and Quakers which had escaped the disruption and animosities of the Great Awakening. If he was a well-poised closet-thinker and expositor, one who avoided overt controversy, rather than a man of action and public achievement, this was all the better for his present role as peacemaker.

From at least three points of view the *Christian Union* warrants careful examination. Its immediate object was the solving of a specific ecclesiastical problem of provincial concern by the union, or reunion, of all Congregational churches in New England. For this purpose Stiles stressed the superiority of Congregational polity for the maintenance of the natural right of private judgment in things religious. Self-defense, if nothing else, he insisted, dictated immediate union. Secondly, he came out for the correctness and sufficiency of presbyterian ordination of ministers, and ranged himself unequivocally on the side of his fellow ministers of Connecticut, Noah Hobart and Noah Welles, in a spirited vindication of the institution against Episcopal attacks in Old and New England.

The most startling aspect developed by this divine was the shifting from the local scene to a far broader view. His acute awareness of the discouraging situation of the English Nonconformists contributed decisively to the vigor of his argument. He not only proposed that all Congregational churches in New England take prompt steps toward union; he also would associate his churches not only with the Presbyterian and Baptist bodies of the Middle and Southern Colonies, and the National Church of Scotland and the three dissenting denominations of the British Isles, but, in addition, with *all* the Protestant churches of Europe. One great universal federation of Protestant churches formed to protect religious liberty is what Stiles hoped for in the *Christian Union;* he stood for religious cosmopolitanism, not a narrow nationalism.

In his proposals for such an eventual unity, Ezra Stiles invoked the law of nature, and indeed the Enlightenment filters through every page of the *Discourse.* For, Stiles was an American *philosophe.* He illustrates, better than almost any man of his time, the way in which an alert intellectual in New England could absorb and acclimate much of the best of European thought. Such a phenomenon was a tribute to the excellence of transatlantic communication, even in that age, which kept most of New England and all of the colonial cities in the midstream rather than in the backwaters of the eighteenth century. The output of the London press, the library at Yale College with its catholic collections, and a steady exchange of correspondence with the most liberal of the English dissenting divines made this possible for those with a taste for letters and science.

Faith in the power of Reason suffuses the *Christian Union.* Its author never doubts that the use of right reason will heal the breaches in the churches and enable all New England to preserve church independence and the right of individual judgment. He makes extensive use of what might be called the raw materials of Reason when he levies on historical scholarship for evidence about the ecclesiastical struggle from 1690 to 1760, and even more so when he introduces demographic statistics into his discussion. The passion for gathering statistics and making calculations from them to apply to social problems is one of the most characteristic innovations of the *philosophes,* and no single person in colonial America so immersed himself in this novel delight as the Reverend Mr. Stiles. "Political arithmetic" enabled men to be more honest, precise, and accurate in their use of right reason.

Constitutionally of an optimistic nature, Stiles readily fell in with the new belief in progress. Americans looking at their surroundings and thinking of the rapid growth of the colonies, found material progress a proven fact — visually and statistically demonstrable. Yet, from a minister trained in Calvinism, no matter how much it was watered-down by Arminianism, progress did not require a complete rejection of original sin and total acceptance of the perfectibility of the human species. But a qualified belief in progress and a deep commitment to the value of the experimentalism of natural philosophy enabled the Newporter to dream of a Heavenly Country on the American continent with New England as its center.

This dream of a place where religious and civil liberties would be forever secure is validated by the natural rights philosophy expounded by John Locke and was widely understood by all Congregational pastors. With a ministerial experimentalism inherited from the Puritan past, Ezra Stiles does not hesitate to attempt to formulate, if we may so put it, an ecclesiastical science.

Virtually every device familiar to enlightened writers of the eighteenth century can be detected in this sermon. But above all, it is the author's prose style — lucid, clear, exact — that makes it such a successful vehicle for propagating his schemes. The vocabulary is simple, the phrasing pungent, and current clichés such as "unalienable right," "this land of liberty," "liberty of conscience," are inserted with psychological certainty at just the right places for true effectiveness. Everything that Stiles has to say, even in the examination of his Biblical text, he sets forth interestingly; he holds his audience's attention to the last sentence. His entire piece is reasonable, conciliatory to those of opposite views, and persuasive. Here indeed was a man of liberal cast.

Though he placed his arguments for Congregational and Protestant union, for religious and civil liberty, in the context of the Protestantism of the entire Western world, the experiences of his own life and times impelled him to give them a colonial — an American — complexion. This American note rings as clearly in the clergyman as in his friend B. Franklin, printer. He saw that religion could contribute mightily to the growth of a healthy New England provincial pride. "You are a secure people, you Yankees, and can sense your strength," he seems to be telling them. "Look upon your religious and civic accomplishments for the last century or more! They are good!"

As one of the first colonials to glimpse the importance of the West, Stiles provided a dimension to the concept of the "manifest destiny" of the American people — a contribution to be made by organized religion to the happiness and welfare of the "millions of inhabitants" who would fill the West during the next hundred years. He borrowed and refined Franklin's demographic formula and considerably elaborated the discussion of the inexorable drive of the colonists for living space in the new provinces won from France, a drive which he foresaw would take them under their charter claims all the way to the Pacific. (California was admitted as a state in 1850.)

His was a tremendously dynamic concept of America's future. It was an agricultural ideal of free land and voluntary religion for farmers, not concentrated settlements of artisans. It was an ideal born of American conditions and needs, not derived from the books of the physiocrats, from which it differs appreciably. It offered a solution suited to the limitless expanses of the New World. Over here would be observable progress — progress achieved under Divine Providence by the efforts of Yankees who feared God but always kept their powder dry.

VI

Thus did the American *philosophe* present his summary of the ecclesiastical history of New England from 1630 to 1760, during which time the Dissenters had evolved their theories of loyalty in diversity and of freedom from civil control. He had written a systematic account of American theory and progress toward religious freedom for the colonists of 1760 and coupled it with a demand for further advance; it was, in fact, a Protestant manifesto calling for something approaching the "universal Protestant liberty" of the minister's own Rhode Island. He hoped that it would be achieved by means of Congregational and ultimately Presbyterian union within the colonies, if not everywhere.

In this notable sermon, Ezra Stiles systematically and successfully fused English Nonconformist ideas about religious and civil liberties with American ideas arising out of a vastly different historical experience. The *Christian Union* sent out a call for continental religious unity which strikingly paralleled the aspiration for imperial political union — one capable eventually of trans-

formation into a call for American unity for Americans. It embodied the ideal of the era of the American revolution, though, of
course, only advanced colonial thinkers of his own stripe grasped
the far-reaching significance of his position.

We have noted the wide circulation of the tract in England. The
English Nonconformists recognized that here was no New England
bigot but a civilized divine who spoke their language and had
delivered a tolerant, cultivated sermon that incorporated their own
views. Though the prophetic quality of the *Christian Union* was
lost on them, Anglicans did comprehend at once the potent implications of the sermon and the clarity with which it disclosed their
open and their secret designs. If the statistical display made by
Mr. Stiles surprised even well-informed Dissenters, the impact upon
the principal colonial Episcopalian, the Reverend Samuel Johnson
of King's College, was enough to make him pay a grudging tribute
to the *Discourse* in a letter to Archbishop Thomas Secker in 1762
in which he refers in the clerical pejorative to the *Discourse* of
"one Mr. Stiles": "Its estimates, page 112, may be of some use,
and I believe he has endeavoured to be exact, but doubtless there
are many more Episcopalians," but for the next fifteen years
Anglican statisticians worked in vain to overset the Newporter's
population figures.[24]

The primate of all England learned in 1763 about the threat
posed by Stiles's "intention to invite all parties and sects in the
Country to unite against the Church of England." It is nothing less
than suppression of the Church that is really aimed at, was the
penetrating comment of the Reverend Henry Caner of Boston:

To . . . these provocations and Insults, our Clergy have made no
reply, avoiding to be thought disturbers of the public peace by encouraging disaffection among the people at a time when their union
was so absolutely necessary. . . . The only reason I can give for the
bitterness of spirit which seems thus of a sudden to break out among
the Dissenters, is that they look upon the war as near a conclusion, and
that a great part of the conquests made in America will probably be
ceded to the British Crown. So remarkable a Crisis, it is natural to

24. Herbert and Carol Schneider, eds., *Samuel Johnson: President of King's College. His Career and Writings* (New York, 1929), I, 231.

imagine, will fall under such regulations as will either greatly establish the Church of England, or the Dissenting Interest, in this part of the world. Their activity is therefore employed to the uttermost, both here and in England, to secure the Event in their favor. And I am sorry to say, that their conduct in this matter is as disingenuous as their diligence is remarkable.[25]

To all colonial missionaries and their hierarchical superiors at Fulham Palace, counter-measures seemed imperative and were soon taken. These, in time, like George Grenville's reform program, helped to pull down the pillars of the first British Empire. The *Discourse on the Christian Union* proved but a prelude to the furious literary debate of the 1760's over religious and civil liberties, for Stiles's exegesis represented the ideal of religious liberty, which was such a powerful factor in the remarkable change of mind that caused Americans to revolt against Great Britain. Anglican bishops became the principal symbol in the American mind of the threatened ecclesiastical tyranny. The American Revolution of 1760–75 resulted quite as much from a *religious* as from a political change in the minds and hearts of the people.

VII

It was no accident that Ezra Stiles delivered his sermon calling for religious unity when he did, for he had an uncanny sense of timing. The high voltage of the Great Awakening had been dissipated, and many believers awaited a mediator. Stiles also fully realized the political actualities of the time. Inasmuch as the fall of Quebec eight months prior to the Bristol Convention seemed to indicate the prompt and victorious outcome of the war, the young minister argued that ecclesiastical union must be achieved in time

25. Six years later some Rhode Island clergymen complained in a report to the S.P.G., "Since the first settlement of Christianity so large a Continent as this was never known without a resident Bishop. We flattered ourselves that such an extensive territory as was heretofore possessed and hath since been added to the British Dominions by the last war would certainly have been followed by some provision of this kind. . . ." William S. Perry, ed., *Historical Collections Relating to the American Colonial Church. Massachusetts* (Hartford, 1873), III, 489-90, 531.

to win the West, or the Episcopalians would not only win there but would also inevitably throttle the religious and civil liberties of New England. United Congregationalism was the only guarantee of freedom.

History supplied the *leit motif* for this discourse. It is constantly alluded to as a reminder of that "errand into America" of "our fathers," whose memory must be perennially invoked in order that posterity may retain their ideals and their desire to build the city on the hill. Reverence for the greatness of this past would buttress the union of the churches, which had to be antecedent to the westward expansion of the people.

A knowledge of the history of the religious strife in the Mother Country was implicit in the sermon, for the ecclesiastical arguments in this forecast of the severe struggle of the 1760's over religious liberty had their origin in the Dissenters' case as worked out in England. The contest began in 1689 when the English Nonconformists formulated and elucidated the case for liberty in diversity and against the Test Act. England's rulers denied them a hearing before 1828, but in the colonies the situation was different, and the London Dissenters dutifully and generously contributed to the cause of their colonial brethren, fearing that what had happened to them would be enacted in the New World. Nor were these fears groundless, for the Anglicans had made great inroads in New England in just two short decades before the Reverend Ezra Stiles delivered his great challenge to the Congregationalists to unite. The unity he called for was designed to halt the Episcopal advance, which was threatening the colleges and churches of the colonies.

The following chapters will trace the succession of events and the progressive unfolding of ideas about religious liberty in England and America after 1689 and show how they worked to produce the state of affairs described by Ezra Stiles in 1760, when victorious Britain set about reorganizing its empire. Succeeding chapters will trace and analyze the mounting conviction in the public mind that its civil as well as religious liberties were no longer safe under the British connection. Both were threatened and both must be defended. The consequences of this conviction were the Declaration of Independence, seven years of war to ensure it, and a series of noteworthy state constitutions guaranteeing religious rights as that age conceived them. To a fundamentally devout people, with one hundred and fifty years of experience with what they knew as religious tyranny behind them, religious liberty was prerequisite to and ultimately encompassed by freedom from the Mother Country.

II

THE ENGLISH DISSENTERS AND EPISCOPACY

1689–1750

In these days when the unity of the "Atlantic Civilization" attracts so much popular and scholarly attention, it is pleasant as well as fruitful to investigate one of its most important phenomena, the transit of civilization from Europe to America. When we examine its nature, however, we usually tend to overlook the fact that America influenced Europe; the relationship was a reciprocal one. People, things, ideas, and institutions crossed the ocean on the westward passage; and, as time elapsed, people, things, and ideas, if not institutions, made the voyage eastward.

The exchange of persons that took place beginning with the Great Migration of the Puritans to the New World involved an exchange of religious ideas as well. From 1629 until the twentieth century there has been a steady interchange of correspondence, printed matter, and ministers, which has profoundly affected religious developments in both Great Britain and America. The first Puritans to settle at Salem wrote home about their exciting, new experiences, and they commented especially on the development of the "New-England Way" of congregational church polity. With the calling of the Long Parliament, more than a few ministers returned to fight in "the good Old Cause," but after King Charles II was restored to the throne and the Act of Conformity ended the ascendancy of the Puritans, some of them went out to New England seeking peace and security. But always, throughout the entire seventeenth century, New England divines and such pious laymen as Samuel Sewall kept in touch with the brethren in England. An exchange of letters took at least three months and generally much longer, but an astonishing amount of transoceanic correspondence took place, and the up-to-date knowledge that persons on both shores possessed is impressive. It is no accident that in the eighteenth century the English Dissenters were better informed about the religious and political, as well as economic, affairs of the colonies than were the Anglicans or the royal officials.

Both New England Congregationalists and the Nonconformists of England had much to hope for when William and Mary came to the throne in 1689. Indeed the Toleration Act did mark a turning point in the religious history of the English people. In 1689 the Nonconformists entered upon a strikingly new course in their relations with each other and with the state in the sphere of religion, a course which was soon evident both in practice and theory. Hopes that the limits of the Church of England could be stretched sufficiently to enable most of the Nonconformists to re-enter and live undisturbed within the framework of the Anglican Church faded with the failure of the House of Commons to pass a "comprehension" bill. Instead, the Dissenters had to accept an act which allowed Protestant Nonconformists who accepted the doctrine of the Trinity to worship in churches and meetinghouses of their own, but under specific and onerous regulations. Originating in King William's Calvinism and latitudinarianism, and conditioned by everyday needs, this solution scarcely reflected any popular acceptance of toleration. Still, henceforth, this practical accommodation was always called the Toleration Act.

To the Nonconformists, however, such a title was a misnomer. It is true that the new law relieved them from the oppressions of the severe religious code of Charles II, and they had gained the right to think, worship, and, after 1694, to publish their thoughts on religion without censorship or official interference. Forthwith the Dissenters began to apply for licenses, and, during the two decades after 1689, they built more than a thousand meetinghouses. The failure to secure comprehension served to etch more sharply the nature of the separatist tradition in English life. Vivid memories of the bitter years subsequent to 1661 and the meagerness of the concession in the Toleration Act, for they still suffered disabilities and exclusion from the universities, did not heighten the Nonconformists' sense of security under the new dispensation.

For many years this very insecurity hindered them from taking the initiative to assist their colonial brethren, to whom the new legislation was soon extended. When one examines certain Anglican activities in the colonies concerning church and state during the reign of Queen Anne, one quickly sees further grounds for the Nonconformists' apprehension.[1]

II

Enjoying widespread popular support and an entrenched legal position at home, the Church of England also had a formidable organization, the machinery of which appeared to outside observers to be well-oiled and running smoothly. For a long time all activities of the Church in the colonies had come under the jurisdiction of the Bishop of London, and so they continued for some years after the Revolution. In 1699, with the founding of the Society for Promoting Christian Knowledge to foster missionary work at home and in the colonies and, more importantly, the establishment of an offshoot devoted exclusively to colonial affairs, the Society for the Propagation of the Gospel in Foreign Parts,[2] the Church acquired two excellent agencies for dealing with those Englishmen still living outside of its communion.[3]

Under the constitution of the S.P.G., the Archbishop of Canterbury served as president. The fine start made by the missionaries was in no small part the work of Archbishop Tenison (1695–1716)

1. The ecclesiastical legislation of the reign of Charles II affecting the Nonconformists is conveniently assembled in the Appendix of Olive M. Griffiths, *Religion and Learning* (Cambridge, Eng., 1935), 168–76; John E. Baur, "English Protestant Attempts at Reunion, 1689–1710," *Historical Magazine of the Protestant Episcopal Church*, XVIII (1949), 444, 449, 450, 452; and for the Toleration Act, 166–7; Duncan Coomer, *English Dissent under the Early Hanoverians* (London, 1946), 4–5.

2. In this work, the Society for the Propagation of the Gospel in Foreign Parts will ordinarily be referred to as: the Society, the S.P.G., or the Venerable Society.

3. David Humphreys, *An Historical Account of the Incorporated Society for the Propagation of the Gospel in Foreign Parts* (London, 1730); Charles F. Pascoe, *Two Hundred Years of the S.P.G.* (London, 1901), I, 4–8; and for the charter, II, 932–5.

who, with Henry Compton, Bishop of London (1675–1713), strongly supported the new undertaking. Propagating the gospel in the plantations could be, and was, implemented by ecclesiastical provisions inserted in the commissions and instructions issued to royal governors in the colonies by the Lords of Trade and Plantations, of which board the Bishop of London was a regular member. Finally, the prelates enjoyed access to the King-in-Council when it dealt with colonial religious matters.[4]

Spurred on by the welling humane and religious spirit of the age and a desire to bring the plantations under Episcopal control, which would parallel contemporary political efforts to unite them and impose royal governments on all of them, the S.P.G.'s missionaries invaded the colonies in force and employed tactics worked out by the prelates in London. This juxtaposing of ecclesiastical and political schemes did not escape the notice of the London Dissenters, who, however, were in no position to take any delaying action at that time.[5]

Upon the accession of Queen Anne, the High-Church Tories gained the upper hand in the House of Commons and, despite three failures, 1702–4, they finally succeeded in 1712 in forcing through Parliament the Occasional Conformity Bill, a measure particularly injurious to wealthy Nonconformists. Dr. Sacheverell's pulpit fulminations, together with the burning of meetinghouses by mobs, served to whip up popular resentment against the Dissenters. A further setback occurred when the Schism Bill, forbidding them to keep schools, passed the House of Commons. Small wonder then that the Dissenters long remembered the dramatic moment on a Sunday morning, August 1, 1714, when, during the sermon, Dr. Thomas Bradbury's brother dropped a white handkerchief from

4. For the early history of Episcopal control in the American plantations, 1607–1714, see Arthur Lyon Cross, *The Anglican Episcopate and the American Colonies* (Cambridge, Mass., 1902), 1–52; Evarts B. Greene, "The Anglican Outlook on the American Colonies in the Early Eighteenth Century," *American Historical Review*, XX (1914), 64–84.

5. Tory attempts to make the proprietary and chartered colonies royal, together with the further efforts at unified control of the plantations are discussed in Louise P. Kellogg's "The American Colonial Charter," American Historical Association, *Annual Report*, 1903, 187–341.

the gallery, a prearranged signal that the Queen had died, enabling the minister to be the first divine in England to end his final prayer with "God save King George!" [6]

Meanwhile, from America, the S.P.G. missionaries pleaded with importunate frequency for one or more resident bishops to transfer episcopacy in its entirety to the New World. For the first time such requests from the clergy of the Middle and Northern Colonies received serious attention in England, and the Society's officers were persuaded of the need to take prompt action. As early as 1703 a committee had prepared "The Case of Suffragan Bishops for Foreign Parts briefly proposed," which won the support of prelates of such divergent views as Henry Compton and White Kennett. Six years later the Society memorialized Queen Anne about an American bishop. Support came in 1712 from a sermon preached by Dean Kennett before the S.P.G. stressing the necessity of having Episcopal government and discipline in the colonies "to compleat the face of decency and order." On March 24, 1713, a comprehensive plan, framed for the Queen by a committee of the S.P.G., was ratified by the Society and delivered to the Archbishop of York to be presented to Her Majesty, who approved the request at the last moment. A bill had even been drafted and was ready for submission to Parliament when her death ended the project.[7]

The effort was renewed in a representation to King George I on June 3, 1715, but it received no consideration, probably because of the Jacobite uprising and the coming to power of Sir Robert Walpole and the Whigs. Moreover, the Hanoverians, who looked with favor on the Dissenters, would scarcely have wished to strengthen the Anglicans in the colonies. Even White Kennett, in a letter to the Reverend Benjamin Colman of Boston, deplored the "Fooleries" of the High-Church Episcopalians. Never again did

6. Because of the Queen's death, the Schism Bill did not become a law. Coomer, *English Dissent*, 6; Edmund Calamy, *An Historical Account of My Own Life* (London, 1829), II, 228; David Bogue and James Bennett, *History of Dissenters from the Revolution in 1688, to the Year 1808* (London, 1809), III, 118.

7. Cross, *Anglican Episcopate*, 92–9, 101; Protestant Episcopal Historical Society, *Collections* (1851), 139; for the Memorial and the bishops petition, Ernest Hawkins, *Historical Notices of the Missions of the Church of England in North American Colonies* (London, 1845), 378, 380.

the Venerable Society in its corporate capacity apply to the Crown for an American bishop, nor did it actively pursue this goal in any other way until 1741.[8]

While the S.P.G. was steadily expanding its missionary activities in the plantations, the leadership in maintaining episcopal rights and arguing the cause for colonial bishops was assumed by Edmund Gibson when he advanced to the See of London in 1723. Because of the indisposition of Archbishop Wake, he also served as president of the Society until John Potter became primate in 1737. Wake and Gibson aspired to tighten the control that the Church of England wielded over spiritual matters, and they spared no energy in furthering this design. In London, Gibson listened sympathetically to the pleading of the "Connecticut Apostates," Timothy Cutler and Samuel Johnson: "With this learned and excellent prelate they conversed frequently, on the state of the Church in the colonies. They urged the necessity, as they had repeatedly done with their friends in London, and at both universities, of sending Bishops to America. . . . His Lordship was of the same opinion with them; and, the next year, on occasion of the Jacobites sending two Bishops over to the colonies, he entered warmly into the affair; but he could not prevail with the Ministry to give his proposal the attention it deserved." [9]

Although the Bishop was unable to influence the Ministry, he succeeded fairly well with his fellow members on the Board of Trade and Plantations and with the Privy Council. As will appear in the next chapter, letters Gibson wrote to the Duke of Newcastle advocating that he oppose the holding of a "dissenting" synod in Massachusetts caused the Government to take steps to prevent that meeting and to censure Governor Samuel Shute for approving the proposal. In his twin capacities as head of the S.P.G. and Bishop of London, Gibson received more than two thousand letters, most

8. Hawkins, *Missions of the Church,* 380–83; Ebenezer Turrell, *The Life and Character of the Reverend Benjamin Colman* (Boston, 1749), 133.

9. Norman Sykes, *Edmund Gibson, Bishop of London, 1669–1748* (Oxford, 1926), 343; Thomas Bradbury Chandler, *The Life of Samuel Johnson, D.D.* (New York, 1805), 38. For the documents on the Jacobite bishops, consult B. Franklin, "Non-Juring Episcopates in the United States," Prot. Episc. Hist. Soc., *Collections* (1851), 87–98.

of them complaints from American missionaries, and the pressure applied by him on the Privy Council and the Crown's legal officers from 1727 to 1732 had much to do with the winning of important concessions for Episcopalians in Connecticut and Massachusetts.[10]

Nor did this energetic and dedicated Churchman ever desist from trying to have one or more bishops sent to the colonies. By 1734 he had earned such a reputation as an ecclesiastical politician that anonymous pamphleteers taxed him with wanting to use the colonies as an outlet for disagreeable clergymen as well as places from which to extract a large revenue from mulcts and fines:

> But I'll transport them for recruits
> Among the poor Plantations bruits,
> Who yet, I fear, will not receive 'em
> Being such dupes as to relieve 'em
> Else what a glorious crop of fees
> Might Spring from foreign diocese.
> Why should remotest nations want
> The pious fraud and solemn cant?
> The Virtues of our Order claim
> The full eclaircissement of Fame.

Despite such attacks and frustrations, Bishop Gibson continued to fight valiantly for colonial bishops to the end of his career in 1748, though his influence waned after John Potter became the Archbishop of Canterbury.[11]

More perceptive and realistic in appraising the situation was a colleague, Mathew Hutton, King's Chaplain, who wrote to the Reverend Samuel Johnson of Stratford in 1736 that "the united interest of the Bishops here is not powerful enough to effect so reasonable and right a thing as sending bishops into America." Years afterwards, Samson Occom, the American Indian preacher, harshly but accurately assessed Gibson's efforts: "The ministry of those days suffered him to play with his project till he had modelled it to his own liking; they then exposed the pernicious nature of it and left both the project and the projector to the contempt and

10. Sykes, *Gibson*, 343, 346–7.

11. *Dr. Codex's Fifth Pastoral* (London, 1734), in Sion College Library, as quoted in Sykes, *Gibson*, 373.

derision of all wise and good men." It was for others in the next decade to reinvigorate the movement for an American episcopate.[12]

On February 20, 1741, the members of the S.P.G. listened to an impassioned sermon by Thomas Secker, in which the Bishop of Oxford resurrected and reformulated an issue which had lain dormant since 1714. Representing uncritically, and far from accurately, the religious attitudes and behavior of the first English colonists in America as having been deplorable, and contending that in the second and third generations the sense of Christianity had so declined in some of the colonies that "there were scarce any Footsteps of it left, beyond the mere Name," Secker proceeded to describe the gains made by the Society's missionaries and thence to "the Prospects of future success." Though the hopes of achieving it "amongst our own People there, are just the same as here at home," he said the heathen Indians and Negroes were in dire need of spiritual aid. He then made his main point: that, for the further ministering to the infidels and the ensuring of the spiritual welfare of the English colonists, resident bishops were essential.[13]

Of the twenty-six ministers "bred among the dissenters" that Edmund Calamy listed as conforming to the Church of England by 1731, the most prominent from a spiritual point of view was Joseph Butler, author of the celebrated *Analogy* and of a plan for an American episcopate; but the most successful as a Churchman was Thomas Secker. This son of a Dissenter of small estate received his early education at Chesterfield before studying for the ministry, first at Jollie's academy at Attercliffe, then with John Eames in London; next, on the advice of Isaac Watts, the writer of hymns, at the academy of Samuel Jones at Gloucester; and finally at Tewkesbury. There he met Butler and Samuel Chandler, who became a famous dissenting preacher. Secker abandoned the ministry in 1716 and took up the study of medicine, for he found dissent unsatisfactory. In 1720 he became a special student at Exeter College, Oxford. The Church of England gave him a living at

12. Schneiders, *Johnson,* I, 86; *London Chronicle,* Jan. 17, 1764.

13. Thomas Secker, Bishop of Oxford, *A Sermon Preached before the Incorporated Society for the Propagation of the Gospel in Foreign Parts. . . . February 20, 1740/1* (London, 1741), reprinted in Frank J. Klingberg, *Anglican Humanitarianism in Colonial New York* (Philadelphia, 1940), 215–17, 218, 227, 228–9.

Houghton-le-Spring in 1724, and in 1727 he was instituted at London. His rise was rapid: Chaplain to the King in 1732, Bishop of Bristol in 1735, and two years later Bishop of Oxford. Nor did he stop short of the top; in 1758 he advanced to the primacy.

Making his way with the intense zeal of a convert, Bishop Secker "shewed no hearty affection to Liberty of any sort," nor any evidence that the experiences of his youth had made him more tolerant than his fellow bishops. Publicly enunciating his views in the sermon of 1741, the Bishop of Oxford thereafter became the most potent champion of a colonial episcopate. Aggressive, fearless, experienced, and tenacious, this prelate used every art of political intrigue to accomplish his designs. The fact that he knew the Dissenters from within gave him an advantage of understanding that other Churchmen lacked, but it did not endear him to his former associates. Thomas Hollis called him "Leviathan" with no complimentary intent, and another Dissenter paid an oblique tribute to the success with which he "juggled for Fame with his own order" — "advancing gradually in the faith of the civil church establishment till he reached the See of Canterbury." However ambitious and worldly his nature, Secker also had administrative ability. He was everything the S.P.G. missionaries in America hoped for in a leader, and to his last day he never failed them, for he devoted much time and energy to the grand strategy of the contest for ecclesiastical and civil power for his church in America.[14]

The Bishop of Oxford's sermon inspired both Bishop Gibson and the Archbishop of Canterbury to hold a series of conferences on the colonial episcopacy question during the next four years; and, once institutional inertia had been overcome, events "began to move actively." In 1745 Bishop Secker opened a correspondence on the subject with Samuel Johnson of Connecticut, who wrote to Gibson on November 25 pleading that he and Archbishop Potter would spare no efforts "in their fresh attempt to secure so great a blessing." About this time, Gibson offered to give £1000 for the support of a resident bishop in America. As the shrewd Secker had

14. Calamy, *My Own Life,* II, 500; *London Chronicle,* Aug. 20, 27, Sept. 1, 1768; *Dictionary of National Biography,* XVII, 1108; Massachusetts Historical Society, *Proceedings,* LXIX (1947–50), 146, 163; Norman Sykes, *From Sheldon to Secker* (Cambridge, Eng., 1959), especially pp. 216–23.

foreseen, however, the opportunity had not yet arrived for any definite move, because the Jacobite uprising had stirred up so much opposition to any kind of Episcopal venture. Much of this resistance came from the Dissenters who, for the first time since 1669, were in a strong enough position to influence the Government.[15]

III

Disappointed and frustrated by the outcome of the Revolution Settlement of the religious question, the English Nonconformists found themselves in a predicament: they lacked an accepted program for united action and, possibly worse, any organization to implement a program. Leadership of the Dissenters ever since the Restoration had been exercised by the ministers of the separate denominations, of which the Presbyterians were the most numerous and influential. On July 1, 1690, a "United Body of Presbyterians and Congregationalists" made a serious effort at union by establishing a fund to train a "succession of fitt persons to propagate the gospel," and these moneys were placed under the administration of a committee of seven members from each denomination living in or about London. Within two months' time contributions collected from wealthy London Dissenters amounted to the huge sum of £2136.12.6. Although auspiciously begun, the union failed to survive, ending in 1693 when the Congregationalists withdrew because they resented what they considered an attempt at "Presbyterian" discipline. Two years later these same members organized the Congregational Fund Board.[16]

The formation of the "General Fund" of 1690 had at least cleared the way for an even more promising effort at uniting the two bodies. The Reverend Nathaniel Mather and his brother Increase, "the foremost American Puritan" who was then in London soliciting a new charter for Massachusetts, together with Mathew Mead and

15. Sykes, *Gibson,* 371, 372; Chandler, *Johnson,* 75.

16. Presbyterian Fund Board, Minutes (Dr. Williams's Library), I, July 1, 14, 1690; Charles A. Briggs, *American Presbyterianism* (New York, 1885), Appendix, lvi–lx; for attempts at union prior to 1689, see "An Essay of Accommodation," Dr. Williams's Library, *Occasional Papers,* Nos. 6, 9, 17 (1957–60).

other prominent Congregationalists, met with the Reverend John Howe and a group of leading Presbyterians. Both Howe and Mead were trustees of the "General Fund," and the initial achievement of this benevolence society seemed to augur well for something more comprehensive. At a meeting in the London area April 6, 1691, where the Reverend Mr. Mead preached, a "Happy Union" was proclaimed. Enthusiasm mounted rapidly as the movement spread to the country Dissenters, and success seemed assured when Increase Mather, with the assistance of Mead and Howe, lent his diplomatic talents to the framing of "Heads of Agreement." [17]

Although in general the Heads of Agreement favored the Congregational church polity, the Presbyterian ministers were willing to accept the agreement; whereas the Independents continued to be uneasy about the arrangement. Even so, the Heads of Agreement could have been the vehicle for the sorely needed union, had not a violent theological controversy suddenly ranged the two denominations against each other and eventually rent the London dissenting interest asunder.

In *Gospel Truth Stated and Vindicated,* published in 1692, Dr. Daniel Williams severely censured the "Antinomianism" of Dr. Tobias Crisp. The Congregationalists, already "offended at several managements in the Union," now determined to secede. Nathaniel Mather, in spite of his brother Increase's efforts to get him to listen to reason, complained, along with five other Independent divines, to the Union about the book. The first minister to resign from the Union was the Reverend Isaac Chauncy who, in November, 1692, thus registered his objections to synodical control by the Presbyterians. In 1694 the Union collapsed upon the withdrawal of the Congregationalists, who, in so doing, also split the General Fund Board. Soon the "heats among the Dissenters grew

17. On the "Happy Union" and the "Common Fund," see Alexander Gordon, ed., *Freedom after Ejection* (University of Manchester Publications, Historical Series, XXX, 1917), 150–64; Griffiths, *Religion and Learning,* 34–97; Williston Walker, ed., *The Creeds and Platforms of Congregationalism* (New York, 1893; Boston, 1960), 441–52, 456–62 (text of the Heads of Agreement); the text is also printed by Daniel Neal, *History of New-England Containing an Impartial Account of the Civil and Ecclesiastical Affairs of the Country to the Year . . . 1700* (London, 1720), II, 656–63.

perfectly scandalous." Pathetically, the Presbyterians half-pretended that the Union still existed until the last attempt to resuscitate it in 1698.[18]

By this unfortunate internecine strife, the Presbyterians forfeited their one chance to assume the leadership, as the largest dissenting body, in bringing English Nonconformists together. Thereafter, for all practical purposes, the English Presbyterians virtually lapsed into a loose association of independent churches. Looking back years later, Edmund Calamy could write of all the Dissenters: "Had they now set up a General Correspondence in all parts of the Kingdom, and regularly kept it up, many good ends might have been answered, and there would have been no such clamours as were raised and spread upon their attempting it some years afterwards." Their inability to subordinate sectarian differences so as to effect some sort of confederation left the dissenting bodies without any kind of organization to further their common purposes, though the ministers of the leading denominations in London (Presbyterian, Independent, Baptist) occasionally met as individuals to exchange views.[19]

Fresh from Harvard College in 1695, Benjamin Colman crossed to England and there took lodgings with Thomas Parkhurst, a Congregationalist whose bookshop in Cheapside was so much patronized by Dissenters. In this shop Colman must have met many prominent ministers including the Presbyterians John Howe, Edmund Calamy, and Dr. Daniel Williams, and from them he must have heard many a tale about ecclesiastical tensions during the abortive negotiations for reconciliation by moderates in both denominations. Before his return to Boston in 1699 to preside over

---

18. For the present purpose it is not necessary to enter into the acrimonious debate about placing the blame for this unfortunate affair. Calamy, *My Own Life,* I, 321–4, 356; Briggs, *American Presbyterianism,* 134–5; Edmund Calamy, *An Abridgement of Mr. Baxter's History of His Own Life and Times* (2nd ed., London, 1713), 537, 539, 549–64; Griffiths, *Religion and Learning,* 97, 105; A. H. Drysdale, *The History of the Presbyterians in England: Their Rise, Decline, and Revival* (London, 1885), 470–76; *History of the Union between the Presbyterian and Congregational Ministers in and about London; and the Causes of the Breach in it* (London, 1698), 9; and Roger Thomas, Librarian of Dr. Williams's Library, to author, Sept. 5, 1960 (Mr. Thomas has in preparation a history of the Body of the Three Denominations).

19. Calamy, *Baxter's History,* 498; and *My Own Life,* II, 408.

the new Brattle Street Church, Benjamin Colman preached in Presbyterian meetinghouses in Bath, Norwich, and London, and accepted ordination by Presbyterian ministers. His long stay abroad had taught him much about English nonconformity, but, above all, he had made lasting friendships with Dissenters of every complexion and with many moderate Anglicans as well — connections which would be vital to the Dissenters' cause in later years.[20]

When Queen Anne came to the throne, the Nonconformists found themselves in a sorry condition with no means of resisting the fierce attacks of the High-Church Tories. Intensified fears for their faiths convinced the pastors that somehow they must concert measures to safeguard against the abridgment of such religious liberties as they already had, rather than concern themselves with winning any future extensions of them. By 1699 the Congregationalists had conceded the validity of Presbyterian objections to "Antinomianism" and unauthorized preaching. Furthermore, Nathaniel Mather and other extremists had died, and the Independents were able and ready to accept the leadership of Dr. Williams. The fact that they had been accustomed from the early days to approach the throne as one deputation pointed the course in 1702, and "The Body of the Protestant Dissenting Ministers of the Three Denominations in and about the City of London" was formed for this purpose. Its first act was to send a deputation consisting of four Presbyterians, three Independents, and three Baptists, headed by Dr. Williams, to address Queen Anne in the interest of their liberties.[21]

As the Body of the Three Denominations was of a "somewhat indeterminate character," it took many years to recover from the effects of the Antinomian Controversy. Faced with very serious local problems, it could scarcely have been expected to take any very large part in American ecclesiastical affairs. Nevertheless individual Presbyterian and Congregational pastors corresponded

20. Turrell, Colman, 5, 18–45, garbles the account of the situation in England but prints important letters now missing from the Colman Mss (Mass. Hist. Soc.); Roger Thomas to author, Sept. 19, 1960.

21. Calamy, My Own Life, I, 460, 621; and Baxter's History, I, 423; Bogue and Bennett, History of Dissenters, II, 148; Roger Thomas to author, Sept. 5, 19, 1960; Coomer, English Dissent, 59; Roger Thomas, "The Non-Subscription Controversy amongst the Dissenters in 1719," Ecclesiastical History, IV (1953), 167.

intermittently with such Boston divines as the Mathers and Benjamin Colman. The exchange dealt principally with matters of divinity, but on occasion each side raised matters of mutual concern such as the difficulties encountered by the infant Presbyterian Church in the province of New York and the demands of London Quakers for the relaxation of the ecclesiastical laws of Massachusetts and Connecticut. The Body of the Three Denominations did, however, keep the channels to the colonies open, if only in a desultory way, during the reign of the last Stuart.

In numbers, the Dissenters of the London neighborhood were far from negligible. They had, in 1711, eighty-eight meetinghouses, whereas the Anglicans had only twenty-eight parish churches and eighteen chapels of ease. Still, buffeted as they were during Queen Anne's reign, their anxieties about the future steadily deepened. Under such a dispensation, many Nonconformist ministers hesitated to use their combined influence politically lest they give offense to their enemies and incur further repression. Though the Committee of the Three Denominations met regularly, it confined its work largely to five formal addresses to the throne between 1702 and 1710, after which it became moribund.[22]

The advent of the Hanoverians presaged better days for Nonconformity. The King, and after 1719 the Walpole Ministry, looked upon Dissent as a bulwark of the new dynasty as well as a political force to conjure with among the commercial classes, particularly in London and the southern-county boroughs. Slowly but perceptibly mercantile laymen began to come to the front as the most experienced and useful political manipulators in Parliamentary circles for the Dissenting Interest.[23]

After its quiescent period during Queen Anne's last years, the Committee of the Three Denominations "again reviv'd" in 1714, and in 1716 showed signs of renewed activity by enlarging its membership to six Presbyterians, five Independents, and five Baptists. It now began to agitate for compensation from the Government for the meetinghouses destroyed in the Jacobite uprising of 1715 and for the repeal of restrictive laws. It also opened a corre-

22. George M. Trevelyan, *Peace and the Protestant Succession* (London, 1934), 55n; Calamy, *My Own Life*, I, 460; II, 25, 51, 63, 93; Coomer, *English Dissent*, 6n.

23. Coomer, *English Dissent*, 6–7, 9, 92.

spondence throughout the country to assess the strength of Dissent. Benjamin Colman used its good offices in 1715 for the presentation of the loyal address of the Boston ministers to King George I. Seven lay representatives were added to the Committee in 1717 (four by the Presbyterians and two by each of the other two denominations). One of them, John Shute Barrington (who, though a Congregationalist, had been selected by the Presbyterians), soon insisted that the Committee try to resolve a theological controversy at Exeter. The celebrated debates, so critical for the future of English Presbyterians, took place in 1719 at Salters' Hall in meetings of the Body of the Three Denominations.[24]

Plans for an even closer union resembling the Heads of Agreement were being discussed in 1719 but, as one divine put it, "the United became the Divided Ministers" after the Salters' Hall meetings. Certainly the debates split the ranks of the Presbyterian ministers and, in consequence, the Body lapsed into another period of inactivity, though it managed to present an address in 1722 and another in 1727 before the death of George I. Not until the next reign did it again come to life.[25]

In distant Boston, Benjamin Colman soon sensed the shifting of power from the pastors to the laymen, a fact of which he may have been apprised by his friend Sir William Ashurst or by the alert Massachusetts agent, Jeremiah Dummer. The New Englanders desperately needed political backers in London who would look out for their interests. So, with this in mind, the Boston minister wrote to Messrs. Calamy, Reynolds, Bradbury, and Tong of the Dissenting Interest on May 16, 1725. He said that he and his associates had reason to believe that these members of the Three Denominations now stood ready to assist the New England churches in meeting the attacks of their enemies and in defeating the recent bill in Parliament threatening Massachusetts with the loss of its

24. Thomas, "Non-Subscription Controversy," 167, 167n, 168; Thomas to author, Sept. 5, 1960; B. Stinton MS (Dr. Williams's Library), folios 16, 55, 71, Aug. 4, 1714; Thomas Crosby, *History of the Baptists from the Reformation to the Reign of King George I* (London, 1740), IV, 107–13, 158, 170–77; Turrell, *Colman,* 83, 86, 91–2.

25. Thomas, "Non-Subscription Controversy," 172, 180; Coomer, *English Dissent,* 73, 77; Thomas to author, Sept. 5, 1960.

charter. Not content with approaching the ministers of the Three Denominations, Bostonians also sent letters to such friendly Anglicans and lay Nonconformists as Lord Chancellor Cowper, Sir William Ashurst, and John Shute Barrington. Although Nonconformists still continued to be very unpopular and their ministers felt the enduring hostility of such prelates as the Bishop of London and the Archbishop of Canterbury, who were seeking by every means to strengthen the spiritual authority of the Church of England, the dissenting laymen, under improved organization, began to exercise greater influence as ecclesiastical issues grew ever more acute.[26]

Nevertheless, the public reputation of the Nonconformists reached its nadir about 1719. That year, in a letter to Colman, the kindly White Kennett conceded that the Anglicans of the High-Church variety had behaved very badly, but he countered the admission quite properly: "You will understand if I say something of the wrong Spirit among our Dissenting Brethren, or the Body of them." Their famed old tender conscience has "visibly abated" (notably in sobriety, daily observance of family prayers, the fear of God in children and servants), and "is wearing off apace, Bibles are less read, and Sabbaths less observed. . . ." In short, the Dissenters are losing the "good Old Puritans' . . . sober Deportment." This "Degeneracy" occurs just when they are in the greatest danger: "Dissenters of late have had the common Cry against them." Kennett said that the law could hardly protect them, and if the Low-Church bishops had turned on them, persecution must surely have followed. And yet, on the positive side, he hastened to add, "the Dissenters (perhaps to a Man) have had one of the greatest Merits, that of being true to their Country, and to the Ballance of Europe, always well affected to the Protestant Succession, and very faithful Subjects of King George, and firm adherents to his Royal Family." Hard upon this came the shattering experience of theological conflict culminating in the Salters' Hall Conference which, at least indirectly, resulted in the spread of unorthodox views in the Presbyterian community.[27]

26. Turrell, *Colman*, 91; Letters were also sent by ten Massachusetts laymen.

27. The entire letter is in Turrell, *Colman*, 133; Griffiths, *Religion and Learning*, 119; for the Salters' Hall Debates, see Thomas, "Non-Subscription Controversy," 172–83.

After 1714 the Nonconformists were assured of freedom from persecution, and in 1719, responding to the pressure of Barrington and other dissenting laymen, Parliament repealed the Tory laws against Occasional Conformity and the nonconformist schoolmasters. The irritating disabilities of the Test and Corporation Acts remained, however. The ministers were also troubled by the decline of piety and the spread of rationalist ideas within their folds as well as by the actual loss of fifty or more of their brethren to the Church of England between 1715 and 1731. Certainly they could not offer much aid to the embattled New Englanders during the 1720's — a time when the Society for the Propagation of the Gospel under Bishop Gibson was spurring the missionaries in the colonies on to new campaigns and winning unquestioned victories.[28]

Actually by 1720 the Committee of the Three Denominations had again lapsed into desuetude. Three years later some laymen of London induced the King and Parliament to make an annual grant of £1000 to the Dissenters for charitable purposes without attaching any conditions, and the pastors set up a trusteeship of this "Regium Donum" to dispense the funds to poor ministers and their widows. Not until the accession of George II, however, did the stimulus arise for them to try to undo the damage done to good relations between their several parties by the Salters' Hall affair. On July 11, 1727, they reconstituted themselves as the General Body of Protestant Dissenting Ministers of the Three Denominations to represent their churches in all public undertakings.[29]

Membership in the revived Body included all ministers within ten miles of London and Westminster, and henceforth none was to represent them "in any publick act" who had not been approved by one or another of the denominations. The General Body convened annually, and the Committee (seven Presbyterians and six each from the Independents and Baptists) met quarterly for executive and administrative purposes. Two years afterwards, through the handsome provision of the late Dr. Williams, an ex-

---

28. Coomer, *English Dissent*, 14n, 93; *A State of the Dissenting Interest* (London, 1734), 73 (Mr. Calamy's copy of a printed confidential report in Dr. Williams's Library).

29. For the *Regium Donum*, see Bernard L. Manning, *Protestant Dissenting Deputies* (London, 1952), 22; Calamy, *My Own Life*, II, 465–8 (a participant's account of the origin of the *Regium Donum*).

cellent Dissenters' library opened in Red Cross Street and immediately became the center for Nonconformist activities in the London neighborhood. The trustees of the library arranged in 1732 for every pastor and his assistant from the Three Denominations to have free access to the collection, and after 1736 the General Meetings of the Body always convened in the attic room of the library.[30]

Notwithstanding such promising beginnings, it was not long before country Dissenters began to hint in formal protests and printed pamphlets: "That of late Years some of the Dissenting Ministers in London, by whom the Management of our Civil Affairs has been undertaken, are publickly and strongly suspected to have abused the Interest they have with Men in Power, so far as to have secretly applied for or received great Sums of Money." Such charges had some basis in fact as to the receiving of the "Regium Donum" but probably little with regard to the administration of the fund. In effect, government agents used their influence to pacify the Dissenters and to keep them from agitating for their "rights." The managers of the "Regium Donum," whom their critics branded "royal almoners," joined with other ministers to persuade the Three Denominations to dodge the responsibility of seeking abolition of the Test and Corporation Acts by bringing in laymen to manage the case. Many laymen and divines in London did deplore the "very low and declining State" of the Dissenting Interest as they saw many able ministers desert to the Church of England, and sensed the great discontent of others with nonconformist policy — or the absence of it. They believed the principal difficulty to be the legal disabilities set up by the Corporation and Test Acts. It is possible, too, that blaming themselves for this sorry situation, many pastors and gentlemen concluded that their political fortunes could be improved only by entrusting them to secular management under men experienced in the hurly-burly of everyday life and well acquainted with those who exercised power in the City and Parliament.[31]

---

30. The approved ministers totaled 168 at the time of the reorganization of the Three Denominations: Presbyterians, 72; Independents, 49; Baptists, 47. Protestant Dissenting Ministers of the Three Denominations in and about the City of London, Minute Book (Dr. Williams's Library), I, 2–3, 4-13, 29, 32, 62; Drysdale, *History of the Presbyterians in England*, 476n.

31. *A Narrative of the Proceedings of the Protestant Dissenters of the Three*

Over many years such resourceful men as Thomas Hollis, Samuel Holden, Lord Chancellor Peter King, Sir Joseph Jekyll, and Sir Thomas Abney had proved themselves willing and able to handle the secular affairs of the Dissenters. Whig laymen apparently took the initiative and approached the ministers through the great Presbyterian, the Reverend Samuel Chandler. At a meeting of the Committee at North's Coffee House, August 29, 1732, Dr. William Harris and Mr. George Smythe informed the members that they were desired by some of the brethren of the Three Denominations to consider the proposal that "a considerable Number of Gentlemen, of Principal Weight and Figure, of the Three Denominations, shou'd meet and consult what Steps are fit to be taken with relation to the Repeal of the Corporation and Test Acts, the next ensueing Sessions of Parliament." Despite the reorganization of 1727, the Body had done nothing more up to this time than address the throne and members of the royal family on stated occasions, and such a decisive step required deliberation and delay. The Committee agreed to take the proposal up with the annual meeting of the General Body in October. A series of negotiations between the ministers and the gentlemen, headed by Samuel Holden, brought agreement by the end of the year in the formation of a lay counterpart of the Three Denominations for consultation over action for the repeal of the restrictive legislation at the next session of Parliament.[32]

The new organization became known as the Protestant Dissenting Deputies. From the first, serious differences arose over the scope of its work: one group held that anything more positive than the usual addresses to the throne and unobtrusive efforts to secure repeal of the Test and Corporation Acts would bring the Dissenters

---

Denominations: relating to the Proposals of the Corporation and Test Acts, from the Year 1731 . . . (London, 1734); A State of the Dissenting Interest, 1, 3.

32. Three Denominations, Minute Book, 30, 31, 32, 34, 39, 40, 42; The Protestant Dissenting Deputies, Minutes (London, Guildhall Mss., 3082), I, 1–6; An Impartial Account of the Late Transactions of the Dissenters in reference to their Committee and Deputations, With Proper Reflections, in Answer to the Remarks on the Letter to the Deputies and Right of the Committee Consider'd (London, 1734). In Dr. Williams's Library, there is a collection of forty some pamphlets (1731–36) about the repeal of the Corporation and Test Acts and the controversy over the founding of the Dissenting Deputies. Norman C. Hunt, Two Early Political Associations: The Quakers and the Dissenting Deputies in the Age of Sir Robert Walpole (Oxford, 1960), is more complete than earlier discussions; Crosby, History of the Baptists, 171–2.

more trouble than they presently had; the other faction favored more positive steps and wanted all the civil activities of the Dissenters placed in the hands of the Deputies. According to the Reverend Isaac Watts, these issues split the London Dissenters "Wretchedly . . . into two parties," which, for three years, indulged in mutual recriminations, much un-Christian wrangling, and more than one "violent discussion." But at last, in 1735, an accommodation was reached and the laymen thenceforth ran their affairs with dispatch and notable success. Consisting of two delegates elected by each congregation of the Three Denominations within ten miles of London, the Dissenting Deputies met at stated times in a General Meeting, while a committee of twenty-one carried on the executive and interim work. The issue over the extent of its jurisdiction was permanently resolved in 1736 by enlarging its instructions "to take care of the Civil affairs of the Dissenters." [33]

At long last the Nonconformist forces possessed an agency through which they could act to forward their cause. The success of a circular letter in 1734 urging Dissenters in the country to support "the Interest of Friends of Civil and Religious Liberty in the ensuing Elections of Members of Parliament" impressed Sir Robert Walpole with the political usefulness of the Dissenting Deputies. Two years later the Deputies resorted to the printed pamphlet for the first time when they distributed several tracts concerning their legal disabilities to members of Parliament. The Committee of the Dissenting Deputies voted on February 1, 1736/7, to establish a subcommittee of seven to correspond with friends in the country about "the Civil Affairs of the Dissenters." This arrangement became institutionalized in 1741 with the appointment of a standing committee of nine "to prepare Answers to the several Letters we may at any time receive from our Correspondents in the Country." In this same year the Dissenting Deputies also appointed a solicitor to attend Parliament regularly as their lobbyist. Here, then, save for the use of the newspaper press to influence public opinion, all the devices available to an eighteenth-century pressure group were being employed by a well-organized body. It is easy to see why the General Meeting in 1737 expressed great satisfaction with "the

33. *Impartial Account*, 5; Dissenting Deputies, Minutes, I, 60; Manning, *Dissenting Deputies*, 24, 25.

great usefulness of the deputation to the General Interest of the Dissenters." [34]

No matter how admirably it is constituted, no representative body can achieve its purpose without leadership. This the Dissenting Deputies got in full measure from Dr. Benjamin Avery who, though a severe critic of Holden's management in the formative period, served with distinction from 1732 until his death in 1762. His election in January, 1737, as chairman of both the General Meeting and the Committee marked the beginning of the effective work of the Deputies. From his portrait that looks down from the walls of Dr. Williams's Library, one immediately senses the intelligence and vigor of the man. A Presbyterian pastor until 1720, he changed his calling, probably because Arian and Arminian outlooks augured difficulties in the ministry, and decided to take up the study of medicine. He accepted an appointment as treasurer of Guy's Hospital, a Baptist foundation, but seemed to find ample time for other work. He was a trustee and one of the principal readers of Dr. Williams's Library, in which he prepared his many polemical tracts. Among his wide acquaintance and his wider list of occasional correspondents, Dr. Avery numbered many public men, statesmen, moderate Anglicans (including bishops) and such prominent Americans as Benjamin Colman and Ezra Stiles. No man could have been better fitted to head the Dissenting Deputies. Most important of all, he understood completely the long-standing hesitancy of the Dissenters about setting up a "National Assembly," which "may draw after it consequences more fatal and more detrimental to the public in the present state of affairs." By exercise of admirable tact, considerable daring, diplomacy, and persuasive skill, he managed to infuse vigor into the Deputies without alarming the members or arousing the Government or public opinion.[35]

Historians have criticized the Dissenting Deputies for their failure

---

34. For a time, in 1737, the Deputies believed the Quakers were inclined to act with them. Dissenting Deputies, Minutes, I, 27, 30–31 (the circular letter of 1734), 68, 83, 90–91, 107, 109, 222–3; on the political side, consult Norman C. Hunt, *Sir Robert Walpole, Samuel Holden, and the Dissenting Deputies* (Oxford, 1957), 1–31; and more fully in his *Two Early Political Associations,* Chapter VIII.

35. From 1738 to 1749, Dr. Avery also served as treasurer. Dissenting Deputies, Minutes, I, 83; on Avery, see *Dict. Nat. Biog.,* I, 746–7; Hunt, *Two Early Political Associations,* 153–78.

to press more forcefully for the repeal of the Corporation and Test Acts and for the greater cause of civil and religious liberty in England. Much can be said for their view. What the Deputies succeeded in doing for their colonial brethren is another story entirely. Never fully exploited on the American side, the minutes of the Dissenting Deputies assist us in piecing together an amazing and complicated story of transoceanic co-operation for the protection and furtherance of religious and political liberties that is without parallel in Anglo-American history.[36]

On July 23, 1740, at a meeting of the Deputies' Committee at the Amsterdam Coffee House, Dr. Benjamin Avery read a letter from Dr. Benjamin Colman of Boston asking the London Dissenters to assist in the case of the Reverend Joseph Torrey of South Kingston, Rhode Island, against whom an appeal was lodged with the Privy Council. The dispute had been building up since 1723 over a gift of glebe land to "an orthodox minister," and it came to a head after 1733 when the *New England Weekly Journal* and other Boston newspapers debated whether Mr. Torrey, the Congregational minister, or the S.P.G. missionary, the Reverend James MacSparran, had the better legal claim to the property. During the litigation, the Episcopalians challenged the entire financial and representative system of the New England churches, and soon the Boston ministers and their Anglican rivals plunged into the affair. Reluctantly the Great and General Court of Massachusetts decided that it could not finance Torrey's defense when MacSparran appealed the local decision to the Privy Council. Dr. Colman and the Reverend Thomas Prince thereupon set out to raise funds; they used the newspapers and hawked broadsides to bring in nearly £2000, and then Dr. Colman made doubly certain of support for Mr. Torrey

---

36. When Dr. Samuel Chandler headed a deputation to remind Walpole of his promise to aid the repeal of the legislation against the Dissenters, he remarked that whatever his private inclination, the time was not yet ripe. "You have so repeatedly returned this answer," said Chandler, "that I trust you will give me leave to ask you when the time will come?" "If you require a specific answer," Walpole replied, "I will give it to you in a word — Never." William Coxe, *Memoirs of the Life and Administration of Sir Robert Walpole* (London, 1816), IV, 94–5; Manning, *Dissenting Deputies*, 19–130; Caroline Robbins, *The Eighteenth-Century Commonwealthman* (Cambridge, Mass., 1959), 231.

by dispatching an appeal to the Dissenting Deputies of London.[37]

The Committee of the Protestant Dissenting Deputies agreed to support the Rhode Island minister, and on October 15, a General Meeting at Salters' Hall voted to notify Dissenters in the country about the case. The Privy Council took up MacSparran's appeal on May 8, 1741. Apparently the Deputies succeeded in getting a hearing with some of the members inasmuch as in August Dr. Avery reported the receipt of a letter "with the thanks of the Reverend Ministers of the Province convened at Boston to the Committee for their care about the South Kingston affair." The Deputies continued to follow the case for the next ten years until the Privy Council finally handed down a decision sustaining the Congregational pastor. The service rendered to their colonial brethren in this instance was of the greatest importance, for an adverse decision would have dealt a virtual death blow to New England Congregationalism at one of the most critical times in its history.[38]

IV

During the half-century of conflict between the Dissenters and the Anglicans after the passage of the Toleration Act, the Nonconformists appear to have declined in numbers. A turning point was reached by 1740, however, and, under the aegis of the lay and ministerial organizations, future prospects appeared brighter. Their own modified attitudes toward toleration, doctrine, church polity, and the whole cluster of ideas bearing on what they called religious and civil liberties contributed to the improvement.

Although the Toleration Act had measurably improved their situation, the Nonconformists fully realized that their newly won position depended almost wholly upon a mild administering of the law. The Corporation and the Test Acts still restricted them, and the influence of the bishops in the House of Lords always prevented

37. Dr. Colman had also solicited aid for Torrey from Samuel Holden in the 'thirties. Turrell, *Colman*, 113; Dissenting Deputies, Minutes, I, 203; Wilkins Updike, *A History of the Episcopal Church in Narragansett, Rhode Island* (2nd ed., Boston, 1907), I, 70–83; Clifford K. Shipton, *Biographical Sketches of those who Attended Harvard College* . . . (Boston, 1951), VIII, 499–500.

38. Dissenting Deputies, Minutes, I, 204–5, 214, 353.

any reform of ecclesiastical courts, or measure of relief from tithes. As previously stated, not until George I mounted the throne did Dissenters have a friend at Court.

Such conditions sobered many Nonconformists who had been softened by some of the ideas inherited from the great religious contests of the previous century. As a result, the dissenting thinkers, both lay and clerical, in working out a theoretical defense of their cause, gradually, and often consciously, expanded their conception of religious liberty. As early as 1691 the more liberal Dissenting ministers had required by way of subscription in the section of the Heads of Agreement entitled "a Confession of Faith" no more than an acknowledgment of Scripture and any one of the three confessions of faith: the Anglican doctrinal articles, the Westminster Confession, or the Savoy Confession. Although many of the brethren came to accept such views and joined in the general reaction of the age against religious persecution and ecclesiastical authority, whether Anglican or Nonconformist, others among them desperately clung to the attitudes of the former century. The showdown came with the Salters' Hall debates of 1719 when the Presbyterians divided almost equally over the question of subscription. The outcome in the long run, however, was a much broader and more tolerant outlook by the leading Dissenters, which created an atmosphere in which improvements in the organization of the Nonconformists might be effected.[39]

As a corollary to this new attitude, these forward-looking Dissenters concurrently evolved, in both belief and practice, the idea of the essential rightness and value to the state of a loyal religious diversity in England. No clearer concise statement of this new position exists than that in *The State of the Dissenting Interest* (1734):

The Interest of the Protestant Dissenters appears to be of very great Importance, both upon Religious and Civil Considerations. As it is uncontroverted, that, from the Make of Humane Nature itself, it is

39. Mr. Roger Thomas shows the connection between the Salters' Hall and Bangorian controversies and demonstrates convincingly that "both controversies are but parts of one and the same story; both deal with allied problems; the same leading ideas are prominent in both; and, in both, the year 1719 marks the beginning of a reaction" against them, "Non-Subscription Controversy," 180.

impossible to bring all Men to think alike of Religion, or to acquiesce in any one particular Establishment; it is highly requisite and necessary, that different Bodies of Men be tolerated and supported, who may be an Asylum, to such as are not able to come up to the Terms required by the National Establishment; whether it be from any Defects in the Establishment itself, or from any Peculiarity in their own Way of Thinking. It will be the Interest of such Men, to study and cultivate the Principles of Liberty (without which they can have no Right to subsist) more than can be expected from any National Clergy; who, as Governors, must undoubtedly often find their Measures thwarted by those very Principles. And in this View, a Body of Dissenters will be found to be of great Service to all the Lay or governed Part of a National Church. In Civil Affairs it cannot be denied, that the Protestant Dissenters in this Kingdom have frequently been very serviceable, in successful Oppositions that have been made to destructive Measures; and that they have, on several Occasions, had the Honour and Happiness, to turn the Balance in Matters of great Importance. They are a most sure Seminary of Loyal Subjects, nor can an Instance be produced (so far as we have been able to enquire among our Denominations) of any, who have had their Education among the Dissenters, who, while they have continued with them, or even in a good Correspondence with them, were ever suspected of being disloyal to his Majesty, or disaffected to the Royal Family, or the Constitution of the Government.

Here is no plea for an ideal separation of church and state, for such was never advocated by the eighteenth-century Dissenters. They no longer desired to erect a new national establishment such as their Puritan forebears attempted in the seventeenth century. Above everything else they wanted equal political rights and an equal share in the economic, legal, and educational privileges still enjoyed exclusively by members of the Church of England.[40]

Nonconformist fear of the Tories, with their high-handed Jacobite and High-Church associates, extended most naturally to the Church of Rome also. Among the Whigs, particularly the "commonwealth-Men" on whom they fastened their hopes for improving their status, the Dissenters found strong and ready allies. Indeed many moderate

40. *A State of the Dissenting Interest*, 1; Robbins, *Commonwealthman*, 228.

Whigs and the freethinkers displayed a fright at the specter of Popery as great, if not greater, than that of the Dissenters.[41]

In 1720–21 there appeared in the London bookstalls fifty-three numbers of *The Independent Whig* which were written by John Trenchard and Thomas Gordon, skilled polemicists and ardent anti-clericals. In their genuine and unfeigned alarm about the spreading of Popish ideas through the Church of England, the authors dedicated *The Independent Whig* to the Lower House of Convocation! "Consider, Gentlemen, that you cannot take as much of Popery as you please, and leave the rest!" They could find no middle ground between Popery and the Reformation: "that is, between the claiming of any Power in Religion; and the renouncing of all Power." Because Catholicism and arbitrary government went together in the minds of most eighteenth-century Englishmen, their warnings were heeded. "The English laity have been us'd pretty much of late, to think for themselves; and we find . . . that the more Men know of Church Power, the less they like it." Reprinted many times in book form in England, and at Philadelphia in 1724 and 1740, *The Independent Whig* became a veritable source book for those who were opposed to a colonial episcopate.[42]

The Dissenting ministers also produced a far-reaching effect through their historical writings. Perceiving that in history they had a potent weapon, they proceeded to use it with marked success in presenting to the public their version of the seventeenth-century struggle of Englishmen over religion. Justice was the professed aim, and they sought learnedly and eloquently to revise the public's image of their Puritan ancestors.

Foremost among the dissenting historians was the Reverend Daniel Neal. His *History of New-England,* published in two volumes in 1720, managed, however, to offend Dissenters at home and in America who, like Samuel Sewall of Boston, grieved "to see New-England's Nakedness laid open in the business of the Quakers, Anabaptists, Witchcraft." "Nor, Sir, need any wonder that Daniel

41. For the "Contribution of Nonconformity," I am very much indebted to Miss Robbins's learned *Commonwealthman,* particularly pp. 19–20, 115–20, 221–70.

42. *The Independent Whig* (2nd ed., London, 1722), v, xi–xii, xx, and for the essays which so profoundly affected the thinking of William Livingston of New York, Nos. 3, 5, 13, 14, 49.

Neal is in request with the Dissenters in New England," said crusty old Timothy Cutler to Dr. Grey, "the more venemous a book is, the more sweetly do Dissenters suck at it." To Isaac Watts's protest that his candor and condemnation of Puritan excesses provided their enemies with opportunities for insults, the author replied "that the fidelity of an Historian requir'd him to do what he has done." In fact Neal candidly admitted in his preface, "I can't help declaring myself sometimes on the Side of Liberty and an Enemy to Oppression in all its Forms and Colours; Accordingly, I have taken the Liberty to censure such a Conduct in all Parties of Christians where-ever I have found it." [43]

Daniel Neal's honest and sweet-tempered modern version of history appealed to such Boston divines as the forward-looking Cotton Mather and the liberal Benjamin Colman; the latter had provided the author with materials not found in earlier sources or Mather's *Magnalia*. The *History of New-England* did much to bring about the gradual modification of New Englanders' ideas about their past. Neal's contribution to the readjustment of English Nonconformist thought came with his great *History of the Puritans,* which appeared in four volumes between 1732 and 1738.

Endeavoring always "to keep in mind the honesty and gravity of an historian," Daniel Neal told the story of the Puritans calmly and, on the whole, dispassionately. He pointed out to the Protestant Dissenters, to whom the book was principally addressed, how important it was to adopt a more liberal outlook as they read his pages. Further, he urged them to recollect the terrible Tudor and early Stuart spirit of bigotry and persecution, and how far they had traveled since the first half of the seventeenth century "to a detestation of all persecuting principles; and to a loyal and dutiful behaviour to the best of kings, under whose mild and just government they are secure of their civil and religious liberties." [44]

43. Mass. Hist. Soc., *Collections*, 5th ser., VII (1911), 251–2; John Nichols, *Illustrations of the Literary History of the Eighteenth Century* (London, 1817–58), IV, 299; Watts to Colman, Feb. 11, 1719/20, quoted by Shipton, *Harvard Graduates*, VI, 594; Neal, *New England*, I, iii, iv.

44. Daniel Neal, *The History of the Puritans or Protestant Non-Conformists, From the Reformation . . . to the Act of Toleration under King William and Queen Mary* (2nd ed. corrected, 4 vols. in 2, London, 1754), I, xiv, xv.

Neal drew certain great lessons from his *History*. Among Christians, he maintained, "uniformity of sentiments in religion" could not possibly be attained; nor could the "cause of truth and liberty" be served by a comprehension within an establishment without a "Toleration of all other dutiful subjects." History shows that all parties of Christians have been guilty of persecution when they were in power: "How narrow their lists of fundamentals. And how severe their restraints of the press!" Therefore the Church should always stand upon a distinct and separate base. Close inspection of past history convinced this author that reformation of religion or redress of grievances against the Church never stemmed from the clergy themselves: "so strange has been the infatuation, so enchanting the lust of dominion, and the charms of riches and honour, that the propagation of piety and virtue has been very much neglected." From these premises he led his readers naturally to the conclusion "that freedom of religion, in subordination to the civil power, is for the benefit of society, and no ways inconsistent with a public establishment" such as existed under King George II.[45]

In spite of the fact that many men who were far from illiberal in their religious views still honestly believed that the good of the kingdom required that church and state be irrevocably united, ideas to the contrary, as set forth by such writers as Daniel Neal, gradually filtered into the minds of many Englishmen at home and in the colonies. These advanced thoughts were propagated at first by the correspondence of liberal-minded clergymen; next they were spread to an interested public in sermons, tracts, books, and histories; and, particularly in the New World, a free press facilitated the circulation of these ideas among many more people. Using the Body of the Three Denominations and the Dissenting Deputies, the Nonconformists thus broadcast their message throughout the British Isles and across the Atlantic, and so eventually won many converts in London and the country, and, far more importantly, gradually swung colonial opinion around to their way of thinking about religious and civil liberty.[46]

An early and impressive example of the influence the Dissenting Deputies could exert for these ideas occurred during the colonial

45. Neal, *Puritans,* II, xvi–xviii.

46. Robbins, *Commonwealthman,* 225.

revival known as the Great Awakening. Late in 1742 Dr. Avery, apparently prodded by some English Baptists or Quakers, wrote a letter to someone in Connecticut lamenting the "confusions" occasioned by some recent provincial laws governing religious matters which seemed to abridge religious liberties and "savour of persecution." This document was publicly read in the Connecticut Assembly. Gratefully acknowledging Dr. Avery's expressed willingness to join with his fellow delegate, Eliakim Palmer (Connecticut agent in London), "in securing the Rights of our Churches and College, as well as the prosperity of our future Civil State," Governor Jonathan Law wrote in November, 1743, a stout defense of the Connecticut laws restraining "Enthusiasm" and "Itineracy" that were directed against the Baptists and Quakers. It contained a long list of the burdensome problems the Great Awakening had thrust on the colonial authorities. All that is needed in London, Law explained, is for the brethren to understand all the circumstances of the religious uproar: "You see Sir in all this there is no Shadow of Imposition but all the Freedom that Heart may wish for." [47]

Dr. Avery communicated Governor Law's letter to the Committee, which directed him to prepare a frank and didactic answer. The reply was submitted to the General Meeting on October 10, 1744. Because the brethren in Connecticut "have before frequently applyed to us for Advice and Assistance," the Delegates voted to send the letter over for "the Strength and Credit of the Dissenting Interest in Generall." [48]

In this missive the members sincerely expressed their sorrow and understanding about the ecclesiastical and other difficulties of the Connecticut government, and they deplored the "delusions" of the great revival as tending to weaken the Congregational churches. Then they came directly to the point: "But great and manifest as those Mischiefs are, Wee cannot be of Opinion that, the Magistrate has any thing to do in this matter; but to see that the publick peace is preserved; that there are no Riots or Tumults, and that his Subjects are not allowed to assault, hurt, maim, wound, plunder or kill one another in those Religious Contests." Laws aimed at unpopular religious opinions can serve no good purpose, however; this

47. Dissenting Deputies, Minutes, I, 265–8.
48. Dissenting Deputies, Minutes, I, 265, 273.

the Connecticut ministers and officials well know from the spectacle here in England of connivance between church and state. The Connecticut law of May, 1742, has been branded a "persecuting" measure by its victims. This hurts you and it hurts us, also, no matter how well you and your Assembly meant by your action. The penalties set for "Dissenters" against the congregational way appear grievious to us, not light as you aver. You fail to give Christianity and the Reformation a fair hearing: thirty years ago here at home we suffered great alarm over the High-Church attempt to deprive us of the privilege of educating our children as we saw fit. In the conclusion of the letter, Dr. Avery read the lesson of toleration to Connecticut. He unreservedly told the Governor and his associates that they had run their ship of state completely off course:

In Short, whether Wee Consider this matter in a religious or political Light, it seems every way most advisable to let these men alone, how wildly Erroneous soever both you and Wee may take their Sentiments to be. Any Penalties, or Incapacities, Fines, Imprisonments, Banishments or Vexatious Persecutions will not fail of being represented here to our, as well as your Disadvantage. And if on such Accounts as these any such Complaints should be made to the King and Council, Wee should not be able, and indeed it would ill become us to endeavour, to vindicate such proceedings. Perhaps Wee don't know every Circumstance that attends your Situation distinctly enough to take upon us to advise you, what part it will be most prudent for you to act on this Occasion. But Wee think nothing can be more Clear, than that it is absolutely necessary you should avoid all kinds of Rigour and Severity in your Methods of Procedure.[49]

Plain speaking such as this coming from London was very much like a strong dose of salts to the Connecticut Yankees. Here were Daniel Neal's ideas served up stark, with no gloss. The incident nicely illustrates the way the Dissenting Deputies and their fellows in London began to line the colonies up for religious — and political — freedom. Though the Connecticut officials, lay and ecclesiastical, were reluctant libertarians, they did realize that their Dutch

49. Dissenting Deputies, Minutes, I, 269–71.

uncles in London kept their best interests constantly before them, and they took the advice to heart.

Actually transatlantic bonds steadily tightened. Handsomely, it would seem, the Connecticut Assembly appointed Dr. Avery as its agent to take the place of the late Eliakim Palmer in 1751. The Deputies' Committee agreed with the physician, however, that he could not properly take the post but concurred with his nomination of a competent and trustworthy man.[50]

It was well for the Dissenters in all parts of the Atlantic Society that by the fourth decade of the eighteenth century they had devised suitable machinery for dealing with the British authorities and with each other across the sea. It was also a happy coincidence that the Nonconformists in the Mother Country had succeeded by the means of private correspondence and the printed word in pushing their American brethren along the way to greater toleration, for in 1748 the advancement of Thomas Sherlock to the See of London inaugurated a long and momentous struggle between the Episcopalians and Dissenters over the relations of church and state in the colonies, a struggle which was terminated only by American independence and complete separation.

50. Led by the liberal Dr. Colman, the Massachusetts ministers were more prone to accept the admonitions of the Dissenting Deputies and to seek their aid. In 1746, after consulting the Duke of Newcastle about proper procedure, Dr. Benjamin Avery took Eliakim Palmer with him when he presented an address from the New England (Massachusetts) pastors to King George II, a service which Colman formally and gratefully acknowledged in January, 1747. Dissenting Deputies, Minutes, I, 291, 294, 323, 324; *Law Papers,* Connecticut Historical Society, *Collections,* XV (1914), 340–41

III

FIRST ANGLICAN FORAYS IN NEW ENGLAND

1690–1740

Westward across the Atlantic in England's North American colonies the Toleration Act forced a profound readjustment in religious life. The nature of this change differed markedly, however, from that in the Mother Country where the Anglican Church was closely allied with the civil power and benefited from the fruits of establishment throughout all England and Wales. In America the Church enjoyed varying degrees of establishment from Maryland southward to Barbados; in Virginia, the oldest dominion of the Crown, it had achieved the most complete and satisfactory arrangements and embraced in its communion the entire population in 1690. In the southern and island provinces prior to 1701, the clergy were legally maintained by the people of their parishes without any outside support, but the Church met with formidable opposition from all other religious bodies.

The accession of William and Mary afforded Churchmen an opportunity to strengthen the position of episcopacy in those colonial regions where it had already taken root and, more significantly, to plant it in the provinces north of Maryland now that active aid from the Ministry seemed certain. Under the direction of such an aggressive Bishop of London as Henry Compton, in whose jurisdiction "the colonial church" belonged, and backed by the awakened interest of such primates as John Tillotson and Thomas Tenison, the future growth and well-being of the Church seemed assured at the beginning of the eighteenth century.

This much at least was certain: henceforth Anglicanism, with all the appurtenances and traditional associations symbolized by mitre and sceptre, ceased to be a regional ecclesiastical activity; it became an intercolonial and a transatlantic institution. Although contemporaries never fully realized the implications, this meant that the Church of England would serve either as a unifying or as a divisive force in the colonies. In truth it was both, but not in any of the ways anticipated by its votaries or by its enemies.

In the Northern Colonies, from Pennsylvania to the Massachusetts province of Maine, virtually all the people, at least after the Restoration, belonged to what the hierarchy at home branded Nonconformists or Dissenters. In a very real sense the New England colonies originated as plantations for religion under the auspices of the Puritans — Calvinist in belief and congregational (later often termed Presbyterian) in church polity.* Organized Episcopalians comprised but a tiny minority of the inhabitants in 1690.

In the great reaches of the New World, these colonists had found safety and freedom in which to worship in their own ways and to conduct their lives under forms of their own devising. During the seventy years after the landing of the Pilgrims, these serious, energetic, and devout people developed the Puritan attitude toward life — an attitude which was at one and the same time religious and civil — in striking contrast to the Anglican outlook. Thoroughly familiar with the English and Continental heritage of the Protestant Reformation, they were skilled in polemical and political controversy, and experienced in self-defense. However, an observer in the last decade of the seventeenth century might have noticed that conflicts between sects had largely degenerated into intrasectarian bickering made possible by a deluding sense of social and religious security.

With good reason historians have emphasized the rise in the eighteenth century of rationalism, of secularism, and the spread of the Enlightenment in the American colonies, but in so doing they have tended to obscure the much larger truth that the English settlements continued to be very religious communities, especially those north of Maryland. This was still an age of faith, of faith in-

---

* Throughout this book the terms *Congregationalist* and *Presbyterian* will be used as designations for American Dissenters or Nonconformists. Congregational is, of course, the American term for Independent.

herited from "our forefathers," faith stiffened by remembered bitternesses, present fears, and suspicions of dangers yet to come from relentless adversaries, themselves driven by like emotions. One must never overlook the fact that religion, politics, and economics in this society were one and inseparable. Religious partisanship was the vogue, and nearly every man still took sides in politics according to his religious affiliation or convictions. Looking backward into these years from 1763, the Reverend Jonathan Mayhew reminded his listeners and readers that "the common people of New England, by means of our schools, and the instruction of 'our able, learned, orthodox ministers,' are, and have all along been, philosophers and divines in comparison of the common people in England, of the communion of the church there established. This is commonly said by those who have had an opportunity personally to inform themselves." [1]

In New England the descendants of the Puritans certainly were not "Dissenters" in the accepted sense. The Congregational or Presbyterian churches were themselves "established by law" in Massachusetts, including Maine, and Connecticut; in New Hampshire they faced no opposition; while in Rhode Island religious liberty prevailed to the great benefit of Baptists, Quakers, Congregationalists, and a number of exclusive and zealous fragmented sects which had fallen away from the larger denominations.[2] In all New England in 1690, only at Boston did a Church of England congregation exist. There the Anglicans were the "dissenters" and indeed they were made to feel so. To extend their church in this land they would have to muscle in, and it may be said that such a gangster term would have seemed more than appropriate to the Mathers, their colleagues of the Standing Order, and to the silent democracy of their congregations.

---

1. Jonathan Mayhew, *Observations on the Charter and Conduct of the Society for the Propagation of the Gospel in Foreign Parts.* . . . (Boston, 1763), 39.

2. On the "establishments" of Massachusetts and Connecticut, see Herbert L. Osgood, *The American Colonies in the Eighteenth Century* (New York, 1924), III, 118, 123, 126–31; Susan M. Reed, *Church and State in Massachusetts, 1691–1740* (*University of Illinois Studies in Social Sciences,* III, Urbana, 1914), 19–34; Maria L. Greene, *The Development of Religious Liberty in Connecticut* (Boston, 1905), 121–52.

II

Aggression by the Anglicans touched off a series of long and bitter ecclesiastical wars in the Northern Colonies. Contrary to Anglican expectations, little or no direct aid came from the British government in these years. Nevertheless in Bishops Compton and Gibson they found strong champions at the See of London, and in 1701 the Reverend Thomas Bray founded the Society for the Propagation of the Gospel in Foreign Parts to send "orthodox Clergymen" as missionaries to the plantations. They were to instruct such of the colonists as "doe want the Administration of God's Word and Sacraments" in the "principles of true Religion," and to take such steps "as may be necessary for the Propagation of the Gospell in those Parts." Significantly, no mention of Indians or Negro slaves occurs in the charter. In the first anniversary sermon, published in 1702, the Bishop of Lincoln explained that the founders' design was to "settle the State of Religion as well as may be among our *own People* there" first; "then to proceed . . . towards the Conversion of the Natives" and infidel Negroes; and finally to carry the blessings of Christian charity to the whites in those portions of America and the West Indies where no ministry had yet penetrated.

This organization, largely and somewhat ironically inspired by the first English missionary society founded to assist John Eliot with the evangelizing of the New England Indians in 1649, was, in essence, the result of joint action by church and state and was chartered by King William. Through its missionaries, who reported to London once a year, and lay members in the colonies, and through the sermons preached annually before the lay and clerical members at the parish church of St. Mary-le-Bow, through the publication of tracts and press notices, and through intimate connections with the hierarchy, the S.P.G. quickly became the central agency for the propagation of the Church of England as well as of the gospel in America. It represented British imperialism in ecclesiastical guise.[3]

3. Pascoe, *Two Hundred Years of S.P.G.*, I, 2, 3, 7; and for the charter, II, 932–5; Klingberg, *Anglican Humanitarianism*, 195–212; and especially E. B. Greene, "Anglican Outlook on the American Colonies," 70–71.

Despite a decision in 1710 to concentrate on converting the heathens and infidels and the allocation of more than half of the Society's income for work among the Mohawks of New York, proselyting for this confessedly sectarian organization came to occupy a much larger place in both the thinking and activities of the missionaries; soon they were to be found all the way from Maine to the Lower Counties on the Delaware. By 1718 Connecticut alone of the continental colonies lacked an Episcopal church.

The march of the Anglicans into New England was impeded and their cause obstructed by the presence of ministers and churches of Massachusetts and Connecticut, whose Congregational Way was established by law. Certain support came to the colonials from their Assemblies and the heavy majorities of the membership in the Councils of all the provincial governments. But an even more potent defensive weapon lay immediately at hand in the form of the public opinion of New England. For sixty years, three and four generations in many instances, a phalanx, which included a few survivors of the Puritan Revolution in Old England such as Increase Mather and Samuel Sewall, had been built up. Indoctrinated by listening to countless sermons and by the perusal of others, as well as tracts, with ideas about government in church and society that may be termed "republican," the emerging Yankees were anti-Episcopal almost to a man.[4]

Formidable as the New Englanders appear to have been in retrospect, they were not as well prepared for the coming wars of the Lord as the aggressive Anglicans seemed to be. Nor were they as yet sufficiently aware of their peril. Actually their chief advantages consisted of the occupancy of their many churches and possession of the minds of most of the colonists.

The Episcopalians delayed launching their attack, and, for a time, even the Anglican leaders were not aware of their objectives. Too, many Congregational ministers of liberal bent welcomed the Society as a Christian body with which they believed they could share in the carrying of the Gospel to the Red Man. But before the close of the first decade of the new century, certain alert Con-

4. Alice M. Baldwin, *The New England Clergy and the American Revolution* (Durham, N.C., 1928), 3–64; Perry Miller, *The New England Mind from Colony to Province* (Cambridge, Mass., 1953), 464–78.

gregationalists began to fathom the S.P.G.'s intentions toward New England. Several ministers kept themselves informed of the Society's activities and aspirations by reading the published reports of the missionaries that were sent over by equally alert London dissenting ministers.

One of these New England men was the Reverend Benjamin Colman, moderate leader of the Boston Association of Ministers, who came to perceive that the Society's officers in London were being misinformed and therefore misled by missionary zealots in America. He opened a correspondence in November, 1712, with White Kennett, then Dean of Peterborough, setting forth his fears of "private Designs and Interests, of Persons and Parties here, to mispend (and so necessarily pervert) great Portions of their noble Charity, to such Ends and in such Manner as do not at all answer the Propagation of the Gospel among us, but which do really break in upon and hinder the spreading and Success of it." As proof he cited the sending of missionaries to Jamaica on Long Island, Braintree and Newbury in Massachusetts on the bounty of the S.P.G. to serve mere handfuls of people when the greater number by far in each of these communities already enjoyed the ministrations of a learned and competent pastor. Mr. Colman conceded that he favored "comprehension," but insisted that "unity" lay not in modes of worship but in charity and mutual esteem. "In short, Sir," he concluded, "there is one sordid Motive which will find you Beggars enough for your Charity in our Country Towns! if you will free them from Rates to any Ministry and maintain it for them." Surely the Society never intended this! [5]

Thus early did the colonial opponents of an episcopate formulate one of their most telling arguments against the work of the S.P.G. That the contention was a valid one, Dean Kennett readily admitted in his conciliatory reply of September 15, 1713, though his proposed remedy for the sending home of misinformation could not have been less acceptable in New England: It is this, he wrote, "in some Ways, that increases our Desires of having Bishops settled in those foreign Parts committed to our Care." Three years later he told Colman that the Society faced two very serious problems: "the

5. Quoted in Turrell, *Colman*, 122–6; and for Cotton Mather's like opinion in 1716, Mass. Hist. Soc., *Collections*, 7th ser., VIII, 327–8.

Want of sober and religious Missionaries; few offering themselves";
and the fact that when men take their position in the colonies, they
frequently "forget their Mission" and contend for "Rites and Ceremonies," or for "Power and Privileges." All hopes for comprehension failed because extremists rather than such moderate and Christian gentlemen as Colman and Kennett called the turns.[6]

Dean Kennett's hint about the possibility of sending out bishops
to the colonies had ten years of agitation behind it. It all started
with Dr. Bray, but it was the missionaries in America who clamored
loudest and longest for an episcopate. After 1702 the voice of John
Talbot was heard above all the rest; on his return from a voyage
to England, where he had petitioned for a bishop, he even went
so far as to select a house at Burlington in West New Jersey for an
episcopal seat — which the Society did purchase in 1712. A convention of 1705 of the clergy of the Middle Colonies held at Burlington petitioned for a bishop, and in 1713 the ministers, church
wardens, and vestry of King's Chapel at Boston, inspired by General Francis Nicholson, brought New England to the support of
their Southern colleagues by addressing the Queen as well as the
Society. Shortly thereafter Rhode Island Anglicans were heard
from. In all these instances the desire for a bishop was circum-
scribed by the internal needs of the Church of England, and on
these grounds the Society made the abortive attempts to procure
them described in the previous chapter.[7]

The failure of the New England ministers to block the advance
of the Society was not solely due to their tardiness in perceiving
the precise nature of its designs. They lacked, as the nascent newspaper press phrased it, "the latest Intelligence, both Foreign and
Domestick," and, in addition, they had no machinery for effective
action. In particular, they were out of touch and out of tune with
the Dissenting Interest in London.

Transatlantic co-operation between the London dissenting ministers and their colleagues in New England began propitiously in
1691 when Increase Mather served with Independent and Presbyterian pastors to frame the Heads of Agreement. Although, as

6. The Colman-Kennett letters are in the Mass. Hist. Soc., *Proceedings,* LIII
(1920), 67–8, 70; and Turrell, *Colman,* 128, 130.

7. Cross, *Anglican Episcopate,* 93–101.

we have seen, all hopes for a lasting union in England faded by 1698, the Heads of Agreement proved so acceptable to the growing presbyterianizing element among the Boston and Connecticut divines that Cotton Mather printed them with an exegetical sermon on *Blessed Unions* in 1692 and advocated them most enthusiastically in his *Magnalia Christi Americana* in 1702. Under the aegis of Benjamin Colman and Cotton Mather, the Cambridge-Boston Association of Ministers sent out proposals to reform the New England churches, stressing particularly the need for better communication between local ministerial associations through correspondence. Known as the "Proposals of 1705," these recommendations have often been represented as being reactionary whereas the Reverend John Wise's later attacks on them are labeled democratic. Rather, it would seem, they arose from a single demand by the Congregationalists and Presbyterians (moving away from their former strict position) for some method of getting things done. The movement toward consociation was certainly in keeping with the contemporary dissenting spirit of the United Brethren in London. Rejected by the Massachusetts churches, it was accepted by the Connecticut divines at Saybrook in 1708, who added a few further provisions to the Heads of Agreement when they drew up their famous Platform of Church Discipline.[8]

With no organization to act in their behalf, individual ministers exchanged letters in order to be informed of any changes affecting their interests. After his return to Boston in 1699, Benjamin Colman wrote regularly to the leading pastors of the three great dissenting denominations; Cotton Mather did likewise, even taking it upon himself in 1701 to publish in London *A Letter of Advice,*

8. The Heads of Agreement and the Saybrook Platform are printed in Walker, *Creeds and Platforms,* 440–49, 456–62, 502–3; for the Massachusetts opposition to the Proposals of 1705, see John Wise, *A Vindication of the Government of the New England Churches,* and *The Churches' Quarrel Espoused; or a Reply to Certain Proposals* [1710, 1717] (Boston, 1860); Cotton Mather, *Magnalia Christi Americana* (Hartford, 1855), II, 272–6. This controversy should have a re-examination in the light of the broader relations of English and American Dissent instead of the purely local or provincial situation. See also Leonard J. Trinterud, *The Forming of an American Tradition: A Re-examination of Colonial Presbyterianism* (Philadelphia, 1949), 29; and especially Clayton H. Chapman, The Life and Influence of the Reverend Benjamin Colman (Ph.D. Thesis: Boston University, 1954), 72–84.

To the Churches of the Non-Conformists, cautioning the brethren against any traffic with "the Babylonish Constitution" or "the Pelagian Apostacy of the Canonical Church of England." To this divine, the High-Church Episcopalianism that was soon to gain ascendancy under Queen Anne was anathema. The passage of the Occasional Conformity Bill in 1712 confirmed his worst fears, and, together with the apparent threat of colonial bishops, so frightened Mather, Colman, and their associates that their ministerial association debated: "How may a minister best deport himself, supposing the Church interest should prevail among us?" The only answer they could give each other was: "Let him be well studied in the point of non-conformity, take care of his life and conversation." [9]

The course of events, time, and distance combined to frustrate much regular overseas communication between dissenting groups. In England the Nonconformists doggedly and unsuccessfully fought for their own rights; whereas their established New England brethren, already in full possession of them, feared the loss of a preferred position. Neither party fully comprehended the view of the other.

Evidence of such misunderstanding came out startlingly in 1703 when a committee of the London Meeting for Sufferings of the Society of Friends solicited the support of the Independent and Presbyterian ministers of the metropolis in a campaign against the severe legal restrictions on Quakers in Massachusetts. With characteristic Quaker directness, the committee wrote the London pastors: "There being several severe Laws made by your Brethren in New England, and in the Massachusetts-Bay Province, against our Friends the People called Quakers, only for their conscientious Dissent from the National Way there, if you are for Liberty of Conscience to those who dissent from you, and are willing our Friends in New-England should enjoy the like Liberty of Conscience there, as you with us do here; we request you to manifest your Sincerity herein, not only by shewing your Dislike hereof to your Brethren there, but also by your concurrent Application with us to the Queen, that she would be favourably pleased to disallow all such Laws." In the meantime the Friends asked for a public

9. Chapman, Colman, 86–92; Mass. Hist. Soc., *Collections,* 7th ser., VII, 312, 326, 549–51; Hamilton A. Hill, *History of the Old South (Third Church), Boston, 1669–1884* (Boston, 1890), I, 362.

declaration by the London Dissenters against the discriminatory laws. Caught in a real dilemma, the Independent ministers replied that they had written two letters to pastors in New England to lay the complaint before them and would therefore have to await an answer before proceeding further.[10]

The letter sent by eleven of the principal ministers of the Three Denominations to Increase Mather for transmittal to his associates gave the New Englanders something to think about:

. . . We pretend not to form a Judgment in the present Case, which would not be just, without a full hearing of both Sides; much less would we presume to dictate Measures to you about it.

We cannot reasonably suppose, but you as well as we are for Liberty of Conscience, as full as it is here established and enjoyed, since you are not so much charged with having lately executed these Laws among you which might now appear to infringe it; whatever peculiar Reasons your Ancestors had for first enacting them.

We conclude, you agree with us, that the Truth is not to be propagated or maintained by external Force or Violence against Errors or Mistakes, but by the gentle Methods of Argument and Persuasion; and we cannot but judge it disagreeing with the Spirit and Principles of the Gospel, and an Encroachment upon the Divine Prerogative, and the undoubted Rights of Mankind, to punish any for their conscientious and peaceable Way of Religion, whilst they are not justly chargeable with any Immoralities, or what is plainly destructive of Civil Society.

Since this is our real Sentiments, and we are called upon to own it, we think ourselves obliged thus to express it, for the avoiding that odious Imputation of denying to others what we claim ourselves. And that we may not give any Handle or Colour for the undermining your and our common Liberties, we would also do whatever may be done with Christian Prudence to engage the Affections of those who differ from us; and at the same Time testify our Abhorrence of the Popish pretended Infallibility and *French* persecution.

We cannot think the Truth to be betrayed, or any Way injured, by the avowing such Principles as secure it the Liberty to speak for itself, and which, if universally espous'd, must open a Way into all Parts and Places of the World.

10. Neal, *New England*, II, 361–2.

Therefore, upon the whole, we conceive, that the Honour of God and the Interest of our Redeemer engage us, thus to appear for Liberty of Conscience; and we persuade ourselves, you will look upon our laying this Matter so freely before you, as an Instance of our brotherly Affection to you, nor is it the wide Distance of Place, or any little Difference of Sentiment that may possibly be, which can lessen our Concern for Members of the same Mystical Body of Christ.

We therefore humbly offer it to the serious Consideration of yourselves, and by you to your Fellow-Labourers in the Ministry, together with other Christian Brethren, what further Assurance may be prudently and fitly given, that in the present Affair you are like-minded with us, and are not to be out-done by any in the Evidence and Exercise of a truly Christian Charity; and that you will rather employ your own Interest, as is here allowed, than that others should be left to try what their Endeavours can do, which we would gladly divert them from, in Expectation of what this Letter may produce.

Finally, Brethren, you will not forget that the Apostle tells us, after the mentioning of Faith, Hope, and Charity, that the greatest of these is Charity; since you are (we doubt not) guided by that Wisdom from above, which is not only pure, but peaceable, gentle, and easy to be entreated, full of Mercy and good Fruits, without Partiality, and without Hypocrisy, &c.[11]

The dismay and uneasiness which this letter stirred up in the minds of the Boston divines may be readily imagined. This was the first instance since the early days of New England when Londoners felt it necessary to advise their American brethren firmly and "without Hypocrisy," but it was not the last. The Londoners wrote with tremendous authority both as ministers and as friends steeped in experience with the great controversy over church and state. They had to be listened to and they had to be answered — and satisfied, somehow.

Daniel Neal, who probably signed the letter, states that Increase Mather replied but that the missive from his son entered more fully and particularly into the merits of the Quaker charges. The Charter of 1691 guarantees liberty of conscience, Cotton Mather points out,

11. Neal, *New England*, II, 362–4; Reed, *Church and State in Massachusetts*, 99–100.

and therefore prohibits severe ecclesiastical legislation. Moreover, all province laws must be approved by the Crown. The Quakers complain of laws requiring all males sixteen to sixty to serve in the militia and others providing for military watches in towns during time of war; they also resent the law taxing everybody for the maintenance of a minister legally chosen and settled. In these respects, Quakers in New England are certainly not under any greater hardship than those in England under Queen Anne, whom they plan to petition. This being the truth, but not the whole truth, the London ministers left further action to the Society of Friends.[12]

In 1705 after another appeal from the Quakers for their support, the Dissenters wrote letters to Massachusetts once more urging that "the Toleration Act by that Government be there admitted by consent in its full force." Agitated by what he considered unwarranted interference from misguided friends, Cotton Mather poured out his spleen in his *Diary:* ". . . the wicked Quakers having made their Addresses and Complaints and Clamours, at home in England against the Countrey, whereof an Account was address'd unto us by the Independent Ministers in London; as if we had persecuting Lawes among us: I thought this a good Opportunity, not only to vindicate my injured Countrey, but also to discover more and more of the wicked Spirit of Quakerism. . . . I composed a Treatise on this Occasion; and sent it over unto the Ministers in London; under this Title: NEW AND REMARKABLE DISCOVERIES OF THE SPIRIT OF QUAKERISM." Ever awake to new devices, Mr. Mather was soon using America's first newspaper, the *Boston News-Letter,* for counter-propaganda directed at the Quakers, thereby introducing the issue of church and state to a wide New England public.[13]

Persistent Quaker protest and pressure, made possible by the well-organized joint efforts of the Yearly Meetings of Rhode Island and London, gradually eroded the Massachusetts establishment and, as a consequence, rendered unplanned aid to the Episcopalians in their fight for rights. This incidentally revealed to the Congrega-

12. Neal, *New England,* II, 364–7.

13. Reed, *Church and State in Massachusetts,* 101; Mass. Hist. Soc., *Collections,* 7th ser., VII, 571–2; *Boston News-Letter,* Oct. 29, 1705.

tionalists their backwardness in both religious outlook and effective organization.

Cotton Mather, who, as we have seen, was always eager to do good as he saw it either at home or abroad, was greatly alarmed over the reports reaching Boston of "the Reproaches and Calumnies" heaped upon the English Dissenters by their High-Church detractors; accordingly, in December of 1711, he decided to send the Independents some advice by which they might "gaine Wisdom from their Enemies." Knowing how bitterly the Nonconformists resented paying taxes for the support of the S.P.G., Mather proposed that the London ministers raise a fund to purchase tracts counteracting the Society's propaganda and distribute them in America, especially to those valiant pastors who were "conflicting with extreme difficulties in our southern colonies." Well-meant, wordy, and cogent advice was one thing; properly timed action was another.[14]

By this time the ministers of New England had learned the first lesson in the hornbook of politics: the need for sound organization. As soon as the news that the Three Denominations at London and the Church of Scotland had addressed King George upon his accession reached Boston, the local pastors hastened to get their country colleagues to assist in consolidating their position in England, politically as well as ecclesiastically.

In late February or early March, 1715, with the approval of the Governor's Council, the Bostonians sent out a call to all Congregational ministers in Connecticut and Massachusetts to send delegates to a convention to prepare an address like that of the English and Scottish divines to the new monarch asking his favor and the continuance of their liberties. They also proposed to work out plans for establishing "such a good Correspondence . . . between us, and our *United Brethren* in the Church of Scotland, and the Dissenters in England, that they may look on what is done unto us, as done unto themselves." Within a few weeks Cotton Mather was informing Nonconformists in England of the New Englanders' "Ambition to be acknowledged as your *United Brethren*." On April 14, the Reverend Mr. Colman wrote to four prominent pastors of the Three Denominations in the name of his Boston associates,

14. Mass. Hist. Soc., *Collections*, 7th ser., VIII, 143, 145, 148.

and soon, for the convention which assembled in Boston in May, 1715, he drafted both the address to the throne and a more specific letter to the Three Denominations.[15]

In the address, Colman related to King George that "We are in Denomination, and so in Principle and Practice, Discipline and Worship, Congregational and Presbyterian; of one Body with the Protestant Dissenters from the Church of England as by Law established in Great-Britain, commonly known by the Name of United Brethren; and like them we have signalized our Zeal for and Adherence to the Protestant Succession in your most serene and illustrious house." [16]

The following year Colman wrote for the Boston clergy to Dr. Edmund Calamy, Mr. Thomas Bradbury, Mr. Thomas Reynolds, Mr. William Tong, and other members of the Three Denominations a letter requesting support for the churches of New England. There are "many Enemies who are continually striking at our Civil and religious Liberties," he pointed out. "Very lately the Charter of our Province was threatened by a Bill in Parliament, and in great Danger of being taken away. This attempt made us sensible, that we need some standing Friends in and about London, who will naturally care for us on like Emergencies, and generously use their Interest in our Behalf." To this prayer the Bostonians added a "true account" of conditions in New England.[17]

That theirs were no idle fears, the Londoners knew full well — "the cry of the city here runs exceedingly against you and they revive the story of 1641" — Daniel Neal wrote them in 1721. Demonstrated loyalty to the Hanoverians and concerted action with English Nonconformists was the New England formula for future success, but it would take years of persistence to assemble and mix the ingredients.[18]

15. Mass. Hist. Soc., *Collections,* 7th ser., VIII, 300–301, 301–3, 310–12, 315–16.

16. Turrell, *Colman,* 83–6.

17. Turrell, *Colman,* 91–2; for the threat to the Massachusetts Charter, see Osgood, *American Colonies,* II, 294.

18. Thomas Hutchinson, *The History of the Colony and Province of Massachusetts-Bay* (Lawrence S. Mayo, ed., Cambridge, Mass., 1936), II, 219.

III

While the Congregationalists were assuming the initiative in proposals for working more closely with the Dissenters in England, the Anglicans won the first great victory in the American wars of religion. Overwhelming in its suddenness and completeness, it occurred not in Massachusetts, where the skirmishing had had its start, but in Connecticut, of which in 1705, Caleb Heathcote of New York reported to the Venerable Society that he believed "that more than half the people in that government think our Church to be little better than the Papist, and they fail not to improve every little thing against us." His estimate was on the modest side, for until 1722 there was not a single Episcopal parish or church; about that time, however, the situation began to change. The Reverend George Pigot believed that many of the ministers could be persuaded to come over to the Church of England if a bishop were present; these pastors could then "secure their parishes now and hereafter. . . ." He also claimed that "there are other gentlemen disposed to renounce their separation, not only in this colony, but also in other provinces of North America, and those of a body considerable enough to perfect a *general reformation*." [19]

The "glorious revolution of the ecclesiastics of this country," as Mr. Pigot was to call it, took place overnight and was revealed in an astounding way on September 12, 1722, at Commencement in New Haven. The Reverend Timothy Cutler, a graduate of Harvard and Rector of Yale College, stunned his audience by the closing words of his prayer, which were these: *"and let all the people say, amen."* Such phraseology was not Congregational; it was Episcopalian, if not Popish. The next day, in the college library, Mr. Cutler confirmed the worst fears of his distressed trustees; he asserted that he, together with Tutors Samuel Johnson and Daniel Brown, as well as James Wetmore and Jared Eliot, could not accept Presbyterian ordination and had decided to conform to the Church of England. Worse still, the Rector admitted that "he had for many

19. Francis L. Hawks and William S. Perry, eds., *Documentary History of the Protestant Episcopal Church in the United States of America. Connecticut* (New York, 1863), I, 9, 53, 57.

years been of this persuasion," and his wife told friends that it had been for a decade, long before he accepted the charge at Yale! Close upon this disclosure came the news that an Episcopal church was soon to be built at Stratford and that three of the "Connecticut Apostates" were departing for England to take Holy Orders.[20]

The aftermath of the great apostacy of Cutler, possibly the most dramatic event in the ecclesiastical history of the American colonies, was dismaying and shocking to the New England Congregationalists, who saw in this duplicity and treachery the approaching end of the Standing Order and the inevitability of bishops. "I apprehend the axe is hereby laid to the root of our civil and sacred enjoyments; and a doleful gap opened for trouble and confusion in our Churches. The Churchmen among us are wonderfully encouraged and lifted up by the appearance of these gentlemen on their side, and how many more will, by their example, be encouraged to go off from us to them God only knows. It is a very dark day with us; and we need pity, prayers and counsel," said the Reverend Joseph Webb of the Yale trustees. It was well, perhaps, that the New England divines did not know of the conversations between Messrs. Cutler and Johnson and Bishop Gibson at London, for the Congregationalists were already concerned about the future.[21]

Any incident that aroused the fears and anger of the ministers could not fail to agitate the entire society of eighteenth-century New England, so intimate and pervasive was their relation to the people. Acting as a *Congregatio Propaganda Fide,* the pastors unhesitatingly resorted to the press as their most potent weapon to combat the Anglican invasion. One Anglican spokesman reported that every town in Connecticut was "glutted" with books,

20. Hawks and Perry, *Documentary History, Conn.,* I, 56, 65–7; 69–70, 72–5; *New England Courant,* Oct. 1, 1722; *Boston Gazette,* Oct. 8, 15, 1722; Franklin B. Dexter, ed., *Documentary History of Yale University* . . . (New Haven, 1916), 226–34; Cotton Mather reported the affair to the great hymn writer, Isaac Watts, who replied regretting the trouble they had had, but saying, "so far as I can hear it makes very little noise in London, and I hope will do you in New England but very little injury." Mass. Hist. Soc., *Proceedings,* XXIX (1894–95), 331–41 for the Mather-Watts correspondence; Eben E. Beardsley, *The History of the Episcopal Church in Connecticut* (New York, 1866), I, 45.

21. Hawks and Perry, *Documentary History, Conn.,* I, 63, 73; Beardsley, *Episcopal Church,* I, 63; Chandler, *Johnson,* 38.

"many thousands of which have been printed off at Boston." "The Mathers are diligent in sending circular letters to all places; exhorting them to trace the pious steps of their forefathers. . . . They have been compelled to take refuge in another more notorious untruth, namely, that there are *two* Churches of England, the high and the low; with the low they pretend to hold full communion, but the high are rank *Papists;* they terming us no less." [22]

Aiming at all levels of public education and intelligence, the Congregational ministers printed letters and pieces seriously reviewing the history on both sides of what one unrestrained Newport divine called "a grand revolution, if not a general revolt, from schism in these parts." Sly allusion, insinuation, sarcasm, and ridicule, coupled with countless hours of pulpit denunciations of the New Haven apostates, provided the rank and file of Yankees with a delectable fare of human interest such as had never previously been set before them; and they ate it up greedily. James Franklin's *New England Courant* carried an anonymous letter about a curious man lately come from England who could be seen at the Greyhound in Roxbury (where Bostonians went for animal shows). "Some say he is a Roman Catholic; others take him to be a Quaker . . . others think he is a Churchman. . . ." Another concludes: "It is nothing but a Pun upon Mr. C[utle]r and the rest of the ministers at Connecticut, that have lately turned Churchmen." A week later appeared a letter from "Jethro Standfast of Nuhaven" who, in the emerging Yankee dialect, banteringly told of a "Jeshuet" who had appeared among them, and that it is "buzd abute, that in order to Salvashn we must beleve the uninteurrupted Sukseshn of Bishops from the Upostels . . . and that all the Churches in the Wurld that any govern'd by Bishops are no part of the Cathalike Church, but are out of the ordnare Rode of Salvashun." Whether this is a doctrine of the Church of England as well, Jethro does not know, but the people are "running mad" about the matter.[23]

22. Cotton Mather informed Thomas Bradbury of London in 1724 that most converts to the Church of England in New England would never have been won "if they had not the Hopes of being Excused from all the Charge of maintaining any Ministry. . . . Mass. Hist. Soc., *Collections,* 7th ser., VIII, 797; Hawks and Perry, *Documentary History, Conn.,* I, 81, 85–6.

23. Hawks and Perry, *Documentary History, Conn.,* I, 91; *New England Courant,* Oct. 1, 8, 29, 1722.

The sole counsel of moderation in the newspapers came from "Silence Dogood," whom we recall was young Benjamin Franklin. Condemning indiscreet religious zeal and partisan invective, he remarked that no word in the English language so wanted precise definition as "church." But he did have this to say of Cutler, Johnson, and company: "Since they have denied the Validity of their Ordination, by the Hands of Presbyters, and consequently their Power of Administering the Sacraments, &c., we may justly expect a further Manifestation of their Repentance for invading the Priest's Office, and living so long in Corah-like Rebellion." [24]

Upon the whole, the Congregationalists won this battle of words. The charge that the Yale group had gone over to episcopacy solely "with a View of Worldly Interest" cut deep into the sensitivity of the converts. However untrue, they never managed to counter it. Nor did Messrs. Wetmore, Johnson, and Brown succeed in dispelling from suspicious Yankee minds "the tragical Representation" planted by comment in the *New England Courant* that for them "to have declared in favour of the Church of England, had been as bad as to have declared for Popery or something worse." In the debate over Bishop Stillingfleet's declaration that no church government is *de jure divino,* the Congregational ministers proved both more learned and agile. Nevertheless, what had been done could not be undone, and Timothy Cutler returned triumphantly from London as rector of Christ Church right in the heart of dissenting Boston.[25]

Fully aroused, first by hysteria and then by resentment, suspicions, and fear, not only by the Checkley affair in their own province but by the Anglican gains in Connecticut, the Massachusetts ministers applied in the spring of 1725 to the General Court of Massachusetts for permission to call a synod to deal with the alarming moral derelictions of society.[26] Without warning, the two Epis-

24. *New England Courant,* Oct. 8, 1722.

25. *New England Courant,* Oct. 15, 22, Nov. 5, 1722; *Bos. Gaz.,* Aug. 2, 1725.

26. John Checkley ran afoul of Boston authorities in 1719 by publishing a work on the apostolic origin of episcopacy; later he brought out other pieces on this subject. Not until 1738 did he succeed in obtaining orders in the Church of England. Never sponsored by the S. P. G., Checkley's case is not immediately germane to the present discussion. Consult Edward J. Slafter, *John Checkley* (Prince Society, Boston, 1891); Clyde A. Duniway, *Development of the Freedom of the Press in Massachusetts* (Cambridge, Mass., 1906), especially pp. 84–6, 108–10, 166–71.

copal divines of Boston, Cutler and Samuel Myles, protested, condemning the synod as illegal and suggesting that its true object was to oppress the Church of England: "and we have little Reason to expect that in such a Synod she will be treated with that Tenderness and Respect which is due to an Established Church." Colman wrote to White Kennett that the "Alienation is like to increase" should a synod be denied, because the Presbyterians at New York have synods, likewise the Irish, and such bodies have a long history of respectable use. Help came from the London Dissenters who procured the insertion of the Boston ministers' address in the London *Flying Post* of August 17, 1725. The proposal for a synod was dropped, however, because, as Colman told Bishop Kennett, their mutual acquaintance at Lambeth Palace, Bishop Gibson, entered the opposition to it. The next move of the crafty Mr. Cutler was to induce an Episcopal convention at Newport to address the Bishop of London and the S.P.G. to press upon the throne their petition for a colonial bishop.[27]

In this same year, 1725, Cutler wrote to his friend, Dr. Zachary Grey in Cambridge, England, about his plans for reforming education in New England commencing with his alma mater, Harvard College: "here is a snotty town of the same name where are near 300 scholars among who[m] a ch[urch]man durst hardly say that his soul is his own, and I think it will never be well till that College become an Episcopal College, or we have one found[ed] th[at] way." The Harvard Overseers had ceased to notify Cutler of the meetings because of his ill-concealed animus against Congregationalism, and Cutler was fighting fiercely though in vain to maintain his right as a "teaching elder" of Boston to sit with them. When John Read, the ablest attorney in the colony, failed to win his case, Cutler sought to carry the fight to London through the Society and Bishop Gibson. Either he must be seated on the Board of Overseers or the College must be new modeled, he told the Secretary of

27. The attempt to call a synod started another newspaper war between Mr. Cutler and the Congregationalists, which may be followed in the *New England Courant,* July 3, 10, 1725; *Bos. News-Letter,* July 8, Aug. 2, 19, 1725; Nichols, *Illustrations,* IV, 271, 273; Hutchinson, *History of Massachusetts-Bay,* II, 245*n;* Perry, *Historical Collections, Mass.,* III, 170–75, 179, 180–81, 191–200; Turrell, *Colman,* 137–8; Sykes, *Gibson,* 346–7; Shipton, *Harvard Graduates,* V, 59.

the S.P.G. in martial metaphor: "For now it is only a Battery planted against the grand Designs of that Worthy Body in Erecting Missions and sending Missionaries into these parts." The Episcopalians won a victory with the quashing of the synod, but the Reverend Timothy Cutler failed to spike the guns of Harvard.[28]

A further attempt to harass their enemies and to curb their power was made when the Anglicans appealed to the Crown for the dissolution of the Massachusetts establishment, which, they claimed, violated the Charter of 1691. Again they failed, for after five years, a decision was handed down in 1732 by the Crown's law officers against the petition of Cutler and the others. The lawyers could find no violation of the Charter and, by implication, declared the establishment legal.[29]

The first breach in the Standing Order's ramparts was made in 1727. Under strong local pressure together with direct threats of interference by the Privy Council inspired by Lambeth and the Board of Trade and Plantations, Connecticut and Massachusetts relaxed their ecclesiastical laws sufficiently to relieve Anglicans from having to pay for the building of Congregational meeting-houses and awarded the rates of those Episcopalians living within five miles of one of their churches to the incumbent missionary. In each of those colonies, however, any deficiency in the salary of the pastor of the Standing Order could be made good by a second assessment in which the Anglicans would be included. The Episcopalians considered such concessions insufficient, but their dissatisfaction was even greater when, a year later, Massachusetts granted the same terms to the Quakers and Baptists and made further concessions to these denominations in 1729, 1731, and 1734. Steady pressure applied by the Society and the Bishop of London induced Governor Jonathan Belcher to persuade the General Court to grant

28. Timothy Cutler failed in 1729 to persuade George Berkeley, Dean of Derry, to locate his proposed college in Boston; he hoped that "this will be some compensation for the loss the Church has sustained as to Harvard College." Nichols, *Illustrations*, IV, 269–70, 284, 289; Cutler to Zachary Grey, April 23, 1723 (Boston Public Library: MS 6 380.27); Perry, *Historical Collections, Mass.*, III, 210–19, 235–43, 257–61; Turrell, *Colman*, 54, 136; Hawks and Perry, *Documentary History, Conn.*, I, 127.

29. Perry, *Historical Collections, Mass.*, III, 274–88.

the Church of England in 1735 the same rights temporarily as were accorded the Quakers and Baptists, rights made permanent in 1742.[30]

Quite as important as these legal advances to the future of episcopacy in the colonies was the emergence of a great leader, an ecclesiastical general. The cause had need of an organizer and strategist more able than Timothy Cutler, whose tactlessness and contentious zeal made him odious to the Congregationalists and impelled them to brand him as a Jacobite and High Church, only a step from Rome itself. He had served the Church well, but he was no longer an asset; he was a liability.[31] Sound judgment, moderation in speech and action, as well as skill in tactics and grand strategy, were essential, and they were found in the Reverend Samuel Johnson, another of the Yale apostates. And Johnson was eager to take command.

In person, Samuel Johnson was rather tall and corpulent. "There was something in his countenance that was pleasing and familiar, and that indicated the benevolence of his heart; and yet, at the same time, it was majestic and commanded respect. He had a ruddiness of complexion, which was sometimes farther brightened by a peculiar briskness in the circulation of his spirits, brought on by the exercise of the benevolent affections. He was happy in an original *calmness* and *sweetness* of *temper,* that was seldom discomposed, and never soured, by the common accidents of life. . . . What was most apt to excite his indignation, was the licentiousness of an un-

30. Reed, *Church and State in Massachusetts,* 178–80; Greene, *Religious Liberty in Connecticut,* 198–201; Osgood, *American Colonies,* III, 138–9; Hawkes and Perry, *Documentary History, Conn.,* I, 124–5; John H. Trumbull and Charles J. Hoadly, eds., *Public Records of the Colony of Connecticut* (Hartford, 1873, 1874), VII, 459; VIII, 123, 334; *Acts and Resolves . . . of the Province of Massachusetts Bay* (Boston, 1874), II, 459–60, 482, 494–6, 543–4, 619–20, 714, 782–3; *Acts of the Privy Council of England: Colonial Series, 1720–1745* (London, 1910), III, 156, 491.

31. Humble folk could take Mr. Cutler's measure too: "I am a poor woman of the other [Trinity] Church at Boston," Madam "Y. Z." wrote to the priest in May, 1726, "and have been sundry times to hear you, and should go very often, but I find you preach up morality, and little of Christ, in your Sermons. I pray you preach more on true conversion, and on the life of Christianity, and not so much on passive obedience and non-resistance." Nichols, *Illustrations,* IV, 279.

principaled age, with respect to both religion and government. The same good temper that rendered him aimiable in private life, marked all his proceedings of a public nature, and may be discovered where such a thing is not often expected, in his controversial writings. These he conducted with decency and candour; and the greatest personal provocations could not kindle him."

Such was the character of the man as delineated by a close friend and fellow divine, Thomas Bradbury Chandler, in 1773. Chandler failed to note the essential conservatism of his hero as evidenced by an inability to measure the drift of his times in matters of church and state, an inability heightened by the fact that he was a pious and energetic convert. Devoted to truth as he saw it, his religious partisanship blinded him to many of the verities of American life. But, taken all in all, his Church could not have had an abler, a more devoted, a more determined, or a more resourceful leader.[32]

Influenced, perhaps, by the Reverend George Pigot in 1722, if not earlier, Samuel Johnson had become convinced that the future of the Church of England in America depended upon the sending over of one or more bishops to lead it, and he harped on this subject. He and Cutler had interested Bishop Gibson in the cause in 1723, and the next year that "excellent prelate" made unsuccessful overtures for political support of the project to the powerful Duke of Newcastle. Back in Stratford, Johnson conducted a frank and importunate correspondence with Gibson and other London Churchmen emphasizing that "the want of a bishop is what is very discouraging to us, and detrimental to our cause." To Francis Nicholson he pointed out that the ministers of the Standing Order in Connecticut habitually "pretend that their schism is the established religion in this colony. . . . From all of which it appears that our chief misfortune is the want of a King's governor and a bishop." Here, at the outset, Johnson advocated a politico-religious policy to which he steadfastly adhered for the rest of his career. He wanted to bring about the union of church and state in Connecticut (ultimately in all America) by unhorsing the "rigid Independents" who manifested such "an inveterate enmity against the established church." Whatever the legitimate internal needs of his Church for

32. Chandler, *Johnson*, 126–7.

bishops were, this man clearly reached far beyond limits acceptable to most Americans.[33]

In April, 1732, Johnson submitted an elaborate plan for an ecclesiastical reordering of the colonies. Asserting, not altogether accurately, that many places lacked "public instruction," and that "people of sense and consideration among them even are sick and weary," longing for religious order, he proposed establishing the Church of England under such a "comprehension" as that attempted in England during the reign of William III. Matters could then be regulated with moderation to soften the blow to the "Independents." Provision was to be made by taxation for the support of one or two bishops with salaries of from £300 to £500 annually, a state of affairs which would undoubtedly encroach on the interests of the existing colonial governments. "Indeed, it would be much happier for the Church," Johnson asserted, "especially if we had a Bishop, if the Charters were taken away," and, he added, "most people begin to think, since they have got into such a wretched, mobbish way of management, that it would be best for the people themselves." Grossly distorting the truth in this last contention, Samuel Johnson lapsed into a form of misrepresentation that became a persistent refrain of the missionaries of the S.P.G. when they wrote letters or reports to their superiors in London.[34]

In the second decade of the eighteenth century, the Episcopalians in the S.P.G. had launched their drive for ecclesiastical power in New England. At New Haven in 1722 they brilliantly ambushed the Congregationalists, forcing them into a rear-guard action as they retreated. During the next ten years the Anglicans gained in

33. Schneiders, *Johnson*, I, 18–19; III, 217, 218, 211–12.

34. Appealing to the new Archbishop of Canterbury, John Potter, in 1737, for help in the propagation of episcopacy in the colonies, Samuel Johnson denied the allegations of some in England that the sending of bishops would "result in our affecting an independency on the government at home." In truth, the exact opposite would ensue; "so that the most effectual method to secure our dependence on the Crown of Great Britain would be to render our constitution here, both in church and state, as near as possible conformable to that of our mother-country, and consequently to send us wise and good bishops to be at the head of our ecclesiastical affairs, as well as governors (I could wish a Viceroy) to represent his most sacred Majesty in the affairs of civil government." Schneiders, *Johnson*, I, 87–8; Hawks and Perry, *Documentary History, Conn.*, I, 153–4, 156.

numbers, and by 1735, with the able and indefatigable Bishop of London back of them, they had broken down the exclusive Massachusetts establishment and severely fractured that of Connecticut. It is no wonder that these victories seemed portentous to the Churchmen.

IV

At the same time that the Episcopalians had been making headway, they were also teaching their enemies that they must recruit their own ranks, plan, and carry out a counter campaign. The Congregational citadel at Cambridge remained intact, and Dean Berkeley, far from setting up a rival college in Boston as urged by Timothy Cutler, responded to the solicitations of Samuel Johnson by giving his books and farm to Yale College. Both the donor and the recipients, who had been advised by Colman, understood that this was a free gift to a still "dissenting" institution. When a truce was concluded in 1735, a viable form of toleration had been won in Massachusetts, which left, unwittingly and ironically too, the Congregationalists there in a far stronger position to repulse the next attack and to take the offensive. The improvement in Anglican status made possible a shift by the New Englanders from bigotry to more advanced views about religious and civil liberty and their interrelations, while their adversaries logically proceeded from actual toleration toward dreams of establishment.[35]

During this initial encounter of the Anglican invasion, and the New Englanders honestly acknowledged it to be just that, the Yankees looked upon the Society for the Propagation of the Gospel, which was present in force, with much more resentment and fear than they did the potential danger from diocesan bishops. In a history of the S.P.G. published in 1730 and widely read in the colonies, Secretary David Humphreys openly conceded, as he told of its work colony by colony, that the Society had to put aside two of "the three great Branches" of its work, namely, the conversion of Indians and Negroes, and the founding of churches where none existed. "The Society began therefore with the English, and soon found there was more to be done among them than they had as yet, any Views of

35. Nichols, *Illustrations*, IV, 289.

effecting." Changing realities produced a change in objective, as is so often the case.[36]

The Congregational ministers of New England knew of this decision through hard experience, and, as they read his pages, they knew at once what Humphreys meant. Using the good offices of Benjamin Colman, who for thirty-five years had served as liaison officer between his colleagues and Englishmen of both the dissenting and established communions, a convention of ministers in rural Hampshire County in Massachusetts forwarded an address to the Bishop of London. In his covering letter, Colman, professing firm faith in the moderation of Edmund Gibson, wrote that he joined in these sentiments of his "remote" brethren, "being fully persuaded of their integrity and uprightness, and that they aim at nothing but what is just and right in the sight of God." The address, drawn up by the already celebrated Jonathan Edwards, "Scribe," is a notable document in this struggle, and an eloquent, accurate, and telling indictment of the Venerable Society and its missionaries. It must be read in its entirety, as much for its tone of restrained emotion and its style, as for its bill of particulars:

Hatfield, Sept. 10, 1734.

My Lord,

We would approach your Lordship with humble Deference and respect, acknowledging our distance and meanness, and hope your goodness will render you a righteous Judge in your own cause and towards your inferiors, as holy Job professes he did not despise the cause of his man servant or his maid servant.

It is the cause of God that we are concerned for, and the well being of our Churches, and which we apprehend our relation to them as pastors obliges us to. And inasmuch as it is more immediately from your Lordship that Missionarys are authorized and sent from England to us, we think no person so proper for us to apply ourselves unto, and humbly beg leave to acquaint your Lordship so far of the state of our Country and Province, and also of the Colony of Connecticut, bordering upon us, with respect to religion, that you may be sensible that the sending of Missionaries hither does not answer the good and noble professed design of the royal Charter of the Society for the Propagating

36. Humphreys, *Historical Account of the S.P.G.*, 23.

the Gospel in Foreign Parts, nor, as we suppose, of many of the generous Donors to that Society, and that they are neither necessary nor profitable, but as to many instances, rather injurious to the interests of the Kingdom of Christ and the good of his Majesty's subjects in these parts.

For 1. We think we may justly claim the name of a Christian Country, or people already (tho' we may blush that we no better honor that worthy name). For we acknowledge the religion which Jesus Christ has graciously taught for the recovery of a lost world to God, His favor and Image.

We believe and own all such Doctrines and Duties as are contained in the Holy Scriptures of the Old and New Testament, consenting to and receiving all the Doctrinal Articles of the Established Church of England, constantly adhering to the Sacred Scriptures as the rule of our Faith and practice, nor dare we call any man upon Earth our father or master in these regards.

2. These Doctrines are openly acknowledged in our Confessions of Faith, and are constantly preached in all parts of the Land. It is our civil constitution that every town in the province shall be provided with a learned and Orthodox Minister, and many of our larger towns have, some 2, some 3 or 4 such. And those who are employed in the ministry are men solemnly separated to that work by the Election of the people to whom they minister, and their own deliberate Act and Engagement and by prayer, with the laying on of the Hands of the Presbytery, and have a solemn charge given them to fulfil the ministry which they have received of the Lord. And we hope that we may say of them in general that they do diligently attend thereunto, Preaching the Word, in season and out of season, and are accepted in the respective Congregations whereunto they are called; and if any are found negligent therein, due Testimony is borne against them, and upon Just reasons are removed, and others are put in their stead.

3. We take care that the doors of our churches be opened to all persons of competent knowledge in the Doctrines of the Christian Religion, and who are of a regular conversation. If any of the members of our churches walk disorderly and fall into scandalous Immoralities, that the discipline of Christ be exercised towards them to bring them to repentance, which so soon as there is a credible appearance of rational Charity, we readily restore them again.

4. The Missionaries that come among us shew a very uncharitable

and unchristian spirit, particularly by insinuating that our Ministry is no Ministry, not having had Episcopal Ordination, and that so all other Administrations are null and invalid, and that our Churches are no Churches of Christ, and that our people are to be looked upon as strangers to the Commonwealth of Israel — a tenet or principle which came from Rome, and which in years past has been disclaimed in England, and is still by all the other reformed Churches in Europe — as also by their Endeavors to render the Government of our Churches insignificant, by receiving into their communion and protection such as lie open to or are under censure in them for immoral conduct.

5. Which things tend to breed disorder and confusion in our Churches, by cherishing a small number of *disaffected persons* in several places, to the ill example of a whole town, produces wranglings, strifes, ill names, needless disputations, instead of Godly Edifying, and tends to lead them to place religion rather in some external *observations and ceremonies* than in love to God and our neighbours and in a life of Faith, repentance and Holiness.

6. We cannot but look upon it as great injustice, it having been often openly declared to the world that our Fathers left their Native Land, and at a vast Expence purchased and subdued a wilderness, that they might in a place of their own serve God according to their Consciences in peace, without giving offence to the then Governing powers — a liberty which we account dearer than any temporal interest whatsoever, which some Missionaries have endeavoured to wrest from us, partly by setting themselves to lay blocks in the way of our having synods convened for the reforming such Evils as have a Threatening effect upon us.

And we have reason to fear that the prospect of a better salary than what our Ministers generally have (which is not, unless in some great towns, £40 sterling per annum, as our Bills are now sunk), has been the great inducement to some of our young men to go over to receive Orders; — that we would not take upon us to judge men's hearts.

But heartily wish that your Lordship and the Honourable Society might not be missled in those weighty affairs, and the Missionaries might have the worthy views of carrying the Gospel among the miserable Heathen who have not known the way of Life, or to search parts of His Majesty's dominions where Ignorance and Error have prevailed, and have no provision made for them.

Relying on your Lordship's candour, and assuring you that we have not any personal views nor Interest that has moved us thus to address you, but from a real desire that the donations from the Honorable Society, in their several Missions, may not be misapplied, and from a sincere regard to the peace and prosperity of our Churches.

We are your Lordship's
most humble servants,
Wm. WILLIAMS, Moderator

Jonathan Edwards, Scribe	*In the name of the* *Associated Ministers of the* *County of Hampshire* [37]

The replies of both the S.P.G. and the Bishop of London to the ministers were defensive and conciliatory in tone; but we have no record of Bishop Gibson's reaction to Benjamin Colman's withering, yet courteous, geographical lesson read to the prelate in his letter covering the address: "The Harvest, my Lord, is Plenteous, from North Carolina to New York, and multitudes are perishing within that long spread of Virginia, Maryland, Pennsylvania, and the Jersies; but from New York northward, Dr. Bray undo [*explains,* in his book of 1700] little need of Missionaries for the propagating of Christianity, the Narragansett [Indian] Country excepted, and in the colonies of Connecticut and Massachusetts none at all, as at the time I was informed." [38]

The Hampshire County document requires no explication: Jona-

37. Everywhere the Congregationalists kept an alert watch. Elisha Williams, Rector of Yale College, "a great Enemy to the Church, and of a very insidious temper," also signed the Hampshire protest. From Fairfield, Conn., in 1736, the Reverend Henry Caner reported to the Society, "The Dissenters among us are busily employed in examining into the conduct of the missionaries in order to have Whereof to accuse us; some instances misinterpreted, I understand they pitch upon." Hawks and Perry, *Documentary History, Conn.,* I, 165; Schneiders, *Johnson,* I, 26–7; Shipton, *Harvard Graduates,* V, 591; for the Hampshire Address, see Perry, *Historical Collections, Mass.,* III, 299–302.

38. Colman here refers to Dr. Thomas Bray's *A Memorial Representing the Present State of Religion on the Continent of North America* (London, 1700), see Osgood, *American Colonies,* II, 30; Perry, *Historical Collections, Mass.,* III, 302. For the Anglican replies, see "The Anatomist," No. II, in *Pennsylvania Journal,* Sept. 12, 1768; and John Holt's *A Collection of the Tracts from the Late Newspapers. . . . On the Subject of the Residence of Protestant Bishops in the American Colonies* (New York, 1769), II, 17–19.

than Edwards presented the indictment with his customary force and clarity. We have already examined the case for the Church of England. Henceforth men of both parties would look upon the Episcopalians, symbolized by mitre and sceptre, as a group whose assumption of ecclesiastical and civil authority would fundamentally alter the entire religious character of the English colonies in America. There was to be no peace in the Commonwealth of Israel until this issue was settled by the sword.[39]

39. The importance attached to the Hampshire Address by both parties in the debate over episcopacy in the colonies is clear from the use made of its arguments by William Livingston in the *Independent Reflector* and "The Watch-Tower" in 1753–54; and in 1768 when Provost William Smith quoted sections of it with the answers of the Bishop of London and the S.P.G. in "The Anatomist," II, which appeared in the *Pennsylvania Journal* and *Pennsylvania Gazette,* Sept. 29, 1734, and in *A Collection of Tracts,* II, 14–19.

IV

Transatlantic Dissent

1740–1760

The ecclesiastical prospect appeared relatively serene to the New Englanders at the beginning of the 1740's; the Anglicans in Connecticut and Massachusetts had won sufficient concessions to enable them to dwell in reasonable harmony with the Standing Orders; the latter, though they had given way more than a little, could congratulate themselves on the preservation of their establishments. Undoubtedly those of the Congregational ministry who, under the impetus of contemporary enlightened European thought, were moving toward a greater theoretical and practical toleration, looked forward to the possibility of guiding their brethren and the people of New England in the direction urged by the Dissenters of England. In spite of the seeming calm, the pastors, still badly shaken by "the glorious revolution" at Yale and its aftermath, slept, like Chaucer's little birds, with open eyes watching for the least sign of renewed Episcopalian reaching for power. And it was a good thing that the parsons did, for they were about to reap the whirlwind.

Before the year 1742 was out, George Whitefield landed at Newport, and soon began the revivals that swept over New England with hurricane force. The Reverend Timothy Cutler of Boston sent a graphic report of the religious excitement to Dr. Zachary Grey of Cambridge in September, 1743:

Whitefield has plagued us with a witness, especially his friends and followers, who are like to be battered to pieces by that battering ram they had provided against our Church here. It would be an endless attempt to describe that scene of confusion and disturbance occasioned by him; the divisions of families, neighbourhoods, and towns, the contrariety of husbands and wives, the undutifulness of children and servants, the quarrels among the teachers, the disorders of the night, the intermission of labour and business, the neglect of husbandry, and of gathering the harvest. Our presses are for ever teeming with books, and our women with bastards; though Regeneration and Conversion is the whole cry. . . . In many conventicles and places of rendezvous there has been chequered work indeed, several preaching and several exhorting at the same time, the rest crying or laughing, yelping, sprawling, fainting; and this revel maintained in some places many days and nights together without intermission; and then there were the blessed outpourings of the spirit. The *New Lights* have with some overdone themselves by ranting and blasphemy, and are quite demolished; others have extremely weakened their interest. . . .[1]

That Congregationalists divided sharply into New Lights who favored and Old Lights who condemned the orgy of emotional enthusiasm is a twice-told tale. Churches also split over the issues of the revival, and, especially in Connecticut, the ministers faced unprecedented problems of church government, modes of worship, itineracy, and kindred matters. To Old Lights these events seemed to be the saddening and frightening result of God's controversy with New England.

All New England Episcopal churches were closed to George Whitefield (notwithstanding the fact that he was an Anglican priest), and the revival did not greatly disturb their communicants, though they could scarcely be oblivious to the convulsions going on around them. Samuel Johnson once went to hear Whitefield, in order to scout his style, so he said, and on another occasion in 1743, he and several missionaries "went one night in the dark, and perfectly *incognito,* among a vast crowd, to see and hear [Reverend James] Davenport's Managements, whom we heard rave about a quarter of an hour and then went away. . . ." If the Great Awakening served the cause of religious liberty in an institutional sense by weakening the structure of the Connecticut churches and like-

1. For the Great Awakening generally, see Edwin S. Gaustad, *The Great Awakening in New England* (New York, 1957); John Nichols, *Literary Anecdotes of the Eighteenth Century* (London, 1812–15), II, 546–7; Osgood, *American Colonies,* III, 407–50.

wise by lessening the authority of the preachers, it also offered the Anglicans a providential opportunity to divide and triumph.[2]

The missionaries themselves could scarcely have dreamed up a situation which would have better aided and abetted their plans for growth and advancement. Nearly everywhere they profited from the enthusiasm raging among the "Independents." From Fairfield, the Reverend Henry Caner truthfully though somewhat pompously reported: "Where the late spirit of enthusiasm has most abounded, the Church has received the largest accession. Many of those deluded people having lost themselves in the midst of error, wearied in the pursuit, as their passions subsided, sought for the rest in the bosom and communion of the Church; and others, reflecting upon the weakness of their former dependence, which left them exposed to such violent disorders, have likewise thought proper to take shelter under the wings of the church." [3]

If there was any doubt but that everywhere the Episcopalians were harvesting a bumper crop and forging ahead during these tumultuous times, the stream of letters dispatched to London pleading for more missionaries and the forming of new churches would substantiate the claims. The response did not, and perhaps could not, keep up with the requests. In Connecticut alone, in 1742, a mere seven clergymen tried desperately to care for fourteen Anglican churches either built or building. In 1748, nine Episcopal clergymen ostentatiously appeared at the Yale Commencement to see three of their best prospects take degrees: Samuel Seabury, William Samuel Johnson, and Thomas Bradbury Chandler. In all, the Church of England students took five bachelor's and five master's degrees. It would be difficult to conjure up a more galling display for the harassed "independents" than the presence of these Anglicans, most of them converts from Congregationalism, headed by Mr. Commissary Barclay of New York and the proud father, Samuel Johnson. "We all consulted the best things We could do for the Church's interest," Johnson wrote home to the Society. One

2. Hawks and Perry, *Documentary History, Conn.*, 203, 204; Gaustad, *Great Awakening*, 110, 119.

3. In 1743 the S.P.G. was supporting sixty-seven missionaries in the colonies. Cross, *Anglican Episcopate*, 33n; Hawks and Perry, *Documentary History, Conn.*, I, 201.

of the designs dearest to all clerical hearts was how to open an Episcopal church on the College Green in New Haven.[4]

The spectacular growth of Anglicanism in New England coincided with the first overt indication by the leaders in England that the S.P.G. would resume its efforts to send bishops out to the colonies, which had been laid aside ever since the failure to interest George I shortly after his accession. The signal came when Thomas Secker, Bishop of Oxford, committed the Society by coming out strongly for a colonial episcopate when he delivered the annual sermon at the parish church of St. Mary-le-Bow in 1741. The following year the Bishop of London received a petition from the clergy in Connecticut bewailing the fact that the want of a bishop had been "a very great obstruction to the propagation of religion." If they could not have a bishop, they desired His Grace to create a commissary for Connecticut, for the one at Boston was two hundred miles distant; this would at least assist them to combat "the strange spirit of enthusiasm" and to shepherd a membership which had recently risen from one thousand to five or six thousand souls. For such an office they proposed Samuel Johnson. The next year Johnson appealed to the Archbishop of Canterbury and added a new reason for a bishop: the missionaries needed assistance against the Moravians.[5]

In the Bishop of Oxford, Samuel Johnson discovered the vigorous ally across the water he had so long sought. Thomas Secker had joined with other prelates in recommending the Connecticut priest for the master's degree at Oxford, conferred on him in 1743. Replying to a letter from Johnson in March, 1745, Secker regretted that "we have been greatly blameable, amongst many other things, to-

4. Gaustad, *Great Awakening*, 116, 117; Franklin B. Dexter, *Biographical Sketches of the Graduates of Yale College* (New York, 1896), 1st ser., 447–50; 2nd ser., 143, 190; Beardsley, *Episcopal Church*, I, 159; Hawks and Perry, *Documentary History, Conn.*, I, 245, and for the applications of the congregations of ten communities for missionaries, 1743–48, see I, pp. 185, 186, 202, 206, 210, 218, 233, 235, 240, 247, 248.

5. Cross mistakenly dates the Reverend Andrew Eliot's able analysis of Secker's sermon *c*.1741, but it was not written until about 1766 or 1767, as internal evidence indicates. Cross, *Anglican Episcopate*, 109; Secker, *Sermon Preached Before the S.P.G.*, reprinted in Klingberg, *Anglican Humanitarianism;* and for Eliot, Mass. Hist. Soc., *Collections*, 2nd ser., II (1814), 190–215; Hawks and Perry, *Documentary History, Conn.*, I, 181–2, 183, 195.

wards you; particularly in giving you no Bishops. But I see no prospect of the amendment of that or any thing, except what arises from the contemplation of his overruling Providence, who brings light out of darkness." Six months later, unwilling to give up his most cherished desire, Johnson again expostulated to Dr. Bearcroft of the S.P.G.: "Would to God we had a Bishop to ordain here. . . ." [6]

The rejoicing at Anglican gains in New England was not only alloyed by the lack of a bishop but also was subdued in December, 1746, by a sudden attack by "the great protagonist of eighteenth-century Connecticut Congregationalism," the Reverend Noah Hobart of Fairfield. In the midst of an ordination sermon at Stamford, in the very heart of Episcopal country, Mr. Hobart opened up a very tender subject. Almost as an aside, he mentioned the "fixed Prelacy" of New England episcopalianism as one of the "Evils of the Times." He contended that a priest of the Church of England could not discipline the most erring of his flock, and that "open Irreligion and undisguised Prophaneness . . . are dreadfully visible where the Church of England has the Ascendant." [7]

Such a charge had to be answered. It elicited a response discourteous very promptly from the Reverend James Wetmore of Rye (one of the "Apostates") to the effect that the Congregational minister had perpetrated a "gross Prevarication and False hood . . . with a wicked Intent, to asperse the Constitution of the Nation." Picturing the Consociated Churches of Connecticut as excrescences and tumors, and their members as bigots, guilty of "Hypocrisy and detestable Vices," he argued hard that episcopacy really came over in the Winthrop Fleet of 1630 along with the common law and the statutes of the realm. Hobart shrewdly addressed his reply to "the Members of the Episcopal Separation in New England" and, in measured phrases, denied the allegation about the common and statute law. To him and his fellow divines, the Church of England was a "Prelatical Establishment in the south part of Britain," made so by the Act of Union of 1707, which recognized

6. Quoted in Chandler, *Johnson*, 75; Hawks and Perry, *Documentary History, Conn.*, I, 217.

7. Shipton, *Harvard Graduates*, VIII, 359, 362; Rev. Noah Hobart, *Ministers of the Gospel . . . Delivered at the Ordination of . . . Noah Welles, at Stamford, December 13, 1746* (Boston, 1747), 20, 21, 24–5.

the Presbyterian as the established church north of the Tweed. Thus, said he, using his advantage to the utmost, the Church is nought but a purely local institution with nothing catholic about it. Turning to the attack, Mr. Hobart flayed the S.P.G. missionaries to New England for invading communities where able, learned, and pious ministers were already established, for taking into communion every disgruntled Yankee, and for outrageous neglect of the welfare of the Indian and the Negro slave. In true Congregational fashion he fortified his whole discourse with cogent citations from the works of liberal Anglican bishops.[8]

In *A Calm and Dispassionate Vindication,* for which the Reverend Henry Caner and the Reverend James Wetmore contributed appendices and Dr. Samuel Johnson the preface, the Reverend John Beach excitedly charged Mr. Hobart with "abusive misrepresentation" and "fallacious argumentations," but he added scarcely anything new, calm, or dispassionate to the controversy. Again holding his temper and with a display of patience suitable to the cloth, Hobart waited at least two years before publishing *A Second Address to the Members of the Episcopal Separation in New England* (Boston, 1751), which was milder in tone than his first essay. Even so, the Reverend Mr. Caner asserted to the Secretary of the S.P.G. that: "Mr. Hobart is not singular in his Ill Nature and Rudeness towards the Church: we think the Profusion of it in his Books is the work of a Junto. However it hath made him so popular, that all his Books are taken up; as I find by our Booksellers [in Boston], of whom I would have got copies to remit to you, if I could, and am still labouring for it, but with little Prospect of Success." [9]

8. Rev. James Wetmore, *A Vindication of the Professors of the Church of England in Connecticut Against the Invective . . . in a Sermon Preached . . . by Mr. Hobart* (Boston, 1747), 6, 7, 29; Shipton, *Harvard Graduates,* VIII, 362–3; Dexter, *Yale Graduates,* 1st. ser., 136; Noah Hobart, *A Serious Address to the Members of the Episcopal Separation in New England, occasioned by Mr. Wetmore's Vindication of the Church of England in Connecticut* (Boston, 1748), 5, 7, 15, 28–35, 64, 65, 72, 100, 130.

9. This particular exchange closed with John Beach's ill-tempered *A Continuation of a Calm and Dispassionate Vindication.* In this second effort, Beach confessed that "I am sensible Mr. Hobart has the Advantage of me both as to his Matter and Manner of Writing; his Business is to load us with Reproaches, and once in a while to shew the Sprightliness of his Wit by breaking a bitter Jest upon us." Rev. John Beach, *A Calm and Dispassionate Vindication of the Professors of the Church*

In this controversy, the Connecticut Anglicans made two serious blunders. Mr. Wetmore's reference to the Winthrop Fleet was bad history, and it caused the Congregationalists to give renewed attention to the refining of their historical myth. Mr. Beach's unrestrained and scurrilous charges did his cause no good but instead made his opponent stand out as an example of moderation. Commenting on the tone and and manners of the Episcopalians in this intemperate debate, a distinguished authority believes "it may well be that this whole unfortunate controversy did more to alienate Connecticut from England than did the Stamp Act." In their zeal to further their faith, the missionaries succeeded only in making it appear to the average Yankee "that the Church of England was a real menace to the social structure of New England." The Yankee sense of humor had not yet been extended to having an appreciation of being regarded as fit subjects for Anglican missionary work.[10]

This battle of the pamphlets called into being a more far-reaching exchange in the newspapers at Boston, which, because they had no competitors north of New York, circulated widely and were read and discussed all over New England. Less than three weeks after Noah Hobart's Stamford ordination sermon, a writer in the *Boston Evening Post* startled the public by saying: "I may almost venture to prophesy, that in a few Years Time *Episcopacy* will generally prevail in this Part of the World." This is probably the earliest newspaper reference to colonial bishops. In April, Thomas Fleet printed in his *Evening Post* an unsigned letter describing the S.P.G. as an institution founded for the noble end of maintaining orthodox ministers in such places as wholly lacked public worship, "But the Truth of the Case is far otherwise; for in most of the Places where the Missionaries have exercised their Ministry, *Gospel Churches have been planted, Ministers settled, and GOD's Word and Sacraments duly administered,* some Scores of Years before this Society had a Foundation." Mildly, though pointedly, the writer remarked

---
of England (Boston, 1749), ii–vi, 38, 48–66, 67–75; and *A Continuation* . . . (Boston, 1751); Hobart, *A Second Address,* 7, 8, 31, 32, 89, 97, 114–26, 144, 146, 150; Shipton, *Harvard* Graduates, VII, 363; Cutler to Secretary, Aug. 31, 1752, S.P.G. Correspondence (Library of Congress Transcripts), Series B, XX, 17.

10. Shipton, *Harvard Graduates,* VII, 364.

on the exaggerated accounts the missionaries sent home to the Society, accounts which contained almost nothing about converting the Indians, Deists, or Roman Catholics. "No, the Missionaries are chiefly engaged in other Work. Their grand Business seems to be, not to convert Men *from Paganism,* to *Christianity,* but . . . to proselyte *Protestant Dissenters to the Church of England!* as if they imagine there can be *no Salvation* out of that Church." [11]

The Hobart-Wetmore-Beach debate over the validity of Presbyterian ordination quickly broadened out to include the larger issue of episcopacy in all its aspects. The Reverend Mr. Hobart had formulated what became the classic colonial case against the Anglicans, and in it he employed all known arguments save that of history. Later controversialists such as William Livingston, Jonathan Mayhew, and Andrew Eliot added little to Hobart's arguments. Moreover, this ecclesiastical exchange soon grew into a public issue through the press, as the discussion attracted attention. Thenceforth the Congregational ministers and their allies would contest in this open forum rather than in the temple. The public, already avid for spirited controversy as a result of its first taste of it in the literature of the Great Awakening, was gradually being prepared for the great struggle for religious and civil liberty.[12]

II

While the public battle of the divines over the nature of ordination and the proper relation of church and state was taking place in Connecticut and spreading to the rest of New England, a more

11. Even Dr. William Douglass, ardent Anglican, wondered in his *History* why missionaries went only to "our most civilized and richest towns." He hinted that they aimed at "getting better livings," a statement which Samuel Johnson resented and denied in a letter of January 15, 1752. William Douglass, *A Summary, Historical and Political . . . of the British Settlements in North America* (Boston, 1751), II, 127–8; Schneiders, *Johnson,* I, 156–8; *Boston Evening Post,* Jan. 12, 19, Feb. 9, Mar. 23, Apr. 27, 1747 (reprinted Jan. 14, 1760); *Bos. Gaz.,* Apr. 21, 1747.

12. The Rev. Noah Hobart emerged from the contest a public figure known widely over the Northern Colonies. Mr. Cutler reported to Bishop Secker in 1754 that the whole impression of Hobart's Sermons had been disposed of and that he could not procure a single copy upon any consideration. Edmund B. O'Callaghan and B. Fernow, *Documents Relating to the Colonial History of New York* (Albany, 1853–87), VI, 907.

important religio-political intrigue was being hatched in England, and the Yankees were immediately drawn into it. No sooner had Thomas Sherlock assumed his duties as the Bishop of London than he told a friend on September 9, 1748: "The business of the diocese, and of the plantations (which last article is immense, and to be carried on by foreign correspondence) sits heavy on me." Six months later he had prepared a comprehensive report relating to the ecclesiastical government of the colonies. This document is notable because it adduces certain points which Anglicans made in every ensuing defense of Episcopacy. The Anglicans in the colonies, said Dr. Sherlock, are not "an inconsiderable party" there, and the Independents and other Dissenters "do by no means . . . make the body of the Inhabitants. . . ." If the Church were properly established, the Independents of New England "could only have a Toleration." Bishops should be sent out, therefore, to complete the establishment of the Church of England, but, inasmuch as it is not intended that they should have coercive powers, nor that they be supported by taxation, the ministers of New England can have no grounds for their usual complaints. Furthermore, he emphatically said, no bishops should be sent to Pennsylvania or New England; the Congregationalists "are not concern'd *themselves* and have no right to judge for *others*" in the plantations where the Church is already established.[13]

At a General Meeting of the Dissenting Deputies held April 5, 1749, Dr. Benjamin Avery, acting upon the efficient intelligence service of Eliakim Palmer, reported to the members that Dr. Sherlock had in mind a bishop for Barbados and another for Virginia "that they may confer Orders there on Persons without giving them the Trouble to come to England to take orders, which if Carried into Execution may be of sad Consequence." The Deputies promptly resolved that their Committee should join with the colonial agents in all proper measures "to prevent the said Scheme taking Effect." Ten days later, Eliakim Palmer wrote to Governor Law about the Bishops' plan, and he promised to bear "the strongest testimony (as your agent) against it" as a measure having "so Direct a Tend-

13. *Tenth Report of the Historical Manuscripts Commission* (Report on the Mss. of the Earl of Eglinton, Sir J. S. Maxwell, Bart., . . . 1885), 302; Chandler, *Johnson*, 166–7; *N.Y. Col. Docs.*, VII, 365–8.

ancy to Introduce Ecclesiastical Tyrany amongst a people whose Ancestors have so severely felt the bad Effects of it as ours have done — I have given the Alarm to our Brethren on this side of the Water who as a Body have Deputed Dr. Avery and myself to attend four Great Men upon the Affair." After they had waited upon the Dukes of Bedford and of Newcastle, Lord Chancellor Hardwicke, and the Honorable Henry Pelham, Palmer reported back to the Committee on May 5 that the officials "all declared the Affair was farr from being Concluded on and that nothing would be done in it without the maturest Deliberations and that they should be willing to hear any Objection thereto from persons of Consequence." Having taken these precautions, the London Dissenters awaited further developments.[14]

Meanwhile, the Bishop of London concentrated on his project for colonial bishops, which some New Englanders suspected, and not without reason, was inspired by certain "restless Churchmen" of Connecticut and Massachusetts. Whatever its origin, Dr. Sherlock strengthened his case by sending one A. Spencer overseas to sound out colonial opinion on his plan. The report, submitted June 12, 1749, concluded that the gentlemen and merchants approached by Spencer in New York and Philadelphia "unanimously" concurred in the sending of a bishop on being assured that he would not be invested with powers inconsistent with colonial privileges. From Boston at about this same time, Timothy Cutler opined that "even many sober Dissenters do think a resident Bishop would be a Blessing. . . . tho' others and the much bigger number, are ready, according to their power to defeat it." [15]

Before Bishop Sherlock had been at Lambeth Palace a year, he regretted having been "induced to leave the quiet and easy See of Sarum," and admitted his "fatal mistake" in supposing that he

14. Palmer also notified Massachusetts in a letter to Thomas Hutchinson, who communicated it to the House of Representatives on June 24, 1749. That body sent a letter of thanks to Dr. Avery and Eliakim Palmer on June 27 signed by Speaker Joseph Dwight. *Journals of the House of Representatives of Massachusetts, 1749–1750* (Boston, 1951), XXVI, 43, 48; Dissenting Deputies, Minutes, I, 314–15, 317; *Law Papers*, XV, 298.

15. *Law Papers*, XV, 325; Spencer's Report, in Cross, *Anglican Episcopate*, 310; Perry, *Historical Collections, Mass.*, III, 433.

"might have prevailed to have bishops already" in the colonies. Sometime between April and August, 1749, he had presented his memorial on plantation bishops to the King, and it had been referred to the principal officers of state for consideration. "But so many difficulties were started, that no report was made to his Majesty." In September, 1749, trying another tack, he approached the Duke of Newcastle, since the latter controlled all ecclesiastical appointments. The Duke's answer was scarcely encouraging: "The appointing Bishops . . . is a great, and national consideration; had long been under the Deliberation of great, and wise men, heretofore; and was, by them laid aside." [16]

Still hopeful, the ever-eager prelate persisted; his next move was to send Newcastle a copy of a Representation that he intended to lay before the King-in-Council. Replying at once, the Duke took serious issue with some of the statements in the Representation about the colonies and expressed the hope that the Bishop would not present it until some of the King's chief servants met with him about it. Such counsel notwithstanding, Sherlock went ahead and submitted his scheme as planned. In a report of progress to the colonial commissaries on September 19, 1750, the prelate stated that the resolution had not yet been acted on because of the King's journey to Hanover. It is apparent that in addition to being stubborn, the Bishop was either overly optimistic or unrealistic — perhaps both.[17]

Always on the alert for any possible action unfavorable to the Nonconformists, Dr. Avery discovered the efforts being made for "introducing Spiritual Power into America" and was able to give the General Meeting of the Dissenting Deputies a full account on March 28, 1750, only three days after Newcastle's second letter of advice. The S.P.G. were agitating again, "intent upon having Bishops sent into those parts," even though the move of the previous year had been blocked. Henry Pelham had told Dr. Avery that the following Thursday there would be a meeting of some

16. Newcastle Papers (British Museum), No. 32, 719, f. 52; quoted by Sykes, *Gibson*, 372; Cross, *Anglican Episcopate*, 320–21; Schneiders, *Johnson*, III, 237.

17. The Sherlock-Newcastle correspondence from the Newcastle Papers is printed by Cross, *Anglican Episcopate*, 320–23; Chandler, *Johnson*, 166–7.

Lords about it. Subsequently the physician learned with relief that Lord Hardwicke "believed there was no Danger at present of such a scheme taking place." [18]

These activities provide the necessary background for understanding Horatio Walpole's long letter of May 29, 1750, written from the Cockpit, explaining to Thomas Sherlock the official attitude of the Government about bishops for the colonies. Whatever the merits of the Representation "abstractly considered," His Lordship has not sufficiently weighed "the consequence of it as a matter of State to our present happy Establishment." Walpole is apprehensive lest carrying the issue to the King-in-Council may cause trouble for the Government, and, besides, he has genuine doubts about the colonials' desire for bishops. They have never asked for one, and many of them have "conceived some jealousy of that Church power." Far better informed about actual conditions in America and the vagaries of British politics, Horatio Walpole politely but firmly read the prelate a prophetic lecture:

I cou'd not forebear letting your Lordship know that I apprehended as soon as a Scheme of sending Bishops to the Colonys altho' with certain restrictions shou'd under your Lordship's Authority and Influence be made publick it would immediately become the Topick of all conversation; a matter of controversy in the Pulpitts, as well as by Pamphletts and Libells, with a Spirit of bitterness and acrimony that prevail more frequently in disputes about Religion as the Authors and Readers are differently affected than on any other Subject.

The Dissenters of all Sorts whom I mention with no other regard or concern than as they are generally well affected, and indeed Supports to the present establishment in State, and therefore shou'd not be provoked, or alienated against it, will by the instigation and complaints of their brethren in the Colonys altho' with no Solid reasons, be loud in their discourses and writings upon this intended innovation in America, and those in the Colonys will be exasperated and animated to make warm representations against it to the Government here, as a design to establish Ecclesiastical power in its full extent among them by Degrees; altho' the first step seems to be moderate and measured, by confining

18. Dissenting Deputies, Minutes, I, 325, 326.

the Authority of the Bishops to be planted amongst them to certain Colonies and Functions.

Permitting himself a little "friendly freedom," Horatio Walpole reminded the Bishop that many people in England are "not without jealousy of your extraordinary Zeal and desire to increase Ecclesiastical Power in this Country," and the introduction of bishops into America will arouse their suspicions. However well disposed the Court may be, if you go to Parliament with the proposal, "heats and animositys" are bound to arise, possibly even creating a division and confronting the Government with a great dilemma. Then, with definite sarcasm, Walpole asked the prelate some searching questions:

Can you undertake to promise that no coercive, or other Ecclesiastical power besides Ordination and Confirmation, shall ever be proposed and pressed upon the Colonys when Bishops have been once settled amongst them, or beyond what is at present exercised by the Bishop of London's Commissary?

Can the Society undertake that the maintenance of the Bishops . . . shall be no Burthen to the Colonys? are they to determine what that expence is to be? and how is it to be supply'd? or is it intended that it shall be done by a Voluntary Contribution out of the Bishopricks in England? [19]

One is bewildered by the Bishop's reliance on the reports of interested American missionaries and surprised at the failure of his Lambeth associates to bring him abreast of the local political situation. That some Churchmen were politically wiser is indicated by the report made several years later by Thomas Bradbury Chandler to Dr. Samuel Johnson while on his trip to London to take Holy Orders: Archbishop Thomas Herring had given him "the true Reason" for Bishop Sherlock's defeat. "It seems that the Duke of New-Castle, Mr. Pelham, and Mr. [Speaker] Onslow can have the Interest and Votes of the whole Body of the Dissenters, upon the Condition of their befriending them, and by their Influence on those Persons, the Ministry was brought to oppose it. Whether it was a

19. For Walpole's letter, see Cross, *Anglican Episcopate*, 324–30.

good Policy in them to submit to such Terms, I will not take upon me to determine; but there does not appear to be any great Matter of Honesty in it. From all Turks, Infidels, and Heretics, the good Lord deliver us. I afterwards had much the same account from Dr. Bearcroft." [20]

The Walpole letter ended any real hope of sending bishops to the colonies for the time being, but still it took some months for this good news to filter down to the Dissenters. Elisha Williams, a Connecticut Yankee who was then in London, wrote back to Governor Law in October, 1750, that the "Arch-Bishop of Canterbury as well as the Bishop of London, with Several other active Bishops, are not a Little Engaged in it, and tis much to be feared will Accomplish it." Williams ardently desired to serve Connecticut well and protect "our" privileges. "There are some who begrudge them to us and Love us not I dont Say, That Such a Man as Dr. Avery may Say, *Treat us hardly because we have them.*" [21]

Such reports did not divert the steady drift of New England into the larger current of dissenting ideas of religious liberty, nor did they affect the high opinion the Congregational pastors and pro-

20. Naturally, Walpole sent a copy of his letter to Newcastle to keep him posted and to suggest that the Bishop's scheme "should be as little known as possible to the Publick." "I always had very good Doubts upon this measure, from the First Proposal," the Duke replied. "There is great Weight, also, in the Consequences, You so judiciously suggest, that This Affair may have at Home, in reviving old Disputes, and Distinctions, which are, at present, quiet; and perhaps, creating new Divisions amongst those Who Sincerely mean the Good of His Majesty's Government and the Good of Their Country. . . . I was extremely sorry to hear, that the Society, for propagating the Gospel, had been concerned in it: But I find Since, that it is Stopped." In May, 1751, Bishop Sherlock complained about the New Englanders to Dr. Philip Doddridge: ". . . they used all their influence to obstruct the settling of Bishops in the Episcopal Church there . . . and I am sorry to add, that some here [Dr. Avery], for whose characters and abilities I have due esteem, have not, upon this occasion, given signs of the temper and moderation that were expected from them." Cross, *Anglican Episcopate*, 327, 329, 331–2; John D. Humphreys, ed., *Correspondence and Diary of John Doddridge, D.D.* (London, 1831), V, 202; Thomas Bradbury Chandler to Samuel Johnson, May 3, 1752, Hawks Papers (New-York Historical Society), II, no. 25.

21. Massachusetts was somewhat better informed. William Bollan, the province agent wrote from London to Secretary Josiah Willard in August that he had seen the Duke of Bedford, who said he was inclined to send bishops to America because too many non-jurors (whom he regarded as Jacobites) had gone over lately. Bollan saw no possibility of this happening very soon, however. Bollan to Willard, Aug. 25, 1750, Mass. Archives (State House, Boston), XX, 643–45; *Law Papers*, XV, 429–30.

vincial officials had of Dr. Avery and the Dissenting Deputies. The latter fully justified this confidence when, in answer to a letter from the Committee of Ministers at Boston "desiring to maintain a correspondence with the Deputation in England," the General Meeting voted on October 10, 1750, to set up a special committee of six including Dr. Avery, Israel Mauduit, and Dennys De Berdt to "keep a Watchful Eye over the Design to introduce Bishops into America, to endeavour to prevent all Encroachments upon the Religious Rights of the people there," as well as to "Correspond with the Ministers in New England." A year later, the churches of New Hampshire, whose leader was Samuel Langdon (later president of Harvard College), sent a letter requesting a regular correspondence and at the same time complaining about the attempts of the royal government of their province "to Discountenance the Dissenting Interest there." At the same meeting, Dr. Avery read another protest from Boston about similar activities of the Episcopalians in Massachusetts.[22]

III

The missionaries of the Venerable Society in the Northern Colonies always had faith that some day a bishop would come to them from powerful England. Unfortunately, some of their superiors in London encouraged them in this hope; one of them, who was born a Dissenter, was the great and spiritual Bishop of Durham, Joseph Butler. Late in 1750, copies of a new plan for an American episcopate drawn up by Bishop Butler arrived in the colonies. The Anglican divine had attempted to anticipate the usual objections to bishops by strictly limiting the ecclesiastical and spiritual authority of colonial prelates. According to a copy sent to William Vassall of Boston:

1. No coercive power is desired over the laity in any case; but only a power to regulate the behaviour of the clergy who are in Episcopal orders; and to correct and punish them according to the law of the Church of England, in case of misbehaviour or neglect of duty; with such power as *commissaries* abroad have formerly exercised [over the clergy in the colonies].

22. Dissenting Deputies, Minutes, I, 328, 329, 342, 343, 360.

2. Nothing is desired for such *Bishops,* that may in the least interfere with the dignity or authority, or *interest* of the GOVERNORS, or any other officers of State. The probate of wills, licenses for marriages, &c. are to be left in the hands where they now are; and no share of temporal government is desired for Bishops.

3. The colonies are to be at no charge in the maintenance of the Bishop.

4. No Bishops are intended to be settled in places where the government is in the hands of dissenters, as in New England, &c. — But authority to be given only to ordain clergy for such Church of England congregations as are among them, to confirm the members of the same, and to inspect into the manners and behaviour of their clergy.[23]

As soon as the Boston Episcopal clergy had studied the Butler proposal, they signified their approval and urged the S.P.G. to collect possible objections. Individually and privately, however, Messrs. Cutler and Caner of Boston protested. They claimed that in New England "the Church itself is peculiarly injured; and there we eminently need a Bishop to appear in our Favor, and upon Occasion to represent our Case at home." Dr. Samuel Johnson, always emphatic, wished that the episcopacy would be in "its full vigor as at home." Insisting that the "Dissenters" were their own greatest enemies, "as well as ours," Johnson went on to reveal his true sentiments: "for their case is very deplorable among themselves since the late enthusiasm hath thrown them into so many feuds, contentions, and separations, which the awe of a bishop would we believe tend much to abate and reduce them to a better state of unity in their own way (as well as reclaim many of them). . . . We verily believe the Dissenters would in a little time be entirely easy under such a scheme as is proposed and that it would be every way of

23. Bishop Secker wrote a long letter on January 9, 1750/1 to Horatio Walpole commending the reasonableness of Bishop Butler's plan and advocating prompt action in sending bishops out to the colonies. The letter was not made public until after Secker's death. Its publication in the *London Chronicle,* June 29, 1769, provoked a spirited discussion; the Butler Plan, as revised by Bishop Sherlock, first circulated in the colonies in manuscript, then appeared in print in *Pa. Gaz.,* Dec. 8, 1768; *A Collection of Tracts,* II, 110–11; and Thomas B. Chandler, *An Address from the Clergy of New-York and New-Jersey, to the Episcopalians in Virginia* . . . (New York, 1771), 21–2.

vast advantage to the Church and the interest of religion in general, *as well as the political interest of the nation."* [24]

The Congregational ministers and the public officials were not at all convinced that the plan was as innocuous as its proponents contended; they were fully aware that one-third of the S.P.G. missionaries in America were in New England devoting their full attention to securing a dominant position for the Church of England. When Lieutenant Governor Spencer Phips, a stout Congregationalist whose wife Mr. Cutler had converted, asked Secretary Josiah Willard what the latter thought of Bishop Butler's project for sending bishops to America, he received a typical Yankee answer: "the universal dissatisfaction to that Scheme among Persons of our Communion is nothing lessened from the Proposals your Excellency was pleased to send . . . of the Restrictions therein contained as to the Exercise of the Episcopal Function here, those Persons expecting that if once Bishops should be settled in America, it would be judged for some Reasons or other necessary to extend their Jurisdiction equally to what that Order of Men are possessed of in Great Britain: However, It is Supposed our Sentiments in these Matters will have but little Influence with those Gentlemen in England who have the Management of this Affair." Had he known of Horatio Walpole's missive to Sherlock, Willard would have realized how well the London Dissenters had performed their duty and would not have been so pessimistic.[25]

IV

"People have no security against being unmercifully priest-ridden but by keeping all imperious bishops, and other clergymen who

---

24. "Our Increase would be out of the Societies of the Dissenters, perhaps breaking up some of them . . . these Colleges [Harvard and Yale] would be Nurseries of Episcopal Clergymen . . . [and] universal experience tells us, That the nearer the Church is to Dissenters, the more it prevails." The letters of Caner and Cutler are given in Cross, *Anglican Episcopate,* 317–18; Schneiders, *Johnson,* III, 240–41, 242 (Italics mine).

25. William S. Perry, *History of the American Episcopal Church, 1587–1883* (Hartford, 1885), I, 410; Henry W. Foote, *Annals of King's Chapel* (Boston, 1896), II, 251, as quoted by Cross, *Anglican Episcopate,* 145n.

love to lord it over God's heritage, from getting their feet into the stirrup at all . . . Rulers have no authority from God to do mischief. . . . In plain English, there seems to have been an impious bargain struck up betwixt the sceptre and the surplice for enslaving both bodies and souls of men." [26]

In such bold, vigorous language, not infrequently spiced with rural Yankee metaphors, the Reverend Jonathan Mayhew made himself the new champion of religious liberty by preaching at the West Church in Boston on the Sunday following the 30th of January, 1750, *A Discourse Concerning Unlimited Submission and Non-Resistance to the Higher Powers.* Ostensibly delivered as an occasional piece to pillory High Church advocates for making King Charles I an Anglican martyr, Mayhew's eloquent outburst was freighted with political implications. It may have been pure coincidence, but the day after the sermon the Reverend Henry Caner wrote to Bishop Sherlock that the news of his efforts to send a bishop to New England would render his name ever dear to supporters of the Church there.[27]

This was not the first time that Jonathan Mayhew had been a "fomenter of contention." In 1748 in *Seven Sermons,* he had come out unequivocally for the right of private judgment, and contended that the essence of the Christian religion was reason. If individual reason was the sole criterion of religion, here at one blow, Mayhew had disinherited the creeds, ministers, and New England establishments which had stood for more than a century. The *Seven Sermons* contained nothing that had not been said by English liberals for fifty years past, but the fact that it came from Boston was of the greatest significance. The London Dissenters detected in the Reverend Mr. Mayhew a new and militant leader who would stand forthright for the kind of religious and civil liberty they had so earnestly sought to inculcate in the minds of New Englanders. They

26. Cross, *Anglican Episcopate,* 145.

27. See the useful unpublished Life of Jonathan Mayhew, by Charles W. Akers (Ph.D. Thesis, Boston University, 1952), and the sketch in Shipton, *Harvard Graduates,* XI, 440–72; Jonathan Mayhew, *Discourse Concerning Unlimited Submission and Non-Resistance to the Higher Powers* (Boston, 1750) in John W. Thornton, ed., *The Pulpit of the American Revolution* (Boston, 1860), 73–4, 101; Caner to Sherlock, Jan. 31, 1750, Fulham Palace Mss, Mass., Box II, No. 193 (L.C. Transcripts).

indicated their support by procuring a reprinting at London of the *Seven Sermons* and inducing the University of Aberdeen to grant the author the degree of Doctor of Divinity.[28]

In Mayhew's own country, however, it was the *Discourse on Unlimited Submission* that brought him unmatched notoriety and fame. To his Congregational listeners and readers — it was published immediately after delivery — it seemed the logical culmination of the Hobart controversy, which they had followed closely in sermon, pamphlet, and newspaper, even though they were ignorant, for the most part, of the intrigues of the Episcopal missionaries and the activities of Bishop Sherlock that were going on concurrently in England. On the other hand, Mayhew's well-directed blows hurt the sensitive members of the Church of England and stirred up a furor in the press; Boston's printing and publishing made it the news center of the English colonies, and its four newspapers broadcast news, gossip, and business advices to all of New England once a week, and printers in the Middle and Southern Colonies clipped their contents.

Jonathan Mayhew now became the center of much comment and abuse in the press, particularly in Thomas Fleet's *Boston Evening Post,* which again set the pace in vituperation and did not let up for six months. The controversy began with a long quotation from a sermon preached before the House of Commons in 1678 in praise of the good and noble character of Charles I, which the contributor trusted would answer "A certain wrangling Preacher in this Town" for "having belch'd out a Flood of Obloquy" upon the martyred king. Boston Anglicans reviewed their Commonwealth history in order to controvert the minister's strictures; others, probably clericals, more specifically spun out the High-Church doctrines of nonresistance and absolute submission. Soon the Boston divine was being censured for traducing not only the memory of King Charles but of Archbishop Laud as well, both of whom were exculpated by a series of quotations dug out of Clarendon, Burnet, Walker, and like authorities. One article warned the public that a comparison of the 10th of January (Charles's birthday) with the

28. Mayhew's London endorsers for the honorary degree were the Rev. George Benson, Rev. James Foster, Dr. Nathaniel Lardner, and Dr. Avery, Mayhew Papers, Nos. 24, 25; Shipton, *Harvard Graduates,* XI, 446, 452.

30th of the same month (his execution) immediately suggested "the great danger of the State, whenever the Ecclesiastical Government is struck at: or in other words it naturally leads us to believe, that *the fall of the Crown is never any farther distant from that of the Mitre,* than the thirtieth of January is from the tenth. And therefore the Good Old saying *No Bishop, no King,* however grating it may be to some people, ought to be the standing maxim of the English Government. And till those *Jesuruns wax fat* by the Repeal of the Test Act, it is impolitick for them to *Kick* lest they should bewray [defile] the GOOD OLD CAUSE." [29]

One of the most arresting communications came from a gentleman who called upon Thomas Fleet to insist upon moderation rather than barbarous and savage quarreling in future interchanges. Though he exempted Mayhew from his blanket charge, the writer did blame him for incendiarism and could find no kinship between the minister and the glorious defenders of liberty in the past. The source of this fiery temper, says this perspicacious anonymous writer, is Mayhew's reading. The latter or declamatory part of the *Discourse* is a very close imitation of the *Independent Whig:* "he may not improperly be said to have taken an Over-Dose of that Author. And thus imbitter'd in himself, he has added Wormwood to Gall, and far out-done his Original in his Faults and Blemishes." Other Episcopalians called the minister a "swaggering Bully," "a vain and arrogant Quack Doctor," and accused him of being "an impudent plagiary." [30]

Wisely, Mr. Mayhew stood on his dignity and declined to descend into the arena. Not so his followers, who pointed scornfully to the "poor Shift these Jacobites are put to, in defending the Character of their pious Martyr," and dared the opponents to shed their anonymity and come into the open rather than smear an honest man in the dark with their newspaper scribbles. Such craven behavior they branded "base, mean, and scandalous, and out of Character, for any one who pretends to be a Gentleman, especially, for one who has obtain'd Episcopal ordination." The acclaim the *Discourse* received in both Boston and Great Britain, where it won Mayhew

29. Daniel Neal was also quoted in the controversy. *Bos. Eve. Post,* Feb. 19, 26, Mar. 5, 12, 19, Apr. 2, 16, 23, 1750; *Bos. News-Letter,* Mar. 1, 22, 1750.

30. *Bos. Eve. Post,* April 16, 23, May 21, 1750.

many correspondents, forced the Boston Association of Ministers to admit that Benjamin Colman's mantle of leadership had fallen on Mayhew's shoulders; however, they could never quite bring themselves to make him a member of their organization. The citizens of Boston and their country brothers applauded the new leader, especially when they read in the midst of the melee the London dispatch telling of the imminent establishment of a bishop in the West Indies "to transact the great Business of the Plantations." Shrill and nasty as these newspapers exchanges were, one can still agree with Jonathan Mayhew's observation to Dr. Benjamin Avery in October, that beneath it all he fathomed "A catholic spirit" such as this "country has hitherto been almost a Stranger to . . . But there are some little Symptoms of an Alteration for the better." [31]

V

The events of 1750 opened a momentous decade for England and her colonies. Beginning in peace, after the fall of Pickawillany in 1752 the primary concern of people on both sides of the ocean was the titanic struggle with France, which affected all other occurrences of the period, including those religious and ecclesiastical.

Fresh from their success in opposing colonial bishops, the London Dissenters stepped up their interest in American affairs, and constant correspondence between New England and London pastors did much to bring the two dissenting groups closer together in outlook. Customarily acting through Dr. Avery and the Committee, the Dissenting Deputies never missed an opportunity to impress the great principles of toleration and religious liberty upon the New England Congregationalists, as when they supported the Presbyterian minister of Newbury, Massachusetts, who complained about his flock's having to pay taxes to maintain the Congregational church. Speaking for the Bostonians in 1753, the Reverend Thomas Prince informed Dr. Avery, "I am as much as any man can be for the largest Liberty of Conscience in Religious matters. . . . And such a glorious universal and happy liberty we enjoy at Boston, without the least inconvenience." He explained that the law did

31. *Bos. Eve. Post*, Mar. 19, Apr. 23, 1750; Mayhew Papers, Nos. 27, 28, 29, 30, 31; Shipton, *Harvard Graduates*, XI, 445.

require everyone to attend some form of Protestant worship, but that each might choose his own way and minister. Prince also adduced several examples of generous treatment of the Episcopalians by Massachusetts Congregationalists. In Connecticut, as late as 1757, however, Dr. Avery and Mr. Sparrow of the Deputies' Committee had to intercede with less liberal members of the Standing Order about the taxing, not of Anglicans, but of those who had separated from their church during the Great Awakening and who had appealed to the English Baptists for support. Such incidents notwithstanding, the New England sentiment was surely moving in the direction of more liberal International Protestantism.[32]

Failure to secure an American episcopate in 1750 left the S.P.G. missionaries in New England bitter and frustrated. Exaggerated reports of "oppressions" experienced by most of them and their flocks, in Connecticut in particular, framed by overwrought clergymen poured in on the Society. At the bottom of one of these sent in 1750, Bishop Thomas Secker wrote: "N. B. These sort of complaints come by every ship almost; there are now some ministers of the Church of England in prison on account of their persecution from the Dissenters." [33]

Undeterred and in spite of the setback, Samuel Johnson continued as the formidable and resourceful leader of the missionaries. Agreeable and courteous on the surface, Dr. Johnson was not above resorting to threats in the service of his Church. He wrote "in the humblest manner" on May 14, 1750, to Governor Jonathan Law in support of a petition to the Connecticut Assembly praying for liberty for the Anglicans to tax themselves for ecclesiastical purposes. Yet there was no humility in his closing paragraph: "I am

32. The Dissenting Deputies aided their American friends in other ways: Dr. Avery presented an address of condolence from the Connecticut ministers to George II on the death of the Prince of Wales in 1751; he gave unofficial support to the Rev. Eleazar Wheelock's Indian School in 1756; and the next year waited on the Earl of Halifax in the interest of Andrew Oliver's candidacy for the office of secretary in Massachusetts. Acting on the suggestion of the Rev. George Whitefield, Dennys De Berdt of the Deputies joined Dr. Avery in a memorial to Lord Halifax for a charter for Wheelock's school in 1757. Dissenting Deputies, Minutes, I, 319, 343, 371, 400, 404, 407; "Letters of Dennys De Berdt," Colonial Society of Massachusetts Publications, Transactions, XIII (1910–11), 410–11; Perry, Historical Collections, Mass., III, 448–50.

33. Hawks and Perry, Documentary History, Conn., I, 266, 267, 292–3, 295–6.

the more solicitous . . . because I am apprehensive of damage to the present constitution of this government unless something is done to remedy these difficulties; which while they remain we cannot avoid complaining to our superiors, and his Grace of Canterbury [Thomas Herring] hath assured us of his patronage. It seems necessary therefore that something be done in our favor. And it would be a great pleasure to me to be able to inform his Grace of our having obtained this favor of the government as on the other hand it would be a grief to me to acquaint him of any hard usage from it for which we could obtain no redress." The epistle closed with the request that the Governor consult on the matter with Johnson's agent and stepson Benjamin Nicholl.[34]

In the light of the recent rebuff of the English bishops by the Government in England, Dr. Johnson's letter was little more than a bluff. Some months later the Connecticut minister wrote to Dr. Bearcroft, secretary of the Venerable Society, reiterating an old theme: "that it would be happy for us if the government of the colony were resumed into the hands of the Crown and a new constitution introduced among us. At least that the Common law were established here that our governor had a negative and that the Council etc., were not so absolutely dependent upon the people." Knowledge among the legislators of Connecticut that this Yale renegade had been holding such opinions since at least 1732 and was now inciting action in England was bound to deepen old resentments and intensify fears; it is not surprising that the petition about taxes was rejected.[35]

Samuel Johnson's energy and devotion to the Church of England made him an ideal conspirator with the Bishop of Oxford, who was as eager for a colonial establishment as the Connecticut divine and far wiser about the timing of Anglican moves. As fully apprised of the work of the Dissenting Deputies as with the dismal failure of

34. Schneiders, *Johnson,* I, 140.

35. Of course, the Connecticut authorities did not know the full extent of Dr. Johnson's duplicity as shown by his letter to Dr. Bearcroft: "With regard to our government it is much too popular. The persons in place absolutely depending on the annual election of the people for their posts, popularity and a servile compliance with all their humors and schemes however so extravagant or unreasonable, is the greatest virtue." Schneiders, *Johnson,* I, 149–50; Hawks and Perry, *Documentary History, Conn.,* I, 270.

Bishop Sherlock's sources of intelligence in the abortive attempt of 1750, Thomas Secker asked Johnson two years later to send over to London promptly anything relating to the Society and its work that should be printed in America. "The Dissenters here have lately had some things of this kind before us; and I think we have had them only through their hands." Secker could give no encouragement about the important "scheme of establishing bishops" but "we must endeavor again when we see opportunity; and pray always. . . ." [36]

The superiority of the Dissenting Deputies' means of information about colonial affairs became evident in their reaction to a report from the missionary Ebenezer Punderson of New Haven to the S.P.G. in 1753 about the whipping of a man at Ashford "for not attending the Presbyterian Worship." Questioned by the Venerable Society, the Deputies promptly investigated the report, "which upon Enquiry appears to have been grossly Misrepresented." Dr. Avery proved this by spreading on the minutes of the General Meeting letters from John Ledyard and Governor Roger Walcott, to whom he had written for particulars. The facts revealed that Pitts, the man whipped by the Justice of the Peace, had never been a Churchman and that, at the next meeting of the Assembly, the offending official had been left off the list of justices. Benjamin Avery justified the Connecticut action and its law in a letter to the S.P.G. When Dr. Johnson learned about Dr. Avery's inquiry, he tried unsuccessfully to see the letter, because it "has inspired the government with a prodigiously venomous spirit against the Church and particularly against Mr. Punderson." Needless to say, Mr. Johnson's account of the Pitts episode differed markedly from the ones forwarded to Dr. Avery, but the Connecticut divine's delay of almost three months in responding to the inquiry on the incident gave the Dissenters a big edge in getting their version to the public. [37]

A few months later, however, Dr. Johnson won a round in the combat. So upset had President Thomas Clap been over Episcopal incursions at Yale, where a tenth of the students were now Angli-

36. About this time, too, Bishop Sherlock wrote to Johnson that there were "little hopes of succeeding at present." Schneiders, *Johnson*, III, 245, 246; Chandler, *Johnson*, 171–2.

37. Dissenting Deputies, Minutes, I, 362, 364, 365–6; Schneiders, *Johnson*, I, 169, 170, 253.

cans, that he forbade all students, even the two sons of Reverend Ebenezer Punderson, to attend the newly opened Church of England. Samuel Johnson refused to accept the excuse that the college statutes required all the students to worship in one place, and adroitly pressed what was a very good case against the president: "Tell it not in Gath! much less in the ears of our dear mother-country, that any of her daughters should deny any of her children leave to attend on her worship whenever they have opportunity for it." He tried to intimidate Mr. Clap by saying that he would notify the Society about the situation and secure from it ample support to take the matter to "our superiors at home," an insincere if not hypocritical threat inasmuch as he had already written. Faced with the possible loss of the College's charter, President Clap capitulated abjectly to Johnson, who blandly told him "in truth the College is ours in proportion as really yours." Clap's only comfort, if it could be called such, was the knowledge that, shortly after this humiliating episode, Samuel Johnson left the colony to preside over the new King's College in the city of New York.[38]

Toward the end of June, Dr. Johnson wrote to his son, William Samuel, about a recent trip to Elizabeth Town: Thomas Bradbury Chandler had taken him to see the Reverend Aaron Burr, and he had learned from the latter that the College of New Jersey would shortly be moved to Prince Town. As for Mr. Clap, "I am glad the president is so mortified and humbled. Burr much condemns him, and says he sees no inconvenience in granting the liberty we contend for." But certainly Johnson did not inform President Burr as to what he went on to enjoin his son in the letter just quoted: Tell Mr. Punderson when you see him that

. . . I beg him to take some pains with those wicked scholars that are so indifferent, and put something into their hands to read that may

38. One senses Dr. Johnson's glee as he ran up the score on the hitherto imperious academician: "But for God's sake do not be so severe to think in this manner, or to carry things to this pass! If so, let Dissenters never complain of their heretofore persecutions or hardships in England, unless they have us tempted to think it their principle, that they ought to be tolerated, in order at length to be established, that they may have the sole privilege of persecuting others." Schneiders, *Johnson*, I, 178, 180–82; III, 253; Thomas Clap to Samuel Johnson, Jan. 30, 1754, Hawks Papers, II, No. 30; Louis L. Tucker, "The Church of England and Religious Liberty at Pre-Revolutionary Yale," *William and Mary Quarterly*, 3d series, XVII (1960), 314–28.

animate and indoctrinate them better. What! are they so mean and abject that having been so long under restraint, they are now come even to hug their chains, and when the prison doors are set open, are they of so low and base a spirit as not to embrace or even accept of liberty? I hope Mr. Punderson will think it a part of his bounden duty to take particular care of the Church Scholars that they be well indoctrinated in the true principles of the Church, they who are the growing hopes of her *future establishment* and prosperity! It is not enough that they be Americans, they must be well instructed in the truth and vast advantage of episcopacy and liturgy.

It thus appears that Samuel Johnson was really out to accomplish exactly what President Clap had feared.[39]

The victory at Yale was too isolated an event, however, to encourage even so sanguine an Anglican as Dr. Johnson. Though Bishop Secker counseled patience, the missionary confessed:

I now almost despair, and very much doubt these more favorable times you hope for will never [*sic*] come. So far from this, that I rather fear the age is growing worse and worse so fast, that the free thinkers and dissenters, who play into one another's hands against the Church will never drop their virulence and activity, by all manner of artifices, till they go near to raze the very Constitution to the foundation, both in Church and State. It is a sad omen that their interest with the ministry should be so much superior to that of the Church, that she cannot be heard in so reasonable and necessary a thing.[40]

In 1755 the London papers announced the second English printing of Dr. William Douglass's *Summary, Historical and Political . . . of the British Plantations in North America.* Both the newspaper reviews and one in the *Monthly Review* were favorable, even while they commented that the author, an Episcopalian, was highly critical of the S.P.G.'s policy of sending missionaries to those colonies where there were already vigorous churches, and that those ministers who conformed to the Church of England aimed at "getting better livings." If setting up the college at New York had not taken up his time, Johnson might have lost all hope for his plan

39. Schneiders, *Johnson,* I, 191 (Italics mine).

40. Schneiders, *Johnson,* II, 333.

except that in 1756 his son William Samuel sent the encouraging
news from England that the Society had got the "affair of sending
bishops over to America . . . upon the *tapis* again." [41]

In 1758 the translation of Thomas Secker, the Bishop of Oxford,
to the primacy of all England raised the hopes of all Churchmen
while at the same time arousing fear among most of the Dissenters.
In defending the appointment to one anxious critic, the Duke of
Newcastle spoke with an optimism that later proved to be unjusti-
fied: "I early sent to him with relation to his conduct towards the
Dissenters. He has explained himself wholly to my satisfaction, and
what I am persuaded will be theirs. He has assured me that he is
well with Dr. Avery and Dr. Chandler. I shall speak to them both
upon the new archbishop's subject, and I shall talk to Dr. Lawrence
and to some who are of a different party among the Dissenters; and
you may assure them all that I will answer for the new archbishop
as far as relates to them." [42]

The new Archbishop of Canterbury acted with circumspection
about the colonial question for several years after taking office, but
his private correspondence reveals that he never once swerved from
his ultimate intention of establishing bishops in America. He did,
however, face up to the charges that the Society had slighted the
Indians and the churchless settlers on the frontiers, "whilst we have
crowded with missionaries, regions which had already a sufficient
number of pastors." Furthermore, he attributed the influence the
Dissenters had with the Government to the success with which they
had alleged against the Society "with remarkable zeal, amongst all
who are indifferent about us, and all who are adversaries to us . . .
that we have unwarrantably changed our object, from the propagation of Christianity and Protestantism, to the propagation of one

41. *London Chronicle,* Sept. 20, 1768; Schneiders, *Johnson,* I, 156–8, 244; *N.Y.
Col. Docs.,* VI, 912–13.

42. The Duke's correspondent, John White, M.P. from Nottinghamshire, continued to be apprehensive, however, because four days later he replied: "Your
Grace undoubtedly knows that the Archbishop has always had strong connection
with the Bishop of London [Sherlock]. and was Strong Advocate (though I think
not a very argumentative one) for the introduction of Bishops into America. I
mention this . . . with some doubt how far weight should be given him in the
Closet during the life at least of the Bishop of London." Newcastle to White,
April 1; White to Newcastle, April 5, 1758, Br. Mus. Add. Mss., No. 32879, f. 74;
Schneiders, *Johnson,* III, 257.

form of it, in opposition to other Protestants; and making the gaining of proselytes from these our chief business." [43]

This politically wise new primate wished "to learn how truly" these charges accorded with the facts, inasmuch as "this accusation hath prevailed so far over all which we can say in our own defense." Secker feared an outbreak of the "epidemic vehemence and wildness which are frequent in this country" should the issue get into Parliament. Consequently he endeavored to bridle the eager Johnson and his associates: "we must be extremely cautious, how we appoint new missions, where Presbyterians or Independents have assemblies." Here Thomas Secker paid the sincerest possible compliment to the success of the Nonconformists in perfecting a transatlantic organization superior to that of his own church: "The Dissenters in America are so closely connected with those in England, and both with such as, under colour of being friends to liberty, are many of them enemies to all ecclesiastical establishments . . . that we have need to be continually on our guard against them." Have patience, we need first to prepare the way "to facilitate what we must ever pray and labor for, till we obtain it, the establishment of bishops of our church in America. This I have long had at heart. . . . Nor shall I ever abandon the scheme as long as I live, but pushing it openly at present would certainly prove both fruitless and detrimental. They alone are judges of opportunities, who know the dispositions and influences of persons and parties, which cannot always be explained to others." [44]

The well-reasoned injunctions of Archbishop Secker were not enough to restrain the impetuosity of the Society's missionaries for more than a year or so. Then in 1759, the Reverend Henry Caner of Boston dispatched to Fulham Palace a personal plea, together with a petition from his colleagues, for the establishing of a mission in "snotty Cambridge." Success at infiltrating Yale in the 1720's had been followed two decades later by the great Anglican victory at King's College in New York. At Philadelphia the Reverend Wil-

43. The prelate also paid tribute to the opposition to episcopacy in 1749–50: "The design, when some years ago it seemed to be in great forwardness, received a most mortifying check, by means of an unseasonable step, which a worthy and able prelate took to promote it, and of which its opposers made their advantage. The time is not yet come for retrieving the ground then lost." Schneiders, *Johnson*, III, 257–8.

44. Schneiders, *Johnson*, III, 258–9.

liam Smith was provost of the College, at least checkmating the Reverend Francis Alison and the Presbyterians. In Virginia the College of William and Mary had always been safely under Episcopal auspices. Only at the young College of New Jersey and venerable Harvard did the so-called Dissenters have undisputed control over higher education. Governor Francis Bernard's attempt to alter the charter of the Jersey institution, so Ezra Stiles later learned, had been narrowly frustrated by the quick-witted Reverend Alexander Cummings. The hope of the petitioners was that in the Congregational stronghold of Cambridge some ground might yet be won by indirection where a frontal attack would certainly fail.[45]

"The College, my Lord, is placed in that Town. It is the only Seminary of Learning for this Province. Socinianism, Deism, and other bad principles find too much countenance among us. To prevent these and like errors from poysoning the Fountain of Education, it will undoubtedly be of great service to erect a Church there, agreeable to the desire of many of the Inhabitants," so argued Henry Caner. To head the mission he strongly recommended the Reverend East Apthorp, University of Cambridge graduate and scion of one of the wealthiest mercantile families of Boston, as one who "may give a right turn to the Youth who are educated there." As one might expect, Dr. Johnson earnestly endorsed the request.[46]

Archbishop Secker consulted several bishops, who were of the opinion that, though opening a mission in Cambridge "might probably furnish a handle for more than ordinary clamor, yet the good to be expected there from the temper, and prudence, and abilities of Mr. Apthorp, was likely to overbalance that inconvenience. Indeed we have so many and so zealous adversaries that our Friends must be as prudent and cautious, and vigilant as possible." In taking this step, Thomas Secker miscalculated, for instead of accomplishing any good, the establishment of the Cambridge mission set off an uproar which only subsided with the outbreak of the War for Independence, and the unfortunate Mr. Apthorp provided the Yankees with one of the most potent symbols in their successful campaign against episcopacy.[47]

45. Perry, *Historical Collections, Mass.*, III, 452.

46. Perry, *Historical Collections, Mass.*, III, 452–3.

47. Perry, *Historical Collections, Mass.*, III, 453.

Down in New Haven, Anglican advances seemed to have reached a stalemate. Proselyting virtually ended when the ablest Yale graduate of the age withstood the alluring call to succumb. Ezra Stiles of the Class of 1746, while serving as a tutor at the College from 1749 to 1755, wavered between the church and the law. In 1753 he pronounced so favorable an oration on Bishop Berkeley that the Episcopalians sought him out. The next January as an enticement to conform to the Church of England, they offered him Trinity Church at Newport — probably the best Episcopal charge in New England — at the munificent salary of £ 200 a year. "I was indeed at this time," Stiles recalled later, "inclined to deism; I was not disposed to profess a mode of religion, which I did not believe, for the sake of a living."

So great were the pressures on him that Stiles decided in September, 1754, to make a religious pilgrimage during which he would examine all faiths before settling down with one. Arriving at New York on September 22, he went to hear Commissary Henry Barclay at St. George's Chapel one day, to the Dutch Reformed the next, and finally to the Jewish Synagogue on Mill Street. Crossing the Hudson to Newark, he attended the Commencement of the College of New Jersey and shared a pew in the Presbyterian Church with Governor Jonathan Belcher while President Aaron Burr conferred an honorary degree on George Whitefield. This experience, together with meeting President Burr and Francis Alison, soon to be vice provost of the new College of Philadelphia, provided a generous sample of learned Presbyterianism. Riding on to Philadelphia next day, Stiles was shown around the Academy by Dr. Alison. He also met Chief Justice William Allen, the foremost colonial Presbyterian layman, and he called on an Episcopal clergyman, the Reverend William Sturgeon of Christ Church. Two days later, he watched as Father Robert Harding, a Jesuit, celebrated the Mass at St. Joseph's in Willing's Alley. Among other Philadelphians, Stiles met Ebenezer Kinnersley, the Baptist minister and electrical experimenter, Presbyterian Dr. William Shippen, and Anglican Jacob Duché.[48]

Back in New Haven, the young academician, having savored in the liberal, enlightened fashion all Christian creeds and modes of

48. Abiel Holmes, *The Life of Ezra Stiles* (Boston, 1798), 40–41; Mass. Hist. Soc., *Proceedings*, 2nd ser., VII (1882), 338–44.

worship from Roman Catholicism on the right to Quakerism on the left, as well as the faith of the Sephardic Jews, sat in the quiet of his study and carefully pondered them all. He reached the not surprising conclusion that the Congregational faith in which he had been nurtured was the best for him.

Quite as important for Ezra Stiles and the religious future of America as the eclecticism of this *Wandermonat* was the opportunity for him to meet and to exchange opinions with the great protagonists of civil and religious liberty of the Middle Colonies, most of whom were Presbyterians. He lodged at Manhattan with Peter Keteltas (Yale, 1752), a "wealthy merchant of literary taste," who introduced him around town and arranged for him to see all the local Yale men. One night William Livingston set out an elegant spread at his house, after which he, Stiles, John Morin Scott (Stiles's classmate), William Smith, Jr., James A. Hillhouse, Thomas Wickham, and Keteltas "settled politics over a generous bottle." Another time, on his return trip, Stiles spent the evening at Mr. Smith's in company with Messrs. Philip and William Livingston, Scott, Hillhouse, and Keteltas. It requires no imagination to surmise that King's College, the New York Society Library, James De Lancey, the *Independent Reflector,* "The Watch-Tower," and other aspects of the struggle then raging between the Presbyterians and the Anglicans were topics of discussion, nor that Ezra Stiles had some of his later opinions shaped on these occasions. He not only settled his religion and his politics and renewed friendships on this journey, but, though he did not realize it then, he had also made connections which would enable him to play a central role in the coming struggle for religious power in America. This he further ensured by accepting a call to the Second Congregational Church at Newport, where he soon became the librarian of the famous Redwood Library.[49]

Between 1755 and 1760, Ezra Stiles began the correspondence with his many friends and acquaintances that he maintained for many years to come. He wrote to the Reverend Francis Alison and Benjamin Franklin in Philadelphia, to several of the New York gentlemen just mentioned, and also to the Reverend Charles Chauncy at Boston. From Newport he kept in touch with his extensive Connecticut acquaintance; in 1756 he promoted the first

49. Mass. Hist. Soc., *Proceedings,* 2nd ser., VII (1882), 339, 344.

convention of Congregational ministers in Rhode Island. Although he had never crossed the ocean, he wrote in 1758 to the Reverend Samuel Chandler, the great dissenting minister at London, to introduce himself, and suggested that they correspond regularly about American ecclesiastical affairs. In like fashion he began writing to the Reverend James Sterling of the Church of Scotland at Glasgow. All of these ministers, it should be observed, were Old-Light or Old-Side adherents, and their European counterparts held the same views, for there had been no ecclesiastical split in the British Isles. Moreover, they were all theological moderates, learned and fully abreast of and interested in the ideas of moral and natural philosophy so popular among English and Scottish intellectuals of the Age of the Enlightenment. They constituted a most congenial group of scholars and divines.[50]

Francis Alison, who had some ideas about retiring to Connecticut in his old age, wrote to Mr. Stiles about his grave concern over the religious division in that colony: "Nothing can be more fatal to their piety, morals, or liberty," he warned; "they will be swallowed up by the Episcopal Church, who envy their prosperity, and will avail themselves of these divisions." He then went on to encourage Stiles to use his influence and interest to unite the factions.[51]

In a lengthy reply to Alison, Ezra Stiles declared:

It is of great Importance that the presbyterian and congregational Interest be strongly united. Plans of Union and Harmony are greatly to be desired and promoted. In this View I am highly pleased with the Union of your Synods of Philadelphia and N. York [1758], and I wish some comprehending Measure was struck into, that might explicitly join to the Union the Confederacy of New England Churches: and the whole be connected with Scotland and the congregational Dissenters in England and Ireland. Such a Junction of lesser and greater Parts would render the whole (perhaps the greater Half of the British Empire) into a much more respectable Figure, than either hold alone and disjoynted. . . . This Combination would be a present Bulwark

50. Stiles to Francis Alison, Nov. 8, 1754; Alison to Stiles, June 20, 1755; Stiles to Chauncy, July 2, 1755; Stiles to Chandler, Mar. 28, 1758; Stiles to Sterling, Nov. 8, 1758, Stiles Papers; Stiles, *Itineraries*, 4; Stiles, *Christian Union*, 127n.

51. Alison to Stiles, May 27, 1759, Stiles Papers.

against a Church which I wish did more Honour to the Law of Jesus.
. . . Your Synods doubtless have, and I wish our Association also
had a annual Correspondence in their public Capacity with the General
Assembly of Scotland — And if it was possible, the Communication
or Publishing the Substance of the Accounts among the people might
animate and corroborate the Cause. And if such an Intercourse was
established with the Churches of Holland, Geneva, and the French
Protestants, it would circulate a great deal of useful Intelligence, that
might serve to keep up and enliven the esprit du Corps as Voltaire
expresses it. . . . It is high Time their [the public's] Attention was
awakened . . . and that the Public Passions were directed to subserve
the Propagation of Truth and Benevolence.

In assuring the Philadelphia divine that the cause was far from
lost, Stiles revealed that he had thought of writing to the Church in
Scotland in the name of his little Rhode Island Convention "to ask
their friendly Protection and Fellowship," and for an annual correspondence. The Newporter failed to mention what he had in
preparation for his fellow Americans, but at that moment he must
have been composing his seminal *Discourse on the Christian Union.*[52]

52. Stiles to Alison, July 2, 1759, Stiles Papers.

V

LUST FOR DOMINION: THE MIDDLE COLONIES
1 6 8 9 – 1 7 5 0

During the early years of the eighteenth century, the struggles of the Congregationalists against Anglican incursions into Massachusetts and Connecticut made New England the colonial center of the church and state issue. The four Middle Colonies, characterized from their inception by religious heterogeneity, which made them more American sooner than the provinces of New England, did not develop the tensions and bitterness ever present in religious rivalry until mid-century. In time, however, this diversity invited ecclesiastical conflict, and contending faiths, injecting religion into every civic issue, tried to line up the citizenry behind them in support of their projects.

To encourage the settlement of their proprietary domain, Lord Berkeley and Sir George Carteret granted freedom of conscience in New Jersey to all who kept the civil peace, and full religious liberty in faith and worship were guaranteed by the Proprietors of West New Jersey in 1677. As is well known, William Penn erected his two colonies of Pennsylvania and the Lower Counties on the Delaware into havens for Europeans with tender consciences. When the Dutch surrendered New Netherland in 1664, the capitulations stipulated that the members of the Dutch Reformed Church should never be molested by the English authorities, and in 1689 the instructions of the first governor sent out to New York by William and Mary provided "liberty of Conscience to all Persons (except Papists)." In a region of so many nationalities — Dutch, Swedes, Finns, French, Germans, English — toleration was vital to the very existence of the Middle Colonies.[1]

1. William Macdonald, *Select Charters and other Documents Illustrative of Amer-*

The only activity of the Church of England in the Middle Colonies in 1690 was the weekly service held at the Fort on Manhattan; in the tiny city of New York, the proportion of Episcopalians to the other sects — Dutch Reformed, Lutherans, Presbyterians, Quakers — was only one to forty. The National Church, so popular in England after the Revolution that it actually endangered the carrying out of the provisions of the Toleration Act, really had no standing at all in this important region of the American colonies. Here was an open field for the application of practical piety and missionary endeavor, one in which the presence of a royal governor seemed to presage ample support for Anglican efforts.[2]

Pressed hard by Governor Benjamin Fletcher, the New York Assembly passed a bill in 1693 providing for an annual levy in the counties of New York, Richmond, Queens, and Westchester for the support of "a good and sufficient Protestant Minister." The county justices were to hold elections in each county once a year for the choice of church wardens and vestrymen who would join with the justices in fixing the rate and would also serve as the agency for calling the minister and disbursing the funds. The act set the salary for the ministry of New York County at £100. The Governor returned the bill to the House with the request that a clause be inserted recognizing his power of presentation to ecclesiastical benefices, but, when the Assembly flatly refused to do so, he allowed the bill to become a law anyway.[3]

The Episcopalian framers of the Ministry Act intended to establish their church in the four southernmost counties of New York, but such was not the understanding or the intent of the members of the Assembly. Words uttered in 1699 by Lewis Morris, able

---

ican History (New York, 1899), 142, 176; Charles M. Andrews, *The Colonial Period of American History* (New Haven, 1937), III, 286; Hugh Hastings, ed., *Ecclesiastical Records of the State of New York* (Albany, 1901–6), II, 991, 1012; *N.Y. Col. Docs.*, II, 251.

2. All members of the Assembly of 1693 but one were Dissenters. *Ecclesiastical Records*, II, 1910; Osgood, *American Colonies*, II, 14; Briggs, *American Presbyterianism*, 144.

3. Hastings prints the Ministry Act, *Ecclesiastical Records*, II, 1076–9; Morgan Dix, *A History of the Parish of Trinity Church in the City of New York* (New York, 1898), I, 79–80.

attorney, strong Anglican, and later both a vestryman of Trinity Church and an active member of the S.P.G., bear this out:

The People were generally dissenters, and averse to the religion of the Church of England; and when the Act was past that provided for the Maintenance of Ministers . . . it was to settle an Orthodox Ministry, which words, were a Governor a Dissenter and would induct Dissenters, would be as favourable in favour of them as the Church; and the people, who ne'er could be brought to settle an Episcopal Clergy in direct terms, fancied they had made an effectual provision for Ministers of their own persuasion by this Act.

Some years later Morris regretted that the Episcopalians had finessed the assemblymen: "I believe at this day the Church had been in a much better position had there been no Act in her favour." This much is true, beginning with the dissension over the interpretation of the Ministry Act, the Church was to undergo eight decades of ecclesiastical strife which might, perhaps, have been avoided.[4]

The vestry elected for New York City and County, called the "Town Vestry," reflected the views of the great preponderance of the Dissenters on Manhattan when, on February 12, 1694, a majority of that body voted "that a dissenting Minister be called to officiate." A year later, however, at the insistence of Governor Fletcher, it chose William Vesey, a recent Harvard graduate and an Episcopalian, as the minister. The Vestry did, however, withhold notification to Vesey while it appealed to the Assembly, which advised that the intent of the law was to allow the choice of a Nonconformist. To this Fletcher curtly replied that the Assembly had no power to decide: "The Laws are to be interpreted by judges," and accordingly Mr. Vesey was called and inducted as New York's first rector. In 1697 the Governor issued a royal charter creating "Parochial and incorporate into one body Politicq in fact and name" the "Rector and inhabitants in communion of the Protestant church of England *as now established by our laws.*" [5]

4. Quoted by Charles W. Baird, "Civil Status of the Presbyterians in the Province of New York," *Magazine of American History,* III (1879), 597; *N.Y. Col. Docs.,* V, 323. For the Presbyterian case against Fletcher's administration, see William Livingston's account in "The Watch-Tower," Nos. 20–21, *New York Mercury,* April 7, 14, 1755.

5. Dix, *Trinity Church,* I, 82–5, 94, 457 (my italics); *Ecclesiastical Records,* II, 1114–15, 1136–65, 1219; and for Vesey, Shipton, *Harvard Graduates,* IV, 173–5.

The forces were thus arrayed against each other at the outset: the Episcopalians seeking religious unity, but unable to achieve it in more than four counties; and the Dissenters striving for the diversity so characteristic of their experience, even to the denial of the legality of the establishment in the four counties.

The return of the Reverend Mr. Vesey from London with Anglican orders in 1697 was the signal for the renewal of political and ecclesiastical activities by the supporters of the Church of England. When Lord Bellomont succeeded Fletcher, the Assembly, hoping the new governor would be more tractable, sent up a bill to settle a nonconforming minister in the City of New York in the place of the anti-Leislerian incumbent, but his Lordship rejected it as contrary to his instructions. More important for the Anglican cause than this minor victory was the founding of the Society for the Propagation of the Gospel in Foreign Parts in 1701, which at once set out to overcome the colonial conditions which had reduced the Church of England to the status of a sect in the colonies north of Maryland. Most of the first group of missionaries dispatched were sent to the Middle Colonies; at New York as early as November, 1702, Governor Francis Nicholson of Virginia convened a meeting of seven of the Episcopal clergy, whose expenses he defrayed, to discuss measures for advancing the fortunes of the Church. This first intercolonial meeting of the Anglican clergy concluded its week-long deliberations with a call for a suffragan bishop from England.[6]

A further strengthening of the claims for Anglican establishment in New York County and City came in 1704 when Lord Cornbury, the most cynical and unscrupulous by far of the province's colonial governors, induced the Assembly to pass an act incorporating Trinity Church and divorcing the church's vestry from the "Town Vestry." Trinity Church was thereby fully established by law; as William Livingston and other legal authorities later argued convincingly and with great learning, this was the only parish legally established in the entire province.[7]

6. *N.Y. Col. Docs.,* IV, 536; *Ecclesiastical Records,* III, 1507–9.

7. A year later Lord Cornbury granted the income of the Queen's Farm to the rector of Trinity Church, and in the same year the Assembly also recognized the Governor's right to induct into livings. *Ecclesiastical Records,* III, 1563–6; V. 3427–32; *Independent Reflector,* No. XLV (N.-Y. H. S. copy, New York, 1753 [4]), 181–4.

Lacking even an iota of piety, Cornbury pandered to the Church of England solely for his own private purposes and without regard for sectarian harmony in his government. An example of this occurred at Jamaica in Queens, a county parish settled by Presbyterians. The town had voted in 1701 to levy a tax under the Ministry Act of 1693, and a year later the vestry built a church and a house and then called the Reverend Mr. Hubbard, a Presbyterian, to serve them. Cornbury ejected the Presbyterian and inducted the Reverend William Urquhard into the living. Thereupon began a contest that went on for years in which the Dissenting and Episcopal ministers contended for possession of the glebe and parsonage.

The Boston divines, led by Cotton Mather, displayed unusual concern over the fate of the meetinghouse and glebe lands at Jamaica, the "Frontier" of Nonconformity. Mather induced Messrs. B. Robinson and Thomas Reynolds of London to represent to the S.P.G. that many towns in New York and New Jersey had no minister at all, and that more than one hundred families of Jamaica had proved exemplary in "Christian knowledge and goodness" and maintained a church with a most worthy parson. Yet when a mere ten families declared for the Anglican way, Governor Cornbury had sent them an Episcopal minister and had ordered the parsonage, glebe, and meetinghouse seized for his use. The people have borne all of this with patience, Mather continued, "but if such things proceed that noble Society for the Propagation of Religion in America will greatly wound religion and their own reputation also, which ought to be forever venerable." In June, 1715, however, Mr. Reynolds had to notify Cotton Mather, "with sorrow of heart," that, notwithstanding all efforts made in London for Jamaica, the S.P.G. proceeds apace; but "we are attempting afresh to represent the case to the Society."

This protracted dispute became a celebrated case, which the Presbyterians brought to the public's notice whenever the opportunity presented. In 1727 the Dissenters seized the glebe and parsonage by force and never again lost possession. The missionary assigned to Jamaica in 1732 declared that the Presbyterians "by their sly tricks and quirks of the common Law, got the Church, the Parsonage house, and lands into their possession," and are resolved next to deprive him of his legal salary of £60 per annum.[8]

8. One of the principal reasons Governor William Cosby removed Chief Justice

The missionaries sent by the S.P.G. to the Middle Colonies devoted as much time and thought as did their New England colleagues to figuring out ways to gain control of education in the colonial colleges and to bring a bishop over from England to complete Episcopal organization, which would, incidentally, elevate the clergy to a higher status. As a graduate of Harvard, William Vesey informed the Bishop of London in 1699 that there were plans afoot for a royal charter for the New England college, "on which I beseech your Excellency to have an intense eye, as it, which if granted, will be of a very fatal consequence to that very glorious work . . . for the . . . good of his Church in all these American parts." He ardently hoped some day to see Episcopal influence at work in Cambridge. Caleb Heathcote, the most prominent lay member of the S.P.G. in New York, while arguing some years later for a colonial bishop, pointed out that a bishop's presence would ensure conformity among the many Episcopalian youths who now go to Harvard and there turn Dissenters. When the Rector and Vestry of Trinity Church thanked Queen Anne for the gift of a communion service in 1712, they used the occasion to request that a bishop be sent over, and, more presumptuously, they asked for the establishment of the Church of England not only in New York but in the bordering provinces also. All that came of these requests, however, was the return of Mr. Vesey from London in 1715 as the Bishop of London's commissary. Nevertheless, it did appear both to aspiring Anglicans and uneasy Dissenters that Episcopal advance had been virtually unimpeded.[9]

II

In some respects the oppression carried out in the name of the Church of England by Edward, Lord Cornbury, exceeded anything

---

Lewis Morris from office in 1733, was his alleged "notorious partiality in the administration of justice," specifically the Anglican jurist's decision in favor of the Jamaica Presbyterians. *Ecclesiastical Records,* III, 1463–4, 1570, 1874, 1892, 1899, 1909, 2043–4; IV, 2392, 2565, 2623, 2643–7; Mass. Hist. Soc., *Collections,* 7th ser., VIII, 132.

9. There were only four S.P.G. missionaries in New Jersey, and any attempt to establish the Episcopal Church there where the overwhelming majority of the people were Presbyterians and Quakers, who agreed with Lewis Morris in calling the Anglican service "Pageantry," would have been unrealistic if not impossible.

attempted against the Nonconformists by High-Church zealots in the England of Queen Anne. Especially resented was his attack on the Reverend Francis Makemie. Though characterized by Lord Cornbury as "a Jack of all Trades, he is a Preacher, a Doctor of Physick, a Merchant, an Attorney, or Counsellor at Law, and which is worst of all, a Disturber of Governments," he is also generally accredited with being the first Nonconformist licensed to preach in Virginia and the founder of the Presbyterian Church in America.[10]

Francis Makemie was born in County Donegal of Scottish parents; he attended the University of Glasgow, and shortly after being ordained he came out to Maryland in 1683. Soon he was in correspondence with both of the Mathers, who encouraged his labors in the Southern Colonies, where the angelic conjunction of his several "trades" was sorely needed. Crossing to London in 1691 in search of support from the English Presbyterians, there Makemie seems to have met Increase Mather as well as many of the leaders of the "United Brethren" and to have been won to the principles embodied in the Heads of Agreement.[11]

The episode involving the Reverend Mr. Makemie which aroused the resentment among most Protestants other than Anglicans began on January 20, 1707, when the minister preached at a private house in New York "in as publick a manner as possible, with open doors." On the same day at Newtown, Long Island, the Reverend John Hampton spoke in the meetinghouse. When Mr. Makemie joined his companion on January 22, they were both arrested by a sheriff bearing a warrant from Lord Cornbury and detained in jail at Jamaica, after which they were carried to New York for a hearing before the Governor and Council. Cornbury based his charges on the fact that the Presbyterian ministers held no licence from him despite their having been accredited by the governor of Virginia. The charges against Hampton were dropped, and an error in the

As for Connecticut, nothing further need be said. Shipton, *Harvard Graduates*, IV, 176; *Ecclesiastical Records*, III, 1611, 1917, 1918, 1924, 1950, 2053.

10. *Ecclesiastical Records*, III, 1669–70; *Dictionary of American Biography*, XII, 215.

11. *Dictionary of American Biography*, XII, 215–16; Trinterud, *American Tradition*, 27, 29–30.

presentment by the Grand Jury to the March term of the court led to a postponement of Makemie's trial until June.[12]

Aided by the best of counsel, Francis Makemie won his case and his freedom on June 7, 1707, but Governor Cornbury's arrogant and illegal conduct in arresting the minister, detaining him, fining and imprisoning him, and causing him inconvenience and expense for a matter of six months was counterbalanced in part by the reaction of the public. The Anglican Lewis Morris wrote to England and deplored "a procedure by no means warrantable, and that alarms all mankind here. My Lord's arbitrary conduct with respect to this man, and his example together, have so soured a great many, that subscriptions are getting to build a Dissenting Meeting House . . . and a support will be provided for one of their Ministers." [13]

The declarations of the Governor and Attorney General that "the Act of Toleration does not extend to any Plantations" were patently wrong and caused many to fear for their rights. Writing to Samuel Penhallow of Portsmouth, New Hampshire, on July 8, 1707, Cotton Mather rejoiced that "That brave man, Mr. Makemie, has after a famous trial, at N. York, bravely triumphed over the Act of Uniformity, and the other Pœnal Lawes for the Ch. of England. Without permitting the Matter to come so far as pleading the Act of Toleration, he has compelled an Acknowledgment that those Lawes . . . are but Local ones, and have nothing to do with the Plantations. The Non-Con[formist] Religion and Interest, is, thro' the Blessing of God on the Agency of that excellent person, Likely to prevail mightily in the Southern [Middle] Colonies." [14]

Immediately after his release from jail at New York, Mr. Makemie had informed Benjamin Colman and other Boston ministers

12. *A Narrative of a New and Unusual American Imprisonment of Two Presbyterian Ministers: and Prosecution of Francis Makemie, one of them, for Preaching one Sermon at the City of New York* (London, 1707), 3, 7, 8, 13, 25, in Peter Force, *Tracts and Other Papers Relating . . . to . . . the Colonies in North America* (New York, 1947), IV, No. 4.

13. *Narrative of a New American Imprisonment*, 25–45; Baird, "Civil Status of Presbyterians," 605-6.

14. *Narrative of a New American Imprisonment*, 9; Mass. Hist. Soc., *Collections*, 7th ser., VII, 599.

about the packed jury of Lord Cornbury, and Colman and his associates communicated their deep concern to Sir Henry Ashurst, Sir Edmund Harrison, and other influential Dissenters. Their interest doubtless procured the publication at London that same year of the *Narrative* of Makemie's trial with its damning evidence for "the ingenuous Reader": "You have here a Specimen of the Cloggs and Fetters with which the Liberty of Dissenters are Intangled at New-York and Jersey Governments beyond any places in Her Majesties Dominions; And when Conditions and Impositions required, are as heavy, and uneasy to be bore; and as great a Scruple of Conscience, as the grounds of their Separation and Dissent, it is next to no Liberty at all." [15]

The attempts at co-operation by English Dissenters through the Heads of Agreement convinced some of the American Congregationalists and Presbyterians that they too could benefit by working together. Acting upon Makemie's suggestion, Philadelphia Presbyterians applied in 1698 for a minister to Increase Mather, acting president of Harvard, who sent them the Reverend Jedediah Andrews. As might be expected, there was a natural affinity between the Scottish Presbyterians and those in the colonies. As early as 1700 the Provincial Synod of Glasgow invited "an intercourse . . . between the ministers of New England and us in Scotland . . . seeing you and we are so much united together" against the common enemies of "popish zeal" and "High-Church Anglicanism." A decade or more later Cotton Mather was writing to Principal Sterling about the Scotch-Irish: "As great numbers are like to come to us from the North of Ireland, the bond between the churches of Scotland and New England will every day grow stronger and stronger." Since the most pressing problem of nascent Presbyterianism was the procuring of ministers and funds for their maintenance, Mr. Makemie sought to promote closer connections with the Presbyterians of London rather than with the Kirk of Scotland.[16]

In London during the summer of 1704, Francis Makemie made a successful appeal for men and money to advance colonial Presbyterianism, and the English Dissenters agreed to support two minis-

15. *Narrative of a New American Imprisonment*, 3, 5.

16. Shipton, *Harvard Graduates*, IV, 219-20; Briggs, *American Presbyterianism*, 129-30; Trinterud, *American Tradition*, 31-2.

ters in Maryland for two years from the Presbyterian Fund. Returning to America, Mr. Makemie strove for an arrangement whereby Puritan ministers from New England and Presbyterians from Great Britain might "act in concert," and he brought this about in March, 1706, by organizing the Presbytery of Philadelphia. As occasion required it, the Reverend Jedediah Andrews wrote on behalf of the Presbytery to charitable London Dissenters, and he often joined his efforts with those of the Boston ministers, who always seemed willing to assist the cause in the Middle Colonies. Andrews began a correspondence in 1710 with Ireland at the request of the Reverend Alexander Sinclair of Dublin, and shortly thereafter opened another with the Synod of Glasgow. From Ireland he hoped to procure funds and the use of Irish Presbyterian influence with Dr. Edmund Calamy of London, while he appealed to the Scots to send over and support one or more ministers. The Reverend Thomas Reynolds of London, at the behest of Cotton Mather, was also active in procuring financial support for the Presbyterian ministers in Pennsylvania and New Jersey. Through his mediation, also, colonial Presbyterians continued to correspond regularly with their English brethren.[17]

Presbyterian organization in the Middle Colonies was completed on September 19, 1716, with the formation of an annual synod at Philadelphia, composed of the three Presbyteries of Philadelphia, New Castle, and Snow Hill. Within two years the Synod had taken the initiative with the English Presbyterians and Congregationalists and had notified Dr. Edmund Calamy, John Nesbit, and James Anderson that "there is nothing we desire more than the honour and comfort of a yearly correspondence with you . . . if it were but to have your countenance, concurrence, and advice, in the great and common work of our Lord and his kingdom." Because their moderator, the Reverend George McNish of Jamaica, was going to Great Britain, the Synod supplied him with letters of introduction to Principal Sterling and the Synod of Glasgow.[18]

Thus it was that about the same time that the Nonconformists in

17. Briggs, *American Presbyterianism*, 139, 161–2; *Records of the Presbyterian Church in the United States of America* . . . (Philadelphia, 1904), 16, 19, 20, 21, 37, 39.

18. *Records of the Presbyterian Church*, 45–6, 54–5; Mass. Hist. Soc., *Collections*, 7th ser., VIII, 318–19.

England were beginning to recover the position lost under Queen Anne, the Presbyterians succeeded in rooting themselves in the Middle Colonies and perfecting their organization with presbyteries and a synod. Henceforth the Presbyterians would take the lead in this region. In 1723, after arranging a meeting with the representatives of ministers of the consociated churches of Connecticut to seek peace in the Presbyterian Church in the city of New York, the Synod resolved:

And if the good ends proposed, relating to New York, be at the conference happily accomplished, the Synod recommends it to those of their members afore appointed . . . to treat with said ministers of Connecticut about an union with us, and empower them to concert and conclude upon any methods that may conduce to that end.

That such a union was not effected for forty-four years was not the fault of these early Presbyterians.[19]

It was fortunate for all denominations in the Northern Colonies that in organizing their ecclesiastical activities they took their cues from the conciliatory Heads of Agreement rather than from strict Congregationalism or rigid Presbyterianism of the Scottish variety. The spirit of the Heads of Agreement made relatively easy, considering the times and the distances involved, an astonishing degree of co-operation among groups exhibiting a high degree of Christian brotherhood in London, Boston, New York, and Philadelphia, and, on occasion, in Dublin and Glasgow also. Notwithstanding the failure of the United Brethren to survive more than a few years in England, their ideals as set forth in the Heads of Agreement did live on in the Saybrook Platform of Connecticut and, even more significantly, in the spirit of the ministry of the Congregational and Presbyterian churches. Much closer together in polity and theology than they perhaps realized at the time, the colonial dissenting divines of 1690–1720 cleared the way for the effective union of 1767 to combat episcopacy.

19. Similarly, though on a much smaller scale, twenty Baptist ministers, meeting at Philadelphia September 13, 1717, thanked the Baptist Churches of London, "especially those concerned lately in writing to us" and sending the books supplied by Thomas Hollis and a Mr. Taylor, for gifts which revived their spirits. Crosby, *History of the Baptists*, IV, 193–4; Briggs, *American Presbyterianism*, 182–3; *Records of the Presbyterian Church*, 76–7.

III

In 1716, Caleb Heathcote could note with delight that "Mr. Vesey hath by his good conduct frustrated all the designs of dissenting ministers from settling among us"; and he added, "a happiness no city in North America can boast of besides ourselves." His pleasure was short-lived, however, for within six months a Presbyterian minister arrived in the city and preached to his flock in the City Hall until 1719, when an edifice was raised on Wall Street near Broadway. As the Presbyterian Church expanded during the two decades, 1720–40, its members in the city of New York learned once again what Episcopalian "establishment" could mean when "dissenters" asked for what seemed to them reasonable favors of the government. Lord Cornbury had set the mode for succeeding officials; and for the remainder of the colonial period they in turn always treated Manhattan Presbyterians as unwelcome guests. Ultimately, as Lewis Morris had predicted, the Pesbyterians raised the money to call and support a minister.[20]

Now possessed of a meetinghouse and ground for a cemetery, the Presbyterians applied to the Council for a charter making them a corporate body empowered to hold property. The petition was referred to a committee which, in the Governor's absence, reported to the President of the Council that it might be granted. Later the Council recommended consulting the Board of Trade and Plantations, and the matter was dropped. Upon the arrival of Governor William Burnet, the Presbyterians tried again. Though Burnet appeared to favor the application, further opposition from Trinity Church prevented any action. In 1724 the petition was presented for a third time, and again the Council requested an opinion from the Board of Trade, whose legal counsel, Richard West, advised (four years later) that "by law such patent of incorporation may be granted." However, Episcopal pressure on members of the New York Council once more caused the petition to be passed over. Angry and frustrated over this series of denials and desperately needing some responsible agency to handle its property, the Wall Street Church transferred title to some Edinburgh ministers, who were to

20. Baird, "Civil Status of Presbyterians," 606.

hold the property in trust for the congregation's use; in 1732 the General Assembly of the Church of Scotland took on the obligation. Though apparently extinguished, the fire of resentment smouldered on, flaming up on several later occasions to the great injury of the Church of England.[21]

IV

The Great Awakening played even more havoc among the Presbyterians in the Middle Colonies than it did in Connecticut. Opposition by ministers educated in Scotland to what they considered inadequate training had led to violent discussions in the Synod, for there was an acute shortage of properly qualified Presbyterian ministers — those educated in either New England or the British Isles. To make up for the deficiency, the Reverend William Tennent founded the "Log College" at Neshaminy, Pennsylvania, in 1736; in five years' time he sent seven capable young men to the Philadelphia Synod for licensing. By 1739 it had become evident that the Presbyterians were splitting into two factions: the "Old-Side" Scottish divines of Pennsylvania headed by Francis Alison, and the "New-Side" Log College men and their New England-trained supporters who were located principally in New Jersey and New York. In 1741 schism came, and four years later the latter group formed the Synod of New York at Elizabeth Town, New Jersey.[22]

Although other differences such as itineracy and attitudes toward the revival contributed to the split, the education of the Presbyterian ministers was the central issue. The Philadelphia Synod had discussed a design for "a seminary of learning" back in 1739 and had sought the advice and help of the Boston Congregationalists. Through Benjamin Colman, support had been assured for the "laudable proposal" of opening a seminary in the Middle Colonies. In March, 1745, "several Gentlemen residing in and near the Prov-

21. Baird, "Civil Status of Presbyterians," 606–7; "The Watch-Tower," No. 22; *N.Y. Mercury*, June 30, 1755; *Ecclesiastical Records*, III, 2173–5; IV, 2601; *Records of the Presbyterian Church*, 89–90, 98.

22. *Records of the Presbyterian Church*, 141–2, 233–4; Trinterud, *American Tradition*, 63–4, 71, 75; *Dict. Amer. Biog.*, XVIII, 370.

ince of New Jersey" met before the new Synod of New York convened to support "Religion and Learning." The Boston pastors,
joined shortly by President Thomas Clap of Yale College, lined up
solidly behind the scheme, leaving the Scots in the Synod of Philadelphia to their own devices. On October 22, 1746, Governor John
Hamilton of New Jersey granted a charter for the proposed college.[23]

The undertakers made such rapid progress with their plans that
the *New York Gazette* of February 2, 1747, carried an announcement about the college in New Jersey, which opened in May at
Elizabeth Town. The public was assured that "equal Liberties and
Privileges are secured to every Denomination of Christians, any
different religious Sentiments notwithstanding." [24]

When the Anglicans learned that the "New-Side" Presbyterians
had stolen a march on them, they protested to the new governor,
Jonathan Belcher, "The Mæcenas of the Age," that the Hamilton
charter had been issued without the advice of the Council. But they
reckoned on the wrong man; Governor Belcher, an enthusiastic
"New-Light Congregationalist," responded: "Pray Gentlemen, make
yourselves easy, if their Charter is not good, I'll get them a better."
Which he did. Fortified with this second royal grant, the New-Side
men not only anticipated the action of their Philadelphia rivals
in the Presbyterian Church but confronted the Episcopalians of the
middle regions with a stunning *fait accompli*. All that the latter
could do was to complain bitterly that they had not been notified
of the plan in time to offer sound objections against it. In sending
an account of this sequence of events, together with a copy of the
charter, to the Bishop of London, the Reverend Samuel Johnson
expressed his great fears that the Church of England would suffer
from the new institution, "it being entirely in the hands of the most
virulent Methodists" (by whom he meant, of course, George Whitefield's Presbyterian followers). Thomas Bradbury Chandler de-

---

23. *Records of the Presbyterian Church*, 149, 153–5, 186–9; *A General Account
of the Rise and State of the College, lately Established in the Province of New
Jersey in America* (New York, 1752), 2; Varnum L. Collins, *Princeton* (New York,
1914), 7, 10, 11, 18, 20; John Maclean, *History of the College of New Jersey*
(Philadelphia, 1877), I, 46; Trinterud, *American Tradition*, 141.

24. *N.Y. Gazette*, Feb. 2, 1747.

clared it to be just "one great part of their design . . . an engine to play against the Church." [25]

The first that the Dissenting Deputies knew about the new college was an appeal from some New England divines in June, 1749, for funds for the institution, the College of New Jersey. In January of 1754 the Synod of New York appointed Gilbert Tennent and Samuel Davies to cross to England and Scotland in search of donations. Though the Dissenting Deputies did not consider it within their corporate competence to participate in the soliciting of gifts, their good will measurably aided the cause, and such well-to-do members as Dennys De Berdt generously contributed as individuals.[26]

The immediate success of the Presbyterian seminary alarmed the Episcopalians and spurred them on to renew their efforts in the sphere of higher education, with, it may be added, some curious and spectacular consequences. At Philadelphia they joined with the Old-Side Presbyterians (!) to carry out Benjamin Franklin's plan for a nondenominational academy. The institution opened in January, 1751, under the leadership of the Reverend Francis Alison, the most learned of the Scottish-trained Presbyterian ministers, who had been instrumental in arousing the interest of Franklin and the Reverend Richard Peters. In 1753, the Reverend William Smith, a Scot in Anglican orders, came to head the Academy, and in March, 1755, the Proprietors of Pennsylvania issued a new charter creating "the College, Academy, and Charitable School of Philadelphia" with Smith as provost and Alison as vice provost. Before long, Provost Smith, reporting on the state of the college to the Secretary of the S.P.G., proudly boasted that "the Church, by soft and easy means, daily gains Ground in it." [27]

Competition and infiltration, by whatever means achieved, were

25. William Livingston to Noah Welles, Sept. 19, 1747, Johnson Family Papers (Yale University), No. 36; Maclean, *College of New Jersey*, 62; Collins, *Princeton*, 18; *Pa. Gaz.*, Aug. 13, 27, 1747; Hawks and Perry, *Documentary History, Conn.*, I, 236–7; Schneiders, *Johnson*, I, 165–6.

26. Dissenting Deputies, Minutes, I, 316, 358, 369; *Records of the Presbyterian Church*, 244, 252, 255, 256, 265, 266.

27. Carl and Jessica Bridenbaugh, *Rebels and Gentlemen: Philadelphia in the Age of Franklin* (New York, 1942), 40–44, 56–9, 61.

more or less expected, but overt intervention in the affairs of the College of New Jersey was considered an outrage. During his first appearance at a Princeton commencement, Anglican Governor Francis Bernard piously declared that it was his duty to "encourage all Institutions, calculated for promoting religious Conversation and useful Learning." The well-informed and truthful Ezra Stiles recorded, however, that "about the year 1759 Governor Bernard of the Jersies proposed to alter the Constitution of Jersey College and introduce half of the Govt. of it to Episcopalians: When in the Remonstrance and Opposition of the Trustees Rev. Alex Cumming[s] asserted that all the Episcopalians did not amount to a Fortieth part of the White Inhabitants." Mr. Cummings's statistics, which were correct, may have been the reason the Governor did not pursue his plan, for no further tampering with the charter took place.[28]

One rather paradoxical situation resulting from the Great Awakening was the Presbyterian invasion of Virginia, a province where the Church of England was established by law. Governor William Gooch, himself a Scot, notified the Synod of Philadelphia in 1738 that he was inclined to favor people west of the Blue Ridge provided they observed the Toleration Act, and accordingly the Synod sent Scotch-Irish preachers to the Great Valley where, in general, no friction developed. Just west of the fall-line in Hanover County, however, where the Anglican Church had long cared for the inhabitants, New-Side Presbyterians from the Synod of New York began to proselyte among Episcopalians disturbed by the preaching of Whitefield. Here was a situation exactly the reverse of that in New England, with this exception: that in the Reverend Samuel Davies, the Nonconformists of the Virginia Piedmont found a champion of marked ability who, with clarity and logic as well as baffling legal skill, openly argued their cause before the local courts and in England.[29]

Mr. Davies, who settled in Hanover in 1748, developed the Presbyterian argument for civil and religious liberty. This he detailed in letters to the eminent London divine Philip Doddridge, to Benja-

28. *Pa. Journal,* June 29, 1758; Stiles, *Itineraries,* 25.

29. *Records of the Presbyterian Church,* 138–9, 147, 185; Osgood, *American Colonies,* III, 470–73.

min Avery, and to the layman Israel Mauduit. Dr. Doddridge communicated such portions of the correspondence as he saw fit to the Bishop of London whose replies he relayed to Virginia. The Dissenting Deputies took up the matter of licensing of ministers in the Old Dominion, which was one of the chief grievances of the colonial Presbyterians. In 1751 that same body requested Israel Mauduit to ascertain from Samuel Davies "the State of the Fact about the Dissenters there" and at the same time ordered an inquiry about the representations sent over by Virginia Anglicans branding the Presbyterians "dangerous People." A year later, after all the facts were in, Mauduit was instructed to tell the Virginia Dissenters that the Dissenting Deputies would render all possible assistance, but to "desire them to be easy for the present, till the Committee be able to give them further instructions." Dr. Avery's next step was to get an opinion from the Attorney General about Davies's contention that the Toleration Act applied to Virginia.[30]

Though the Dissenting Deputies comprehended the views and position of colonial Presbyterians, much of the information that circulated widely in England was misconceived, as Samuel Davies discovered when he and Gilbert Tennent went to London to try to collect funds for the College of New Jersey. He reported going into "Hamlin's coffee-house among the Presbyterians, where they are generally very shy and unsociable to me. They have universally, as far as I can learn, rejected all tests of orthodoxy, and require their candidates, at their ordination, to declare only their belief of the Scriptures." I was told that the report that "we would admit none into the ministry without subscription to the Westminster Confession . . . would hinder all our success among the friends of liberty. I replied that we allowed the candidate to mention his objections against any article in the Confession, and the judicature judged whether the articles objected against, were essential to

---

30. Bishop Sherlock's reply to Dr. Doddridge was moderate and conciliatory, though he did not let the opportunity pass to condemn the New Englanders for proselyting in Virginia when they complained of the S.P.G. in their own country. "Was this consistent with a spirit of toleration?" Like most English officials of the eighteenth century the good Bishop was unable to distinguish between Congregationalists and Presbyterians; it was the synod of the latter which sent Davies to Virginia. *Correspondence and Diary of Doddridge*, V, 199–202; Dissenting Deputies, Minutes, I, 336, 347, 349, 354; *Records of the Presbyterian Church*, 247, 258.

Christianity; and if they judged they were not, they would admit the candidate, notwithstanding his objections. The Englishman seemed to think that we were such rigid Calvinists, that we would not admit an Arminian into communion." [31]

While in London, Davies appeared before the Committee of the Deputies to discuss the complaints of the Virginians. It was proposed that he draft a petition to the King, which, when the members approved it, was sent to Virginia for signatures. This document, produced out of London experience, came back but was not presented, for in the meantime Dr. Avery had taken counsel with the Earl of Halifax, who had advised that the Presbyterians should go on preaching in Virginia without licenses and, if they were prosecuted, then to appeal to the King and Privy Council. Instructions sent out to the Old Dominion to this effect were carefully followed. Probably no other single action of the Dissenting Deputies so nicely reveals the skillful handling of a critical ecclesiastical problem on both sides of the ocean. Involving Davies and his associates in Virginia, the Synod of New York, the London divines, the Bishop of London, and the principal officers of state, it was a complicated maneuver requiring careful planning, prompt action, long waits for ships and mail to arrive, finesse in dealing with men, not to mention perfect timing. The success attending Dr. Avery's and the Deputies' actions contrasts sharply with several contemporary Episcopalian efforts. [32]

The steady immigration of thousands of Palatine Germans into the Middle Colonies after 1729 built up a large group whose ecclesiastical ties with the homeland were so weak that it was ripe for proselyting. To a certain degree this was also true of members of the Dutch Reformed Church with whom the German Calvinists loosely affiliated in America. Both Anglicans and Presbyterians vied for the religious allegiance of these newcomers, but the close con-

31. In 1759, Dennys De Berdt wrote a preface for, and procured the publication of, a sermon by Samuel Davies. It was dedicated to Lord Halifax. In the preface he said that Mr. Davies revealed "the Genuine Sentiments of a Heart full of Zeal for the Honour of His Majesty King George, and a just Indignation against a base, cowardly, Neglect, to defend the Civil and Religious Liberties of British America." Col. Soc. Mass., *Publications*, XIII (1910–11), 296–7; William H. Foote, *Sketches of Virginia, Historical and Biographical* (Philadelphia, 1850–55), I, 257.

32. Dissenting Deputies, Minutes, I, 370, 371, 372, 378, 380, 381.

nection of the Presbyterians with the New England Congregationalists, made possible by the acceptance of the principles of the Heads
of Agreement, and the common bond of Calvinism offered a better
basis for a union of the English Presbyterians, Dutch, and German
bodies than did the Anglican church. Actually, in May, 1744, the
Reverend Henry Dorsius of the Dutch Reformed Church at Neshaminy presented the Synod of Philadelphia with letters from the
deputies of North and South Holland inquiring whether the Dutch
and German churches "may be joined in communion with the said
Synod." Though the Synod undertook further discussions through
the synods in Holland and the Scottish ministers of Rotterdam "indicating our willingness to join with the Calvinist Dutch" (High
and Low), the schism in colonial Presbyterianism balked the proposal. Thus, unfortunately, was lost an unexcelled opportunity to
unite all Calvinist denominations in one great compact organization.[33]

For a time it seemed as if the Anglicans might succeed in winning over the Lutherans. At New York in 1751, Chief Justice James
De Lancey and Commissary Henry Barclay talked with the Reverend Henry Melchior Mühlenberg about the similarity of their
two communions, and Mr. Barclay pointed out that any properly
ordained Lutheran minister could preach in an Anglican church
if recommended by an archbishop. Frequent exchanges of opinion
by pastors of the two denominations brought some form of union
closer in 1756 when a Lutheran minister (probably Mühlenberg)
gave the Reverend William Sturgeon of Philadelphia "some un-
digested thoughts" on the subject, a copy of which the Anglican
forwarded to Dr. Bearcroft for the governors of the S.P.G. Four
years afterwards, the Reverend Thomas Barton of Lancaster, Pennsylvania, wrote to the Secretary for an organ, stating that "many
of the Lutherans who gladly embrace the opportunity to teach
their children the Religion, Manners, and Customs of England,
would come to our Church if we had but an Instrument to celebrate
the praises of God in the manner that they have been used to."
Small wonder then that Presbyterian suspicions were widespread,
particularly on the occasion in 1761 when the missionaries in the

---

33. A second effort to merge the Germans with the Presbyterians failed in 1751.
Records of the Presbyterian Church, 176; Briggs, *American Presbyterianism*, 284,
287–9; Trinterud, *American Tradition*, 136.

city of New York took Mr. Mühlenberg to their church and admitted him to a session of their ministerial convention.[34]

English and colonial fears of the Roman Catholic enemy during the French and Indian War inspired an interesting joint effort of Anglicans and Dissenters on both sides of the Atlantic to provide education for the Germans of Pennsylvania. A group of Pennsylvanians under the leadership of Provost William Smith of the College of Philadelphia, among whom were prominent Presbyterians and Episcopalians, planned in 1754 to open six charity schools to teach German children not only the English language and the usual subjects but also "the Constitution and Interest of the Colonies." The money for the project was raised by "a Society of Noblemen and Gentlemen in London," who turned out to be mostly Nonconformists, including Dr. Benjamin Avery and the Reverend Samuel Chandler, though the Bishop of Exeter displayed genuine interest in the undertaking. Most of the money was spent directly by the Pennsylvania trustees, but some was disbursed by the Synod of Philadelphia to such schools conducted by Presbyterians for educating German pupils as that of Sampson Smith at Chestnut Level. This first attempt at "Americanization" of non-English immigrants lasted about five years. The nonsectarian project was finally terminated because the Palatines, prodded by Christopher Saur of Germantown in his newspaper, grew increasingly suspicious of the intentions of the projectors, who never included any Quakers or Germans in their councils, and because the Reverend Richard Peters and Provost Smith tried to use the charity schools to promote the Anglican cause.[35]

V

The center of agitation for an Anglican bishop shifted from Connecticut to the Middle Colonies in April, 1754, when Dr.

34. Theodore G. Tappert and John W. Doberstein, *Journals of Henry Melchior Mühlenberg* (Philadelphia, 1942), I, 282, 323, 456; Perry, *Historical Collections, Pennsylvania,* II, 268–9, 294.

35. Parliament acknowledged the Moravian Episcopate on June 6, 1749, and encouraged members of the United Brethren to settle in America and Britain. *Ecclesiastical Records,* IV, 3084; Bridenbaughs, *Rebels and Gentlemen,* 52–5; *N.Y. Gaz.,* Mar. 17, 1755; *Records of the Presbyterian Church,* 219, 226, 227–8, 231, 290, 315.

Samuel Johnson moved to New York to head the new college. "If these dissenting governments in New England, who scarcely tolerate the Church, must be indulged," he grumbled to the Bishop of Oxford in October, "yet why may not one [bishop] be allowed to be sent to New York or Maryland, or Virginia, or South Carolina, in which colonies the Church is established by law? This is extremely hard indeed!" Mr. Chandler's good news four months later that the munificent Bishop of London had offered the King and Council £10,000 on condition that "an American Bishop might be sent over in his Time" hardly allayed the good Doctor's melancholy.[36]

That colonial Dissenters could always count on potent friends in England shows up again on the occasion when Israel Mauduit communicated a letter to the Committee of the Dissenting Deputies on September 25, 1754, from the Boston Congregationalists complaining that their missionaries to the Iroquois in the province of New York had been obstructed because they were not episcopally ordained and requesting that the Committee use its influence with "some Proper Persons in Power" in their behalf. Dr. Avery responded by taking the matter up with Lord Halifax.[37]

Young Episcopal clergymen of Manhattan, who were openly more aggressive than Dr. Johnson, had no scruples about meddling in politics, and they too made a practice of appealing to friends in London. In January, 1755, they asked the Archbishop of Canterbury to use his influence in procuring the appointment of "Religious and Exemplary Governors, who are well attached to the Church," as long as a bishop could not be sent over. Specifically, because Jonathan Belcher was a prominent Dissenter and was approaching the close of his life, they urged that a devout Anglican, Colonel John Schuyler of New York, be appointed the next governor of New Jersey. Within a year the Dissenting Deputies received letters from the Presbyterians of New York and New Jersey asking them to intercede with Lord Halifax in the matter of the New Jersey governorship.[38]

36. Schneiders, *Johnson*, II, 334; Chandler to Johnson, Feb. 26, 1755, Hawks Papers, II.

37. Dissenting Deputies, Minutes, I, 377.

38. New York clergy to Archbishop of Canterbury, Jan. 29, 1755, S.P.G. Correspondence, ser. B, II; Dissenting Deputies, Minutes, I, 397, 398; Governor Belcher did not die until 1757.

VI

New-Side Presbyterians, lay and clerical, had borne the brunt of the battle at New York, but the schism in their church had kept them from presenting a united front to the opposition. As early as 1751, proposals for reunion had been sent from the Synod of New York to Samuel Hazard in Philadelphia for delivery to the Old-Side Synod of that city. Hot heads had to cool and issues change before agreement could be reached. It took seven more years — in all seventeen — to end the schism. Finally, by the summer of 1758, a plan of union passed both synodical bodies, and the strengthened new Synod of New York and Philadelphia provided a confident leadership for the denomination. Henceforth, as Professor L. J. Trinterud tells us, "a truly American Presbyterianism was distinguished by its tone, discipline, and spiritual vitality." [39]

39. Trinterud, *American Tradition*, 134.

VI

TRUMPETS BLOW IN ZION: NEW YORK AND NEW JERSEY

1750–1760

The province of New York seemed fated to be the scene of ecclesiastical strife, for as far back as 1690 friction between the Anglicans and Dissenters confused every public issue; ecclesiastical and civil politics were never actually separated. Indignant that an Episcopalian minority, aided and abetted by royal governors, could thwart the Assembly, as it did in the administration of the Ministry Act, and could deny them the right to incorporate, the Presbyterians could not be apathetic about the increasing power of the Church of England. The strong personalities of the leaders of the opposing forces made it inevitable that New York should become the cockpit in which the champions of the various denominations contended for power and prestige more than for souls.

William Livingston, the ablest of several sons of the second lord of Livingston Manor, was graduated from Yale College in 1741 at the age of eighteen. Like Timothy Cutler and Samuel Johnson before him, Livingston was more influenced by the books in the library at New Haven than by the orthodox Congregationalism of the tutors and Thomas Clap, who became rector in 1740. Whatever the official curriculum, Yale's severest critics must admit that the students were free to browse in the library and to form their own opinions, and that they were independent enough to do so. Saturating himself with Locke, Addison, Steele, *The Independent Whig,* and like philosophical and critical writers, William Livingston became a liberal dissenter of the type of so many of the English Nonconformists who have peopled these pages. No person of his strongly rationalist bent could accept the "New-Light" enthusiasm of the

Great Awakening, but, on the other hand, he openly deplored the narrowness and bigotry of many of Connecticut's Standing Order.

Livingston's closest intellectual companion after graduation was Noah Welles, sometime tutor at the College, whose ordination at the Congregational Church in Stamford afforded the Reverend Noah Hobart the opportunity to deal with the Anglican clergy of New England. Just at this time, Livingston, seeking to persuade Welles to visit Manhattan, "our second Sodom," proudly emphasized the hospitality maintained by some kindred spirits — "not to say that it reflects no little honour on our place that we allow a Liberty of Conscience to all people, and a Man here may Serve his Maker after his own fashion without running the Risque of fine or imprisonment, which, perhaps, is more than can be said of your highly privileged and indulgent Government." [1]

Upon publication at Boston in 1747 of Noah Hobart's sermon, *Ministers of the Gospel . . . Delivered at the Ordination of . . . Noah Welles*, the Stamford divine sent a copy to his New York friend, probably with the intent of showing him that religious liberty was being stoutly upheld in Connecticut. Acknowledging its receipt on July 23, Livingston replied: "I think that Parson Hobart is very Smart upon the Church . . . but that there is not so much vital piety &c. in New England now as there was before the Church gained so much ground, I don't take to be a Conclusive Argument, that the Church has introduc'd that looseness and Immorality. . . ." Not that he approved of the Church of England: "It has I think too many popish relicks, not to say, gross Superstitions." And, he continued, "it must further be owned that the Church of England clergy by what Charter I know not, do actually assume greater Libertys, and indulge themselves in a much more licentious course of Life than the Dissenting Ministers; and the Generality of them, if not really vicious, seem to make little Conscience of approaching to the very extremity of Vice." This, more than endless debate over Episcopal and Presbyterian ordination or the sin of nonconformity, "with whole folios of the like nonsensical inconsequence," is your great argument against them. [2]

In spite of these strictures, the New Yorker followed the ex-

1. Livingston to Welles, Sept. 17, 1746, Johnson Family Papers, No. 27.
2. Livingston to Welles, July 23, 1747, Johnson Family Papers, No. 34.

changes in the Hobart-Wetmore-Beach debate with the deepest interest. Having studied the law (he was admitted to the bar in 1748) Livingston took special note of the forcefulness of the arguments and the presentation. "The Rector of Rye [James Wetmore] burnt his fingers in meddling with your ordination Sermon," he told Welles. "Mr. Hobart proceeds (as the Lawyers say) upon the Gist of the Controversy. He is a masterly Reasoner, and, when he thinks fit, a sound Satyrist. He says the most galling things with an air of good humour and is sharp without Virulence. This dispassionate temper gives him a prodigious Advantage over his Antagonist. This wrathful Gentleman is apt to besprinkle his Writings with a profusion of Scandal, Ribaldry and Billingsgate. But his *Salt* instead of *preserving* unfortunately *spoils* his Works. . . . To be serious, in a preacher of the humane and benevolent Religion of Jesus, it is abominable." William Livingston, as an avid reader of the colonial press, could not have missed the progress of this altercation in the Boston papers nor have failed to draw a sound lesson from it; the same lesson that he found in the rougher Mayhew controversy of 1750. A few years later, when Livingston emerged as the lay champion against an American episcopate, he paid Mr. Hobart the prime compliment of taking over all of his arguments. The Connecticut parson had forged the link joining Massachusetts and New York.[3]

Nor did the pamphlet battles over church and state going on concurrently in England escape the attention of William Livingston and his New-Side associates. In 1747 Livingston sent Noah Welles a "little Pamphlet against the spiritual Jurisdiction of the Church of England" with the comment that he had offered to be a subscriber, if it were reprinted, "to Encourage a Work that will expose Ecclesiastical Tyranny, vindicate the dissenting principles, assert Liberty of Conscience, and prove the inherent and unalienable Right (not of what is profanely honour'd with that splendid Title, but what in reality deserves the Name) of Free Thinking." When a second and longer *Letter from the Dissenting Gentleman,* sent to

---

3. For the Hobart-Beach-Wetmore exchange, see also p. 87. Livingston to Welles, July 23, 1747, No. 49, Feb. 24, 1747/8, No. 41; Feb. 19, 1749/50, No. 57, Johnson Family Papers.

William Peartree Smith (Yale College, 1742) by a London book-seller, came to Livingston's attention, he thought that it contained the "most exquisite humour." Accordingly he recommended it to his friend Noah Welles for distribution in Connecticut, "where the Candidates for the Ministry seem of late inordinately fond of large Salaries and are more intent upon tickling a dainty Palate than maintaining sound principles." These two pamphlets by Micajah Towgood, which attacked the Anglican record in ecclesiastical and public affairs, were reprinted at New York by James Parker in 1748 under the title: *The Dissenting Gentleman's Answer, to the Rev. Mr. White's Three Letters; in which a Separation from the Establishment is Fully Justified; The Charge of Schism is Refuted and Retorted; and the Church of England and the Church of Jesus Christ, are Impartially Compared, and found to be Constitutions of Quite a Different Nature.* The fact that at least two editions were printed in the colonies in addition to the three in England proves that the New Yorker was not alone in his appreciation of this "Admirable piece." [4]

In the decade after leaving New Haven, William Livingston had continued to read widely and deeply in theology and the philosophers of the Enlightenment. Always interested in polite literature, the classics, literary criticism, and wit, William Livingston wrote a clear, trenchant, and often elegant prose. His letters are among the best surviving from his day, and his long poem, *Philosophic Solitude* (1747), celebrates in Virgilian vein the pleasures of country life. Much of his later success as a controversialist was due to his

4. Livingston expected the pamphlet to be "a timely barrier" to check the boasted Anglican progress in Connecticut, and "beat down that furious intolerance, which some of its furious Champions seem to be full of." Rogers and Fowle of Boston also reprinted Towgood's tract in 1748. When the Reverend James Wetmore first heard that his Congregational opponent was preparing a reply to his *Vindication of the Professors of the Church* (1746), he published with Rogers and Fowle in 1748, *The Englishman Directed in the Choice of His Religion, Reprinted for the Use of English Americans. With a Prefatory Address, Vindicating the King's Supremacy and Authority in Parliament, in Matters of Religion, and thereby demolishing all Pleas for Separation, according to the Concession of the Dissenting Gentleman's Answer to the Rev. Mr. White's Letters. . . .* On Towgood, see Robbins, *Commonwealthman*, 227, 231, 340–41; Livingston to Welles, July 23, Sept. 19, 1747, No. 39; Dec. 10, 1747, No. 39; Mar. 12, 1747/8, No. 42; April 16, 1748, No. 43, Johnson Family Papers.

superior literary skill. On February 18, 1749, he confided to Noah Welles that the William Smiths,* Scott, and he planned, as soon as possible, to publish essays after the type of the *Spectator* "for correcting the taste and improving the Minds of our fellow Citizens." Each contributor would write a paper a month until 150 were ready, and then they would publish one or two a week. He asked for contributions on religion and morality from Welles. Further, this "formidable and brilliant lawyer, shambling and slovenly in appearance, whose height and thinness, combined with the cutting quality of his writings," had early earned him the sobriquet the "Whipping Post," had already fearlessly and pugnaciously made it clear to the Episcopal clergymen round about that he considered them and their ecclesiastical designs fair and ample subject matter for his gifted, mordant pen.[5]

At Yale College, Livingston had nourished a thorough dislike of prelacy along with his brand of "Free Thinking," and by 1747, if not before, had decided that a union of church and state was bad in any form, anywhere. Sometime prior to 1750 he changed his religious affiliation from the Dutch Reformed to the Presbyterian Church, where his Yale friends and legal associates — the William Smiths (father and son), William Peartree Smith, and John Morin Scott — all worshipped. Although he continued to find the theological position of Old Lights more acceptable, he considered the character, the New England respect for learning, and especially the anti-Episcopal bias of many of the New-Side ministers of the Synod of New York most compatible; Livingston was never the bigoted type of Presbyterian his enemies charged; he was, in reality, an eighteenth-century rationalist.[6]

* There were, unfortunately for the reader, *four* William Smiths on the New York scene at this time, who will be distinguished as follows: William Smith, senior; William Smith, Jr.; plain William Smith, the Anglican, soon to take Orders; and William Peartree Smith, Yale, 1742.

5. Livingston to Welles, Feb. 18, 1748/9, No. 49, Johnson Family Papers; George Dangerfield, *Chancellor Robert R. Livingston of New York, 1746–1813* (New York, 1960), 22.

6. Livingston discussed with Welles in May, 1746, establishing at Yale a "Livingstonian Professor of Divinity" named after his father, to form the minds of the students and "to root out" any "latent Seeds of Superstition and Fanaticism." Letters 1–22, Johnson Family Papers, discuss Livingston's views on religion.

The widening rift between the Dissenters and Anglicans of the city of New York is revealed in a seemingly trivial bit of local tattle. For Welles's edification, Livingston told of the return from England of the Reverend John Ogilvie (Yale College, 1748) in November, 1749, with some "tattling" talk about a New York merchant who kept a mistress in London; challenged, the gossip proved false. Livingston also forwarded a paper, "The Memoirs of Thomas Rant," which delineated the "Character" of the scandal-mongering vicar in good London fashion. Word got around Manhattan that Livingston had sent copies of the paper to all the ministers in New England, and it was therefore deduced that he and William Smith, Jr., were the authors. Livingston denied authorship but promised that, when the facts were all known, "I shall not spare the Gown and Cassock." One fact emerged from the "terrible uproar" caused among the High-Church adherents: "it hath been the means of discovering a much greater number than I imagined we had among us." [7]

As the decade of the 1750's opened, the clashes between the representatives of the Church of England and the Dissenters became more frequent and more bitter. Nearly every political maneuver was immediately interpreted as a device to gain influence and prestige for one or the other of the ecclesiastical groups. William Livingston and his Yale associates at Manhattan deliberately fused religion and politics, and thereafter the Livingston and De Lancey factions were labeled Presbyterian and Anglican with reasonable accuracy. William Livingston made the ecclesiastical side of the contest for power peculiarly his own.

The petition of the Anglican clergy for the exclusive right to perform marriage ceremonies is a specific instance of attempts to aggrandize their position and the type of political action that impelled Livingston to attack the Churchmen every time they showed signs of playing politics. William Smith, Jr., in his *History of New York,* said that the Church of England sought "to enlarge the sphere of their secular business." But this effort on the part of a minority to grab the lucrative fees hitherto enjoyed by all ministers and justices of the peace could only exacerbate the already marked

7. Livingston to Welles, Nov. 30, 1749, No. 54; Jan. 3, 1749/50, No. 55, Johnson Family Papers.

resentments of the Presbyterians and the Dutch Reformed. "A great clamour ensued, and the attempt was abortive." [8]

Dear to the heart of William Livingston was a scheme to found a provincial college. By an act of 1746, supplemented by legislation in 1748, the New York Assembly authorized the raising of funds by public lottery for a college. After his first enthusiasm for the project had cooled down somewhat, he wrote to the Reverend Mr. Welles: "The College in New Jersey goes on but slowly, and that intended for this province is, I suppose, by this time, wholly forgotten, unless, which is possible, the Design is postponed on account of the perplexity of our public Affairs." As to the possible failure to establish a college, Livingston went on to say: "I should be glad if it did, because I think it impossible for three Colleges to be so near one another, without clashing and interfering with each others Interest. So that the Design of building the Jersey College bids the fairest for being carried into Execution." Apparently the New Yorker took heart again, for the following year, 1749, he revealed that he had a pamphlet in press: *Some Serious thoughts on the design of erecting a College in the Province of N. York, shewing the Advantages of a public liberal Education more especially with regard to Religion and politicks humbly offered to the public for the encouragement of so useful an undertaking. By Hippocrates Mithridates Apoth.*[9]

In November, 1751, the Assembly vested the £3443 raised in the lottery in a board of trustees, among whom were six Anglicans, two Dutch Reformed, and Presbyterian William Livingston. The following March, when the Board of Trinity Church offered "to give any Reasonable Quantity of the Church's Farm" on Manhattan for a college, the Episcopalians seized the lead. Their next step, one that proved decisive, was the publication by William Smith, a young Scottish tutor fresh from the University of Aberdeen, on October 24 of *Some Thoughts on Education: With Rea-*

8. The Anglican clergy's petition was apparently killed in a committee of the Council, New York Council Minutes, May 2, 1748 (New York State Library, Albany), V, 21; William Smith, Jr., *History of the Late Province of New York from the Discovery to the Appointment of Governor Colden in 1762* (New-York Historical Society, *Collections,* 1st ser., IV, 1829), I, 349.

9. John Zenger published the college pamphlet in 1749. Livingston to Welles, Sept. 19, 1747, No. 36; Feb. 18, 1748/9, No. 49, Johnson Family Papers.

sons for Erecting a College in this Province and fixing the same at the City of New York. . . . with a Poem. Being a serious Address to the House of Representatives. "Philomathes," as Smith signed himself, argued hard for establishing a college under Episcopal auspices, and suggested that two tutors be employed at once with the lottery funds and that the erection of an edifice be postponed until more money should be available. More important, Smith nominated the best-known Anglican of the colonies, the Reverend Samuel Johnson, as the first rector of the new institution. An unnamed writer, "Philopatriae" in the *New York Gazette,* took up the idea, and, also assuming Episcopal control of the college, proposed that, in order to ease the strain on the lottery fund, the provost might also serve as minister of the new St. George's Chapel, and then intimated that "perhaps Dr. Johnson of Stratford, may give Satisfaction at both." From Livingston's legal associate, William Smith, Jr., masquerading as "Goose Adrianse," came a devastating and sarcastic attack on the author of *Some Thoughts on Education,* which closed by asking why this William Smith had been so modest as to avoid offering himself for the presidency — Some thought you did so in the preface, but it was "too delicately hinted." [10]

Only a few months before this exchange, the Reverend James Wetmore of Rye had reported to London that the Hobart controversy "is yet subsisting." Now, with the Anglicans maneuvering to control the projected institution at New York, it seemed to William Livingston and his circle that the time had come for them to stand forth against the High-Church group in defense of both the religious and civil liberties enjoyed in the province. Though only 20 of the 150 numbers planned for the new periodical were ready by November, 1752 (half of which he had written himself), Livingston decided to launch the long-delayed publication. Accordingly the first number of the *Independent Reflector,* printed by James Parker, came out on November 30, 1752. [11]

The reforming of "public abuses" was the intent of the *Inde-*

10. *Ecclesiastical Records,* V, 3207–8, 3220; Osgood, *American Colonies,* III, 483–4; Dix, *Trinity Church,* I, 258; *N.Y. Mercury,* Nov. 6, 1752; Jan. 1, 1753; *N.Y. Gaz.,* Nov. 6, Dec. 4, 1752.

11. Hawks and Perry, *Documentary History, Conn.,* I, 293.

pendent Reflector, who frankly avowed his "principal Design of Opposing Oppression, and vindicating the Liberty of Man." Corruption, ignorance, and indolence are rife in our society, said he, but "none of these Discouragements shall, however, deter me from vindicating the *civil and religious* RIGHTS of my Fellow-Creatures." Under no obligation to any party, the *Reflector* does not propose to enter the New York political lists. Moreover, "the Espousing of any polemic Debate between different Sects of Christians shall be the last Charge against him; tho' he shall be ever ready to deliver his Sentiments on the Abuses and Encroachments of any, with the Freedom and Unconcernedness becoming Truth and Independency." [12]

The *Independent Reflector* very shortly found a receptive public, and before two months were up James Parker advertised that he had run out of back numbers and would have to make a larger printing to meet "the great and unexpected demand." A knowing and calculating manipulator of public opinion, Livingston, at first, while his circulation built up, published articles dealing only with local civic problems. Not until January 4, 1753, did he make good his announcement that he would unburden his sentiments on religious abuses with a spirited defense of the Moravians, or United Brethren, whom his own church opposed. "The Pulpit-Scold is the most despicable Scold in the World. He is a cowardly Scold, that gives his Antagonist no Opportunity of scolding back. From this paper, therefore, I will preach against every such Preacher, and make the Press reverberate the Calumnies of the Pulpit. . . . Never did any Sect spring up in the Christian World, void of superstitious Rites, and holy Gimcracks, but it gave great Offense to a High-Church." Two weeks after this truculent utterance, Livingston explained privately to Welles that the *Reflector's* vindication of the Moravians "has made a most prodigious noise amongst the High-Church of all kinds, several Bigots having refused to take the paper any longer, but curiosity has since procured more Subscribers than Bigotry has drawn off." But before the author can "Rise in his Spirit . . . he must gradually pave the way for bold Strokes.

12. *Independent Reflector,* No. 1 (November 30, 1752), 1–3 (I have used Samuel Hazard's copy, now in the William L. Clements Library. It lacks the preface. Ordinarily citations will be by page rather than number or date of issue.

The Town is not yet ripe for seeing plain Truth. The Veil must be removed from their eyes by slow degrees." [13]

In style, subject matter, and attitudes on public questions, the *Independent Reflector* did not offer the New Yorkers the mildly satirical Addisonian essays on manners, morals, and taste that its projector had contemplated in 1749, save in an occasional issue. This crusading paper openly took as its model Trenchard and Gordon's famous London periodical of 1720. In "A Defense of Ridicule" (No. XLI), Livingston declared that "The Independent Whig has gone further toward shaming Tyranny and Priestcraft with downright Banter, than would have been effected by austere Dogmas, or formal Deductions." Written by "one of the finest pens in Europe," The *Independent Whig* enjoyed such a great popularity at New York in these years that it was natural for Livingston and his coterie to imitate its hard-hitting, derisive style and to borrow heavily from its anticlericalism. And they turned to other English rationalistic works as well. "There is scarce anything of note written by the freethinkers, as they call themselves, to the detriment of Christianity," the perturbed Samuel Johnson informed Fulham Palace, "but what is transmitted hither and propagated among us and greedily read and imbibed by many conceited unthinking people. . . . Among other pernicious books the *Independent Whig* grows much in vogue and a notable set of young men of figure in New York have of late set up for writers in a weekly paper called the *Independent Reflector.*" As he and his fellow clergymen employed their pens to combat the effects of the local periodical, they tried at the same time to counter Trenchard and Gordon by reprinting at New York in June, 1753, Francis Squire's *An Answer to Some Late Papers entitled The Independent Whig.* Here, as in so many instances in colonial history, English ideas were appropriated and either refurbished or transformed for American purposes.[14]

13. *Independent Reflector*, 20, 21, 22, 36; Livingston to Welles, Jan. 17, 1753, No. 68, Johnson Family Papers.

14. William Smith, the Episcopalian, charged in July, 1753, that the Reflector "continues to pilfer from the *Independent Whig, Henry on Prayer,* &c. . . . Any old Woman could also have copies of the Independent Whig. . . ." *N.Y. Mercury,* June 11, July 9, 1753; *Independent Reflector,* 163; Schneiders, *Johnson,* III, 247; IV, 3; Henry Barclay to Samuel Johnson, Apr. 16, 1753, Hawks Papers, II, No. 21.

Writing anonymously in the *New York Mercury* in April, 1753, the Reverend Samuel Seabury, the elder, of Queens ascribed the *Independent Reflector* and the "inundation" of letters to the New York press on religious issues to "a Club, who are known to be more fertile in Schemes than in Prudence." Years later, Judge Thomas Jones insisted that the periodical was hatched in the King's Arms Tavern by members of the Whig Club. Who were the authors? The Livingston-Welles correspondence quoted above makes it certain that William Livingston was its moving spirit, laid down the policy, and performed most of the writing. Other contributors were the lawyers William Smith, Jr., John Morin Scott, and William Peartree Smith, in addition to Noah Welles — all of them graduates of Yale College. They were not all members of the Whig Club of Manhattan, nor were they even agreed on secular politics, but they did agree on matters ecclesiastical. They were religious liberals and dedicated to maintaining what they fervently regarded as their liberties against Anglican encroachments.[15]

When he wrote on February 18, 1753, thanking his friend at Stamford for a contribution to his paper, Livingston admitted that in his Moravian piece "the Reflector goes rather too far in his Notions of orthodoxy and some other Points, and has not been particular Enough in distinguishing the Clergy he writes against from those who [like Welles] are an Ornament to Mankind. But be this as it will he is attacked in one of our News Papers almost every Week, so rudely and unfairly that I could not forbear [*sic*] to answer a Church Parson who appeared in Print last Week on that Subject. My answer will come out in Parker's Paper of this Day. You will find I have used very little Ceremony, as he appears of a down right slavish Disposition with respect to civil Power, and a furious Bigot in Religion, both of which I hate as the Sin of Witchcraft. He would persecute if he dared." Then Livingston completely disclosed in the privacy of the letter the motives which impelled him

15. The most satisfactory discussion of the difficult question of the authorship of the *Independent Reflector* is by Lyon N. Richardson, *History of Early American Magazines, 1741-1789* (New York, 1931), 79n-80n; *N.Y. Mercury*, April 30, 1753; Thomas Jones *History of New York during the Revolutionary War* (edited by Edward F. De Lancey, New York, 1879), I, 6; Livingston to Welles, Feb. 18, 1753, No. 69, Johnson Family Papers.

to forgo the gradual educating of the public for what may be called literary direct action:

There is a thing Mr. Welles which has long been the Subject of my thoughts and which I should be glad to transmit to the Reflector in a Course of Letters, could I obtain your assistance. The Case is this — Our future College will undoubtedly be of great Importance to this Province, and is like to fall without a vigorous opposition, under the sole management of Churchmen. The Consequence of which will be universal Pries[t]craft and Bigotry in less than half a Century. The Trustees lately proposed were every one a Churchman, and many of them the most implicit Bigots. The Churchmen can assign no colour of Reason to have the Direction of the Affair in preference to any other Sect, but *I would not have it managed by any Sect.* For that reason I would have no Charter from the Crown, but an Act of Assembly for the Purpose. Nor, for the same Reason should Divinity be taught at College because whoever is in the Chair will obtrude his own Notions for Theology. Let the Students follow their own Inclinations in the Study of Divinity and Read what Books they please in their Chambers [as we did at New Haven] or apply themselves to it after they leave the College. Their religious Exercises should consist of reading the Scriptures, and hearing a Prayer in which all Protestants may join. I know that if it falls into the hands of Church men, it will either ruin the College or the Country, and in fifty years, no Dissenters, however deserving, will be able to get into any office. Pray, honour me with Your thoughts on the Matter and you'l increase the obligations under which you have already laid

Your most obedient and sincere
friend.[16]

"The Noise and Uproar about the *Independent Reflector,*" are to him no astonishment, said Livingston on February 8, but he admitted to being unprepared for the "devout Rage, and monkish Indignation" of the Episcopal clergy — "Men of Awful Function . . . For my Part I bless my Stars, that I live in a Country, where their utmost Efforts cannot exceed hard Names, and unorthodox Cursing." "Tis the Cause of Truth and Liberty" for which I con-

16. Livingston to Welles, Feb. 18, 1753, No. 69, Johnson Family Papers (Italics mine).

tend, and in so doing, I will defy "all Tyrants civil or ecclesiastic," and resist all attempts at advancing ecclesiastical domination over this province.[17]

This challenge, flung at the Episcopal clergy with such rhetorical force, was perhaps premature, for the New York audience was hardly as well prepared for the coming "war of words" as Livingston had intended it to be. The very next week, "Layman" Samuel Johnson opened fire in Hugh Gaine's *New York Mercury* with a "profound criticism" of Livingston's latest effort. "I am glad that people begin publicly to animadvert on the Reflector," Thomas Bradbury Chandler wrote to Johnson, and he sneered at the defense made by "Philo-Reflector" (William Smith, Jr.) in Parker's *New York Gazette* as being "as weak and impertinent a thing as ever was published." Nevertheless, the *Independent Reflector* frightened as well as maddened this cleric, who perceived that to try to use sound arguments against him "would be like charging a cannon for the destruction of a vermin. . . . The suppression of the Church seems to be aimed at in every shape in these parts, by a set of men who although they have not the understanding yet have the activity and some of them almost the craft of Jesuits." [18]

It was not until March 29th that Livingston began to comment on the great issue of education in his Number 17: "Remarks upon our intended College," in which he elaborated the views he had earlier expressed to Noah Welles. His contention that sound public policy requires the college to admit members of all Protestant denominations "upon a perfect Parity as to Privileges," and that the danger of "an Academy founded in Bigotry, and reared in Party-Spirit," could be avoided by a charter from the Assembly for a publicly supported college, instead of a royal grant for a denominational institution, startled New Yorkers. The founders of the other colonial colleges had followed the European tradition and placed them under sectarian auspices. What Livingston was proposing was not only a new and radical departure born of the American Enlight-

17. *Independent Reflector*, 43–6.

18. The principal newspaper exchanges are in: *N.Y. Mercury*, Feb. 12, Mar. 12, Apr. 16, 1753; *N.Y. Gaz.*, Feb. 19, 26, Apr. 9, 16, 1753; see also Schneiders, *Johnson*, I, 165–6.

enment but also, be it noted, a rational and practical solution for a problem of unprecedented denominational complexity. "Besides English and Dutch Presbyterians, which perhaps exceed all our other religious Professions put together, we have Episcopalians, Anabaptists, Lutherans, Quakers, and a growing Church of Moravians, all equally zealous for their discriminating Tenets. . . ." To give one sect the preference — and that a minority sect — would create "a Nursery of Animosity, Dissention, and Disorder." [19]

The genuine concern for humane learning expressed by Livingston in his private correspondence shines through the anti-ecclesiastical arguments of his published papers. Nor can anyone who reads the *Independent Reflector* doubt his insistence to "the clamorous Trumpeters of the Coffee-House" that he is not writing against the Church of England. "I have only exposed her unreasonable encroachments" when her agents acted "in defiance of the equal rights of the rest" against law and reason. "I am no sectary." Talk such as this excited a public already aware of the brute facts of the situation.[20]

II

The appearance, intensity of argument, and telling effect on public opinion of the *Independent Reflector*'s crusade against the Episcopal plan for the college dumfounded its supporters. Fortunately for them, an able young Scot, William Smith, was at hand, and he was eager to win a place for himself in America. A witty, well-informed, and lucid writer, Smith declared in his celebrated *A General Idea of the College of Mirania* that, because the Church of England was the established faith in New York, Anglicans should control the new institution. In July of 1753, Smith entered the arena as "X. Z." in the *Mercury*. His first piece denied the mounting circulation claimed for the *Independent Reflector* — "It DIES

19. Harvard and Yale were Congregational; William and Mary in Virginia, Anglican; The College of New Jersey, Presbyterian. For the essays on the college question, *Independent Reflector*, 67–90; Schneiders, *Johnson*, IV, 3–4.

20. *Independent Reflector, Preface* (published separately, New York, 1754), 25, 30–31.

DAILY" — and he pilloried Livingston for plagiarizing the *Independent Whig.*[21]

Using arguments sent to him by Samuel Johnson, William Smith argued in a second letter to the *Mercury* that *"National Establishment* can alone diffuse, thro' a Country, the full social Advantages arising from Religion and Men set aside to explain and inculcate it. If, according to the *Reflector's* Scheme, all Religions were equally favor'd by the Civil Power, none establish'd, and every Man left at Liberty to preach and practise what he thought proper, what a Scene of Confusion would thence arise . . . from such unbridled Liberty of Conscience. . . ." In this Smith expounded the traditional view powerfully, but he also displayed the newly arrived European's ignorance of American conditions and opinions when, in the next paragraph, he continued:

As to the Political Uses of national Establishments, he must indeed be a very shallow Politician who does not see them. The Statesman has always found it necessary for the Purposes of Government, to raise some one Denomination of religions above the Rest to a certain Degree. *This favor'd Denomination, by these Means, becomes as it were the Creature of the Government, which is thus enabled to turn the Balance and keep all in Subjection.* [Italics mine.] For as such Establishments may be made in favor of one Party as well as another, the Party that is uppermost becomes a Balance for all the tolerated Sects; and these last, in hopes of that Preference in their Turn, are always tractable. But let a Government once give away the Power of bestowing its own Favors, and let all Sects and Persuasions be equally favor'd, equally independent of the Constitution, how shall they be influenc'd or how rul'd?

Then came the unkindest cut:

This levelling Notion, that a perfect Equality among all religious Persuasions, is the true Basis of *British Liberty,* the *Reflector* seems to have borrow'd, but, according to Custom, misconstrued from Voltaire.[22]

21. Jones, *History of New York,* 12–15; *N.Y. Mercury,* July 9, 1753; William Smith, *A General Idea of the College of Mirania* (New York, 1753), 84–5.

22. Smith makes clear in his second newspaper piece that he knows who the Reflector is; and in one place says a future Hudibras may write:

When William Smith sailed to England in mid-summer of 1753, he hoped to return to New York as a tutor in the new college though "great revenge is threatened against me." He carried with him a manuscript by Samuel Johnson, which was published at London under the title *Elementa Philosophica*. Appended to the treatise was a letter "by the Author and Some of his Brethren" setting forth the dire need of an episcopate for America in the event that all the Calvinists in the English colonies — English, Dutch, German — "unite in power, as has been long projected by some enterprising spirits." Such a coalition of Englishmen and "foreigners" would do more mischief to government and promote a greater ecclesiastical tyranny than could ever be apprehended from a full Episcopal jurisdiction over *all America,* which has unjustly been charged as the aim in settling bishops in the colonies. When Dr. Johnson first saw a copy of his book with the ill-advised inclusion of this letter, he was so appalled that he wrote at once to England to explain that, though he had discussed all the points mentioned with William Smith, the young man had written and published it without his permission. But once the colonial Dissenters read the missive, the damage done could never be repaired.[23]

Meanwhile, the Society's missionaries in New York and New Jersey had come to their own and their church's defense against the Reflector's forays. One of the ablest clerical controversialists was the elder Samuel Seabury of Queen's County, whose "smart piece" in Gaine's *Mercury* "spoke home to the *Reflector* and has madded them not a little." This occasions no surprise when one reads how far he descended below the pulpit level to write that for all the *Reflector's* "BRAYINGS" the "Proper Receptacle" was "Cloacina's Office." Seabury accused the *Reflector's* authors of trying to pull down the English and Dutch churches and to aggrandize the Presbyterian on the ruins. The fact that Parker refused to print four or five replies to these allegations did not endear him to Seabury's adversaries. Then there was the Reverend James Wetmore,

He rose, dread Foe to Priests, and Fetters,
Deep-skill'd in Church *and civil Matters;*
For he'd read all Cato's Letters.

N.Y. *Mercury,* July 9, 23, 1753; Schneiders, *Johnson,* IV, 4.

23. Schneiders, *Johnson,* II, 333; III, 248, 250–51; IV, 5.

who wrote the preface for Squire's *Answer to the Independent Whig;* the clergyman was hard at work on a series of papers defending the establishment in New York, but Anglican lawyers advised against publishing them. Henry Barclay, Rector of Trinity Church, the Reverend Samuel Auchmuty, and Thomas Bradbury Chandler of Elizabeth Town, New Jersey, complete the circle of missionary writers.[24]

The published utterances and the doings of the Episcopalians were well known to "The New York Triumvirate" — Livingston, Scott, and Smith — and their friends among the pastors as well. But it was William Livingston who the cause of episcopacy in America found to be its most redoubtable lay opponent. Anglican machinations struck at the very roots of that religious and civil liberty he cherished so much, and which he believed the large majority of the inhabitants of New York held dear. The vituperation, name-calling, and abuse he had to take from the Anglicans in pamphlet and newspaper, from the pulpit and coffeehouse, and to which the essay form of the *Independent Reflector* prevented him from replying, drove Livingston to neglect the college issue for a series of excursions against orthodoxy and priestcraft in the summer of 1753. He wrote powerful indictments "Of the Veneration and Contempt of the Clergy," of "The Absurdity of the civil Magistrate's interfering in Matters of Religion," "Of Passive-Obedience and Non-Resistance." Always in the forefront of his thinking was the conviction that in John Locke's civil compact men had not yielded to the ruler in their religious ideas: "Matters of Religion relate to another World, and have nothing to do with the Interests of State. . . . The civil Power hath no Jurisdiction over the Sentiments or Opinions of the Subject . . ." until they become prejudicial to the community. He reached a climax on September 27 with a long and learned historical article refuting the claim that the Church of England was ever legally established in the province of New York.[25]

Episcopalian pressures on the Manhattan printers, quite as much

24. Schneiders, *Johnson,* IV, 4, 6; I, 169; *N.Y. Mercury,* April 30, 1753; Barclay to Johnson, April 16, 1753, Hawks Papers, II, No. 21.

25. In No. 22 (April 26, 1753), Livingston advised his "dear Countrymen: You, I hope, will consider the least Infraction of your Liberties as a Prelude to greater Encroachments. Such always was, and ever will be the Case." *Independent Reflector,* 29, 134, 143–6, 147–50, 151–8, 175–80.

as the ferocity of the attacks in the columns of Hugh Gaine's *Mercury,* impelled the backers of the *Independent Reflector* to lash out at the printer as a "Tool of a Party" who abused the freedom of the press by denying slandered persons space to reply to their traducers. Though James Parker and William Weyman still would not open their *Gazette* to the Triumvirate, they continued to issue the *Independent Reflector,* and in September agreed to print a new set of fifty-two papers. Still indignant at their treatment, the authors of the *Reflector* announced in the *New York Gazette* that "the Enemies of Liberty . . . having by the most Iniquitous Acts, engrossed the *New York Mercury,* and utterly excluded their Antagonists from a fair Hearing in that Paper and the Printers of the *Gazette* declining the Insertion of any Thing that savours of political or religious Controversy, another Paper, entitled *The Occasional Reverberator,* has been set up to be published every Friday, as often as Occasion may require. . . ." In this sheet, William Smith, Jr., essayed to defend his friends, but intimidation caused Parker to refuse further publication on October 7 after printing only four issues. Then, without so much as notifying Livingston of his intention, Parker also stopped printing the *Independent Reflector* with the fifty-second number on November 22, 1753, though he had agreed to publish it until June 1, 1754, or give due notice. Some weeks later Parker admitted "that he had been threatened with the loss of the public business if he continued the publication of my papers," said Livingston, who blamed James De Lancey for being behind "such insidious and indirect practices to suppress the truth." [26]

In a preface of thirty-one pages for the bound issues of the *Independent Reflector,* Livingston described the trouble he had had with the printers. When Philadelphia and Boston printers declined to undertake it, he persuaded Henry De Foreest, the Dutch printer, to do it for him, but the job was badly botched. The preface appeared for sale at Robert McAlpine's Book Shop in February, 1754, with a statement on the title page: "Printed (until tyrannically suppressed) in MDCCLIII"; on the final page the Reflector warned

26. *Independent Reflector,* 159–62; also *Preface,* 2–3; *N.Y. Gaz.,* Sept. 17, 1753; *Occasional Reverberator,* September 7–October 5, 1753. For Hugh Gaine's side of the affair, see Paul L. Ford, *The Journals of Hugh Gaine, Printer* (New York, 1902), I, 9–12, 211–22. The Episcopalian attacks, some of them scurrilous, are in *N.Y. Mercury,* July 30, Aug. 17, Sept. 3, 10, 17, 24, Dec. 3, 1753.

that he would view the local scene quietly for a time, but none should conclude that he had been silenced. "I am preparing a History of this province and its politics," which I will offer to the public when "the press is restored to its former liberty." [27]

It appeared to many New Yorkers in 1754 that the demise of the *Independent Reflector* marked a great triumph for the members of the Episcopal party. Yet further consideration indicates that the real victory lay with the Livingstonians. Through the *Independent Reflector,* they had brought to a boil the church-state controversy, which had been simmering since 1690. They had defined clearly and penetratingly, with an abundance of detail, the cardinal issue involved — the intimate connection between religious and civil liberty. On ecclesiastical questions they had ranged themselves with liberal English writers, the so-called Freethinkers, not with narrow, bigoted partisans of either episcopacy or presbyterianism. They had attracted intercolonial attention, for Parker circulated their weekly paper through the Northern Colonies from Philadelphia to New Jersey, to Connecticut, and Boston, where, for example, Richard Draper, printer of the *Boston News-Letter,* received a complete set of it and also of the *Occasional Reverberator.* Both friends and enemies sent copies of the *Independent Reflector* to England. For more than a year the "war of words" fed discussions in pulpits, taverns, coffeehouses, private homes, and on street corners. The frequently foul-mouthed personal exchanges indulged in by the men of the cloth probably did more to keep the exchanges going than dignified rebuttals would have done. Not infrequently the *Independent Reflector* displayed great adroitness in drawing its opponents into statements that greatly injured their cause — even with some Episcopalians — as when William Smith wrote of the political uses of establishment. One may conclude, therefore, that the "New York Triumvirate" and their allies succeeded remarkably well in transferring an ecclesiastical controversy over to the public arena, where it received unprecedented publicity among the laity. This was no small achievement.[28]

27. *Independent Reflector, Preface,* 26, 31; Isaiah Thomas, *History of Printing in America (Archaeologica Americana,* Albany, 1874), VI, 125.

28. Draper's files of the *Independent Reflector* and *Occasional Reverberator* are in the Boston Athenaeum (Walter Whitehill to author, November 1, 1760).

Because of its literary quality, the *Independent Reflector* survived; while the ephemeral pieces in the *Mercury* disappeared with yesterday's newspapers. At Boston in 1758, Benjamin Meccom reprinted Nos. XXVII and XL on the Thirty-Nine Articles and on the Freedom of the Press in his *New-England Magazine*. Bound copies of the periodical were quickly bought up, and in 1759 Dr. Johnson could not find a single one to fill Archbishop Secker's request. In truth, the *Independent Reflector* ultimately became as much the American debater's manual of anti-Episcopal argument as the *Independent Whig* had been for the English. No better testimony to the lasting influence of the *Independent Reflector* exists than that of James Madison in a letter to the biographer of William Livingston in 1831:

In my youth I passed several years [1769–1772] in the college of N. Jersey, of which he was a trustee. . . . I recollect, particularly, that he was understood to be one of the authors of a work entitled "The Independent Reflector," and that some of the papers in it ascribed to him, being admired for the energy and eloquence of their composition, furnished occasionally to the students orations for the rostrum [of the American Whig Society], which were alternately borrowed from books and composed by themselves.[29]

III

For ten months after the final issue of the *Independent Reflector* came out, neither the *Gazette* nor the *Mercury* mentioned the ecclesiastical strife. Behind the scenes, however, both the Anglicans and the Triumvirate were actively maneuvering. On March 5, 1754, the Reverend Henry Barclay advised Dr. Johnson at Stratford about the appearance of the Reflector's Preface "Summing up all that he had wrote against Biggotry, Priestcraft, a Party Colledge, and Exceeding if possible his former Scurrility. He tells us what wonders he would have done had not his paper been Tyrannically Suppress'd. And amongst other Things that he would have pointed out (I think) 39 Lyes that have from time to time been wrote to

29. Richardson, *Early American Magazines,* 139; *New-England Magazine* (August, 1758), 33–41; (October, 1758), 19–22; *Ecclesiastical Records,* IV, 3745–6; *Letters and other Writings of James Madison* (Philadelphia, 1867), IV, 161, 163.

the Society. I have just had a Glance of the Book and shall endeavour to Send it next post." It is evident that the New York clergy both feared and respected William Livingston and had not been lulled to sleep by the suspension of the *Independent Reflector*.[30]

Never at any time, even during the period that he was preoccupied with the printers, did Livingston give up hope of preventing the creation of a party college under "ecclesiastic Domination." In December, 1753, he reported to Noah Welles that he and the other trustees of the college fund had agreed unanimously on calling Samuel Johnson to be the president. The Anglican members, however, continually delayed meeting to complete the transaction so as to avoid appointing Chauncy Whittelsey, a Yale Congregationalist, as first tutor, which they had also assented to. Livingston, aware of their scheming, declared that "if the Reflector had not been suppressed by a villainous Collusion with the Printers I would have defyed them to carry it into execution." On February 1 the New Yorker notified Welles that Dr. Johnson had accepted.[31]

Early in 1754, at "an evening convention of a few private friends," including the Triumvirate, William Alexander, and several Livingstons, members all of the Dutch and Presbyterian churches, it was decided to raise money for a "Publick-Library." Intended to unshackle the minds of New Yorkers by means of its books, the New York Society Library at once became the center of politics, as John Morin Scott explained later in No. 25 of "The Watch-Tower":

No sooner were the Subscriptions compleat, and a Day appointed for the Election of Trustees, than a dirty Scheme was concerted, for excluding as many English Presbyterians as possible, from the Trusteeship; concerted not by Trinity Church in this City, but by some of her unworthy Members: Which Distinction is here carefully taken, to prevent those contracted Bigots from misrepresenting the Sentiments of an Author, who . . . holds that, and all the other Protestant Churches, in the highest Veneration.

John Chambers, "a jealous envious Bigot," made up his own list, circulated it, and advised many of the subscribers "carefully to

30. Barclay to Johnson, Mar. 5, 1754, Hawks Papers, II, No. 22.

31. Livingston to Welles, Dec. 15, 1753, No. 70, Feb. 1, 1754, No. 71, Johnson Family Papers.

avoid electing any Presbyterians. . . . [but] the Subscribers were so obstinately impartial, as to chuse Persons who, from their Acquaintance with Literature, they imagined were able to make a proper choice." William Smith, Jr., adds that his party "ran through the town" with their list before the Anglicans could mobilize against them.[32]

About this time, the Episcopalians began once again to agitate for a royal charter for the college. As a countermeasure, Livingston appealed to the New York Assembly to issue a charter, and on May 16 read a list of "twenty Unanswerable Reasons" about the proposal to the trustees. The matter was once more in the public domain when the trustees applied to the Governor and Council for incorporation on May 20, 1754.[33]

Deprived of an outlet in the press, the Triumvirate resorted to every available means to arouse the anti-Episcopal members of the New York Assembly against the scheme. They distributed copies of the *Independent Reflector* and Livingston's protest against a royal charter to convince the Dutch Reformed and Presbyterian country folk that the Anglicans aimed ultimately at complete establishment. They hoped thereby to flood the Assembly with petitions against the royal charter and to maintain such unremitting pressure on "irresolute" members that they would join the anti-Episcopal opposition.[34]

The "Presbyterian Party" did thoroughly alarm Samuel Johnson and his sons with this final drive to defeat the plan of a "partisan college." William even warned his father not to talk with the postriders in New York, "for they are pumped very carefully at their return [to Stratford], and if any thing is found that will make a noise, it flies like lightning." Another son, the judicious William Samuel, advised his father not to try to have an answer made to Livingston's protest: "I am generally averse to disputes of this kind, as tending more to irritate the passions than to convince the under-

32. Smith, *History of New York,* II, 207–8; *N.Y. Gaz.,* Apr. 29, 1754; "The Watch-Tower," No. 25; *N.Y. Mercury,* May 12, 1755; Carl Bridenbaugh, *Cities in Revolt* (New York, 1955), 181–2; Austin B. Keep, *History of the New York Society Library* (New York, 1908), 130–40.

33. *Ecclesiastical Records,* VI, 3478–99, 3516–17; Schneiders, *Johnson,* IV, 12.

34. Livingston to Whittelsey, Aug. 22, 1754, Letter-Book A (1754–1770), Livingston Papers (Mass. Hist. Soc.); Milton Klein, "Democracy and Politics in Colonial New York," *New York History,* XL (1959), 239.

standings of people. What is wrote in this way, is most generally read only by those persons who are before possessed on one side or the other of the question." The old gentleman, now president of the proposed college, fumed as he kept silent, but, when he wrote to the Bishop of London in July, he blasted the "active Faction of presbyterians and Freethinkers, that do violently oppose such a Charter and do all they can to disaffect the Dutch, without whom they can bear but a small proportion in the province." [35]

Because of an internal split in the Presbyterian Church in the city of New York, and the pro-De Lancey sympathies of most of the Dutch Reformed, this campaign failed to accomplish what was expected of it. The lack of a press was crucial. "Had the printers not been overawed from publishing anything on the subject," Livingston told Chauncy Whittelsey in August, "I am confident we should have raised so great a fervor in the provinces, as nothing but a catholic scheme would have been able to extinguish. However, a new press will be set up in the fall, and then I am persuaded (if not then too late) the trumpet will not cease to blow in Zion." [36]

When Lieutenant Governor De Lancey and his Council approved the royal charter on October 31, 1754, the only course remaining to the Triumvirate was to introduce a bill for chartering a public seminary by an act of the Assembly. It was stipulated therein that "no particular religious profession, Church or denomination whatever shall be established in the said College." There would be no religious test and no system of divinity publicly taught, and any Protestant might attend. It is difficult to believe that Livingston thought he could ever get this bill accepted; probably he sought merely to prevent public money from going into the new King's College. Fortune favored him in one thing, however, for just at this juncture the New York press again opened its columns to both parties.[37]

President Johnson reported to his sons in December "that the Reflectors have made such a great stir among the Dutch that it was not thought advisable to try for a vote of the Assembly this ses-

35. Schneiders, *Johnson*, IV, 13-14, 17; Johnson to Bishop of London, July 6, 1754, Hawks Papers, II, No. 54; *Ecclesiastical Records*, IV, 3483.

36. Schneiders, *Johnson*, IV, 22.

37. *Ecclesiastical Records*, IV, 3484, 3506–15, 3523–5.

sions" on the charter. The next day he wrote to Dr. Bearcroft of the S.P.G. that "I have never in all my time known such a violent struggle against the Church as now and of late. The spirit is bitter to the last degree." William Samuel Johnson thought "the enemy has . . . gained ground" on the Episcopalians because "the opposite party are incredibly industrious and busy in fortifying . . . themselves against a fresh attack. Their publications, however little real weight there may be in their arguments, will, it is probable, much influence the people, and I fear raise no small clamor against the proposed establishment of the college." [38]

What so troubled the Episcopalians and "brought a great bundle of petitions from Tom, Dick and Harry, of several counties against the college's having that money" was the cumulative effect of the past summer's rural campaign, capped by a new and effective publication. As usual, Noah Welles learned the inside story from his classmate on December 7:

We have at length with great trouble got Mr. Gaine to enter into Agreement with us to allot us the first page of his News-paper for the publication of our thoughts which we do under the name of the Watch-Tower. As this Paper will be a kind of medium between the Reflector and the Spectators . . . I should be extreamly glad if you would bear a part in the Compositions. We propose indeed to write cheifly upon Politicks, and to open the Eyes of this Province respecting many measures the Concealment of which is the only Thing that keeps them from being defeated. . . . The affair of the College is not yet settled. The Governor has passed a Charter for a Church College, and the Assembly voted to print a Bill which was brought in by my Brother for a free one. [Livingston is not sure that it will be safe to bring it to a vote now; printing it will give the public the facts.] So that we intend to improve the time between this and next Session to keep the Province warm in so momentous an Affair. The Dutch begin to see, and the Designs of our Adversaries give a more general umbrage than ever.

As almost all of the Authors of the Watch-Tower are men of Business, I hope you will not refuse us your Assistance, for we would by no means suffer a Week to slip without something, tho' we could not, always furnish a Paper on our public Controversies. For if we once drop it,

38. Schneiders, *Johnson,* IV, 27, 30–31.

it may be difficult to get the Printer in the same humour. He is a fickle Fellow and easily intimidated by our opponents. However we have entered into Articles of Agreement in Writing, which we hope he will not break thro'.[39]

Hugh Gaine had addressed the readers of his *New York Mercury* on November 18, 1754, concerning the complaints made during the publication of the *Independent Reflector* on his "Refusal to publish any Thing that was offered by that Author or his Friends." Now, because the controversies have risen rather than subsided since the discontinuance of his labors, and have "become vastly more extensive and interesting — as almost universal Discontent now appears for want of a FREE PRESS" — Gaine has been importuned, and is "determin'd to give both Parties an Opportunity of being heard in his Paper." The next week he ran Number 1 of "The Watch-Tower" on the *Mercury*'s first page and continued to feature it there for a year. The first two "Watch-Tower" essays offered an account of the college question and a dialogue between a Churchman and a Dissenter. In the next issue of the newspaper there were reflections on the first essay signed "Z" but now known to be a joint effort "hatched up" by the Reverend Samuel Auchmuty and Thomas Bradbury Chandler, and before long the Reverend James Wetmore joined the pack assailing the feature. Samuel Johnson had reason to exclaim, "It seems we must be in a state of war." [40]

As with the *Independent Reflector,* it fell to William Livingston to write most of the "Watch-Tower" pieces. Welles contributed possibly one article; Smith and Scott several, and a few other friends helped out. The form of the new publication permitted its authors greater freedom for dealing severely, even roughly, with personalities than had the *Independent Reflector.* They asked no quarter, and they gave none. They used both the rapier and bludgeon. Furthermore they turned out to be as resourceful in defensive arguments as aggressive on the attack; and they also proved to be more learned and better informed on public issues than the clergy they fought. In Number 4, the author stated the position of the Triumvirate:

39. Schneiders, *Johnson,* IV, 39; Livingston to Welles, Dec. 7, 1754, No. 73, Johnson Family Papers.

40. *N.Y. Mercury,* Nov. 18, 25, Dec. 2, 9, 1754; Schneiders, *Johnson,* IV, 33.

It is easy to conceive, that a Person may, in a religious View, be a Dissenter from the Church, and at the same Time, as good a Member of the Community, a cordial Well-Wisher to its Prosperity and Happiness. There is still less difficulty in Apprehending, that a Man may expose the Conduct of a little assuming Party in the Province of New-York, without being an Enemy to the Church established in *South Britain.*

He may even wish to see the Church of England flourish as he censures some of its "factious Spirits" and he deplores "only those degenerate Members of Trinity Church, in New York, who were said to be instrumental in the late dishonorable Attempt, to render a legislative Body, Dupes to a private Project." [41]

The most effective literary device employed in "The Watch-Tower" was an imaginary dream that Livingston fell into while ruminating on the state of the province *twenty years hence,* "should a certain faction" methodically encroach on "our liberties." He read in the *New-York Journal,* No. 15, "publish'd by Authority," February 3, 1775, a letter from an Albany County clergyman to "the Bishop of New York":

I make no doubt but by the blessing of God, and your Lordship's rigorous measures, we shall reduce this obstinate colony to the obedience of the Church. They are a stubborn, contumacious generation, and naturally averse to prelacy. Hence the business of tithes goes much against the grain. . . .

Another extract reports the passage of acts in the Assembly for better collecting of tithes; against reading Calvinistic and other "heretical" books; and disabling Dissenters "from sitting in the Assembly." With such satire, he played with sure effect upon the fears, prejudices, and memories of many readers of the *Mercury.*[42]

But the most telling points scored in "The Watch-Tower" were the hard facts served up in a series of historical articles (as Livingston had promised in the Preface of his former periodical) narrating treatment accorded by the government-backed Episcopalians to the Dissenters — "which by the way, as we have no Ecclesiastical Establishment in this Province, is an improper Appelation." From

41. *N.Y. Mercury,* Dec. 16, 1754.

42. *N.Y. Mercury,* Feb. 3, 1755.

April 7 to July 15, 1755, all but one of "The Watch-Tower" essays educated New Yorkers in the ecclesiastical history of their "Forefathers": the Ministry Acts, Lord Cornbury's misrule, the Jamaica case, the arrest of Francis Makemie, the denial of incorporation to the Presbyterian Church. To admit the partisan nature of this account is not to deny it the quality of good history: its author was erudite; he printed many damning documents and gave references to others. His essays have the persuasiveness not found in other accounts and are rather more moderate and temperate than might be expected in such a controversialist. Moreover, they have withstood the test of time as a reliable source for the church history of New York. Because the persecutions of Hampton and Makemie required too much space for a four-page newspaper, the Triumvirate reprinted Makemie's now-famous account separately. Concluding his history, Livingston remarked:

> I have uncontestibly shewn, that the happy Circumspection of the Representatives of our Forefathers foiled even Bigotry herself, a Monster, hedious and insatiate; and amidst the pious Wiles of the renowned Fletcher, secured to their Posterity, the Enjoyment of their invaluable religious Liberties.[43]

Fear that the Triumvirate would win over the Dutch led the Anglican clergymen to publish a two-page sheet called *John Englishman* for ten weeks from April to June, 1755, with Parker and Weyman. This paper sought to explain "John Englishman's true Notion of Sister-Churches," and it charged "The Watch-Tower" writers with attempting to make out of the Dutch Reformed and Presbyterians "a Sect of Reflectarians," who would load the province with the burden of a second college. Denials notwithstanding, Livingston was right in his conviction that "J. E." was the product of "a Conclave of Eight Reverend Clergymen." Scurrility seems to have come easier to these divines than to the laity, as for example, in commenting on the authors of the *Independent Reflector* and "The Watch-Tower," all *John Englishman* could muster was: "The worst Wh . . . cries Wh . . . first."[44]

43. *N.Y. Mercury,* April 7–July 14, 1755.

44. *John Englishman,* Nos. 1–10, April 9–July 5, 1755; *N.Y. Gaz.,* Apr. 7, 1755. "John Englishman" first appeared in the *N.Y. Mercury,* Jan. 27, 1755, with an

A new and greater and much more urgent matter began to absorb William Livingston's attention as early as July 21, 1755. This was the French menace. After concluding a fifth paper on the Assembly's bill against a royal charter for the college, Livingston had this to say: "The highest Hopes of my Antagonists are entirely blasted, and our Representatives ever tender of the Liberty and Privileges of their Constituents, have sufficiently demonstrated their Aversion to a Party-College; and even its most vigorous Advocates, have, in a Manner, given up the Cause, no valuable End can therefore be attained at present by the Continuation of my Labours." [45]

Privately the Anglicans were inclined to accept Livingston's claim of victory at face value, for on November 3, the Manhattan clergy reported to the S.P.G. that "the opposition still continues, and has so far prevailed as to have hitherto prevented the application of the money raised by lottery . . . and disingenious methods have been used to prejudice the common people in the several counties, whom they have endeavored to persuade, that the test imposed on the president will infallibly be attended with the establishment of bishops and tithes, and will end in the loss of all their religious privileges and even in persecution itself. . . ." The entire letter is an unintended tribute from the very best of authorities to the long-range success of the propaganda of the authors of the *Independent Reflector* and "The Watch-Tower." The trumpets had indeed blown in Zion.[46]

IV

The controversy over the founding of King's College (now Columbia University) was of supreme importance in the history of liberty in America, because it raged over an actual institution; ideas translated into reality in the New York arena. Because he was so close to the events, Livingston occasionally had doubts about his success. As he wrote to Welles on August 8, 1757, he related: "We

attack against the Reverend Noah Hobart's opinion that the colonies stood in the same relation to the Crown as did the Channel Islands.

45. *New York Mercury*, Nov. 17, 1755.

46. Schneiders, *Johnson*, IV, 40.

stood as long as our legs would support us, and, I may add, even fought for some time on our Stumps, but to recount, at present, the particular manner in which we were Vanquished, *Animus meminisse Horret Luctuque refugit"* — the mind trembles to remember and flees in distress. The absence at King's College of the strife that plagued the College of Philadelphia in the 'sixties and 'seventies was due in no small measure to the work of "the Reflectors" in forcing the Episcopal party to liberalize its constitution somewhat during these years of "naked warfare." [47]

William Livingston had served America well (not merely his city and province), and in 1755 stood pre-eminent as the New-World penman of religious liberty; he knew what he was doing and what he was saying, and he had no contemporary equal in the great eighteenth-century art of pamphleteering. No small part of his success as a propagandist was his patent sincerity and what might be termed his estimate of the popular situation. He adopted the reasons for civil and religious liberty developed by the liberal English Dissenters, the theological and ecclesiastical arguments of "the profound and elaborate Hobart" (as Thomas Bradbury Chandler put it), added something from his own fund of "Freethinking," and brought them all to bear in the great public debate. It is something of a miracle to the modern observer to discover how he and his faction succeeded in treating an ecclesiastical controversy so vividly in newspaper and pamphlet that they kept not merely a local but an intercolonial public's attention for three long years — an attention diverted only by the shock of the final episode in the struggle of England and France for the control of North America. There can be no question of the indelible impression that this debate made on the emerging "American" mind.

V

Late in the spring of 1756, William Smith, Jr., completed his *History of the Province of New York* and dispatched it to his friend Dr. Avery. Printed by Thomas Willcox of London in 1757, though it was not advertised in New York until March, 1758, this version of New York's turbulent political and ecclesiastical history found

47. Livingston to Welles, Aug. 8, 1757, No. 76, Johnson Family Papers.

many readers on both sides of the Atlantic. Written, as Provost William Smith of Philadelphia later said, by "the impartial Presbyterian Historian," it told about the general discontent in the province over the Ministry Act":

. . . Not so much that the provision made by them is engrossed by the *minor sect* as because *the body of the people are for an equal, universal, toleration of protestants, and utterly averse to any kind of ecclesiastical establishment.* The dissenters, though fearless of each other, are all jealous of the episcopal party, being apprehensive that the countenance they may have from home, will foment a *lust for dominion,* and enable them, in process of time to subjugate and oppress their fellow subjects. . . . The episcopalians, however, sometimes pretend, that the ecclesiastical establishment in South Britain extends here; but the whole body of the dissenters are averse to the doctrine.[48]

The best witness to the effect the book produced is Dr. Johnson's agitated animadversion in a letter to Archbishop Secker in 1759:

One book indeed which has, I imagine, been a principal occasion of the present complaints against the Society and missionaries is the history of New York published in England lately which was wrote by one Smith of this town, a virulent enemy, which doubtless your Grace has seen, upon which Mr. [Henry] Barclay has made some very just remarks which were sent about two months ago and I hope are now in the Secretary's hands. . . . I believe one of the chief ends of his writing his history was to abuse the Church and Society and missionaries, as it contains a summary of what they had before published in those [Reflector] papers as far as the Society is concerned. But your Grace will see by our controversy with Hobart and by Mr. Barclay's papers compared with Smith's history that it is indeed fencing against a flail to hold any dispute with them as there is nothing that they will stick at, however so false and injurious, in opposing and discrediting the Church, and which they will not cease to repeat and inculcate over and over again however so thoroughly it was answered. . . . It is indeed, my Lord, a thing of most melancholy consideration that by such unaccountable methods our adversaries should have secured such

48. Roger A. Wines, "William Smith, The Historian of New York," *New York History,* XL (1959), 7; *N.Y. Mercury,* Mar. 27, 1758; *Pennsylvania Chronicle,* Oct. 24, 1768; Smith, *History of New York,* I, 336–8.

a formidable multitude at home to be disaffected to the Society, and that any should treat it with such insolence as to use even threatening intimations, when at the same time there never was the least ground for that which it seems is their grand complaint as though the Society have *unwarrantably changed their object from the propagation of Christianity and protestantism, to the propagation of one form of it in opposition to other protestants.*[49]

As the close of the French and Indian War and victory approached, the only cloud in the New York Dissenters' sky was the denial on March 30, 1759, by Lieutenant Governor James De Lancey, who had led them to expect approval, of incorporation for the Presbyterian Church because of the machinations of Manhattan Anglicans. Before long the cloud would turn into a thunderhead and the lightning would flash.[50]

49. Schneiders, *Johnson*, I, 283.

50. Mass. Hist. Soc., *Collections,* 2nd ser., I (1814), 151.

PART TWO

NO BISHOP, NO KING, 1760–1775

VII

WORKING THE ECCLESIASTICAL ENGINES

The contest for ecclesiastical dominion in America intensified with every decade after 1690 as both parties worked out and clarified their positions and improved their organizations. The brief interlude which occurred after the delivery of Ezra Stiles's great sermon of 1760 affords us an opportunity to examine the issues as they were drawn and to review the assets of each side prior to the final struggle, during which the Church of England's aspirations for a bishopric were ended by America's separation from Great Britain.

Though not always clear at the time, it is now evident that in number, fertility of ideas, and organization, the colonial Nonconformists were better off than their adversaries. Furthermore, they had a formidable weapon right at hand in a usable past, in which the large majority of the Americans living north of Maryland were well versed and which they cherished; there existed also the machinery needed by their leaders for the dissemination of their version of history and cognate ideas. Moreover, a succession of unpopular actions and political blunders made by the authorities at home gave rise to and perpetuated a prolonged crisis from 1760 to 1776, throughout which countless appeals to American tradition served to transform the attitudes of the proponents and opponents of episcopacy alike. These years vividly illustrate the interplay of ideas and events, which is the essence of the history of ideas. No aspect of the American Revolution holds more fascination for the historian than the adjusting, part conscious and part unconscious, of the colonists' view of their past to meet the requirement of the changing social and political conditions of the age.

Before 1760 the principal colonial Dissenters developed a powerful and persuasive case against episcopacy. The Reverend Noah

Hobart first brought all the points together into a consistent argument in his several tracts defending Presbyterian ordination; and through the *Independent Reflector* and "The Watch-Tower" papers, William Livingston and his circle turned the preacher's ideas into common currency. The salient feature of their grand argument was the use of a particular interpretation of the colonial past, to which they constantly referred for authority and support. These gentlemen knew very well that no ideological weapon in their armory possessed the striking power of history rightly interpreted.

II

For more than a century, the colonists had been constructing the version of history employed during the debate of the 'sixties; and some of its concepts reached back into Europe for another hundred years at least. The Americans' view of themselves and of their history can be understood only when it is fitted into the larger framework of their attitudes toward Christian and, more immediately, English history. It thus becomes necessary to investigate the origins of several of the basic ideas and interpretations of decisive events of the colonial past, and then to see how they were corrected, changed, added to, and even distorted by succeeding generations in the making of the mighty historical instrument of 1760.

The Puritans brought with them to New England a well-developed theory of history: they looked upon their enterprise as the culmination of a long, historical process, evolving according to divine ordinance. In other words, their legend had already crystallized before they landed on the western shore to perform the final act of the Christian drama of salvation in "the good land." These first New Englanders, their descendants, and all who emigrated from Europe thereafter, whether they came from the British Isles or continental Europe, shared in common the international heritage of Calvinism, which stretched back from England to the Rhineland and Geneva. All were protestants against the Church of Rome, and anti-Catholicism was the staple of their religious diet.

These immigrants to the Northern Colonies, because of their experience in the New World environment, fashioned a unique interpretation of English history which differed from the two versions accepted in the Mother Country in the eighteenth century: one by the Anglican majority, the other by the Nonconformist minority.[1]

The standard colonial version of New England's origins drew upon both the English and American accounts. It began with "the errand into America," when, as Edward Johnson later described it in 1650, the Lord directed his "praysing Saints" to forsake "a fruitful Land, stately Buildings, goodly Gardens, Orchards, yea, deare Friends, and neere relations, to go into a desart Wildernesse, thousands of Leagues by Sea, both turbulent and dangerous . . . all which they underwent, with much cheerfulnesse that they might enjoy Christ and his Ordinances in their primitive purity." They fled to this "howling desart" to establish a new and godly state. Some of them agreed, in truth, that God had moved Archbishop Laud and the Anglican hierarchy to persecute them in order to carry out His plan for them to erect a city on the hill.[2]

As time passed and the Puritan society rooted itself, the ministers began to call for a history of the Lord's work in New England: "It were well," the Reverend Urian Oakes advised in 1673, "if there were a memorial of these things faithfully drawn up, and transmitted to Posterity . . . that the memory of them may not dy and be extinct, with the present Generation." The Reverend William Hubbard prepared the first official history, and in 1682 the General Court of Massachusetts gave him £50 for his "paynes." Compiled from the early journals of William Bradford and John Winthrop, Hubbard's manuscript — for it was not published in the colonial period — served as an original source for more than a century. Thomas Hutchinson acknowledged in 1765 that "it has been of great use to me: It was so to Dr. [Cotton] Mather in his history, of which Mr. Neale's is little more than an abridgement." In this manner, Hubbard, by his influence on the *Magnalia Christi Americana* and subsequent histories, inaugurated that propensity for ancestor worship so notable among New Englanders, a propen-

1. "International Calvinism Through Locke and the Revolution of 1688," *Collected Papers of Herbert Darling Foster* (priv. pr., 1929), 77–105, 147–78. See in general the thoughtful study of Wesley F. Craven, *The Legend of the Founding Fathers* (New York, 1956).

2. Edward Johnson, *Wonder-Working Providence of Sions Saviour in New England* (J. Franklin Jameson, ed., New York, 1946), 21–2.

sity which has made outside observers compare them with the Chinese. Thenceforward, *our forefathers,* denoting the Puritans of the Great Migration, becomes a stereotyped expression in sermons, newspaper essays, and formal history — in fact an everyday Yankee household phrase. Our ancestors are "the forefathers," and we must remember to revere them always.[3]

In the *Magnalia* (1702), Cotton Mather quotes an election sermon preached before the General Court of Massachusetts-Bay early in the 1690's, which both poses the question and concisely supplies the classic interpretation of early New England history in the form current at the end of the seventeenth century:

"What went ye into the wilderness to see?" And the answer to it is not only too excellent, but also too notorious, to be dissembled. Let all mankind know, that we came into the wilderness, because we would worship God without that Episcopacy, that common-prayer, and those unwarranted ceremonies with which the 'land of our forefathers' sepulchures' had been defiled; we came hither because we would have our posterity settled under pure and full dispensation of the gospel, defended by rulers that should be our selves.[4]

In the early eighteenth century, new ideas and fresh events caused a change of emphasis on the nature of the mission of "our fore-fathers"; John Locke's famous essays and the writings of the English Republicans stressed civil as well as religious liberty. Complex political and ecclesiastical conditions directly connected with the great question of the relation between church and state arose from the Toleration Act of 1689 and the Massachusetts Charter of 1691; the latter stipulated that "for ever hereafter there shall be a liberty of Conscience allowed in the Worship of God to all Christians (Except Papists)." Thus was the door to religious diversity un-locked, though not yet ajar. The new charter came to be regarded as the palladium of provincial liberties at the same time that the

3. Perry Miller and Thomas H. Johnson, *The Puritans* (New York, 1938), 81; John L. Sibley, *Biographical Sketches of Graduates of Harvard University* (Cambridge, Mass., 1873), I, 55–6; Hutchinson, *History of Massachusetts-Bay,* I, xxvii; William Hubbard's *A General History of New England from the Discovery to MDCLXXX* was first published in Boston in 1815; Miller, *New England Mind,* 135–6.

4. Mather, *Magnalia,* 240–41.

public conception of those liberties widened until they were commonly referred to as "our religious and civil liberties." [5]

With the publication by Daniel Neal in 1720 of *The History of New England*, and even more with his *History of the Puritans* (1732–38), the Dissenters on both sides of the water acquired a potent revisionist version of English history which was a synthesis of actual experience, of the rationalistic ideas of the Enlightenment, and of the Nonconformists' desire to justify the deeds of their ancestors of the Puritan Revolution against the calumnies of Anglican chroniclers. This challenging point of view was rapidly absorbed into New England historical tradition. About the same time, Thomas Gordon, the Independent Whig who contributed so much to colonial thought, fulminating in a lay sermon directed at the establishment of ecclesiastical tribunals in the New World, followed closely the New England explanation of the errand of the forefathers, "who were many of them first driven thither by the Oppression and Barbarity of such courts here, especially in Archbishop Laud's Reign." The ultimate effect of such writings was to liberalize, and, in part, secularize the once-narrow, seventeenth-century legend of the forefathers and to make it both palatable to and usable for English Nonconformists, and also for many members of the National Church. An amusing instance of Anglican acceptance of the myth occurred in 1730 when Secretary David Humphreys remarked of the New England Puritans, in his *Historical Account of the Society for the Propagation of the Gospel in Foreign Parts*, that "it ought to be owned to the just Honour of this People, that the first Settlers who left their native Country England, appear to have done it out of a true Principle of Conscience, however erroneous." [6]

The new version of the legend had become official in New England

5. Macdonald, *Select Charters*, 209.

6. [Thomas Gordon] *A Sermon Preached before the Learned Society of Lincoln's-Inn, on January 30, 1732. By a Layman.* (London, 1733); also in *Weekly Miscellany*, March 10, 1733; Humphreys, *Historical Account of the S.P.G.*, 36. For the later development of this version, see the Hampshire County, Mass., Petition on page 78 of this work; and for an excellent specimen of Nonconformist revisionist history, William Harris, *An Historical and Critical Account of the Life and Writings of James, the First, King of Great Britain. After the Manner of Mr. Bayle. Drawn from Original Papers and State-Papers* (London, 1753).

by 1736 when the Reverend Thomas Prince could refer to Governor Jonathan Belcher, the House of Representatives, and the Council in the dedication to his *Chronological History of New England* as being descended from "the worthy FATHERS of these Plantations: whom Yourselves and Posterity cannot but have in everlasting Honour, not only for their eminent *self Denial* and *Piety,* wherein they set Examples for future Ages to admire and imitate; but also for their great Concern that the same vital and pure Christianity and LIBERTY both *Civil* and *Ecclesiastical,* might be continued to their successors; for which they left their own and their Fathers' Houses in the most pleasant Places then on Earth, with many of their dearest Relatives, and came over the Ocean into this then hideous Wilderness." One fancies that on hearing this, the shades of "our forefathers" uttered a ghostly "Hear, hear!" [7]

In numberless weekly sermons, Congregational and Presbyterian divines recounted the glorious history of their "Country," and the pressing need to keep the memory of the forefathers alive. Thereby they spread the legend throughout rural communities seldom reached by newspapers and books. When, in 1750, Jonathan Mayhew invoked the past in his celebrated discourse *On Unlimited Submission,* he could be certain in advance that his remarks would reach a people steeped in the same historical tradition, and, since he clothed his arguments in a vivid colloquial style, he could be equally sure of their ready acceptance.

At New York in 1755, in "The Watch-Tower" No. 42, William Livingston shrewdly aligned the Dutch Protestant forefathers with the English when he publicly explained to Sir Charles Hardy, the new governor, "that the greatest number of our inhabitants, are descended from those, who with a brave and invincible spirit, repelled the spanish tyranny in the *Netherlands;* or from those, who for their ever-memorable opposition, to the arbitrary measures of King CHARLES Ist, were constrained to seek a refuge, from the relentless sword of persecution, in the then inhospitable wilds of AMERICA. From such ancestors, we inherit the highest relish for

7. Thomas Prince, *Chronological History of New England in the Form of Annals* (Boston, 1746), I, Dedication, ii; also John Callender, *An Historical Discourse on the Civil and Religious Affairs of the Colony of Rhode-Island* [1738] Rhode Island Historical Society, *Collections,* IV (1838), 61–7.

civil and religious LIBERTY." This very year, 1755, youthful John Adams gave evidence of the prophetic uses of history as he was writing to a kinsman that "soon after the Reformation a few people came over into this new world for conscience's sake. *Perhaps this apparently trivial incident may transfer the great seat of empire to America.*" [8]

By the time Ezra Stiles came out for union, the Dissenters' historical weapon had been hammered and tempered, and Stiles brandished it with certain effect. Occasional history had been published by William Smith, Jr., to aid in the hot New York contest, and his friend Livingston had more in preparation. At Newport, Stiles started to gather the materials for a full-dress ecclesiastical history of New England which would, if completed, be a master's account in the style of the *essai sur les mœurs* of "our worthy and venerable ancestors (be their memories dear to posterity)." In the opposite camp, however, the champions of episcopacy had no version of history, no legend, with which to counter in 1760, but they were well aware of the need to produce one.[9]

This first American venture in applying history to present purposes was of profound importance in the controversy over an Anglican episcopate. The dissenting writers possessed not merely the learning to evolve their myth with only minor distortions of the basic facts, but both the ministerial and lay forensic skills to propagate the legend. Their creation of the part-truths men live by compels admiration. So well had they prepared the public mind, that by the time of the great debates of the 'sixties, it is not too much to say that, of all the arguments employed, the appeal to history was used the most, because the people would react to it without taking further thought. So certain were the writers of the familiarity

8. In declining the honor of having the first building of the College of New Jersey named Belcher Hall after him, the Dissenting governor asked the Trustees to name it "Nassau Hall" to celebrate "in this remote part of the Globe," the deliverer of the British Nation "from those two monstrous Furies, *Popery* and *Slavery*," and who procured the act of Parliament guaranteeing "true Religion and . . . English Liberty" through the present royal family. "The Watch-Tower," No. 42, *N.Y. Mercury*, Sept. 8, Oct. 6, Sup., 1755; Charles F. Adams, *The Works of John Adams* (Boston, 1856), I, 23 (Italics mine).

9. Although Stiles never completed his history, his voluminous notes indicate its probable authoritative nature.

of their readers with the accepted legend of the forefathers that they seldom found it necessary to allude to it in more than a few cliché-studded lines. For them, brevity was the soul of propaganda.[10]

III

However compelling ideas may be in the determination of history, it is well to remember that equally important are the means and the men through which and by whom the ideas are transmitted and, not infrequently, transformed.

The rich and powerful episcopal organization of the National Church enabled it to stand secure against the Dissenters in England in these years and placed it in a favorable position to support further extension of its influence in the colonies. Renewed Anglican interest in sending bishops to America became evident immediately upon the election of Thomas Secker as primate in 1758, which also placed him at the head of the Society for the Propagation of the Gospel in Foreign Parts. Access to the King could always be had by the Archbishop of Canterbury, and in the House of Lords the bishops kept a weather eye on all proposals pertaining to the colonial church. The Bishop of London (in whose diocese the American churches belonged), as a member of the Lords Commissioners of Trade and Plantations, was in a strategic position to influence the framing of instructions for governors of royal provinces and the oversight of their activities. Such proconsuls as Francis Bernard of Massachusetts, John Wentworth of New Hampshire, and the several governors of New York gave the Church of England support on many occasions. And, in addition, after 1760, the overwhelming majority of placemen sent over to America were Anglicans. Finally, by requiring regular annual reports in addition to a sustained correspondence, the Venerable Society kept in touch with the needs and doings of its missionaries in the Northern Colonies.

On the American shore, the Church of England loomed ever-

10. Typical for 1760 was the Reverend Nathaniel Appleton's declaration: "It is grievous to think that when *our Pious Ancestors* came over into this Land, when an *howling wilderness, to enjoy the Gospel* in the *purity and simplicity of it,* that the Church of England should thrust it self in among us." Franklin B. Dexter, *The Literary Diary of Ezra Stiles* (New York, 1901), I, 125. (Italics mine)

more threatening to the Dissenters. Though still inferior in number to the Presbyterians and Quakers in the Middle Colonies and to the Congregationalists of New England, the Episcopalians had grown, according to the calculations of Ezra Stiles, from a mere handful in 1690 in the latter region to 12,600 souls worshipping in forty-seven churches under the care of twenty-seven missionaries by 1760. The missionaries themselves claimed much larger numbers but offered no statistics.[11]

Whatever the prestige and might of the Church in the Mother Country, its outward appearance of strength in America proved deceptive, for colonial Episcopalians enjoyed no organic, intercolonial union and were wholly dependent upon such support as they could get from England. From Maryland to Georgia, where it was established by law, the Church was served by parochial clergymen whose professional and material interests made them nearly as indifferent to episcopal control as were their parishioners. To the northward, save in a few instances, all members of the clergy were missionary pensioners of the S.P.G. The commissaries appointed by the Bishop of London lacked authority to govern the American clergy, and, of course, all candidates for Holy Orders had to cross the ocean for ordination by a bishop. Because the recruiting of colonial college graduates was made very difficult by the requirement of the arduous and dangerous journeys to England, and because they realized that clerical laxity necessitated the discipline of a bishop, leading missionaries understandably began to step up requests for an American bishop. They knew their deficiency in leadership; commissaries were not enough.

The same year that Thomas Secker became Archbishop of Canterbury, 1758, his favorite colonial missionary, Thomas Bradbury Chandler, established a yearly convention of the New Jersey clergy. Though positive proof is lacking, Secker's previous record, his correspondence with Dr. Johnson, and his deep interest in the colonial ecclesiastical situation all point to his support of the convention movement, if, indeed, he did not actually set Chandler about it. Before long the clergy of other provinces followed the New Jersey lead: Pennsylvania and the Lower Counties on the Delaware headed by Provost William Smith in 1760; Connecticut

11. Stiles, *Christian Union*, 113.

under Dr. Johnson in 1765; and northern New England in 1766. These meetings, held once a year and occasionally oftener, were always described as voluntary. Much of their time was spent memorializing London authorities for an American bishop, for the missionaries were convinced that only by completing episcopacy in the colonies could they solve their internal problems.[12]

When Provost Smith was in London in April of 1764, he called the attention of Bishop Osbaldeston to the urgent need of some efficacious plan for conducting the Venerable Society's affairs in America. Smith suggested a division of the Northern Colonies into three regions, each of which would have an "agent" assisted by a "corresponding Society" composed of some of the principal gentlemen of the area; their duties would be threefold: to transmit to London "faithful accounts" of Church affairs, to solicit larger subscriptions from the laity, and to aid in the establishment of schools among the Indians. The clergymen believed that "much good may also be expected from the corresponding Societies" when the time for bishops should come, and he ventured to hope that his share would be to institute the agency for Pennsylvania, the Lower Counties, and New Jersey. At Perth Amboy in October, Smith broached the scheme to the New Jersey Convention as having the approval of the S.P.G. Though strongly backed by the Reverend Samuel Auchmuty of New York, Smith's plan was rejected because it placed too much power in the agent (who obviously might be the Provost himself), and also because the orthodox Jerseymen feared the Methodist influence of the Philadelphia clergy.[13]

The Episcopal conventions attracted attention through notices in the public prints, and they aroused curiosity and alarm. The day after commencement at King's College on May 21, 1766, when fourteen of the clergy of New York, New Jersey, and Connecticut were in Manhattan, Dr. Samuel Johnson presided over a joint convention at the house of Dr. Samuel Auchmuty. The members

12. N.Y. Mercury, June 12, 1758; Samuel A. Clark, The History of St. John's Church, Elizabeth Town, New Jersey (Philadelphia, 1857), 118; Perry, Historical Collections, Pennsylvania, II, 295–6, 364, 404–5; Perry, Historical Collections, Mass., III, 524; New Hampshire Gazette, June 21, 1765.

13. Horace W. Smith, Life and Correspondence of the Reverend William Smith, D.D. (Philadelphia, 1880), I, 348–9; Perry, Historical Collections, Pa., II, 364.

of the Convention listened to an address of welcome by Governor Sir Henry Moore, to which they replied that, "as the Church of England requires her Clergy to inculcate the great Principles of Loyalty and Submission to Government," they commended the churches in New York to his protection and patronage. That same day they adopted a resolution:

The Clergy of the Province of New York taking into their serious Consideration the Present State of the Church of England in the Colonies, where it is obliged to struggle against the Opposition of Sectaries of various Denominations, and also labours under the want of the Episcopal Order, and all the advantages and Blessings resulting therefrom; agreed upon holding voluntary Conventions, at least once in the Year and . . . oftener if necessity required; as the most likely means to serve the Interest of the Church of England; as they could then not only confer together upon the most likely methods, but use their joint Influence and Endeavours to obtain the Happiness of Bishops, to support the Church against the unreasonable Opposition given to it in the Colonies, and to cultivate and improve a good Understanding and Union with each other.[14]

The next day Dr. Auchmuty read a letter to the meeting that he had received from the Bishop of London relating "the Intention of the Presbyterians in this Country (as credibly reported), to make Application to the Kirk of Scotland, for their Influence with the King and British Parliament, to obtain a Charter of Incorporation." After thanking their host for his good work, the members ordered a full report of their actions and future intentions dispatched to the Society, together with arguments against the "pernicious" design of the New York Presbyterians to win incorporation through pressure from Scotland.[15]

New England also witnessed the meetings of Anglican missionaries. When the first annual convention of the Massachusetts clergy assembled at Boston early in June, 1766, the fourteen divines "made something of an appearance for this Country, when we walked to-

14. Schneiders, *Johnson*, I, 47; "The Seabury Minutes of the New York Clergy Conventions of 1766 and 1767," *Hist. Mag. Prot. Episc. Church*, X (1941), 132–9.

15. Schneiders, *Johnson*, I, 47; "Seabury Minutes," 140; N. Y. Clergy to Secy. of S.P.G., May 22, 1746, S.P.G. Correspondence, ser. B., II.

gether in our Gowns and Cassocks" to hear the Reverend Henry Caner preach at King's Chapel. There they learned that the Bishop of London endorsed their convening, and Governor Francis Bernard showed his approval by joining them at a dinner. Two days later at Stratford, Dr. Johnson, assisted by Dr. Auchmuty, presided at a gathering of the Connecticut clergy, and "the affair of the bishops for America was again strenuously solicited in an address to the Bishop of London." These were but the first of many meetings of Anglicans in New England which gave concrete evidence of the growth of episcopacy.[16]

Other agencies existed for propagating the gospel in the episcopalian way. As the founders had expected, King's College provided a good rostrum for President Samuel Johnson and his successor, Myles Cooper, as well as for the clergy of the city of New York. At Philadelphia, Provost Smith and the Reverend Richard Peters had succeeded so well in steering the College and Academy in the Anglican direction that by 1764 Archbishop Secker deemed it advisable to caution the trustees against displaying excessive zeal. The progress made through episcopal intrigue so embittered Vice Provost Francis Alison, who had sought equal treatment for all sects, that he confessed to Ezra Stiles, "I am ready to resign my place in the College, and retire into the country meerly thro' Chagrine. The College is artfully got into the hands of Episcopal Trustees. Young men educated here get a taste for high life and many of them do not like to bear the poverty and dependence of our ministers." Another lure, besides the "high life," was used to bait these seekers after status when the English prelates, acting on a suggestion of Dr. Johnson, began to use their influence with

16. Meetings of Episcopal conventions are reported regularly after 1767 in the Boston, Portsmouth, Providence, Newport, and New York newspapers, accompanied occasionally by an editorial gloss. "It is suspected by many, that a principal design of the late and frequent and numerous Conventions, is in order to a spirited application to the powers at home, upon some supposed abuses of the Church, in two neighbouring Colonies [Massachusetts and Connecticut], which is pretended to amount to persecution. Is it not to the last degree cruel and mean, to take this opportunity to attack us on this matter at a time when the united efforts of all sects, are so necessary in the Common Cause of Liberty." Daniel Fowle's *N.H. Gazette,* Nov. 11, 1768; Perry, *Historical Collections, Mass.,* III, 524; Schneiders, *Johnson,* I, 47.

Oxford and Cambridge to procure honorary degrees for outstanding missionaries; this balanced the similar honors conferred on Dissenters by Scottish universities, Yale, and Harvard. Degree-hunting is not a twentieth-century innovation. Finally, by enlarging the S.P.G.'s lay membership in the colonies, the missionaries won valuable political and financial support from such officials as Sir William Johnson, Governor John Wentworth of New Hampshire, Joseph Harrison of the Customs Service, and wealthy Godfrey Malbone.[17]

All these efforts and the power of the hierarchy at home notwithstanding, the Church of England in the colonies continued in leading strings. Such British colonial agencies as the Board of Trade recognized the need to strengthen it, but the Church remained "the weak side" when compared with the Dissenters, whose organization improved with every year.[18]

After 1715, as we have seen, the Nonconformists gradually enhanced and expanded their means of communication, until, by the time of Ezra Stiles's sermon calling for union, they had the first effective transatlantic and intercolonial intelligence network. The direction of most activities had centered in the Dissenting Deputies at London, but now, because of the prolonged illness of Dr. Benjamin Avery, the Deputies no longer played the active part in colonial affairs that they had in previous years. Besides, the energies of the new officers were absorbed by a long and costly litigation before the House of Lords in which they won exemption from serving in "burdensome offices in corporations." Furthermore, Jasper Mauduit, who succeeded Dr. Avery as chairman, lacked the physician's vigor and address in dealing with the politicians. From 1762 to 1765 he took on the duties of colonial agent for Massachusetts, and, as he wrote to Mr. Mayhew in 1762, he found "an increase of the Care of our affairs perpetually falling" on him. Still he managed to help out the Massachusetts Congregationalists in several in-

17. Stiles, *Itineraries,* 428; Bridenbaughs, *Rebels and Gentlemen,* 61–2; Schneiders, *Johnson,* I, 46–7; III, 280.

18. Rev. James Lyons to Secy., Nov. 12, 1764, S.P.G. Correspondence, ser. B, II; Dora M. Clark, *British Opinion and the American Revolution* (New Haven, 1930), 183–4.

stances. Fortunately for colonial Nonconformity, other and more useful means of intelligence and sturdy support came from England at critical times in the 1760's.[19]

The real strength of American dissent lay in its substantial numerical superiority over the Church of England, in both laity and clergy. According to Ezra Stiles, the "Coalition" consisted of about seven hundred churches. A New York newspaper of 1768 listed 586 Congregational churches (one for each town), and of these, one hundred and fifty affiliated with the General Assembly of Churches in Connecticut under the Saybrook Platform. The balance were Presbyterians and Separatists. All groups, but especially the Boston ministers, had long since organized into associations or conventions to deal with common ecclesiastical problems. The Reverend Henry Caner recognized this fact when he explained to the Archbishop in 1763 why the Episcopalians had failed to answer the tracts of Ezra Stiles and Charles Chauncy: "We are a Rope of Sand; there is no union, no authority among us; we cannot even summon a Convention for united Counsell and advice, while the Dissenting Ministers have their Monthly, Quarterly, and Annual Associations, Conventions, &c., to advise, assist, and support each other in any Measures which they think proper to enter into." [20]

Every year, able, pious, and well-educated young men entered the ministry from the colleges at Cambridge and New Haven, and toward the end of the colonial period from those at Providence and Hanover. Through them, new blood and the latest religious and political ideas were infused into an already active ministry, whose influence penetrated to every Yankee town, no matter how remote. Of 1586 ministers who served the Congregational churches of New England during the entire colonial period, only seventy-nine had not

19. After April 21, 1761, the Body of the Three Denominations was known as "The General Body of . . . The Protestant Dissenting Ministers in and about the Cities of London and Westminster." Three Denominations, Minute Book, I, 253, 460, 467, 476, 478, 479, 480–557 (the Corporation case); J. Mauduit to J. Mayhew, July 31, 1762, Mayhew Papers, No. 64; Andrew Eliot to J. Mauduit, June 1, 1763, Mass. Hist. Soc., *Collections*, LXXIV (1918), 119.

20. *N.Y. Mercury*, Sept. 12, 1768; Hawks and Perry, *Documentary History, Conn.*, II, 125; Perry, *Historical Collections, Mass.*, III, 490; William W. Sweet, *Religion in the Development of American Culture, 1765–1840* (New York, 1952), 3.

graduated from a college. Tractarian boasts of an educated ministry were not exaggerated.[21]

"We are not half so bad as our Enemies make us, nor near so good as our friends would make the world believe," Chief Justice Allen, the leading Presbyterian layman of Pennsylvania, told Jonathan Mayhew in 1761. Reunited in 1758, the Presbyterians controlled about one hundred and forty churches spread from New York to the Carolinas in local presbyteries under the centralized supervision of the Synod of New York and Philadelphia. The College of New Jersey at Princeton supplied most of the ministerial candidates for this rapidly mounting denomination, and its influence south of Pennsylvania was growing noticeably. As the College of Philadelphia took on more and more of an Anglican complexion after 1769, Vice Provost Alison came to look upon New-Light Princeton as a bulwark against episcopacy: "I should rejoice to see her Pistols, like honest Teagues, grown up into great Guns." In 1770 he joined with William Allen, Hugh Williamson, Charles Thomson, and other Presbyterians to secure a charter from the Penns for an academy he had founded in the 'forties at New London, but which later moved to Newark in the Lower Counties (the present University of Delaware). Upon the eve of the Revolution, it could be said that the Presbyterians were as well provided with facilities for higher education and the training of ministers as the Congregationalists.[22]

21. English interest in colonial education is reflected from Totnes, Devon, by the Reverend John Reynolds's letter to Jonathan Mayhew in 1763: "I rejoice to find that new Seminaries for education of youth are from time to time erecting in the American World, and especially where they are on a catholick Plan, as I apprehend that at Philadelphia is. The other at New York, I fear, will be too much under the Influence of our English bishops from whom little good is to be expected — the keeping up of their authority and furthering of a Worldly Interest too often disposes the more Part of them to take Measures that would not suit our Colonies." Reynolds to Mayhew, March 26, 1763, Mayhew Papers, No. 65; Sweet, *Religion in the Development of American Culture*, 6–7.

22. William Allen reported to Mayhew in 1763 that in Pennsylvania the Presbyterians were "the most numerous . . . of any of the Societys of his Majesty's natural born subjects, and among the Germans the Reformed [Calvinists] are rather of the greater number. The Quakers . . . are esteemed the more wealthy, but are not equal in numbers to the Presbyterians, and this state of things likewise prevails in New Jersey." Allen to Mayhew, March 12, 1761, April 2, 1763, Mayhew

Although colonial Presbyterianism had been materially modified by its contact with Congregationalism, the Synod kept open its connection with the National Church of Scotland. By virtue of the presence of lay elders at meetings of the presbyteries and synod, the denomination made good use of such prominent citizens of the Middle Colonies as Chief Justice Allen, the Philadelphia merchant Samuel Purviance, Judge George Bryan, and, of course, the New York Triumvirate.

IV

Without any thought of justifying his own voluminous correspondence to posterity, Cotton Mather wrote to a Scotsman in 1715 that "when the distance of the huge Atlantic, separates Brethren from one another, one Method unto which we must resort for Maintaining, the communion of Saints, is the Epistolary." Certainly the eighteenth century, more than any other, deserves the title of the epistolary age. The number and variety of letters exchanged between the members of the cloth appear remarkable today and seem to have been exceeded only by those between merchants. Improvements in the official overland post made during the Old French War were retained after 1759 and supplemented by many private services. Letters to and from England crossed on the "packets" that sailed once a month between Falmouth and New York.[23]

The S.P.G. acted as the clearing house for missionary intelligence at London. The clergy of the Northern Colonies wrote regularly to its secretary, and once a year submitted reports of numbers, membership gains, the state of churches and parishes, and other pertinent information, which was abstracted and published as an appendix to the Society's annual sermon. Naturally, too, the missionaries corresponded with each other about ecclesiastical affairs, and by this means such vigorous leaders as Dr. Samuel Johnson, Thomas Bradbury Chandler, Henry Caner, and Provost Smith sought to

---

Papers, Nos. 57, 66; Donald R. Come, "The Influence of Princeton on Higher Education," *William and Mary Quarterly*, 3 ser., II (1945), 359–96; Stiles, *Itineraries*, 433, 435; Bridenbaughs, *Rebels and Gentlemen*, 62–4.

23. Mass. Hist. Soc., *Collections*, 7 ser., VIII, 327; Bridenbaugh, *Cities in Revolt*, 290–91.

promote the Anglican welfare. When Mr. Chandler was preparing his *Appeal* in January, 1767, he alluded in a letter to Samuel Johnson to special privileges granted him by the Episcopalian in charge of the northern district of the Post Office: "I am much obliged to Mr. [James] Parker for consenting to, as well as to you for contriving a method of communication, that will probably be safe, expeditious and free from expense." [24]

Lack of such special privileges did not deter the Nonconformists from flooding the mails to relay information, ideas, and messages of encouragement and support to their brethren. Between 1755 and 1760, Ezra Stiles systematically established a periodical exchange of news and sentiments with eminent ministers of the British Isles, and by 1766 his "Directory for Correspondence" among English dissenting preachers, including addresses and honorary degrees with dates, consisted of nineteen Independents, eighteen Presbyterians, and seven Baptists, among whom were Dr. Samuel Chandler, Nathaniel Lardner, George Benson, and Caleb Fleming. As in former years, a host of divines in Massachusetts and Connecticut were in direct communication with their fellows on the other side of the ocean, and Charles Chauncy could inform Stiles in 1768 that the associated ministers of Boston had "for more than 20 years corresponded with the Committee of Deputation of Dissenters in London and by means of this Correspondence we have effectually secured the whole Dissenting Interest in England in favor of our Churches." To a Bostonian in the same year, Dennys De Berdt gave pointed advice: "We have always maintained a friendly Correspondence — I leave it to your consideration whether it might not be expedient (as the Dissenters now do here in England) to present one of the Clerks of the House of Commons ten Guineas per annum to give early intelligence when any Act may be brought in which affects America — for these [of which he writes] slipd thro' the House without our having any notice of the matter." [25]

From his post at Newport, Ezra Stiles added to his already long

24. Schneiders, *Johnson*, I, 385, 388.

25. A Directory for Correspondence with English Dissenting Clergymen, 1766, Stiles Papers (Mass. Hist. Soc., 101.7); Chauncy to Stiles, June 13, 1768, Stiles Papers (Yale University); Col. Soc. Mass., *Publications*, XIII, 332.

list of correspondents up and down the coast, from Dr. Samuel Langdon at Portsmouth, New Hampshire, to the Swiss Congregationalist John Joachim Zubly of Savannah, Georgia. After the death of Mayhew, Stiles depended chiefly on Chauncy and Eliot for news of the activities at Boston; his Connecticut reporters were Noah Welles and Chauncy Whittelsey; while at New York the Reverend John Rodgers and in Philadelphia Francis Alison were his principal informants about the Anglican skirmishing. The large collection of his letters at Yale University supplies abundant evidence both of the wide extent of his connections and of his potent influence. For his achievement in these exciting years after 1760 as one of the master minds in the defense of colonial dissent, he may well be dubbed the chief of staff or executive secretary of the anti-Episcopal forces.[26]

The distinct advantages gained by the New Englanders from their network of correspondence were not lost upon the Presbyterians. At its first meeting in May of 1758, the new Synod of New York and Philadelphia appointed "a committee to correspond in the name of the Synod with the churches of our persuasion in Britain and Ireland, and in these colonies and elsewhere, by means of proper persons in these churches." Each year thereafter there were similar committees set up, and by the time of the Stamp Act the Presbyterian ministers, like their Congregational fellows, had experienced committees which they were ready to use to bring about the union against their common enemy.[27]

By land and by sea, the volume of travel by Americans of the eighteenth century never ceases to amaze historians. Foremost among those who ventured forth on horseback or by tiny ship were the men of the cloth. The necessity of going to England for ordination ensured a wider knowledge of the Mother Country by the Episcopalians, though not a few Dissenters, chiefly laymen be it noted, made the voyage to England, too. The Honorable William Allen, Andrew Elliott, Esq., and Dr. Hugh Williamson, all of Philadelphia, conferred in London with the eminent Nonconformists, Benjamin Avery and Samuel Chandler, between 1763 and 1766; and several Bostonians had long talks with Dennys de Berdt

26. Stiles, *Itineraries*, 523–8, 597–602.
27. *Records of the Presbyterian Church*, 336, 343, 353, 354, 356, 361–2.

and Thomas Hollis. The trip of Henry Marchant, Rhode Island lawyer and member of Ezra Stiles's congregation, to the British Isles in 1771–72 resulted in discussions of a highly important nature with the principal Dissenters, and his journal supplied his minister with some very useful propaganda.[28]

A major factor in fostering a common spirit of dissent among colonial ministers and laymen, regardless of denominational affiliation, was the heavy travel overland between Philadelphia and Boston and midway points during the 'sixties. Newport's reputation as a summer resort attracted travelers to Rhode Island, and Stiles met them all. "Mr. Purviance has been a Feast of Intelligence to me," he wrote to Alison in August, 1766, and he added that he was sending the Presbyterian merchant on to Boston with an introduction to Charles Chauncy as "a Pillar of the Western Churches." On another occasion it was the Reverend John Ewing and Reverend Patrick Alison, the educator's brother from Baltimore, who called on him. William Livingston not only crossed the Hudson to meet Noah Welles at Elizabeth Town, New Jersey, in 1766 to patch up a "coolness" but also had an interview in a tavern with the great Episcopal champion Thomas Bradbury Chandler, to which he had been invited by mutual friends. A significant feature of the entire controversy from 1689 to 1776 is that, through college affiliations and travel, all the contestants knew each other, a fact which explains why Samuel Johnson "urged on by the anxiety of my mind," warned Archbishop Secker that the Dissenters "know our weaknesses as well as their own strength." [29]

V

"They are all Politicians, and they are all Scripture learnt," a British official declared after a visit to rural Connecticut. The

---

28. Samuel Miller, *Memoirs of the Rev. John Rodgers, D.D.* (New York, 1813), 108; *Records of the Presbyterian Church*, 333, 366–7; on Marchant, Stiles, *Literary Diary*, I, 72, 83, 221, 238, 304.

29. Alison to Stiles, May 18, 1756, Gratz Collection (Hist. Soc. Pa.), Univ. and College Presidents, A–B; Stiles, *Literary Diary*, 173; Alison to Stiles, May 29; Stiles to Chauncy, Aug. 26, 1766, Stiles Papers; Livingston to Welles, Dec. 12, 1766; Apr. 23, 1767, Johnson Family Papers, 84, 85; *Records of the Presbyterian Church*, 307; Schneiders, *Johnson*, I, 378.

juxtaposition should surprise no one who is familiar with the taverns, town meetings, and churches of New England. But it should be noted that though the Yankee picked up his practical politics in the local forum, he very likely got his political theory in ecclesiastical form from the minister on the Sabbath or at the weekly lecture. Dean Alice Baldwin has shown in a remarkable and too little read book that for eighty-five years prior to the revolt of the colonies the Congregational divines used their pulpits to instill in the minds of a highly intelligent and interested townsfolk the connection between the law of God and the law of nature; and they also taught them, until they knew almost by rote, the ministers' views of the history of the forefathers and the terrible threat of episcopacy. They had made the word *bishop* stand for everything hateful in the Yankee past.[30]

The pastor, who assumed responsibility for educating his flock, was the town's prime luxury. Respect was accorded him for his superior education and intellectual eminence, and he had to be good or he was apt to incur biting censure from a village critic, like the Windham brother who declared, "I had rather hear my dog bark than Mr. Billings preach." Few facts or ideas appeared in newspaper, tract, printed sermon, or book that were not rehearsed and elucidated in the pulpits of the inland towns. Often, too, excerpts were read in the taverns to receptive patrons. To a lesser degree, these same conditions held in the Presbyterian and other Calvinist communities of the Middle and Southern Colonies, where many an American picked up more by ear than from the printed page. It was thus, that by 1760, a majority of New Englanders and a very large number of the inhabitants to the southward had become, over the years, fully prepared for the coming ecclesiastical debate on religious and civil liberty. On this score, "Massachusettensis," the ablest of the Tory pamphleteers, said in 1775:

What effect must it have had upon the audience to hear the same sentiments and principles which they had before read in a newspaper, delivered on Sundays from the sacred desk, with a religious awe, and

30. Anne Hulton, *Letters of a Loyalist Lady* (Cambridge, Mass., 1927), 105; Baldwin, *The New England Clergy and the American Revolution*, especially xi–xiii, 3–12, 90–92, and see also her "Sowers of Sedition," *Wm. & Mary Quarterly*, 3 ser., V (1948), 52–76.

the most solemn appeals to heaven, from the lips which they had been taught, from their cradles, to believe could utter nothing but eternal truth? [31]

VI

The pamphleteer, Daniel Leonard, was correct in linking the pulpit to the newspaper. In nearly every New England town and in the hamlets of the Middle Colonies, the preacher received his newspaper from the post rider once a week, and such universally inquisitive urban ministers as Stiles and Chauncy subscribed to several journals. North of Maryland in 1760, the printers of seven communities published fourteen weekly gazettes (customarily so-called); when the ecclesiastical dispute reached its peak, 1766–68, twenty newspapers came out weekly at eleven places, and just before the outbreak of hostilities with England the number published in the Northern Colonies amounted to twenty-nine in fifteen towns. Boston, New York, and Philadelphia newspapers had an average circulation of 1475 in 1765, which rose to 2530 by 1774; those of smaller places ranged from seven to eight hundred each. British newspapers often commented during the pre-revolutionary years that the colonial newspapers reached a markedly higher proportion of the population than those in the Mother Country.[32]

If the English had wanted an explanation of this circulation, they

31. For a precious example of this hard-thinking type who was "no grate reader of antiant history," and for Samuel E. Morison's statement, which agrees with Harold Laski, "that with the sole exception of England of the Commonwealth, no community in modern history has been so fecund in political [and religious] thought as America, in the revolutionary generation," see William Manning, *The Key of Libberty* (Billerica, Mass., 1922), xiv, 3–5; Ellen D. Larned, *History of Windham County, Connecticut* (Worcester, Mass., 1874), I, 281; Carl Bridenbaugh, "The New England Town: A Way of Life," American Antiquarian Society, *Proceedings*, LVI (1946), 15–18. The last quotation is from [Daniel Leonard] *Massachusettensis* (Boston, 1775), 16.

32. Most London newspapers were dailies. In 1763 the *Public Advertiser* claimed a circulation of 2000, and five years later, of 3000; the leading journal, *The Gazetteer and New Daily Advertiser*, reached 5000 in 1769. These and other figures are given by Arthur M. Schlesinger, *Prelude to Independence: The Newspaper War on Britain, 1764–1776* (New York, 1958), Appendix A. For the founding of colonial newspapers, see Clarence A. Brigham's *History and Bibliography of American Newspapers: 1690–1820* (Worcester, Mass., 1947).

could have found at least one good reason in a reprint in their own *London Chronicle* taken from a *Boston Gazette* — that in New England there was a grammar school in every town. This was brought home to Thomas Hollis in a letter of 1761 from the Reverend Andrew Eliot stating that because of the excellence of the common schools of New England, "Scare any are to be found among us, even in the obscurest parts, who are not able to read and write with some tolerable propriety." The parson might have added that the rate of literacy was only slightly less in the middle regions of America. William Livingston recognized the importance of these facts when he spoke of the immense utility of the public prints in combating the movement for episcopacy in 1768: "these are almost universally read and from the greater latitude one may give himself, will prove more effectual in alarming the colonies." The S.P.G. missionaries were quite as much aware of the force of the press as the Presbyterians, for they too made every effort to see that the New York, Boston, and Philadelphia papers were "circulated through the Country with the greatest Zeal and Industry." [33]

Ever since 1689 religion had been the most absorbing question before the public. In the 1720's, when the Boston papers had become firmly established, they took up the question of an episcopate in a fumbling way, and again in the 1740's, their columns reflected the public's interest in the excitement over the Whitefield revival. Hard upon the Awakening came the remarkable advance in the art of religious propaganda made by the New Yorkers with the *Independent Reflector* and "The Watch-Tower" in 1753-55. The printers had learned that the public had an insatiable curiosity about the burning issue of church and state, and the amount of space allotted to that subject in the news columns of the Northern press exceeded that for any other kind of American advices including politics. Such men as John Holt, James Parker, and even Hugh Gaine, of New York; William Bradford and William Goddard of Philadelphia; the Fleets and Edes and Gill at Boston; and others in New Hampshire,

33. Thomas Hollis, Diary, 1759-1770 (Typescript, Institute of Early American History & Culture, Williamsburg, Va.), II, 681, 690; Eliot to Hollis, Jan. 29, 1769, Mass. Hist. Soc., *Collections,* 4 ser., IV (1858), 436; Livingston to Rev. Samuel Cooper, March 26, 1768, William Livingston Letterbook A (Mass. Hist. Soc.); Chandler to Secy., June 24, 1768, S.P.G. Correspondence, ser. B, XXIV, No. 94, 277-83.

Rhode Island, and Connecticut stood ready to play the printer's essential role in the dramatic and fateful decade of the 'sixties.[34]

There were, besides the newspapers, many other products of the press that influenced colonial and English opinion on ecclesiastical affairs: sermons, pamphlets, broadsides, and books by proponents of both sides of the controversy. Those printed on one side of the Atlantic were distributed and not infrequently reprinted on the other, and the audience for such publications was large. The cumulative effect of this constant rehearsing of religious arguments was that colonial readers and listeners became familiar with all the facts and points of view, and they were trained not merely to think through to the conclusion of a problem but to delight in the examination of the subtleties of the debates. More and more they began to think about these issues that transcended provincial boundaries, even continental ones. This prolonged experience with doctrinal exegesis and religious disputation educated the American colonists for political thinking after 1760.

The press of the British Isles also had learned that a vast number of the public would lap up any news about a lively debate over religion. The Anglicans had always enjoyed access to the press; most London and provincial newspapers and magazines treated the National Church with friendliness and deference. Besides the normal outlets, the Church aired the colonial question in the reports of the S.P.G. and the printed annual sermon, in the latter case often with unfavorable results. Nor was the press closed to the Nonconformists, who had their own booksellers and connections with well-disposed printers of books and newspapers. Then there were the neutral craftsmen whose interest could be won by a conveniently bestowed guinea or two. The Dissenting Deputies had long been making adroit use of the London press, and in Thomas Hollis the Nonconformists uncovered a propaganda genius whose work calls for special comment.

VII

In any age the effective manipulating of ideas and the machinery of organization requires the services of able men. Leaders to operate the ecclesiastical engines were not wanting as the decade of the

34. Osgood, *American Colonies,* III, 409–10.

'sixties opened; both parties produced them: men of ability, energy, dedication, even passion. The veterans of previous contests continued their good work — among the Dissenters there were in the New World the ministers Ezra Stiles, Noah Hobart, Francis Alison, and Noah Welles, and the formidable lay figure of William Livingston; while at the same time in London, Dr. Benjamin Avery, Samuel Chandler, and Israel Mauduit labored for the cause. Among the Episcopal missionaries, the aging Samuel Johnson and Henry Caner had eager and vigorous coadjutors in Samuel Seabury the younger and Provost William Smith. In England, the secretary and other S.P.G. officials always guided the colonial clergy. In the great Thomas Secker, Archbishop of Canterbury, the Church of England in America possessed a leader whose tact and political astuteness matched his compelling determination to see episcopacy fully established in the colonies during his time in office. When the American clergy lost Secker, they also lost their cause.

Many more committed individuals of capacity, lay and clerical, came to the fore in this period, the most critical in the struggle for ecclesiastical supremacy in the colonies. Three of them were of particular importance: a private gentleman of London, Thomas Hollis; a dynamic Boston Congregational minister, Jonathan Mayhew; and the ablest of the missionaries of the Venerable Society, Thomas Bradbury Chandler of Elizabeth Town in New Jersey.

An odd mixture of exceedingly strange parts, Thomas Hollis (1720–73) was what his century knew as an original. His primary concern in life was liberty, which he was convinced was being hunted round the globe and fast disappearing in his beloved England; he looked back nostalgically to the great proponents of liberty of classical antiquity and the seventeenth-century republicans for spiritual sustenance. All his intelligence, energies, and funds, for he inherited and increased a fortune, went exclusively into a one-man campaign to shore up the sagging foundations of liberty. A great believer in mottoes, he could well have taken for his own: I am a libertarian; nothing about liberty is foreign to me.[35]

A descendant of a Yorkshire Baptist family long noted for its

---

35. Thomas Hollis, III, made numerous gifts to Harvard and founded the Hollis Professorship of Divinity in 1721. The lives of few Englishmen of the eighteenth century are so well recorded as that of the fifth Thomas Hollis: he left a full and

philanthropic interests, this "strenuous Whig," fifth of his name, kept bachelor quarters in "Palmal." Possessed of means and leisure, Hollis devoted many hours to reading and study; he was a frequent visitor at Dr. Williams's Library. Though he read widely in the literature of Nonconformity and mastered Locke, histories and classical writings appealed to him above all else — "Finished Robertson's history of Scotland, which is ingeniously written, and in favor of civil, and religious liberty," reads an entry in his diary of June 12, 1759. Unlike many strongly prejudiced persons who fail to scout the enemy, Hollis dipped into the writings of Roman Catholics and High-Church Anglicans, whom he lumped together as enemies of freedom.[36]

It is unlikely that the booksellers of London had a better customer than Thomas Hollis. Volumes for his own use constituted but a small part of his purchases: one day he was sending Milton's prose works to the University of Groningen, the Leyden Public Library, and that of the Canton of Berne; another day he dealt with Millar about reprinting Locke on Toleration in a handsome new edition at his own expense. Copies of the editions that Hollis financed usually found their way into appropriate hands, and not infrequently he made a point of depositing one in the library of the British Museum. At one time, J. Almon was persuaded, for a consideration, to bring out a series of tracts relating to America.[37]

A philanthropic interest in New England and particularly in Harvard College might be said to have been a part of his inheritance. He went regularly to the New England Coffee House to read the colonial newspapers, "some of which are wonderfully spirited and fine," and sometimes, when the printed word failed him, he would

revealing diary of which Professor Robbins has made a typescript; much of his American correspondence is in the Mass. Hist. Soc., the letters to Andrew Eliot and Mayhew being printed in its *Collections* (4th ser., IV, 1858) and *Proceedings* (LXIX, 1956); Francis Blackburne compiled the *Memoirs of Thomas Hollis* (2 vols., London, 1780). Miss Robbins has revived his reputation in "The Strenuous Whig," *Wm. & Mary Quarterly,* 3 ser., VII (1950), 406–53, and in her *Eighteenth-Century Commonwealthman,* 260–68; and has analyzed the books donated to Harvard in *Harvard Library Bulletin,* V (1951).

36. Hollis to Harrison Gray, May 16, 1768, Hollis Papers (Mass. Hist. Soc.); Hollis, Diary, I, 7, 23.

37. Hollis, Diary, I, 144, 321, 364; II, 512.

go "down the River among the New England Vessels to get information concerning N. E. matters." His active concern with New England's religious destiny and educational institutions dated from his
reading of Jonathan Mayhew's "sermon on Government." Through
Israel Mauduit of the Dissenting Deputies, Hollis arranged in February, 1755, to ship anonymously a box of books containing some
prints and two sets of the works of "that great statesman Algernon
Sydney" to Boston with the request that Mayhew accept one of them
and give the other to the college. Two years after, the philanthropist
again made an anonymous gift through Mauduit, but in November,
1758, he let down his guard so far as to send a large collection direct,
which drew an immediate letter of thanks from the Bostonian and
opened a notable correspondence. By 1761 they had become sufficiently intimate for the thrifty Englishman to direct Dr. Mayhew
thereafter to send copies of his publications in parcels, "not as
letters," to save Hollis the heavy postal charges.[38]

This passion for anonymity would have made Hollis the despair
of the public relations men of our times. He assiduously shunned
the public, and after 1767 believed, almost pathologically, that his
enemies were having him followed every time he went abroad on the
streets. Though he was very careful to conduct his affairs "anoni-
mously," Hollis managed, however, to circulate freely among all of
the gentlemen of the day who really counted, or whom he hoped to
make count, in the grand strategy of his libertarian enterprises. He
ran the gamut of the politicians — from Speaker Onslow and the
Lord Chief Justice at the top of the scale to John Wilkes; and likewise, among the cloth, from lords and bishops to an obscure dissenting preacher of Honiton in Devon.[39]

As long as an organization shared his liberal outlook and humanitarian sensibilities, Thomas Hollis made no distinction between Nonconformist and Anglican bodies, and he joined many of the volun-

38. Captain Bruce of the *John & Sukey* out of Boston, "a plain, worthy, intelligent
Person," met Hollis by appointment at the Three Tuns in Grace Church Street,
September 24, 1766, and gave him "much information relating to the People of
Boston and Cambridge . . . and the late Dr. Mayhew." Hollis, Diary, II, 445,
447, 448, 463, 464, 516, 520, 521, 524; Jasper Mauduit to Mayhew, Feb. 28, 1755,
Mayhew Papers, 42; Mayhew to Hollis, Aug. 16, 1759; Hollis to Mayhew, Oct. 27,
1761, Mass. Hist. Soc., *Proceedings,* LXIX, 109–10, 126.

39. Hollis, Diary, I, 202, 318, 356; II, 559.

tary associations for promoting good causes that spawned in London. Active in the Society of Arts and the Society of Antiquaries, he also served on the boards of governors of both St. Thomas's and Guy's hospitals — when he visited the latter on January 15, 1760, he observed "Dr. Avery dirty as usual." To other organizations he made generous contributions. Thus it was that "this immaculate Whig" knew intimately such virtuosi as the painters Hogarth and Reynolds, the architect Adam, Wilton the sculptor, Vaillant the mezzotinter, and Cipriani the maker of medals. Upon the payment of ten guineas in 1767, the Free Society of Artists made him "an honorary, perpetual Fellow." [40]

The methods Hollis chose to recall, perpetuate, or disseminate his ideas of liberty did not seem as bizarre to his contemporaries as they may today — he ordered medals, mezzotints, and prints of the likenesses of the champions of freedom, paid for them from his own purse, and distributed them, always anonymously, where he thought they would do the most good. Such Hollisiana were the pin-ups of his times. In 1767, for example, when Vaillant's mezzotint of Jonathan Mayhew failed to please Hollis, he had Cipriani make an etching from a crayon likeness sent over by the widow and then dispatched three hundred impressions to persons all over the British Isles.[41]

Odd though he might have been, Thomas Hollis was both well informed and intelligent, and perhaps no single person had a better understanding of the sudden rise and nature of public opinion in England and of the means by which it could be managed. In this respect, as in his methods, he resembles Benjamin Franklin, who spent many years in London at this very time and who met Thomas Hollis.

Hollis became sufficiently acquainted with such prominent printers as Almon, Cadell, and Kearsley of Southwark, to induce them to publish items in which he was interested. Knowing that the "hacks" of the *Critical Review* were secretly influenced by Archbishop Secker and never "critical," he informed Jonathan Mayhew that those of "the *Monthly Review* are of a different stamp. They are more impartial, know their business better, and are more

40. Hollis, Diary, I, 13, 36, 38, 40, 73, 115, 127, 140, 179, 202, 318; II, 557, 575, 580.
41. Hollis, Diary, II, 564, 575, 602.

dextrous in the execution of it." Among dissenting ministers he picked out such able journalists as the Reverend Caleb Fleming, and from the liberal Episcopalians chose a man of the caliber of Archdeacon Francis Blackburne (who compiled Hollis's *Memoirs* after his death), to direct their pens against the Roman Catholic advance in England, or the threatened invasion of the colonies by Anglican bishops. In August, 1769, he presented ten guineas to Fleming "as my mite, for having continued to serve the cause of Liberty and the Revolution, now fast waining, as a Writer in the public prints in its behalf." [42]

With two of the principal London printing houses, Hollis's relations became personal and direct. Franklin's friends, the Strahans, father and son, were Hollis's also. As early as June, 1762, the senior Strahan inserted in his *London Chronicle* a paid advertisement that the libertarian had written against the Roman Catholics. Two years later, upon request, Strahan ran extracts from a pamphlet by Jonathan Mayhew of Boston, and a few days after that Hollis spent all morning "preparing for dispersion in Town and Country, a dozen of the Extracts from Dr. Mayhew's 'Remarks.'" Again and again, both Strahans "incerted" squibs and pieces submitted by Hollis in the columns of their paper. Though he always paid for each item, the shrewd propagandist thought it wise in March, 1765, when he found himself alone with "Mr. Strahan, jun," to present him with "Two Guineas, for attentions which [he] had obligingly shewn me of late, in respect to divers papers which it appeared right to me to have made public in the *London Chronicle.*" [43]

The connection between Thomas Hollis and Noah Thomas, "Director of the *St. James's Chronicle,*" and his printer, Baldwin, began in 1764. Before much time passed, Thomas accepted thanks for his attentions, and five guineas, "my Mite towards enabling him more effectually to assert the Cause of Liberty occasionally in that Paper." Money, indeed, inked the type. Soon an anti-Catholic article by the donor appeared, to be followed by many more "relating to the Popish Controversy now on foot in the St. James's Chronicle." The diarist recorded on June 29, 1765: "Busied all the morning writing

42. Hollis, Diary, II, 464, 629, 669, 740, 749, 781, 824, 831; Blackburne, *Memoirs of Thomas Hollis,* I, 260–61.

43. Hollis, Diary, I, 199, 326, 349, 350, 357, 392.

out articles for the S. J. and L. Chronicles"; and on July 4: "Busied in the evening drawing up a Letter for the S. James's Chronicle signed an English Accoucheur; to ridicule Popery." For "having assisted the Cause of Liberty stoughtly, on all occasions," Hollis tipped Thomas eight days later with four more guineas "to keep him steady to the Cause of Liberty in the Mother Country and Colonies." With frequency and regularity, this curious little man waited on the Strahans and Thomas to give them "their Clue" on public affairs.[44]

Few, if indeed any, Englishmen actively engaged in exercising power or making propaganda remained unknown or unvisited — one might almost say unpaid — by Thomas Hollis. He studied his opponents as if he were a military commander. His acquaintance with Thomas Secker and admiration of his talents was of twenty years standing when he wrote Mayhew about the prelate. He is not anti-Roman Catholic or strong for liberty, said Hollis, and now that I understand his plan for bishops in America, "and the extreme poorness of his conduct in having fixed a Spy [East Apthorp] upon you . . . in the center of your Land," I am resolved "to drop him wholly." Hollis ventured on a different course with the Marquis of Rockingham: on October 23, 1765, he showed him Dr. Mayhew's account of Boston's attitude toward the Stamp Act without saying who wrote it. His Lordship was most civil, "Read the Letter attentively; but did by no means appear to feel the importance of it nor the very imminent danger there is at this time of losing our Northern Colonies. That being the Case with respect to him; and also, it should seem, by his talk with his Brother Ministers . . . My little Power of action among the great, Mr. Pitt [a close friend] being far in the Country, has however been faithfully exerted." [45]

While Hollis resisted Dr. Mayhew's efforts to involve him in Massachusetts politics and to increase his list of correspondents, this doughty champion of liberty privately and in his own way gave every

44. Hollis often got his squibs for the two newspapers from the colonial gazettes he read in the coffee houses. In the New York Gazette for Nov. 14, 1766, he found "a high 'address from the Genius of Liberty to the Inhabitants of N. York and the British Dominions in N. America,' which I design to get printed in the L. Chronicle." He copied out the entire address the next day. Hollis, Diary, I, 314, 315, 343, 356, 396; II, 403, 406, 416, 417, 426, 433, 442, 444, 464.

45. Hollis to Mayhew, Apr. 4, 1764, Mass. Hist. Soc., Proceedings, LXIX, 146; Hollis, Diary, II, 443.

support to the cause in New England. Knowing all of the prominent Dissenters of London, he put Dr. Mayhew in touch with them and saw to it that his overseas correspondent received all the latest intelligence, whether by tract, book, newspaper clipping, or letter. Even the gossip he dispensed had its point, as in his report that Governor Bernard was "said to have been an officer in an ecclesiastical court before his appointment" in the colonies. "On this view of his qualifications for government it is natural enough to suppose, he might have a predilection for episcopal jurisdiction and episcopal discipline; and that he might endeavor to promote the designs of archbishop Secker and others, of establishing bishops in America, with alacrity." [46]

With characteristic independence, Thomas Hollis applied his standards of toleration and religious liberty to New England as well as to his native land. When in 1764 Dr. Mayhew presented him with a copy of Thomas Hutchinson's *History of Massachusetts-Bay,* which he commended as a "judicious and impartial" account of the persecutions carried out by the "Fathers of this Country," Hollis replied, after reading the book, that "the Fathers of New England were *Persecutors* with the Stigmata of persecution fresh bleeding upon them." He would not accept the New England legend in its entirety. Periodically he gave more books to the Harvard Library and contributed liberally to the Reverend Eleazar Wheelock's Indian School and to the Reverend Morgan Edwards for Rhode Island College. Upon the death of the Reverend Samuel Chandler, he declined the request of Mr. Timothy Hollis to become agent in England for the College of Philadelphia, because he never accepted public posts, but he said he would send over some books. [47]

Thus it happened that almost by accident and with genuine reluctance Thomas Hollis became, despite his obscurity, the most outstanding and useful link joining the Dissenters of both Atlantic shores. For Hollis to step from the wings to act as a one-man intelligence and propaganda agency at the very time that Doctors Avery

46. Hollis, Diary, I, 26, 73, 95, 152, 155, 207, 250, 252, 257, 258, 316; II, 457; Blackburne, *Memoirs of Thomas Hollis,* I, 163.

47. Mass. Hist. Soc., *Proceedings,* LXIX, 163, 170; Hollis, Diary, II, 526, 536, 537; Dennys De Berdt to E. Wheelock, Aug. 31, 1761, Col. Soc. Mass., *Publications,* XIII, 420.

and Chandler left the stage was a singularly fortunate occurrence for Imperial Dissent. The man and the moment coincided and determined history.

By championing religious and civil liberty, Jonathan Mayhew earned the title of "Master Spirit" fastened on him by the admiring Hollis. He is no newcomer to these pages, though his most important contribution did not occur until the six years before his untimely death in 1766. The eloquence and courage with which Mayhew proclaimed his liberal Arminian religious views and defended Dissenters made him a natural leader in New England. Among many colonial correspondents, he numbered most of the influential public Dissenters from Pennsylvania to New Hampshire. Long after his death, even so determined an opponent as Thomas Bradbury Chandler referred to him as "a man of distinguished abilities and assurance," who always showed his "address as a disputant, availing himself in the best manner of every little accidental advantage, and pushing his antagonists with vigour on every turn." Of the Nonconformist ecclesiastical pamphleteers, Jonathan Mayhew was equaled only by Noah Hobart for reasonableness, fairness, and the fundamental decency of his manners.[48]

No small part of the unique position that Mayhew held may be attributed to the fame his friend Thomas Hollis procured for him in the British Isles. Curiously though, while the New Englander exhibited boundless self-assurance in his native land, in his correspondence with Hollis he felt it necessary, unlike Stiles, to apologize for his colony and its people. He always remained the colonial. This attitude, however, rendered Mayhew peculiarly receptive to suggestions from London, as in the instance when Hollis pointed out the propaganda advantage of linking the Roman Catholic to the Episcopal threat and urged him on to a greater use of the press in the campaign against the bishops.[49]

During the years 1760–66, Thomas Hollis spent many hours arranging for the reprinting of Mayhew's published pieces. In his

48. Akers, Jonathan Mayhew is essential; see also the treatment in Shipton, *Harvard Graduates,* XI, 440–72; and Alden Bradford, *Memoir of the Life and Writings of Rev. Jonathan Mayhew, D.D.* (Boston, 1838), which contains many letters. Mass. Hist. Soc., *Proceedings,* LXIX, 115; Chandler, *Johnson,* 111–12.

49. Mass. Hist. Soc., *Proceedings,* LXIX, 112, 118, 148, 154.

diary for August 7, 1763, is the entry: "Busy all the morning in reading over a tract of Dr. Mayhew . . . and correcting it according to his instructions." He thought the piece "much too prolix," and "unlikely to have a current sale," but nevertheless hoped to induce Millar to reprint it. "An aid of five guineas given him out of my own purse towards defraying the expense" was sufficient to persuade Millar. Six guineas were needed in 1764 to launch a second tract, which Millar wisely brought out under another printer's name, he being "Printer in Ordinary to the Episcopal propagators [S.P.G.]." Hereafter Hollis advised Mayhew to adhere strictly to brevity and clarity, for few tracts will sell in England if the price exceeds a shilling a copy.[50]

The busy libertarian supervised the publications at every step; he read and corrected all proofs, and, when the finished work came from the press, he assiduously attended to the distribution to influential persons and such strategically placed libraries as the Advocate's at Edinburgh, the Scottish universities, the Radcliffe and Bodleian at Oxford, Christ College at Cambridge, and in London to Dr. Williams's and the British Museum.[51]

The extent of Jonathan Mayhew's contribution to the defeat of episcopacy in America was large. The *Boston Gazette* came very close to the truth when its obituary extolled Mayhew as "one of the great polemical writers this or any other country has seen." The part he played in civil politics is germane here only in one instance, but that was of the first importance. No one knew better than he how effective the communication between ministers, both in the colonies and across the water, had been since the earliest times. Since 1689 they had gradually perfected the committees of correspondence, and naturally Mayhew thought of turning this highly successful device to a political issue. Shortly after rising on "Lord's-day Morning," June 8, 1766, the preacher's thoughts strayed from his coming sermon; it was difficult to separate religious and civil matters, and he dashed off a suggestion to James Otis:

50. Hollis, Diary, I, 272, 277, 278, 286, 306, 315, 348, 351, 356, 359, 362; Mass. Hist. Soc., *Proceedings,* LXIX, 109, 118, 145.

51. Hollis, Diary, I, 286, 315, 316, 351, 356, 359, 362; Hollis to Harrison Gray, May 16, 1768, Hollis Papers.

Sir, — To a good man all time is holy enough; and none is too holy to do good, or to think upon it. Cultivating a good understanding and hearty friendship between these colonies, appears to me so necessary a part of prudence and good policy, that no favorable opportunity for that purpose should be omitted. I think such an one now presents.

Would it not be proper and decorous for our assembly to send circulars to all the rest, on the late repeal of the stamp act, and the favorable aspect of affairs? Letters conceived at once in friendship and regard, of loyalty to the king, filial affection towards the parent country, and expressing a desire to cement and perpetuate union among ourselves, by all laudable methods. A good foundation for this measure has been already laid by the late congress in New York [six colonies] which, in my poor opinion, was a wise measure, and contributed not a little towards our obtaining lately a redress of grievances. Pursuing this course, or never losing sight of it, may be of the greatest importance to the colonies, perhaps the only means of perpetuating their liberties.

It is not safe for the colonies to sleep; for it is probable they will always have some wakeful enemies in Great Britain. But if they should be such children as to do so, I hope there are some too much men, and too great friends to them as well as to liberty, to rock the cradle, or to sing lullaby to them.

You have heard of the communion of churches; and I am to set out tomorrow morning for Rutland, to assist at an ecclesiastical council. Not expecting to return this week, while I was thinking of this in my bed, the great use and importance of a communion of colonies appeared to me in a strong light; which led me immediately to set down these hints, to transmit to you. Not knowing but the general court may be prorogued or *dissolved* before my return, or my having an opportunity to speak with you, I now give them, that you may make such use of them as you think proper, or none at all.[52]

Of the several sources from which proceeded the inspiration of those formidable organizations, the revolutionary committees of correspondence, none had been tried out so successfully over a long period or were more obviously right at hand than those of the Congregational and Presbyterian ministers, as Samuel Adams was quick

52. Quoted in Bradford, *Mayhew*, 428–30; *Bos. Gaz.*, July 14, 1766.

enough to perceive. The nonconforming divines of England and America had invented and proved this device: "This is the foulest, subtlest and most venemous serpent that ever issued from the eggs of sedition." When the colonial opposition to royal authority, which numbered in its ranks so many dissenting ministers, found itself maneuvered into the forming of a revolutionary organization, it did not indulge in a miraculous improvisation. It took the tried-and-proved ecclesiastical organization of the Nonconformist churches and adapted it to secular affairs with great though hardly surprising success.[53]

Dr. Samuel Johnson, the Nestor of the missionaries of the Venerable Society, was sixty-seven in 1763 when he resigned the presidency of King's College. Though resolved to seek retirement at Stratford, for his remaining nine years he resumed his duties as rector, participated actively in the episcopate controversy, and published an English-Hebrew grammar. All this we learn from the biography prepared by the man he designated his successor and biographer, and who, understandably, turned hagiologist on the eve of the colonial revolt.[54]

Born into the well-known Congregational family of "Chandler Hill" at Woodstock in 1724, Thomas Bradbury Chandler followed the Connecticut custom of attending the college at New Haven, from which he graduated in 1745. Though his parents' social position entitled him to be ranked seventh in a class of twenty-one, "his Learning and Merit" placed him at the top in the eyes of Tutor Noah Welles, who gave him a letter of introduction to William Livingston in New York the next year. But Dr. Samuel Johnson, always on the lookout for promising youths from Yale, had already persuaded Chandler to read theology with him at Stratford, and before long joined with the elder Samuel Seabury in procuring the proselyte a place as catechist at St. John's Church in Elizabeth Town, New Jersey. As Ezra Stiles recalled the incident two decades later (doubtless from his voluminous notes): "it was, as I understood, in 1748, by Letters of Correspondence between Dr. Johnson and this said

53. *Massachusettensis*, 35; for other, but in my opinion less directly traceable, sources, see Edward D. Collins, "Committees of Correspondence of the American Revolution," Amer. Hist. Assn., *Annual Report* (1901), I, 243–72.

54. Chandler's *Life of Johnson* was written about 1773.

Dr. Secker Bishop Oxon., that Thomas Bradbury Chandler was proselyted, learning or imbibing then an assurance that in his day the Hierarchy would be erected here and that the young Adventurers had a fair chance of becoming Bishops and other Dignitaries in the Church. This same Bait was at that time offered to me." [55]

In the spring of 1751, after a passage of nine weeks, young Chandler arrived in London and in July received ordination at the hands of Bishop Sherlock. Dr. Johnson arranged for him to meet the Bishop of Oxford, whom he impressed as one who could go far in ecclesiastical circles. Returning in November he settled down to the two tasks of caring for his parishioners and propagating epis-copacy with unrestrained zeal. Two years later, Oxford awarded him a master's degree and, in 1768, a doctorate in divinity; honors also conferred by King's College in 1758 and 1767, but never matched by his alma mater.[56]

The Reverend Mr. Chandler was a large man, who grew portly on good living as the years passed. His portrait, painted by his brother Winthrop, shows a man of vigorous appearance. Con-temporaries remarked on his uncommonly fine blue eyes, command-ing voice, and love of music. Cheerful in temperament, sociable to a degree, he quickly took his place in the Jersey gentry by marrying a niece of the Presbyterian Elias Boudinot. All these qualities, so useful in a vicar, did not dampen those of the scholar. Dr. Chandler was "remarkable for his extensive learning," fond of study, and col-lected a library of more than 1600 titles. Like his Newport rival, Ezra Stiles, he served his community as librarian at the Elizabeth-Town Library Company, founded in 1755.[57]

55. Reliable testimony like that above reflects upon the sincerity of Dr. Johnson's insistence to Archbishop Secker, March 1, 1759, that at Stratford "I never once tried to proselyte dissenters, nor do I believe any of the other ministers did." Schneiders, *Johnson*, I, 284; Albert H. Hoyt, "The Rev. Thomas Bradbury Chandler, D.D., 1726–1790," *New England Hist. & Genealogical Register*, XVII (1873), 230; Livingston to Welles, May 26, 1756, Johnson Family Papers, No. 22; Stiles to Chauncy, Mar. 19, 1770 (Mass. Hist. Soc., 41F, 104).

56. Hoyt, "Chandler," 231; Samuel C. McCulloch, "Thomas Bradbury Chandler: Anglican Humanitarian in Colonial New Jersey," *British Humanitarianism* (Phila-delphia, 1950), 104, 105, 108.

57. McCulloch, "Chandler," 111; Schneiders, *Johnson*, IV, 104; Hoyt, "Chandler," 236; *N.Y. Gaz.*, Mar. 21, 1766.

Whatever "Bait" Dr. Johnson and Bishop Secker may have held out to the young clergyman, he fulfilled his promise. In 1752 he invaded the New-Light stronghold of eastern Connecticut and preached at his native Woodstock, where, he reported to the Society, he thought only the opportunity was lacking for the assembling of "a large congregation of conformists." His position as the principal Churchman in New Jersey was never questioned. When he inaugurated the first annual convention of the clergy in 1758, he gave evidence of far more than pulpit talents. More and more the aging Johnson leaned on the younger man, and by 1766 the Dissenters as well as Episcopalians recognized Thomas Bradbury Chandler as the foremost American missionary and a man well fitted by experience and connections overseas to lead the final all-out push for colonial bishops, of whom, conceivably, he might be the first.[58]

Leaders of the ecclesiastical hosts like Chandler and Mayhew had need of steady support from secondary leaders in the last fifteen years of British rule in the colonies. There were, of course, other important missionaries who devoted all their energies to the cause of the Church of England. Samuel Seabury, the younger, and Charles Inglis eagerly followed Chandler's lead; while Samuel Auchmuty, who was not supported by the Society, frequently attempted to curb their activities. In Pennsylvania Provost William Smith and the Reverend Richard Peters completed the Episcopal high command for the Middle Colonies. Only in New England did the Anglicans lack men of real ability after the departure of East Apthorp for England. To the Church this was fatal, for the Dissenters, in the learned and prolific Charles Chauncy and Andrew Eliot of Boston and such colleagues as Stiles in Rhode Island and Welles and Hobart in Connecticut, built up a talented and aggressive leadership which needed to be countered if bishops were ever to come among the Yankees.[59]

58. T. B. Chandler and Isaac Brown to Archbishop of Canterbury, Jan. 29, 1755, Hawks Papers, II.

59. Eben E. Beardsley, *Life and Correspondence of the Right Reverend Samuel Seabury, D.D.*, (Boston, 1881); John W. Lydekker, *The Life and Letters of Charles Inglis* (London, 1936); Albert F. Gegenheimer, *William Smith* (Philadelphia, 1943); Hubertis Cummings, *Richard Peters* (Philadelphia, 1944); and for Chauncy, Eliot, Hobart, and Auchmuty, see Shipton, *Harvard Graduates,* VI, 439; VII, 359; X, 128; XI, 115.

VIII

THE ANGLICAN PLOT

From all who dare to tyrannize
May Heaven still defend us,
And should another James arise
Another WILLIAM send us —
May Kings like GEORGE for ever reign
With highest Worth distinguish'd
But Stuarts who our Annals stain
May they be quite extinguish'd.

Then let us sing, &c.[1]

These lines from "The Revolution Ode," inserted by Edes and Gill in their *Boston Gazette* in January, 1760, accurately reflected the mood of many Americans when George III ascended the throne, and not far ahead they could see the victorious end of the long contest against the "Gallic Menace." However, the new reign brought with it new moves by new men with the approach of peace, and religious affairs inevitably became entangled in the confused politics of the day both in England and America. In the latter, a succession of happenings, nearly always involving Anglican missionaries intimately, took on for suspicious Dissenters — and not without reason — the semblance of an ecclesiastical plot connected with the policy of the ministry, which culminated in the Stamp Act. There is no reasonable doubt that in 1765–66 the colonies verged on armed rebellion, nor that religious fears quite as much as political sentiments and economic distress during the five years immediately preceding the crisis contributed to the excited state of public opinion.

1. *Bos. Gaz.*, Jan. 21, 1760.

II

It seemed to the Dissenting Interest in the colonies that clerical interference in American affairs more often than not conflicted with the expressed wishes of the citizenry. As a result, an uneasiness coupled with resentment pervaded the land, and the pastors, who saw more than temporary harassment in the activities of the missionaries, moved to defend their countrymen against Anglican encroachments.

Even in the land south of Mason's and Dixon's new boundary line, a colonial form of anticlericalism had been smouldering for a long time in the Old Dominion, where the parochial clergy were established and supported by law, and no S.P.G. missionaries were stationed. As early as 1736, Governor William Gooch sensed that malice toward the clergy lay at the base of the opposition to the law concerning the payment of clerical salaries in tobacco. When Governor Fauquier first arrived in Virginia, he, the royal appointee, was so indignant at the arrogance of the Reverend John Camm that he instructed his white servant to call in all the Negro slaves to look on Camm so that they would never allow him to set foot in the Governor's palace again. News reached Virginia in the summer of 1760 that the Two-Penny Act of 1758, which permitted vestries to commute tobacco payments into money at two pence per pound, had been disallowed by the Privy Council. The ensuing dispute, known as the Parson's Cause, came to a head in 1763 amid widespread antagonism against the Churchmen and, incidentally, thrust Patrick Henry into the public view.[2]

In some instances, clerical intervention from overseas in matters outside of ordinary parish preserves contributed to the Dissenters' belief that an Anglican cabal sought civil as will as religious control. In New Hampshire, the Board of Trade's 69th instruction of June, 1761, forbade Governor Benning Wentworth to permit any schoolmaster crossing from England to teach there who could not produce a license from the Bishop of London. At New York, the Presbyterians smarted over the failure of Lieutenant Governor De Lancey

2. Sir William Gooch to his brother, enclosure, Aug. 25, 1736, Letterbook (Typescript, Colonial Williamsburg, Inc.); Perry, *Historical Collections, Virginia*, I, 464.

to support their fourth application for a charter to allow them to control their own property; for he "had frequently expressed his abhorrence of the illiberal and unjust refusal which their former applications had met." And the Lutherans had experienced a similar turndown.[3]

As soon as the outcome of the French War was assured, in fact several years before the treaty was signed, both the Anglicans and Congregationalists in New England began to consider methods of converting the Indians to their ways of worship. Before any official plan was adopted, some of the Roman Catholic Indians in the Penobscot region of Maine asked Governor Bernard for a priest, but he, fearing conversion of near-by white settlers, procured through the S.P.G. an Anglican chaplain, who turned out badly. Though made in another connection, a comment of Dennys De Berdt's is apropos: "You can have no better rule to judge of the society than by the persons they send you. The single point they keep in view is Episcopacy." [4]

"To show gratitude to God, who has crowned the King's arms with success, and to take advantage of the French being driven out of Canada, we proceed to spread the knowledge of His religion" — so stated the Great and General Court of Massachusetts when it chartered "The Society for Propagating Christian Knowledge among the Indians of North America." Ezra Stiles had called for such a move, and Nonconformists in England and America took the initiative in the religious contest for the territories conquered in the late war. The new body would have at its disposition, without any requirement to publish annual accounts, "an Evangelical Treasury . . . chiefly supplied from England and Scotland, but applied," as Caner was to charge, "at the pleasure of a Junto here." Actually the Boston ministers and their European backers intended that this Massachusetts Society should counter the Roman Catholic influences among the newly acquired tribes and carry out the century-old

3. Leonard W. Labaree, ed., *Royal Instructions to British Colonial Governors, 1670–1776* (New York, 1935), II, 492; William Gordon, *History of the Rise, Progress, and Establishment of the United States of America* (London, 1788), I, 147; Baird, "Civil Status of Presbyterians," 607–8.

4. John E. Sexton, "Massachusetts Religious Policy with the Indians under Governor Bernard, 1760–1769," *Catholic Historical Review*, XXIV (1938), 310–28; Col. Soc. Mass., *Publications*, XIII, 417.

ideal of Christianizing them. They had manifested this in the charity school conducted by Eleazar Wheelock at Lebanon, Connecticut, which such eminent Englishmen as George Whitefield, Dennys De Berdt, and Dr. Benjamin Avery had commended to Lord Halifax as worthy of a royal charter.[5]

Even though the Governor approved the act and sent it to England for review, Jonathan Mayhew, writing to Hollis, predicted "that our *good* Friends of the Church of England will endeavour to obstruct this scheme." Several of the Boston ministers wrote to Jasper Mauduit to solicit the aid of the Dissenting Deputies in promoting their project, and that body appointed Dr. Avery, Mauduit, and one other deputy to take any necessary action.[6]

In the meantime, as Mayhew had foreseen, the Anglicans were at work trying to prevent royal approval of the charter. "The real design of it is to frustrate the pious designs" of the S.P.G. to convert the natives, Caner wrote the Archbishop. As for the new society being allowed to hold property up to £2000 sterling in real estate, that would be dangerous, and he urged the prelate to work against it. Provost William Smith, then in London, submitted a series of "Remarks" against the organization which his superior used to good effect, for in March, 1763, Jasper Mauduit reported that his committee had failed in its application to the authorities. In May the Privy Council (with no bishops present) disallowed the act. "From the beginning there was a strong prejudice conceived against this New Society," Israel Mauduit wrote to Mayhew. "The word had been given, that it was set up in opposition to the Society here. . . ." Even the most moderate bishops "had all been spoke to, and with a

---

5. From the Mohawk country, Sir William Johnson covertly opposed Moor's Indian Charity School because it was not under Anglican auspices, but Eleazar Wheelock suspected that the baronet was not being straightforward with him. After Sir William became a member of the S.P.G. in 1766, Wheelock remarked that he "designs the Six Nations shall be supplied with Episcopalians." Lord Halifax approved chartering the institution but advised that a provincial one would be less expensive. Alexander C. Flick, *Papers of Sir William Johnson* (Albany, 1927), IV, 17, 47, 72, 73; James D. McCallum, *Eleazar Wheelock: Founder of Dartmouth College* (Hanover, N.H., 1939), 120–21; Leon B. Richardson, *History of Dartmouth College* (Hanover, N.H., 1932), I, 34–5, 38, 53; *Mass. Acts and Resolves,* IV, 520–23; Perry, *Historical Collections, Mass.,* III, 487.

6. Mass. Hist. Soc., *Proceedings,* LXIX, 130–31; Dissenting Deputies, Minutes, I, 460.

The Bishop's Palace at Cambridge

This elegant seat, possibly designed by Peter Harrison, was erected in 1761 by the Reverend East Apthorp in Cambridge, Massachusetts. It quickly became the symbol of threatened Episcopal magnificence and tithes, because rumor had it that its owner was to be the first American bishop. Apthorp House is now the Master's Lodging for Adams House, Harvard University.

Notion, that it might interfere with the Designs of the Church here." Mauduit concluded with the plea that Mayhew and his friends would "keep up the Society in a more private way." When the Episcopalians successfully scuttled the charter, anger welled up in the New Englanders, and they were convinced that a diabolical clerical plot was in the making.[7]

III

The resurgence of Anglican activity in Massachusetts coincided with the arrival at Boston in August, 1760, of the Reverend East Apthorp and Governor Francis Bernard. These two personages turned out almost at once to be the unwitting *agents provocateurs* of church and state. In its reply to the new governor's speech on the capitulation of Montreal, which had emphasized the blessings of loyal membership in the British Empire, the House of Representatives of Massachusetts, on its part, agreed on the advantages but reminded Francis Bernard of the vital colonial contribution of blood and treasure, without which "the common Enemy" might never have been defeated. The members expressed the hope that "the Acquisitions of British Power may be attended with the Improvement of her Policy, and that his Majesty's Gracious and Paternal Example may be always kept in view, and civil liberty may be ever considered as the great end of all true Policy." Such publicly expressed interest in liberty and concern about its future in the colonies, while far from palatable to Englishmen in general and royal officials in particular, originated in an old and continuing attitude, one to fathom and propitiate, not to antagonize, lest it grow to unmanageable proportions.[8]

Once the Church of England had decided to invade Cambridge, it proceeded with speed and flamboyance. Founding the mission in April, 1759, the Episcopal leaders soon had a committee of dis-

7. *Mass. Acts and Resolves*, IV, 562–3; Perry, *Historical Collections, Mass.*, III, 472; Dissenting Deputies, Minutes, I, 467; Israel Mauduit to Mayhew, April 3, 1763, Mayhew Papers, No. 67; Mass. Hist. Soc., *Collections*, 6 ser., IX, 9–10, 14, 15–16; *Acts of Privy Council*, IV, 559–60.

8. *Journals of the House of Representatives of Massachusetts, 1760–1761* (Boston, 1761), 115–16.

tinguished public figures negotiating with Peter Harrison of Newport for the design of a church in "the modern taste." Upon arrival a year later, East Apthorp, aged twenty-eight, wealthy, traveled, and a cultured Cantabrigian, fitted perfectly into the Brattle Street gentry. When the youthful rector made a brilliant marriage with Elizabeth, daughter of Judge Eliakim Hutchinson of Boston, the following August, he took her to live in his new mansion near Harvard Yard. The elegance of this "Seat" so impressed Ezra Stiles on a visit to Cambridge that he measured it, described the interior, sketched details of pedestals and pilasters, and drew an elevation, all of which he inserted in his diary for future use.[9]

As if such ostentation were not sufficient to dazzle the simpler Congregationalists of New England, already in a state of shock over the mere presence of an English church within sight of Harvard College, Episcopal exuberance shortly led to a classic blunder. The Reverend Jonathan Mayhew was not the only reader to be astounded by "A Letter from Cambridge" in a *Boston Gazette* of January, 1761, which exhibited such a complete misconception of New England opinion that one may wonder whether the recently arrived and inexperienced Mr. Apthorp was not responsible for it.

Hail, my happy Country men! upon the hopeful Prospect of being freed from the Shackles of Bigotry, which their Fathers brought into this Land, and with which their Posterity have been so long fetter'd —

Having thus inverted the Yankees' version of their history, the writer continued:

The time perhaps will soon come, when Party Distinction will be at an End, and we shall all call aloud with one Heart and Voice, for One Way (and if it be not inconsistent with my Character, I would speak in Time for the *Established Way*) — 'Till Things are ripe for this happy State, I have a few Proposals humbly to make.

Because he aimed at "reconciling the different Sectaries," this author suggested that good relations between the members of his communion and those of "The Independent Meeting-House" could be

9. Carl Bridenbaugh, *Peter Harrison: First Colonial Architect* (Chapel Hill, 1949), 112–17; Perry, *Historical Collections, Mass.*, III, 457; Ezra Stiles, Diary (MS, Yale University Library), I, 124–5.

inaugurated by holding one of the two customary services on Commencement Day at Harvard College in Harrison's new Christ Church, and by introducing one or more Episcopalians to the Board of Overseers! Such concessions "would be but a just Return for that unlimited Charity and Condescention which the Clergy have always expressed towards Dissenters from the Beginning, even unto this Day." [10]

During the three previous decades throughout the Northern Colonies, noticeably in the cities, an intercolonial aristocracy had been entrenching itself and consolidating into a conscious American class by means of commercial connections which reached across provincial boundaries, and by almost dynastic marriage alliances. Increasingly a segment of this gentry drew toward the Church of England and allied itself with the growing number of Anglican placemen newly arrived from the Mother Country. According to the Reverend Arthur Browne, who had lived in Boston and presided over churches at Newport and Portsmouth, "even being a member of the Church of England gave a kind of distinctive fashion." From Albany in 1762, Colonel John Bradstreet sent out a plea to the S.P.G. to send over a missionary who is "a man of Fashion and weight with abilities and Character" to enable his communion to surpass the Dutch.[11]

The aura of social snobbery attaching to the Church of England grew so notorious that the Reverend Noah Welles dealt with it in a trenchant satire, *The Real Advantages which Ministers and People may enjoy Especially in the Colonies, By Conforming to the Church of England, Faithfully considered, and impartially represented in a Letter to a Young Gentleman,* which he published anonymously in 1762. Masking as an Episcopal clergyman raised a Dissenter in England, and displaying a wit rare in ecclesiastical disputes, Welles lampooned the social distinction of Anglicans.

This then is the principal advantage of the Church of England, that the religion which is generally practised by her members is perfectly agreeable to polite gentlemen; whereas no gentleman can belong to

10. *Bos. Gaz.*, Jan. 12, 1761.

11. On urban aristocracy, see Bridenbaugh, *Cities in Revolt,* 137, 334–50; Col. John Bradstreet to Secy., July 2, 1762, S.P.G. Correspondence, ser. B, II.

other persuasions, without meeting with a great deal of uneasiness from their doctrines, but more especially from their discipline. . . . The church of England-College at New York will doubtless prove a relief to polite young Gentlemen, who are sick of the severities they are oblig'd to suffer at other colleges. . . . But especially they'll make great proficiency in politeness and get the airs of citizens.

The missionaries also were upset by the discussion of the Episcopal search for political power. Dr. Samuel Johnson did not quite know how to handle this American Hudibras and, try as he might, never discovered that the author lived but a few miles from Stratford. When Archbishop Secker wrote that he found the piece framed "in a ludicrous manner, yet with strange virulence," and that it "seems likely enough to do great mischief," Johnson persuaded the Reverend Mr. Beach to answer it.[12]

In 1762 the news that Governor Francis Bernard was considering issuing a royal charter for another institution, to be called Queen's College, in the Berkshires stirred up the Harvard Board of Overseers. Convinced that he favored the application because of the Congregationalists' tight control over Harvard, Boston ministers appealed to Jasper Mauduit and the Dissenting Deputies to take action against any charter for a new college on the grounds that it would be "ruinous to the Province in a religious as well as a civil respect." Apparently a committee of Overseers forced Governor Bernard to "suspend" his approval, and the project never advanced any further, but the bitterness engendered on both sides never completely abated.[13]

IV

Transatlantic clerical scheming and intrigue from 1760 to 1764 provided abundant evidence to substantiate the Dissenters' fears that under the leadership of the Archbishop of Canterbury the mission-

12. No place of publication was given for Welles's *Real Advantages* (1762), 5–7; Schneiders, *Johnson*, III, 265; *Ecclesiastical Records*, VI, 3833, 3841, 3864.

13. *Mass. Acts and Resolves*, IV, 562–3; Mass. Hist. Soc., *Proceedings*, LXIX, 129–30; Dissenting Deputies, Minutes, I, 476; Mass. Hist. Soc., *Collections*, LXXIV, 72; Bradford, *Mayhew*, 195–6n, 231; Josiah Quincy, *History of Harvard University* (Cambridge, Mass., 1840), II, 105 ff.

aries would "episcopize" America. The constant proselyting, the aspersions on their ministry, the attack on the charters of the colonies — all these, plus the fear that the Episcopalians would succeed in foisting bishops upon unwilling communities, convinced Jonathan Mayhew and his fellow ministers that they must mount a perpetual guard over their civil and religious liberties.

On the eve of East Apthorp's arrival at Cambridge, Dr. Johnson hinted that the young cleric was "reserved for yet higher and better things." The missionary was hopeful that "bishops should be sent into America for the accomplishing which I hope you will be continually using your influence in the manner the Archbishop advises, that the Church may apply in full her government." Henry Caner considered a bishop "an expedient too remote to be thought of," but he did ask the Secretary of the Society to designate an archdeacon periodically to supervise overseas work. If we do not have a bishop or two, the Reverend George Craig of Chester declared, "our Church will always be a Jumble of confusion, especially in Pennsylvania." [14]

It was President Johnson, however, who drafted actual plans for establishing the Church of England in America. "Having little to do" during a long winter's stay in Stratford and looking upon Connecticut and her eastward neighbors as "little more than a democracy . . . of republican mobbish principles and practices," Dr. Johnson refurbished and elaborated his old scheme for a constitutional reordering of the colonies. In July of 1760, he sent a copy to his friend Archbishop Secker with the suggestion that, if it met with his approval, it might be published in the *London Magazine*.[15]

The ideas or suggestions were presented in the form of rhetorical questions entitled: "Questions Relating to the Union and Government of the Plantations." In the fourth query, Johnson asked

Whether it is for the best public good, that the Charter Governments should continue in their present republican form, which is indeed pernicious to them, as the people are nearly rampant in their high notions of liberty, and thence perpetually running into intrigue and

14. Schneiders, *Johnson*, IV, 69–70; Perry, *Historical Collections, Mass.*, III, 459–61; *Pa.*, II, 293.

15. Schneiders, *Johnson*, I, 293, 295–6.

faction and the rulers so dependent on them that they in many cases are afraid to do what is best and right for fear of disobliging them?

The thirteenth was more positive:

Whether it is not very dishonorable . . . that the church which is established in England and consequently an essential part of the British constitution and hath ever been the greatest friend to loyalty, should not be, at least, upon as good a foot as the other denominations, as complete in her kind as they in theirs? . . . can any good reason be given why the Church should not have bishops, at least two, or three . . . to ordain and govern their clergy, and instruct and confirm their laity . . . ?

The missionary also had suggestions for the consolidation of Connecticut and Rhode Island under Massachusetts, and he reiterated his old plea for "some gentleman of great dignity and worth" to be appointed by the Crown "to be in the nature of a Vice Roi, or Lord Lt. to reside in New York." [16]

In the accompanying letter, the old missionary told the Archbishop confidentially: "It is of the utmost importance for the best good of that colony [Connecticut] that the Church be propagated and if possible supported; and if at the same time their charters were demolished and they could be reduced under the management of a wise and good governor and council appointed by the King, I believe they would in a little time grow a good sort of people and it would be one of the best of all the provinces." This in spite of his assertion in the "Questions" that "it is not proposed that the episcopal government should have any superiority or authority over other denominations, or make any alterations relating to, or interfering with any civil matters as they now stand." [17]

The experienced primate at Lambeth wisely vetoed Johnson's proposal that the "Questions" be published and explained to the author why he did not follow his further suggestion that copies be sent to William Pitt and Lord Halifax. "The things said in them are, in the main, right, so far as they may be made practicable, but

16. For "Questions," see Schneiders, *Johnson,* I, 297–301.

17. Dr. Johnson asked Archbishop Secker in the same letter to use his influence to see that a governor favorable to the Church of England be sent to replace James De Lancey, deceased. Schneiders, *Johnson,* I, 295–6, 297, 300.

publishing them to the world beforehand, instead of waiting till the time comes, and then applying privately to the persons whose advice the King will take about them, is likely to raise opposition, and prevent success." [18]

News about the "Questions" circulated all over New England like smoke, for Samuel Johnson had conferred with "several gentlemen of good understanding and public spirit" before he drafted them. The ministers were not too startled about these stories, for they knew Johnson's views, but they were perturbed about the rumors coming out of Massachusetts and Rhode Island that a foreign-born faction of Newporters headed by Martin Howard, George Rome, the Harrison brothers, and their Anglican associates, and supported by Governor Francis Bernard, who by this time had begun to urge the creation of a colonial "Nobility appointed by the King for life," were planning an assault on the Rhode Island charter. Bernard wrote home that "in Rhode Island the sensible people neither expect nor desire their charter should be continued." [19]

A little more than a year later Samuel Johnson sent off a draft of an address for the bishops. To Thomas Secker, both the end of the war and bishops for America seemed far distant in December, 1761, and he replied rather curtly: "The right time to try is certainly when a peace is made, if circumstances afford any hope of success. But there is a matter of which you in America cannot judge; and therefore I beg you will attempt nothing without advice of the Society, or of the bishops." Similarly the Archbishop deplored the address to the King on his accession, in which the Boston clergy prematurely mentioned bishops; therefore, he did not present it. By spring, however, cheered by the news of "the good disposition of Lord Halifax towards our being in due time provided with Bishops," Samuel Johnson headed the New York clergy in an address to the Bishop of London for colonial suffragan bishops.[20]

Although the dissenting ministers of New England were not privy to the appeals and plans of the Anglicans, they knew from past experience and could surmise from news items and rumors that there

18. Schneiders, *Johnson*, IV, 72.

19. Schneiders, *Johnson*, I, 293; Bridenbaugh, *Cities in Revolt*, 309; Francis Bernard, *Select Letters on the Trade and Government of America* (London, 1774), 89.

20. Schneiders, *Johnson*, I, 319; III, 261.

was increased Episcopal activity. On April 6, 1762, Jonathan Mayhew dispatched a Macedonian call for advice on ways and means to frustrate any designs of the Churchmen to Thomas Hollis:

We are apprehensive, Sir, that there is a scheme forming for sending a Bishop into these parts; and that our Governor, Mr. Bernard, a true church-man, is deep in the plot. This gives us a good deal of uneasiness, as we think it will be of bad consequence: at the same time that we are much at a loss, how, or in what manner to make opposition to it. If you should happen to hear it discoursed of, I believe I may assure you, that you could not do the body of the people in New England a more essential Service, or lay them under stronger obligations, than by using your influence, in such ways, as may appear proper to you, to prevent this project's taking effect. And I snould be glad if you would take an opportunity to hint something as to this affair, to Mr. [Jasper] Mauduit, and other leading Dissenters in England; who might be likely, as occasion offered, to appear in opposition to such a proposal.[21]

That the ministers' alarm was widely shared by the politicians came out when James Otis and "a Number of other firebrands" privately insinuated to members of the House of Representatives that the dissenting churches stood in danger of tithes and bishops, and that the colony's agent, Anglican William Bollan, was unsuitable to represent the province in such a time. Accordingly on April 19, 1762, the House discharged Bollan and gave his place to Jasper Mauduit, whom Thomas Hollis commended as "a worthy and active Gentleman, a leader among the dissenters, and in connection with People in Power." [22]

V

The newspaper readers of New England received their first inkling of the Episcopal drive for power in 1760 when the *Boston Evening Post* reprinted its assertion of 1747 that the Anglicans' "grand business seems to be . . . to proselyte dissenters." A piece in the *News-Letter* purporting to come from a London sheet describing Massachusetts and "the other American provinces" as "a factious disorderly sort of people," whose magistracy sorely needed strength-

21. Mass. Hist. Soc., *Proceedings*, LXIX, 128–9.
22. Mass. Hist. Soc., *Collections*, LXXIV, 66–7; *Proceedings*, LXIX, 131.

ening, elicited a forceful reply in the *Boston Gazette*. Pointing out that the critic would place ecclesiastical courts on an equal footing with others, the author continued ironically:

Through favour, we in this country, are unacquainted with those courts; their power hath never yet reached this part of the world, and I pray it never may; we know what persecution the fathers of this country, the good old puritans suffer'd, in the *Stewart* reigns, when party and church faction ran high, from the rigor of *ecclesiastical* laws. Severity was then called *wholesome,* as our author would have it called now: the loss of ears, unmerciful whippings, perpetual banishment and imprisonment, were the *usual* sentences given in those courts, and those were the blessed times when it was holden that a man might be indicted for reflecting on the sentences of ANY court, whether ecclesiastical or temporal. Religious liberty has, however, since those times, been better understood by the people of *Great-Britain;* and it is a question whether *ecclesiastical* courts will ever be suffered to plague the nation any more; at least I hope, we shall never feel the *rigor* of their laws here. I shall therefore leave them and their sentences, together with the sentences of all such courts, wherever they are, to be *reflected* upon by all sober men, as they ever have been and ever will be to all posterity.[23]

A long letter in the *Boston Gazette*, February 21, 1763, a sort of sardonic obituary describing the career of a recently deceased missionary at Braintree, opened a decade of torrid controversy. In the "Apostolic Service" of the Venerable Society, this account stated, the Reverend Ebenezer Miller:

Continued upwards of 30 Years; travelling about the rugged Wildernesses, and Lakes of Braintree, and from Cottage to Cottage, with incredible Toil; endeavouring to turn the miserable Barbarians 'from Darkness to Light and from the Power of Satan', Etc. . . . The poor Natives, aforesaid, are now, alas! left destitute of the Means of Grace and Salvation, according to the Rites and Ceremonies of the Church of England. . . . They fear they shall not have another Missionary sent among them, in which Case, they may perhaps, in the Course of a few Years, relapse into the same savage and barbarous State, in which they were before there was an Episcopal Minister settled here. . . .

23. *Bos. Eve. Post.,* Jan. 14, 1760; *Bos. Gaz.,* Sept. 7, 1761.

P. S. Most of the Natives, spoken of above are of the same Colour, or but very little blacker skinn'd than the English generally are: So that they are often mistaken for English, till you converse with them.[24]

In the *Boston Evening Post* and *Boston News-Letter*, writers rushed to combat such satire and protest the "uncharitable insult" to the memory of a good man.

The author, "T. L.," a resident of Braintree, and not Dr. Mayhew, as his enemies charged, easily overmatched the Anglican contributors in popular appeal and rough tactics. Though he insisted that he had not meant to calumniate the worthy Mr. Miller, he did not deny that he "intended to ridicule the *episcopal Missions* in N. England, than which, all Circumstances being considered, I hardly know of a more proper Subject for Ridicule." An attack on the Venerable Society and its policies was thus mounted, and criticisms of the misrepresentations in its annual sermons and printed abstracts of missionary reports became common fare for the reading public.[25]

VI

No sooner had the Treaty of Paris been signed than the Archbishop of Canterbury prepared to launch his campaign for an American episcopate. On March 30, 1763, he alerted Samuel Johnson:

Probably our ministry will be concerting schemes this summer against the next session of Parliament, for the settlement of his Majesty's American dominions; and then we must try our utmost for bishops. Hitherto little hath been said to them, and less by them, on the subject. Our Dissenters give out the Contrary, and endeavour to raise an alarm. God prosper us, if it be his will.[26]

In the meantime, the Reverend Thomas Bradbury Chandler had been puzzling over the fact that the Church seemed to be neither gaining nor losing in the middle region of America. "This appears

24. *Bos. Eve. Post.*, Feb. 28, Mar. 7, 14, 1763; *Bos. News-Letter*, Mar. 31, 1763; *Bos. Gaz.*, Mar. 7, 1763.

25. *Bos. Gaz.*, Mar. 14, 1763.

26. Schneiders, *Johnson*, III, 269. The peace was concluded February 10, 1763.

to me," he had written the Secretary in the spring of 1761, "in some Measure to be owing to that general Harmony and good Understanding which subsists between the Church and the Dissenters. The Point in Controversy between us, some years agoe was disputed with warmth and some Degree of Animosity. Then the Church visibly gained Ground." Now the Dissenters charitably think "there is no material Difference between the Church and themselves," which is "an effectual Bar against Conformity." By the same token, he feared the moderation of the Church too. "Possibly in Time we may come to think, that the Unity of Christ's Body is a chimerical Doctrine — that Schism is an Ecclesiastical Scarecrow — and that Episcopal, is no better than the leathern Mitten Ordination; or in other Words, that the Authority derived from Christ, is no better than that which is given by the Mob." The best way "to prevent this evil," Chandler thought, would be to bring together "in a manner that is very plain and pathetic" an account of the nature and constitution of the Church of England and the "necessity of authority derived from Christ in the Ministers of it — the nature and guilt of Schism, &c." Here we have the first overt hint of the celebrated *Appeal* he would write in 1767.[27]

In the same newspaper as T. L.'s last sally, Thomas Fleet announced the publication by Green and Russell of *Considerations on the Institution and Conduct of the Society for the Propagation of the Gospel in Foreign Parts,* by the Reverend East Apthorp. His purpose in this tract was to tell the public the truth about the Society, its missionaries, and activities. He declared that he had been forced to write his tract by the frequent mention of the subjects in print and conversation as well as the insult to the memory of Dr. Ebenezer Miller. Brief and mild on the whole, for it was intended to be explanatory only, it irritated the readers to whom it was addressed because of the condescending tone, laced with injured innocence, with which it discussed the S.P.G.'s charter and kindred matters. But when Mr. Apthorp touched on the topic of "our forefathers," he provided a tempting target for any well-charged Congregational pamphleteer:

27. Chandler to Secy., Apr. 6, 1761, S.P.G. Correspondence, ser. B, XXIV; Clark, *History of St. John's Church*, 87–8.

Everyone who knows the history of this Country must acknowledge, that in many respects the Religious State of it is manifestly improved. . . . Religion no longer wears among us that savage and gloomy appearance, with which Superstition has terribly arrayed her.

Though "Fanaticism" and "Hypocrisy" be gone, "much indeed remains to be done in Manners and Piety." [28]

The reaction to the Apthorp pamphlet was immediate, and the Boston journals published many communications from those who felt that their ancestors had been maligned. One "N. H." posed a series of penetrating questions about the "primary intention" of the Venerable Society and concluded that it was a public religion and a tithe-supported clergy. Branding the charges against the Dissenters as false, he did not neglect to emphasize the clergyman's ill-concealed contempt for "the Fore Fathers of this Country." A noble Roman, "P. Q. R.," used an interesting device on April 4, when he claimed to have found a letter in the street from Pierre Le Prenoque of Boston to his brother Jon, "Barper at Kwebek." The anti-Catholic temper of his readers was shrewdly played upon by an early use of French-Canadian dialect. Pierre pretends, like all Roman Catholics, to love the Church of England, "Caus tis so neer kin to our vun." Nevertheless, rumors that "vun Toctur Mayu" will "knock up" East Apthorp and "de Jurch ov Hinclant" proved to be only too correct. This "license of the press" alarmed the rector of Christ Church, for he complained to Dr. Johnson that "I have myself been treated with much rudeness in the public newspapers." Mr. Apthorp, it seems, had learned nothing from the newspaper controversies of 1761; even his correspondent admitted that the young cleric "does not seem yet enough used to writing." [29]

From Stamford in Connecticut came a more considered answer to one part of the *Considerations*. Noah Welles did not have East Apthorp specifically in mind when he preached on the *Divine Right of Presbyterian Ordination* to his congregation on April 10; rather, he aimed candidly and severely at all of the missionaries when he

28. *Bos. Gaz.*, Mar. 14, 1763; East Apthorp's *Considerations* was published at Boston, and in London with Mayhew's *Observations* by W. Nicoll in 1763. The copy cited here is in Library of Congress, Misc. Pamphlets, Vol. 358, pp. 153, 154, 159, 163.

29. *Bos. Gaz.*, Mar. 28, Apr. 4, 1763; Schneiders, *Johnson*, III, 268, 273.

explained to the people, more cogently than anyone had before, the real reasons why the Nonconformists opposed the Church of England:

Had our episcopal neighbours been contented with the peaceable unmolested profession of their own peculiar principles, in a government, remarkable for its lenity, even generosity to dissenters [from the Congregational establishment]; as I trust, you would not have requested it, so I am sure, I never should have thought of introducing this subject into the pulpit, much less of publishing any sentiments upon it. But the restless endeavours of some among them, to draw away persons from our communion, and their unwearied attempts to increase their party, by constantly insinuating to you, the danger of continuing in fellowship with churches, in which (as they would bear you in hand) there is no authorized ministry; no regular gospel administrations; at last convinced me that it was high time something should be publickly offered for your satisfaction, in this important point.

Aware that few of his fellow Congregationalists possessed books vindicating ministerial power, while their Episcopalian neighbors had a general supply of arguments, Mr. Welles clearly assumes that the New Englanders will argue this matter not only as a vital concern of the day but as recreation.[30]

The preacher spoke with moderation and restraint; he avoided all irony, sarcasm, or invective; he made no attempt, however, to conceal a mighty indignation, if not fear, at Anglican hypocrisy in deliberately casting suspicion on the dissenting ministry everywhere. With vast learning, rigorous logic, and use of Scripture, Noah Welles demonstrated that it was the Episcopalians, not "the whole Protestant World," who were out of step in the matter of Presbyterian ordination, which is "no upstart doctrine in the world however its contrary may be." In the face of the irrefutable evidence of history, the minister demanded:

Is it not solemn trifling (or is that too soft a name?) for many among us, who yet would be reputed persons of sense and discernment, still to continue the old clamour against us . . . ? Can we think they are in

30. Noah Welles, *The Divine Right of Presbyterian Ordination Asserted, and the Ministerial Authority, Claimed and Exercised in the Established Churches of New-England, Vindicated and Proved* (New York, Holt, 1763), ii.

earnest who act such an uncharitable part? Who upon every occasion plumply deny, that we have any ministerial power, and so in effect, nullify all gospel administrations among us, and unchurch and unchristianize not us only, but all of our profession and communion throughout the whole world?

In his summation the minister castigated the Yale apostates:

You have no liberty, no right, to forsake the communion of these churches, under the pretence of want of ministerial authority in them; you cannot do it without breaking the covenant, particularly despising the institutions of Christ, and incurring the awful guilt of schism.

This exposition by Noah Welles was of the kind that the hierarchy in Britain could not parry but which allowed free play to the English Dissenters.[31]

Although many people, including East Apthorp, had known that Jonathan Mayhew was preparing a reply to the *Considerations,* Ezra Stiles heard that Mr. Mayhew had given it up. When he observed that the advertisement had disappeared from the public prints, Stiles wrote to the Boston minister to implore him not to abandon his efforts to start a public "opposition to the System Mr. Apthorp so openly avows." Proselyting is as serious over here as if they had tried it in Scotland, Holland, or France. And in this connection the Newporter made a timely observation: "So far as Episcopal Influence can take place the Assignment of all civil, military Lucrative Offices and Honorable Imployments in the Plantations are and will be more and more improved to subserve the proselyting to the Mother Church and while they are using Carnal, may we not use Spiritual Weapons of Defence?" He concluded his exhortation by telling Mayhew that he calls upon him as "a bold and open Advocate." [32]

Ezra Stiles had been misinformed by his Episcopal friends, for one week later, on April 21, three Boston printing houses simultaneously brought out Mayhew's *Observations on the Charter and Conduct of the Society for the Propagation of the Gospel in Foreign*

31. Welles, *Presbyterian Ordination*, iii, 11, 71, 73, 76, 78.

32. Stiles to Mayhew, Apr. 15, 1763, Stiles Papers.

Parts; Designed to Shew their Non-conformity to each other. With Remarks on the Mistakes of East Apthorp, M. A., Missionary at Cambridge. Here was a frontal attack on the Society itself, which the writer sustained in 176 pages "stich'd in blue Paper," with only occasional attention to the author of the *Considerations.* Fired up by the actions of the Episcopalians, open and covert, since 1760, Jonathan Mayhew approached his subject in a mood of high seriousness as one of real importance involving "the prosperity, if not the very being of our New-England Churches." [33]

Beginning in the usual Yankee manner with an inspired text from Galatians, 2:4–5, Dr. Mayhew described the Society's missionaries as:

False Brethren unawares brought in, who came in privily to spy out our liberty which we have in Christ Jesus, that they might bring us into bondage: To whom we gave place by subjection, no, not for an hour; that the truth of the gospel might continue with you.

He added nothing new in his arguments against the S.P.G.'s conduct, which he admittedly drew from Noah Hobart's discourse of 1751, but Apthorp's tract had made it necessary to repeat them. Mayhew stressed the Society's misapplication of nearly £35,000 sterling in New England over a thirty-year period, when the Southern and insular provinces, not to mention the natives, sorely needed assistance. He also introduced and used with telling effect the Puritan version of history. The first New England settlers "fled hither as to an asylum from episcopal persecution, seconded by royal power; which often condescended to be subservient to the views of domineering prelates, before the glorious revolution." Far from being of a loose character and of "a savage and gloomy appearance," our ancestors were a noble and pious people, whose first act was to make provision for the public worship of God. Over here they showed few, if any, of those vices so "common" to Old England. They and their descendants always kept the covenants, and, as Mr. Hobart had proved, "there was very little, or rather no occasion for Missionaries in New England." Still the Society sent them out, and their conduct ill becomes them. As for "this outrage" of Mr.

33. *Bos. Gaz.,* Apr. 25, 1763; Mayhew, *Observations,* 7.

Apthorp's, he is not only "too harsh, but a little impolitic in giving such an account of our Forefathers." [34]

At this point Jonathan Mayhew showed true genius as a propagandist by manufacturing a visual image so potent that no Anglican efforts ever eliminated it from the public consciousness. In berating the S.P.G. for sending its missionaries into the most "populous and richest towns," to set up "altar against altar," he fastened on Cambridge, where there lived only ten Episcopalian families to form the new Christ Church:

The affair of Bishops has lately been, and probably now is in agitation in England. And we see the Society spare neither *endeavours, Application, nor expense,* in order to effect their grand design of *episcopizing* (if I may use the term) all New-England, as well as the other colonies. And it is supposed by many, that a certain *superb edifice* in a neighbouring town, was even from the foundation designed for the *Palace* of one of the *humble successors* of the apostles.

From that day to this Apthorp House has been known as the "Bishop's Palace." This was the kind of distasteful image that stuck in the minds of those simple Yankees who did not concern themselves with the fine points of theological controversy. What would our forefathers think of these "mitred, lordly SUCCESSORS of the fishermen of Galilee," riding in gilded coaches and lording it up at the festive board in the Bishop's Palace? "Will they never let us rest in peace," Mayhew exclaimed as he finished his tract, "except where all the weary are at rest? Is it not enough that they persecuted us out of the old world? Will they pursue us into the new to convert us here? — compassing sea and land to make US proselytes, while they neglect the heathen and heathenish plantations! What other new world remains as a sanctuary . . . in case of need?" [35]

The response to Dr. Mayhew's effort depended, as one might expect, on the faith of the reader. Treasurer Harrison Gray notified Jasper Mauduit that it received the general approbation and applause among all "excepting . . . some bigoted high Churchmen, who most sincerely Curse it." Dr. Samuel Auchmuty of New York

34. Mass. Hist. Soc., *Collections,* LXXIV, xxiv; Bradford, *Mayhew,* 320–21; Mayhew, *Observations,* 9, 13, 39–42, 45–6, 48, 89–96, 114, 116–25.

35. Mayhew, *Observations,* 53, 56, 107, 155, 156.

showed restraint, as he referred to Mayhew as a "person of undaunted Assurance and Impudence," but Henry Caner's fury overcame him as he wrote to the Archbishop of Canterbury that Mayhew "has insulted the Missions in general, the Society, the Church of England . . . in so dirty a manner, that it seems to be below the character of a gentleman to enter into controversy with him." Perhaps this explains why many of the attacks on Mayhew that filled the papers were anonymous. One such writer, later identified as an Episcopal lawyer, John Aplin of Rhode Island, sent some verses to the *Newport Mercury;* a few stanzas mirror the whole:

> Ungrateful Mayhew's desperate Hand,
>   Foul Libels dares to write
> To prove her [the Church's] Charities are Crimes,
>   Her Favors all a Bite.

> By Nature vain, by Art made worse,
>   And greedy of false Fame;
> Thro' Truth disguis'd, and Mobs deceiv'd,
>   Thou fain would'st get a Name.

> Thou who can'st hate for Bounties past,
>   And fresh ones would'st controul;
> The Unborn shall curse thy slandring Pen,
>   And scorn thy narrow Soul.[36]

These lines, reprinted in Providence and Boston newspapers and later in pamphlet form, are but a sample of the abuse that poured on Dr. Mayhew for months, and for every attack there was a counterattack. "Never, sir," wrote the Reverend Edward Winslow to the Secretary of the Society, "did a malignant spirit of opposition to the Church rage with greater vehemence than of late." In the midst of it the Reverend John Beach attempted to answer Welles's still anonymous satire on conformity with *A Friendly Expostulation,* but the storm over Mayhew's *Observations* blew it aside; Samuel Johnson doubted if any reply would be made to it, and he also re-

---

36. Mass. Hist. Soc., *Collections,* LXXIV, 103; Auchmuty to Secy., June 9, 1763, S.P.G. Correspondence, ser. B, II, Pt. I, 15; Perry, *Historical Collections, Mass.,* III, 497, 498, 500–2; *Newport Mercury,* June 6, 13, 20, 1763.

ported that Apthorp, whose tract instigated the row in the first place, knew himself to be an "unequal antagonist" to Dr. Mayhew and "utterly declines any reply." [37]

Nothing was heard from Jonathan Mayhew for six months; then, on October 13, 1763, the *Boston News-Letter* announced his intention to answer his critics and at the same time reported the anonymous publication of *A Candid Examination of Dr. Mayhew's Observations*. Known to be written by the Reverend Henry Caner, its main features were an unfavorable estimate of Mayhew's character and a defense of the motives of the Society. Late in November three Boston printers sponsored *A Defence of the Observations on the Charter and Conduct of the Society . . . against an anonymous Pamphlet falsely entitled, A Candid Examination of Dr. Mayhew's Observations,* and any reader of these exchanges must give the victory to Jonathan Mayhew.[38]

Fully aware of the importance of getting in the first word when propagating the faith, Jonathan Mayhew had sent off a copy of Apthorp's tract and a copy of his own *Observations* to Thomas Hollis as soon as they came from the press, with the comment that reprinting the latter in London "might be of Service in more respects than one." The Englishman went promptly to work but did not publish them that summer because "the Town was Empty"; however, he brought them both out in December.[39]

The Reverend Henry Caner saw to it that the Archbishop of Canterbury also received copies of the two tracts, and after reading them, the prelate discussed the *Observations* "with approbation" of its author at a meeting of the S.P.G., without any mention of East

37. The Reverend Arthur Browne of New Hampshire said Mayhew had licked up the spittle of his Oliverian predecessors "and coughed it out again, with some addition of his own filth and phlegm," but at the same time admitted the design of the S.P.G. to settle bishops, because they were an indispensable part of the British ecclesiastical system. *Remarks on Dr. Mayhew's Incidental Reflections. . . .* (Portsmouth, N.H., 1763), 24, 26, 28–9, cited by Cross, *Anglican Episcopate,* 150–51; *Providence Gazette,* May 28, June 4, 11, 25, 1763; *Bos. Gaz.,* June 20, Sept. 5, Oct. 17, 1763; *Newport Mercury,* Oct. 31, 1763; Schneiders, *Johnson,* III, 268, 272, 273; Hawks and Perry, *Documentary History of Conn.,* II, 47–8.

38. Schneiders, *Johnson,* I, 43–4; Cross, *Anglican Episcopate,* 150, 352; *Bos. Gaz.,* Nov. 28, 1763.

39. Mass. Hist. Soc., *Proceedings,* LXIX, 137, 142; *Collections,* LXXIV, 105, 106.

Apthorp. Furthermore he admitted the truth of Dr. Mayhew's statements and in substance adopted his views about the Society's activities by deciding that no more missionaries should be sent to New England. This news was sent over to Boston on August 8 by Israel Mauduit, who had it from "my friend who went to the Society" — "a chiel amang 'em takin notes." [40]

Writing to Samuel Johnson in September, Secker said that he had read Mayhew carefully and feared that his complaints about the Society's "episcopizing" of New England had some foundation, and that, rather than to try to justify all of the missions, it might be better to excuse them and press the adversaries on other points, especially their un-Christian invective. He also expressed uncertainty about colonial bishops, even though Johnson had been writing that "now must be the time" for them. Lord Halifax was friendly to the idea, but "in the present weak state of the ministry," he will not dare "to meddle with what will certainly raise opposition." To the Reverend Jacob Duché at Philadelphia, the primate added that Dr. Mayhew's pamphlet had increased the probable obstacles that Lord Halifax would confront. The Archbishop understood far better than his missionary followers that, before another attempt for bishops could be made, Jonathan Mayhew had to be answered, and "answered with great mildness else no good will be done. The Dissenters must be treated with no asperity, but assured in the strongest manner of what is very true, that we mean solely to provide for our own Church and not to hurt them." He also comprehended that the Dissenters had succeeded in making a public issue of his plan for American bishops, and that this issue affected imperial politics; without making any announcement, he decided to answer Mayhew himself.[41]

40. Israel Mauduit to Mayhew, Aug. 8, 1763, Mayhew Papers, No. 72.

41. Schneiders, *Johnson,* III, 273, 277–8; Perry, *Historical Collections, Pa.,* II, 390; Israel Mauduit to Mayhew, Feb. 11, 1764, Mayhew Papers, No. 74.

IX

Bishops and Stamps

1764-1766

Most accounts of these three crucial years of American History tend to focus upon certain political decisions taken by the British Ministry and Parliament under the leadership of George Grenville and their reception in the colonies. The First Lord of the Treasury introduced his new program for reorganizing the Empire on March 9, 1764, with a bill for revenue; this passed and was followed by another that became the Currency Act. By May news of the legislation reached Boston and created greater alarm, Governor Bernard thought, "than the taking of *Fort William Henry* did in 1757." On March 22, 1765, Parliament passed the Stamp Act, which was to go into effect on the first of November. Mob violence at Boston, culminating in the wanton destruction of the property of Thomas Hutchinson, and rioting at Newport in August indicated the rising tide of colonial anger, and, had not the objectionable act been repealed on March 18, 1766, there most certainly would have been open and armed rebellion.[1]

These events require no further examination in their purely political and financial aspects, but it is highly important to remember that, pregnant and absorbing as they were, they never wholly diverted public attention in the Northern Colonies from the ecclesiastical question. To long-standing religious grievances, fresh civil ones were now added, and it was the conjunction that produced the crisis. Proof of this assertion can best be demonstrated by tracing one thread, the ups and downs of the scheme for erecting

1. Bernard, *Select Letters,* 9; and in general, Edmund S. and Helen M. Morgan, *The Stamp Act Crisis* (Chapel Hill, N.C., 1953).

an Anglican Episcopate in the colonies, in the London and colonial press from the spring of 1763 to the summer of 1766.

II

Most of the facts and rumors about bishops for the colonies came out of London; they crossed to America via private correspondence, newspapers, magazines, or pamphlets and appeared one to three months later in reprints or in the newspapers at Portsmouth, Boston, Rhode Island, New York, and Philadelphia. As a rule little effort was expended on distinguishing fact from hearsay; contradictions, retractions, and rebuttals followed so closely one upon another that the colonists never knew what to believe.

The news items and rumors of 1763 differed little from earlier ones, but the well-organized committees of correspondence relayed all pertinent communications to their colleagues, and the newspaper printers, now more numerous, were only too glad to reprint them to keep the discussion at a white heat. The agitation had accelerated with Mayhew's attack on the Venerable Society in April, 1763, when he declared that there was "a formal design to carry on a spiritual siege of our churches." In May came the word that a Mr. Fisher of Bristol, England, had left a bequest for the first American bishop. On June 16, the *Boston News-Letter* reprinted an article from London papers signed "Americanus" which contained an exaggerated account of the strength of the Anglicans in the colonies, and that same paper, on June 23, reported that advice from the Hartford Post was that the news of a bishop being sent to America was gaining credit and that the two colleges of New York and Philadelphia had met with great encouragement. The London report that a bishop for North America was to be sent to Quebec was reprinted in several newspapers and was denied just as unequivocally. The Reverend Mr. Craig of Chester, Pennsylvania, wrote to the Secretary of the S.P.G. on July 11 that he was "glad to find in the public prints that the Government intends a Bishop for America." Jonathan Mayhew heard from Dr. Lardner of London by a letter written July 18 that "I think it probable that before long there will be an American bishop; but whether he will be fixed at Boston, or some other place, cannot be foreseen or guessed." The *Boston Gazette,* a paper widely copied, had over two columns in the issue of August 8 demonstrating the close resemblance between Roman and Anglican priests in comparison with the colonial ministers. Using the historical argument as ably as anyone thus far, the writer drove home his point that the excellent religious constitution bequeathed from "our ancestors" must be protected from subversion quite as much as the civil constitution. Another paper stated on August 25 that in London "the Appointment of a Bishop for America, is now talked of more than ever, which, if carried into Execution, must greatly promote the Interests of Religion and Learning," a state of affairs which did not bode any good for Harvard, Yale, and the College of New Jersey.[2]

So it went, week after week, and month after month, serving to keep interested parties in both England and America in a continual state of suspense or expectation. In answer to the inquiry of Stephen Ayrault, Newport Anglican, whether there was any "intention of new Modeling the Provinces," Thomas Collinson, a London merchant, reflected what may be termed the Anglo-American Nonconformist view of the religio-political situation:

There was an intention to effect an ecclesiastical Change thro' out all the Provinces on the Continent. This was to be done by erecting one or more Bishopricks. However I believe the general Design is at present suspended, and part of it only will be executed, in the new acquisition of Canada, where they seem determined to establish the Church of England upon the same Laws and basis as it is here, and one Smith [the Bishop of Down] . . . will be the first Bishop. It will be well if this Erection of a Spiritual Prince prove virtually either productive of any moral or political Good, in the late conquered District. . . . History and Experience evince the contrary. . . . Moreover a Bishop must have a See. This will call for the Allotment of a large Tract of Land. . . . To support all this . . . the Laity must be taxed . . . and sooner or later the Party must submit to Laws fram'd by itself, in its own Spiritual court. . . . If Inconveniences occur upon establishing a Hierarchy in Canada, how much more so if executed in Boston and the other Colonies,

2. Mayhew, *Observations,* 56; *London Chronicle,* March 1, 1763; *Bos. News-Letter,* May 19, June 16, 23, 30, Aug. 25, 1763; Perry, *Historical Collections, Pa.,* II, 350–51; Bradford, *Mayhew,* 269; *Bos. Gaz.,* Aug. 8, 1763.

inhabited by the immediate Posterity of those very Persons who fled from their native Land to avoid a Persecution inflicted upon them by this kind of Church Power.[3]

The effect of this constant threat to their churches and colleges upon the colonists is incalculable, but John Adams, the profoundest of all students of the American Revolution, always insisted that "the apprehension of Episcopacy contributed . . . as much as any other cause, to arouse the attention not only of the inquiring mind, but of the common people, and urge them to close thinking on the constitutional authority of parliament over the colonies." To him this was "a fact as certain as any in the history of North America." [4]

The year 1764 gave no promise of being any freer from tensions than the one just past. Thomas Hollis wrote to his friend Jonathan Mayhew on December 6, 1763, with the positive statement that "You are in no real danger, at present, in respect to the creation of Bishops in America, if I am rightly informed; though a matter extreamly desired by our own Clergy and Prelates, and even talked of greatly at this time. . . . You cannot however be too much on your guard." Before this letter was received, the *Boston News-Letter* carried an extract from a letter from London with the news that the Dean of Bristol, Dr. Tucker, would soon be given the title of Bishop of Albany and be sent over to New York Province to reside in a "Palace" on a salary of £2000 per annum to be paid out of royal quit-rents. This startling news went the rounds of the press. Before long the *Newport Mercury* broadly hinted at what might ensue by reprinting Archbishop Laud's commission of 1634 to supervise the colonies.[5]

At London the readers of the *St. James's Chronicle* enjoyed a lively exchange. It was started in May, 1764, by J. Philiber in reply to an article in the *London Daily Advertiser* which had charged that prelatical influence had voided the charter for the New England

3. Collinson to Ayrault, Sept. 23, 1763, *Commerce of Rhode Island* (Mass. Hist. Soc., *Collections*, LXIX), I, 101–2.

4. Adams to Jedediah Morse, Dec. 2, 1815, Adams, *Works*, X, 185.

5. Mass. Hist. Soc., *Proceedings*, LXIX, 142; *Bos. News-Letter*, Jan. 26, 1764; *N.H. Gaz.*, Jan. 27, Feb. 3, 1764; *Newport Mercury*, June 11, 1764.

Society for Christianizing the Indians. He told them, that though "Liberty is the popular Cry" and one could not conceive of oppression in England, they should look at the injustice done to the New Englanders "only because they are not of our Episcopal Church." Philiber commented severely on the costliness of the S.P.G. in New England, where Dr. Mayhew had said "it is so little needed." The current collection for "an Episcopal College" in Philadelphia also came in for harsh treatment, and the writer concluded that "the Church of England, without a Change in her Articles, cannot properly be admitted in that free Country." Only thirty-six days elapsed before the *Boston Gazette* reprinted the *St. James's Chronicle* account, a lead picked up by the *New London Gazette* in August. Edes and Gill set other advices of London origin before the New England audience at this time, the most savory being a remark from the April issue of the *Monthly Review* which recommended that the first colonial bishops go to the West Indies where there are no sectaries, "for if they should send one, yet a while, to New England, he may perchance find it hotter living there than in Jamaica." [6]

In August news came from London that plans were presently under review for the speedy appointment of one archbishop and twelve suffragan bishops "for the religious government of that country." Such reports stirred up so much excitement that the Strahans deemed it necessary to assure the public on August 14 that there never was a scheme for an archbishop or more than four bishops for America, and those four would be sent only to the Episcopal colonies where they would have no power to tax or to govern Dissenters. One can easily imagine the great relief with which New Englanders greeted this news when it reached Boston in October.[7]

The year of the Stamp Act opened with an announcement in the *London Chronicle:* "It is said the affair of introducing church dignities into North America will soon be investigated," to which ten days later the Strahans added that "a strenuous opposition is

6. *St. James's Chronicle,* May 26, 1764; *Bos. Gaz.,* July 2, 9, 23, 1764; *New London Gazette,* Aug. 17, 1764.

7. *London Chronicle,* Aug. 11, 14, 1764; *Bos. News-Letter,* Oct. 11, 1764; *Prov. Gaz.,* Sept. 29, 1764; *New London Gaz.,* Oct. 12, 1764.

intended to be made." By April fast sailing vessels had conveyed the news to Philadelphia and Portsmouth, from which William Bradford and the Fowles spread it far and wide, along with the ominous report that a commission of eminent clergymen would soon arrive to make "an Enquiry into the general State of Religion, that the Ministry may judge how far it will be necessary to favour them with Indulgences, or to check them with Restraints." Some London sources said George Whitefield might be among those sent because he knew the colonists so well. Such were the ecclesiastical reports reaching America at the very time colonial resentment against the Stamp Act burst out in mob violence.[8]

Meanwhile, a number of anonymous writers used the columns of the *St. James's Chronicle* in August, 1765, to educate the English public in matters of civil and religious liberty. "Philocolonus," reviewing the history of Archbishop Laud and the Puritans, pointed out that "It is an unlucky Coincidence enough of the Politics of the two periods [then and now], that while our Statesmen were laying the Incumbrances upon our Colonies of the *Civil* kind, our *Ecclesiastical Physicians* should be projecting to send them Bishops for their *better Government.*" Favoring colonial bishops, though deploring the methods proposed, "X. Y." also comprehended "the just Fears and Jealousies which the People of America entertain of such an Appointment," but he also deemed it unjust to deprive the colonial Episcopalians of what they wanted and needed if it were of "a private and indifferent Nature." But no hierarchy would ever do for America, "the last smooth and superficial Answerer [Thomas Secker]" notwithstanding. The Americans have been treated very badly, and the English will hear more from them about the Stamp Act and the Admiralty Courts, "A Christian" declared prophetically in October:

But there is a Snake in the Grass, seen or considered by few here, a still great lurking Evil, ready, they fear, to fall upon them, the Establishment of a lordly Prelacy, so justly abhorred and dreaded by Men, who forsook their native Country, beloved Friends, and fair Estates, to enjoy

8. A North Carolina law establishing an orthodox clergy was reported in a newspaper extra at Boston, August 1. *London Chronicle,* Jan. 26, Feb. 9, 1765; *Pa. Journal,* Apr. 11, 25, 1765; *N.H. Gaz.,* Apr. 12, May 10, 24, 31, June 7, 1765; *Bos. News-Letter,* May 16, June 6, Aug. 1 *Extraordinary,* 1765.

the liberty of worshipping the God that made them in the Way they believed he required them, and to avoid the cruel Laud and his slavish Associates, who basely envied them that Liberty. . . . What though a few old Women, here and there, struck with the Pomp of Vestments, have bequeathed Sums more or less, for the Establishment of a Mitre in North America . . . some Men's priestly Ambition . . . [hazards] the Repose and Union of the Mother-Country and her Colonies . . . without precipitating the Independence of the latter, which has been, may be demonstrated by History and Fact, would be the sure Consequence of a lordly Episcopacy introduced among them.[9]

At the same time that the English were being instructed on American matters, all kinds of news about the "amazing increase of Popery" got into the London prints. The success of the English Papists in conversion and in procuring of patrons, items about a "new Mass House" at Bristol — all were gaining attention in the newspapers. Thomas Hollis, who dreaded the Romanists even more than the High-Church Anglicans whom he sincerely believed were inexorably moving toward popery, procured the insertion of the following in two London gazettes:

The leaders of the Episcopal Society for the Propagation of the Gospel in Foreign Parts may consider, whether it might not be more proper to employ their Wisdom and Revenue, for some Years, in recovering their own thinned Flocks from Popery at home, lurking, intolerant Popery, than in Missions abroad, and in episcopizing Protestant Dissenters, and converting the Indians.[10]

When the New Englanders read of the great popish advance in the Mother Country, they shuddered as they thought of the potential threat of the Roman Church in the neighboring province of Quebec. Scarcely had the bonfires of the celebrations of the repeal of the Stamp Act died down when, in July, 1766, there arrived from the metropolitan press by way of New York information that not only would Canada receive a Roman bishop but that "the

9. *St. James's Chronicle,* Aug. 8, Oct. 31, 1765.

10. *London Chronicle,* Feb. 14, 16, May 8, 1764; Feb. 14, 1765; *St. James's Chronicle,* Sept. 10, Oct. 1, 1765; Jan. 7, 14, Feb. 13, 1766; Mass. Hist. Soc., *Proceedings,* LXIX, 167, 169; *Newport Mercury,* Jan. 21, 1765; *New London Gaz.,* July 6, 1764.

Pope's galleys will be employed this summer in carrying over the Bishop . . . together with a proper cargo of relicts, indulgences, and other popish valuables." The semi-official *Boston News-Letter* even published a description and lament over the arrival of the Bishop at Quebec — though he came not in a papal galley. To many colonials every day now seemed to be the fifth of November.[11]

Anti-Episcopal intelligences did not flow merely westward, however. There appeared in the *Boston Gazette*, commencing August 12, 1765, four installments of a masterly essay on religious and civil law, which impressively traced the growth of the "desire of dominion." The author contended that the canon law, "the most refined, sublime, extensive, and astonishing constitution of policy that ever was conceived by the mind of man, was framed by the Romish clergy for the aggrandisement of their own order." The worst possible calamity a people could suffer would be the fusing of the canon law and feudal (aristocratic) law into "a wicked confederacy." The history of New England teaches that the colonists escaped this dire eventuality in the past because of the precautions they took to propagate and perpetuate knowledge in town grammar schools at the public expense.[12]

The writer appealed to the printers to spread the word of the impending fusion of the canon and civil law in America to all readers. "A native of America who cannot read and write is as rare an appearance as a Jacobite or Roman Catholic, that is, as rare as a comet or an earthquake. It has been observed of us that we are all of us lawyers, divines, politicians, and philosophers." This still holds true, even though a party of recently imported High-Church men and high-statesmen "oppose the education of our youth." "Let the pulpit resound with the doctrines and sentiments of religious liberty — Let us hear the danger of thraldom to our consciences, from ignorance, extream poverty and dependence, in short, from civil and political slavery. . . . In a word, let every sluice of knowledge be opened and set a-flowing," for "there seems to be a direct and formal design on foot, to enslave America." The attempts of "a certain Society" to introduce the canon law over

11. *N.H. Gaz.*, June 27, July 4, 1766; *Bos. News-Letter*, July 3, Aug. 7, 1766; *London Chronicle*, Aug. 2, 1766.

12. Adams, *Works*, III, 448, 450.

here have already been exposed by "a writer of great abilities," but further attempts can be expected any day by the Society, the Ministry, or Parliament.[13]

Under the impression that Jeremiah Gridley had written these papers, Jonathan Mayhew sent them to Thomas Hollis, who hailed them as powerful and masterly. A year after Hollis received them, when he was gravely concerned over the outcome of the Stamp Act, he gave the title of "Dissertation on the Feudal and Canon Law" to the essays and caused them to be "incerted in the London Chronicle." The *Dissertation* met with good reception, despite the *Critical Review*'s opinion that it was "a flimsy, lively rhapsody," and in 1768 J. Almon thought it worth republishing as part of "The True Sentiments of America." The real author was John Adams, who, as he explained to Catherine Macaulay in 1770, wrote them "at random, weekly, without any preconceived plan," and sent them to the newspaper "without any correction, and [they were] so little noticed or regarded here, that the author never thought it worth his while to give . . . [them] either title or signature." [14]

In the *St. James's Chronicle* of November 23, 1765, "Americanus" reiterated for the English public the contentions of other protagonists of the colonial position:

It may be undeniably proved, that a great Share of the present Alarms and Commotions in our Northern American Colonies is owing to the Scheme of establishing an Ecclesiastical Hierarchy amongst them, which Scheme has been so blindly and superstitiously persued by some as to divert them from all humane and equitable Attention to the religious Rights and Liberties of their equal Fellow-Subjects; and the Dread of this Scourge, aided by some other unhappy Causes, has driven this brave People almost to Despair and Madness; Nor let any imagine that their Fears were vain, of seeing their Country episcopized; for they had certain Information, that the Point was nearly carried by their restless Adversaries, who had almost obtained for it the Consent of those whom it is not fitting for me to name . . . And whatever milder Notions of

13. Adams, *Works,* III, 448–9, 456, 463, 464.

14. Adams, *Works,* X, 332; Hollis, Diary, II, 450; *London Chronicle,* Nov. 21, 1765; Blackburne, *Memoirs of Thomas Hollis,* I, 291.

episcopal Government their Brethren in the Mother Country may entertain, from having seen it long restrained within bounds by the Civil Power, *they* can never be brought to see it in any other Shape than that in which their Ancestors felt its gloomy Power . . . this very Plea of *uninterrupted Succession* is the thing they dread, as what must inevitably unchurch and unchristianize them, and turn them all into Pagans, Heretics, or worse. . . . These are not fanciful Consequences.[15]

There were, of course, other writers, like "Il Modrato," who claimed to have been "much amused" by the "tragical outcries" and was certain that colonial bishops would be "learned, decent, and charitable," and if not, "May I be buttered like an Uxbridge Roll." Nevertheless the burden of most of the pieces in the two *Chronicles* resembled that of "No Powow," who insisted that since the anxieties of both Englishmen and Americans reached a climax just before the repeal of the Stamp Act, that "these Distresses have first been brought on, and uncommonly aggravated, by the Apprehensions of a prelatical Hierarchy at their Door. The fact is not denied by the cool Authors of their Miseries." "Homolgistes" got in the deadly last word:

When in the Reign of a late Tory-Ministry, the Humiliation of America was determined, it would not have been decent for the Projectors to exclude their trusty Friends, the High-Churchmen, from a Share of the Despotism over their new Subjects, in their own peculiar Way. Accordingly, the Stamping and Episcopizing our Colonies were understood to be only different Branches of the same Plan of Power.

The Stampers needed only the sanction of a law; "the Churchmen, who cannot always carry their Points with the same Tranquility that Statesmen do, are expected to prepare the People for the Reception of their Impositions, by something which has the Appearance of Reasoning." [16]

III

The peaks and depressions on this fever chart indicate accurately the periods of activity by American and English Nonconformists

15. *St. James's Chronicle,* Nov. 23, 1765.

16. *St. James's Chronicle,* Nov. 28, 1765; Feb. 11, Mar. 22, June 14, 1766.

working behind the scenes to protect their religious liberties, as they viewed them, and equally the doings of the hierarchy and the S.P.G. in their campaign for colonial bishops.

London bookshops offered for sale late in January, 1764, *An Answer to Dr. Mayhew's Observations on the Charter and Conduct of the Society for the Propagation of the Gospel in Foreign Parts.* For more than a year the identity of the author remained in doubt, though as early as February 11, when he sent a copy to Mayhew, Israel Mauduit correctly surmised that Thomas Secker had written it. The Archbishop had launched his answer to Mayhew at a time when the London press was full of criticisms of the Society's policy and of the part played by the prelates in the disallowance of the charter of the New England Society: J. Philiber called the action worse than the attacks on John Wilkes! Writing moderately and courteously, the Society's champion sought to defend the Church, to ease Dr. Mayhew's "Horror of its enormous Hierarchy," and to excuse the charge of East Apthorp being "right-reverently inclined." The tract did very little to dispel the suspicions raised by the New Englander, even though the *Critical Review* considered that it was written with "more temper, as well as greater abilities, than the doctor has discovered." And, as one might expect, it earned great applause from the missionaries, who subscribed to having it reprinted at Boston in the spring.[17]

Dr. Mayhew knew that a Boston reprint of the *Answer* was due in May, and so he worked hard to prepare a rebuttal, which came out in June. Facing his opponent frankly and openly, the minister said he found the Butler plan for bishops the least objectionable so far, but he did not think he could depend on its not being enlarged in the next reign or by the next ecclesiastical administration. "People are not usually deprived of their liberties all at once, but gradually, by one encroachment after another, as it is found

17. Dr. Johnson, overjoyed that the Archbishop had taken on our "mighty giant," believed the pamphlet would do more good than any other publication. Thomas Hollis also guessed the authorship of the tract. *An Answer to Dr. Mayhew's Observations on the Society for the Propagation of the Gospel in Foreign Parts* (London; reprinted at Boston, 1764), 4, 56–7; I. Mauduit to Mayhew, Feb. 11, 1764, Mayhew Papers, No. 74; Schneiders, *Johnson*, I, 345; Hollis, Diary, I, 317; *London Chronicle*, Jan. 17, 21, Feb. 11, 28, 1764; *St. James's Chronicle*, Feb. 25, 1764; *Monthly Review*, XXX (Jan., 1764), 45–8; *Critical Review*, XVII (June, 1764), 473; *Bos. News-Letter*, Apr. 13, May 17, 1764.

they are disposed to bear them." It is not strange for us Americans to oppose the plan at its inception; "all prudent men act upon the same principle." He envisaged a drive for Episcopal majorities in the assemblies, which would then impose a sacramental test and perhaps exclude Nonconformists from political preferment and civil office "as in England." Taxation for the support of the bishops and clergy would soon follow. The author did not imagine these evils to be near at hand in New England, "but even remote evils may be reasonably apprehended . . . and are to be guarded against, as much as may be." [18]

For the most part the *Remarks on an Anonymous Tract* were politely though forcefully presented. Once more Mayhew made much of the symbol of East Apthorp's "Bishop's Palace." "As to the *place* of episcopal residence," assuming New England would have one bishop to confirm and ordain, "let me add; since a mission was established at Cambridge, and a very sumptuous dwelling-house (for this country) erected there, that town hath been often talked of by episcopalians as well as others, as the proposed place of residence for a bishop." When he dealt with Anglican proselyting activities among persons under Congregational censure for disorderly or un-Christian conduct, Mayhew grew very indignant. In concluding, he had this to say:

I own, that early in life, I imbibed strong prepossessions against diocesan bishops; i.e., if a full persuasion, the result of free enquiry and reading, that the order itself is unscriptural, and that they have been a pernicious set of men, both to church and state, may be properly called prepossession.[19]

As soon as his *Remarks* came from the press, Dr. Mayhew dispatched several copies to Thomas Hollis. He acknowledged his indebtedness to the Englishman for suggesting that he point out

18. Jonathan Mayhew, *Remarks on an Anonymous Tract, Entitled An Answer to Dr. Mayhew's Observations on the Charter and Conduct of the Society for the Propagation of the Gospel in Foreign Parts* (Boston, 1764), 62–3.

19. Dr. Mayhew also struck hard at the Boston Episcopalians who would not lend him the S.P.G. abstracts, "as if they apprehended, there were some things in them, which should not be too narrowly looked into." In 1759 he had written for twenty-five anniversary sermons to a London bookseller, who replied they could not be bought. Mayhew, *Remarks*, 51, 52, 58, 80.

"the strange impropriety of Episcopal Propagators attempting the conversion of foreign Protestants to Churchism, when their own People at home were perverting yearly to Popery, by hundreds and thousands." It was Hollis's opinion that "this is the sore of sores, by which to gaul at Pleasure and beyond expression our Prelates and Commendamists, when touched by a master," and extracts from the *Remarks* on the prevalence of Papists in England and even of "Popish Bishops" appeared in the London papers. By this time the Boston minister had won for himself a transatlantic reputation as the champion of British Nonconformity, and it is doubtful if even Benjamin Franklin had as many readers.[20]

The angry response of the Anglicans indicated that Dr. Mayhew had earned the title of "master." The Reverend Solomon Palmer of New Haven wrote to the Secretary that "the invidious Dr. Mayhew, of base principles, and it is to be feared, a dishonest heart, has raised a dust to blind men's eyes and stir up a popular clamor." Clamor there most certainly was; East Apthorp frankly admitted to Dr. Johnson that "the affair of soliciting the settlement of bishops among us, is, I perceive a matter of too great consequence and difficulty for me to engage in singly." Soon he departed for England, and he never returned to contest with Yankee Dissenters or to occupy the "Bishop's Palace." [21]

After the passage of the Stamp Act in March, 1765, Jonathan Mayhew withdrew from active participation in the contest. He felt no need to answer East Apthorp's tame *Review of Dr. Mayhew's Remarks,* and refused to comply with the request of some Londoners who wanted him to take up the cudgels against Archbishop Secker, whose authorship of the *Answer* was now well known. He did bring out his Dudleian Lecture at Harvard, *Popish Idolatry,* but, as he wrote Hollis, "I was sufficiently weary of the controversy as I intimated at the close of my 'Second Defence,' not that I thought I had a bad cause to manage; but because I had written three large pamphlets on the subject." He was absorbed now by "the present circumstances of my Country." [22]

20. Mass. Hist. Soc., *Proceedings,* LXIX, 142, 143, 149–50.

21. Hawks and Perry, *Documentary History, Conn.,* II, 62; Schneiders, *Johnson,* III, 284.

22. Mr. Apthorp did leave a wide opening for a reply by counseling the colonial Episcopalians to avoid "rather too much shew and expence in the structure and

The Mitred Minuet

Four mitred bishops, holding hands in the form of a cross "to show their approbation and countenance of the Roman religion," dance a minuet around the *Quebec Bill*. Four other seated bishops watch approvingly. At the left, three figures direct the dance: Lord Bute in kilts provides music with his bagpipes; in the center, Lord North, author of the act, points to the prelates; on the right, an unidentified minister wears a ribbon; while above and behind them the Devil whispers satanic suggestions. Paul Revere, silversmith and celebrated horseman, engraved the satire for Joseph Greenleaf's *Royal American Magazine* (Volume I, October, 1774, at p. 365). He copied it from the *London Magazine* (Volume XLVIII, May, 1774, facing p. 312); the *Hibernian Magazine,* Dublin (Volume IV, November, 1774, facing p. 680) also reproduced the plate.

The relationship between the religious disputations and the "alarming crisis" which pre-empted Dr. Mayhew's energies was depicted by Micajah Towgood in his letter to the dissenting minister in which he felicitated him on the end of the Stamp tax and the fine spirit displayed by the Americans:

Perhaps the reluctance you have shown to have episcopal bits put in your mouth, may have hastened your being saddled with that disagreeable tax. If that order of men had been established, you would probably have found not only the saddle fixed, but riders also mounted on you. How seldom has that order been favourable either to the religious or civil rights of mankind. We think we see a flourishing and great empire rising upon your continent; where civil and religious liberty will be better understood, and more fully enjoyed than ever it has been on this side of the Atlantic. You must increase, but we must decrease.[23]

In June of 1766, Thomas Hollis wrote to his old friend Dr. Mayhew in hopes of persuading him to re-enter the lists, spelling out the merit of securing an "Influence over the Public Prints, which influence has been of the highest Utility on both sides of the Water and may and will and must be again." But probably the Bostonian never saw the letter, for he died prematurely on July 9, 1766. Hollis had been largely responsible for promoting the reputation and renown of Jonathan Mayhew in England, and the Dissenters there, as well as in America, knew that they had lost one of their ablest leaders.[24]

Although several letters sent over to the Dissenting Deputies from New England set forth colonial religious and political difficulties during these crucial years, this body, for the first time, had failed to render signal assistance. From his desk in the Redwood Library, Newport, Ezra Stiles threw out new lines by inviting British authors to contribute books to his institution and by sending

---

ornaments of our Church," and to seek "the just limits of decent simplicity." What of Apthorp House? East Apthorp, *A Review of Dr. Mayhew's Remarks on the Answer to his Observations on the Charter and Conduct of the Society for the Propagation of the Gospel in Foreign Parts* (London, 1765), 48; *Bos. News-Letter,* June 13, 1765; *Bos. Gaz.,* May 27, Aug. 19, 1765; Bradford, *Mayhew,* 367; Mass. Hist. Soc., *Proceedings,* LXIX, 173, 175, 178.

23. Bradford, *Mayhew,* 371.

24. Mass. Hist. Soc., *Proceedings,* LXIX, 190; *N.H. Gaz.,* July 18, 1766.

them such works as Noah Welles's *Presbyterian Ordination*. At other times he gave letters of introduction to young colonials whom he desired should meet the leading Nonconformists of England. On June 20, 1764, he dispatched a letter full of information to Dr. Nathaniel Lardner, in which he disclosed that, while Dr. Mayhew's *Observations* uncovered the S.P.G. plan to episcopize America, "he has not told half the invidious truth nor developed half of this Mystery of Iniquity." Then he put out a feeler for an important extension of his favorite project:

I have tho't that a Connexion between the Brethren in Europe and America would be of no Disservice to either; a Junction or voluntary Coalescence of Interest, or only a friendly Intercourse and harmony between us would cement and form a body in the British Empire too respectable to be dispised or treated with antichristian Rigor and Infringements of Liberty, for that Body bids fair in fifty years Time to become the bigger half of the King's Subjects — and Subjects too of the firmest Loyalty.[25]

Another of the Newporter's correspondents was the Reverend William Gordon of Southwark, a strong proponent of American rights who had access to all kinds of confidential information when he wrote his famous *History*. He tells us that at Portsmouth in April, 1764, the Reverend George Whitefield sent for Dr. Samuel Langdon and Mr. Samuel Haven, the Congregational ministers, and told them in private:

I can't in conscience leave the town without acquainting you with a secret. My heart bleeds for America. O poor New England! There is a deep laid plot against both your civil and religious liberties, and they will be lost. Your golden days are at an end. You have nothing but trouble before you. My information comes from the best authority in Great Britain. I was allowed to speak of the affair in general, but enjoined not to mention particulars.

Dr. Langdon repeated this startling information later in a sermon before the New Hampshire Convention. Gordon believed that the

25. Stiles to Rev. M. Gibbons, Nov. 23, 1763; to N. Lardner, June 20, 1764; to Jos. Jennings, Feb. 26, 1766; to B. Franklin, Feb. 26, 1766, Stiles Papers; Lardner to Stiles, Feb. 28, 1764, Gratz Collection, Case 11, Box 8.

details of the plot were identical with those communicated by an Anglican layman of Newport to Ezra Stiles the next year: general taxation of the colonies, alteration of the chartered governments, the introduction of bishops, tithes for the support of the clergy, and public offices for Episcopalians only. This was the usual set of ideas talked about in the Bernard-Harrison-Howard group, and which Joseph Harrison took with him when he crossed to London in the mast ship.[26]

Writing from Southwark in August, 1764, William Gordon himself had warned Dr. Joseph Bellamy:

There's a general apprehension among our brethren [of the Three Denominations] that the government will send over some Bishops to settle in America. If it is only in the Episcopal colonies, I can't see that the dissenters will have any right to blame, tho' they will have cause to fear, for when once Episcopacy has got a footing, there's no knowing where it will stop. It will be well, should it not prove even a wen to our American territories. . . .[27]

In his twin capacities of agent and leading Dissenter of London, Dennys De Berdt performed many useful acts. One of them was his explanation of the religious origins of the American provinces to Lord Dartmouth, the new president of the Board of Trade in 1765; thereby he put the legend of the forefathers to work in exactly the proper quarter:

All the Colonies but Georgia and Nova Scotia, were originally settled by persons drove from their native Country, in those regions which by oppression stain'd the glory of Britain; though by the like oppressive measures she was supply'd with manufactures from the neighbouring continent to our unspeakable advantage.

Yet oppression was so much the taste of those times, that it drove out a number of the King's subjects, who took shelter in a Desart that they might enjoy their Civil and Religious Libertys, uncontroul'd and unmolested; they were then in a state of nature, under no civil government but what they form'd themselves, when they had establish'd their several

26. William Gordon's work has been criticized for overuse of the *Annual Register;* here, where he had personal knowledge I consider him reliable. *History,* I, 143–8.

27. Baird, "Civil Status of Presbyterians," 617.

Settlements, out of regard to their mother country they sent home their several agents to tender their new acquisitions to their mother country, on certain conditions then agreed on by the several parties; and ratified by their respective Charters, which they look'd on as sacred; and make boast of like our Magna Charta of England.[28]

IV

The behind-the-scenes maneuvers of the Society's missionaries, as well as those of the English hierarchy, did much to confirm the English and American press reports about colonial bishops. Convinced that their long-awaited opportunity had come finally, they used every means to have Bishop Butler's plan put into operation. Though ostensibly in retirement at Stratford, Dr. Samuel Johnson still headed the missionaries, but Thomas Bradbury Chandler, highly esteemed by the Archbishop of Canterbury, now came to the fore as the strategist and organizer of the American clergy. At New York he found young and able coadjutors in Charles Inglis and Myles Cooper, who succeeded to the presidency of King's College in 1763; while Samuel Auchmuty frequently offered wise counsels which did not always please the firebrands. With Samuel Seabury, Jr., of Westchester, and the Smith-Peters coterie of Philadelphia completing the forces, Chandler was ready to open an aggressive campaign for an American episcopate.

The first move was to snow the new Bishop of London, Richard Terrick, and the Venerable Society with facts and arguments in favor of an immediate demand for bishops. Alternately the missionaries reasoned and pleaded; then they inquired when the first bishop would arrive. They also wrote to each other about ways to ensure cohesion. In August, 1764, Dr. Chandler sent Samuel Johnson the good news that both archbishops favored prompt action, and that Dr. William Smith thought another year would bring results. Just five months before the passage of the Stamp Act, confident that an episcopate was only a matter of a few months away, the sanguine Dr. Auchmuty spoke of seeking an act of Parliament for New York "to erect every County at least thro'-out

28. Col. Soc. Mass., *Publications,* XIII, 437.

the Government, into a parish, and make the Inhabitants pay Taxes, toward the support of a minister of the Established Church." A firm eighteenth-century believer in the power of Reason, and an optimist, Thomas Bradbury Chandler thought the way for bishops could be prepared easily by spreading a pamphlet "carefully throughout this Country, fairly representing the only Plan on which American Bishops have been requested." Then, he hoped, "the Affair might be carried without *open* Opposition." [29]

Although the missionaries did not foresee the extent of the colonial reaction to the Stamp Act, they did restrain themselves somewhat and did not express as much confidence in the immediate granting of an episcopate for America after the passage of the act. In July, Dr. Chandler did not anticipate any trouble over its enforcement, but promised to exert himself to "allay the Ferment, and to promote a peaceable Submission to the Higher Powers" if anything should develop. By September, however, after the terrifying August riots at Boston and Newport, Dr. Johnson sent a discouraging report to London. He had been told that John Huske, actuated by Mayhew and his English correspondents,

made such a violent clamour against sending us bishops, that it will probably intimidate our friends from attempting it again. These people will stick at nothing to gain their point. It seems they make gentlemen believe that $1\frac{9}{20}$ths of America are utterly against it themselves, and that it would make a more dangerous clamour and discontent than the Stamp Act itself, etc., than which nothing can be more false.[30]

When the clergy of New Jersey met in their annual convention at Perth Amboy, New Jersey, in October, the younger missionaries, undiscouraged and with great expectations, pushed toward their goal with ever greater vigor. With Thomas Chandler presiding and supported by Messrs. Auchmuty, Cooper, and Seabury from

29. Clark, *History of St. John's Church,* 103; Schneiders, *Johnson,* I, 343–4; Hawks and Perry, *Documentary History, Conn.,* II, 72; Shipton, *Harvard Graduates,* XI, 120; Auchmuty to Johnson, Oct. 26, 1764, Hawks Papers, II; Perry, *Historical Collections, Pa.,* II, 368; Chandler to Bishop of London, Dec. 10, 1764, N.Y., Rhode Island, &c. Fulham Palace MSS, No. 14.

30. Chandler to Secy., July 5, 1765, S.P.G. Correspondence, ser. B., XXIV, 88; Schneiders, *Johnson,* I, 353, 354; Bernhard Knollenberg, *The Origin of the American Revolution, 1759–1766* (New York, 1960), 148, 345.

New York, the members joined in the unanimous decision to send addresses to the king, the two archbishops, the Bishop of London, the S.P.G., and the two English universities about the urgent need of bishops for America. In drawing up the representations, Chandler and Cooper used great freedom with their superiors, as the former confessed to Dr. Johnson in his report of the Convention: "It appears to us that bishops will never be sent us, until we are united and warm in our application from this country — and we can see no reason to expect a more favorable time by waiting." Like Mr. Auchmuty, he feared lest Archbishop Secker think it prudent to delay the application.

The address the Jerseyman wrote to the Venerable Society is typical of the rest. In strong language it asked for a hearing. The missionaries were doing their very best at present, but a bishop had been wanting ever since 1701. Lamenting "the Indulgence of the Government to every other religious Denomination," the Convention argued that "near a Million" professors and friends of the Church of England spread over the continent "continue to be an Episcopal Church without Bishops, and to have Canons without Discipline." Why will the Government not aid us now?

We firmly believe that its best Security in the Colonies does, and must always arise, from the Principles of Submission and Loyalty taught by the Church. The Clergy in general are constantly instilling these great Principles into the People. . . .

Otherwise, "if the Dissenters and Their Adherents at Home must not be offended" by any such "reasonable Request," then the future of the Church of England will indeed be deplorable. The Nonconformists may grow and keep bishops from America and eventually "exterminate Episcopacy throughout the Kingdom and subvert the Church; in which Case the State must again shift for itself as well as it can." [31]

After the strongly worded representations were sent off, Samuel

---

31. "I fear our Friends on the other Side of the water, are too lukewarm. I wish I was there to Rouse them. They should have no peace till it was done," Auchmuty wrote to Johnson, Sept. 2, 1765, before the Convention met. Hawks Papers, II, No. 6; Convention at Perth Amboy to Secy., S.P.G. Correspondence, ser. B., XXIV, 314; Schneiders, *Johnson*, I, 356–7.

Auchmuty began to have doubts about the plan's success, because, as he told Samuel Johnson, "alas! The Southern Clergy, as far as I can learn, are really averse to it. They are now their own pastors." It is "Notorious" that "no Bishop, unless a very abandoned one, could put up with the Lives they in general lead." Even more realistic was the observation of Commissary Charles Martyn of South Carolina: "The Principles of most of the Colonists in America are independant in Matters of Religion, as well as republican in those of Government. . . . I can venture to affirm that it wou'd be as unsafe for an American Bishop (if such should be appointed) to come hither, as it is at present for a Distributor of the Stamps." [32]

Thomas Chandler admitted to being depressed also, for he wrote home that the role of the missionary was increasingly difficult to perform. "It is hard to dissemble any Truths or Precepts of the Gospel; and some of them, relating to Civil Society, it is now become dangerous to declare. . . . Such an Opinion of Oppression, prevails throughout the Colonies . . . and it seems to be the determined, inflexible Resolution . . . never to submit to, what they esteem so great an Infringement of their essential Rights." He hopes for a relaxation of Parliamentary severity, but he does not intend that this should be interpreted as excusing the conduct of his "Countrymen." Still, he believes the Government should have instructed them better:

If the Interest of the Church of England in America had been made a national Concern from the Beginning by this Time a general Submission in the Colonies to the Mother Country, in every Thing not sinful, might have been expected . . . And who can be certain that the present rebellious Disposition of the Colonies, is not intended by Providence as a Punishment for that Neglect.[33]

Thomas Chandler, it seems, placed the failure of the British colonial policy in its religious as well as its civil aspects squarely on the Government, but he joined Dr. Johnson in endorsing the Reverend Jeremiah Leaming who attributed the restlessness and

32. Auchmuty to Johnson, Oct. 7, 1765, Hawks Papers, No. 7; Martyn to Bishop of London, Oct. 20, 1765, Fulham Palace MSS, No. 250.

33. Chandler to Secy., Jan. 18, 1766, S.P.G. Correspondence, ser. B, XXIV, No. 90, 258–62.

temper of the colonials to their resentment of the rapid growth of the Anglican Church, and was agreeable to making "a calm defence of Episcopacy." Mr. Leaming's efforts were "executed to the entire satisfaction of those that put it" upon him, and he managed to incorporate a reply to the Reverend Charles Chauncy's Dudleian Lecture and the several tracts of Noah Welles with it in *A Defence of the Episcopal Government of the Church: Containing Remarks on two late noted Sermons on Presbyterian Ordination,* which John Holt issued at New York in March.[34]

One of the bits of information circulating in 1764 that exercised the New Englanders was Governor Francis Bernard's plan for a colonial aristocracy. Of the proposed independent class of royal placemen, they had certain knowledge from information industriously gathered by Ezra Stiles. The plan also tied in with the secondary plot for resuming the charters of Rhode Island and Connecticut. In the *Newport Mercury,* "Z. Y." (possibly Martin Howard), openly condemned the party strife of Rhode Island and urged every reader to join in facilitating "the general reformation of the colonies, which, we have reason to think, is now under the consideration of our rulers at home." When Francis Alison first heard of this, he was alarmed, for some such "madness" had possessed Pennsylvanians. Within a month of the time that Joseph Harrison sailed out of New London in October, 1764, bearing a petition for the resumption of the charter of the smallest colony, Martin Howard of Newport and Samuel Johnson of Stratford each wrote to Benjamin Franklin, who was about to go to London to have Pennsylvania made a royal colony, for his support. "Would to God you were charged with pleading the same cause in behalf of all governments. . . . that the Government at home, when they take yours in hand may make one work of it," was the cleric's fervent wish.[35]

34. Hawks and Perry, *Documentary History, Conn.,* II, 86.

35. "The Episcopal Party being uneasy that their power here is not equal to what it is in England," Alison said, and fears that the colonies will seek independence ". . . will I fear, induce the English Parliament to produce a test; or at least confine all offices in the army and Revenue to members of the Episcopal Church." Alison to Stiles, Apr. 15, 1764, Stiles Papers; *Newport Mercury,* Apr. 23, Oct. 15, 1764; *Bos. News-Letter,* May 3, 1764; Schneiders, *Johnson,* I, 349; Howard to Franklin, Nov. 16, 1764, Franklin Papers (American Philosophical Society, Phila-

Hard upon the passage of the Stamp Act, intelligence from London arrived at Boston of two schemes "now on the carpet": one was for "introducing temporal dignities" for North America, with Sir William Johnson and General Thomas Gage the first to be honored. The second referred to:

the great talk . . . about the alteration of the Governments to be made in the next Session of Parliament in the Northern Districts of America; it is said there will be but four, viz: Nova Scotia, Province of Main, New Hampshire and New-York — the Massachusetts, Rhode Island and Connecticut are to be divided between New-York and New Hampshire.

Proposals for a colonial nobility, deprivation of charters, and bishops served as added incitements in the August stamp riots at Boston and Newport; indeed the stamp officers came off much easier than those gentlemen suspected of complicity in these intrigues.[36]

The idea of altering the Pennsylvania charter grew out of internal dissensions and provincial politics. The Presbyterians, tired of being "a Body of very little Weight and and Consequence" in spite of their increasing numbers, determined to defend their religious and civil liberties. Meeting on March 24, 1764, at Philadelphia, William Allen and his sons, George Bryan, Dr. John Redman, Samuel Purviance, William Henry, Captain John MacPherson, and other prominent Presbyterian laymen, together with twenty-seven of their ministers, framed a plan for correspondence with friends to give and receive advice for "our Union and Welfare," and they also decided to hold annual meetings. They assembled that August at Lancaster to settle matters for the approaching election, "but the Germans who carry every Thing in that Country that goes by Vote," kept apart and "laughed in their Sleeves at the long Bands and Yellow Whigs," said a hostile observer, who in 1769 charged the Presbyterians with a great con-

delphia), I, 108; II, 127; "Ecclesiasticus," New London, to Joseph Harrison, Aug. 10, 1764, Papers relating to New England, Sparks MSS (Harvard College Library), I, 89.

36. "It is said the subject of divers appeals from North America is the expediency of annexing their several proprietary governments to the Crown of Great Britain." *Lloyd's Evening Post* reported Aug. 14, 1765. *Bos. Gaz.,* Apr. 22, May 27, *Sup.,* 1765. For the August riots, see Bridenbaugh, *Cities in Revolt,* 307, 309–10.

spiracy to dominate the Middle Colonies. He was, indeed, right about the entry of the denomination into Pennsylvania politics as the principal support of the Proprietary party against Benjamin Franklin, Joseph Galloway, and the Quaker Party, which sought a royal charter for the province. As a third force in Pennsylvania, the Anglicans looked upon this contest as a grand opportunity to establish an episcopate, because the Quakers would use it as a check on the Presbyterians, and the latter would not dare to object openly, lest they lose the assistance the Church could offer them against the "combinations of the Quakers." This was the local situation that so perturbed Francis Alison, William Allen, and Samuel Purviance. Failing in politics, frightened by the move for bishops, and deeply agitated over the Stamp Act, the Presbyterians even ventured to approach the Quakers about joint action against the Church of England.[37]

At New York the Anglicans still kept the upper hand with the Presbyterians. An attempt to extend the Ministry Act to the Manor of Philipsburg failed in 1763, but the very idea of it infuriated the Presbyterians. They had grown numerous enough to open a second church, collegiate with the Old Brick, in 1766. On March 18, the Reverend John Rodgers and Joseph Treat, the elders, and a number of deacons and trustees sought a royal charter for the fifth time, indicating in the petition, as before, their need to own land and buildings, and to hold funds. They pointed to the proved loyalty of the English and Dutch Presbyterians who "are a great Majority of the whole number of inhabitants." Only eleven days later, Samuel Auchmuty dispatched a report to the Society about this "Artful Scheme" and its "fatal Consequences" for the Church. He boasted that since he came to Trinity Church several such applications to the governors had been denied and would continue to be unless the new Presbyterian game of having "their dear Sister," the Church of Scotland, use her influence at Whitehall

37. In arguing for a royal charter, Benjamin Franklin considered the demand for bishops reasonable and discounted the effect on colonial opinion as he did so often at this juncture. Moreover, he was in London when the dispute was the hottest. *Cool Thoughts on the Present Situation of Our Public Affairs,* in Sparks, *Franklin,* IV, 88–9; *N.Y. Mercury,* Sept. 25, 1769; *London Chronicle,* Nov. 10, 1764; Perry, *Historical Collections, Pa.,* II, 368; John Stephenson to Dr. John Fothergill, Nov. 14, 1766, Pemberton Papers (Hist. Soc. Pa.), XXXIV.

should succeed. This ought to be prevented. President Cooper has written to the Archbishop on the subject, and Dr. Burton must lend assistance. "The Enemies to Church and State, in these Colonies, have too much power already; to vest them with more, must be very bad policy. Depend upon it, if they once get it, they will make a bad use of it. I know them well." Warned by William Smith, Jr., Dennys De Berdt made every effort to further the petition through his friend Lord Dartmouth, but to no avail. When the New York Council recommended against the charter and the prelates of the Church of England did likewise, the Board of Trade advised the Privy Council to dismiss the petition on the grounds that the coronation oath did not allow the King to consent. No action was taken at this time, which was August 26, but it is worth noting that in the previous April, three of the petitioners, whom we encountered earlier as the Triumvirate, by some means not known, had procured a copy of one of the Perth-Amboy Convention's addresses for colonial bishops. Vengeance would soon be theirs! [38]

The opposition of the militant Mr. Auchmuty to the chartering of any religious body save his own worked at cross purposes with the efforts of Pennsylvania Anglicans to bring the foreign-language denominations into the fold. Having lost out on incorporation in 1759, the Lutherans in the city of New York renewed their application in 1763, only to be refused again because Lieutenant Governor Cadwallader Colden ruled that his instructions did not allow him to comply. Applications for incorporation by the French Huguenots and the Dutch Reformed met a similar fate that year. Concurrently over in Pennsylvania at Reading, the missionary Alexander Murray discussed a coalition of the Lutheran and Episcopal churches with the Reverend Henry Mühlenberg. At Philadelphia the Reverend Richard Peters and Jacob Duché courted the German ministers, and the former made overtures to Pastor Mühlenberg a year later.

38. *Ecclesiastical Records,* VI, 4046–8, 4067; Auchmuty to Secy., Mar. 29, May 5, 1766, S.P.G. Correspondence, ser. B, II, Pt. I, 63–4, 71–3; Col. Soc. Mass. *Publications,* XIII, 316–17, 324; *Acts of Privy Council,* 1745–66, pp. 758–61; Auchmuty to Johnson, Apr. 30, 1766, Hawks Papers, II, No. 8; *The Case of the Scotch Presbyterians of the City of New-York* (New York, 1773) gives the pertinent documents in an appendix, 10–36; for the memorial to Scotland, see Historical Manuscripts Commission, 14th *Report,* App., Pt. X, 38.

When a Lutheran accepted Episcopal ordination and went to Nova Scotia to shepherd the German settlers there, Dr. William Smith took hope for a union. He thought that many Lutheran ministers would unite with the Church if prospect of the ocean voyage (which they had experienced in coming to America) for ordination did not stagger them. But the embittered Lutherans of New York remained hostile to any such merger, and their countrymen of the Reformed Church found it necessary to place Johannes Rohrbach, baker, and William Corcelius, "Pot-Baker," under bonds to administer their property at Manhattan. The only Episcopal success with the foreign Protestants occurred when Provost Smith endorsed the petition of St. George's German Reformed Church of Philadelphia to affiliate with the Church of England after Easter, 1766, when only an episcopally ordained and licensed clergyman would conduct services from the Book of Common Prayer. The Venerable Society had failed to take advantage of a great opportunity, and, worse, had angered many of the German pastors and their congregations.[39]

V

As one reads through the colonial newspapers for the postwar years, one senses a gradual awakening of what not inaccurately may be called a national feeling. For the most part unconscious, this emerging temper occasionally took tangible form, notably in the election sermon that Noah Welles preached to the Connecticut Assembly, May 10, 1764, on patriotism. "We must not only wish, but act for our country's good," said he. The times demand of the patriot "public-spirited actions and services, equal to our abilities. . . . But wherever public-spirit prevails, liberty is secure." Fully aware of transatlantic and intercolonial religious issues, the minister looked beyond the borders of Connecticut, even beyond those of New England, in his exhortation. Many other men, lay and clerical, were commencing to articulate for the first time what they had long been thinking; all that was needed was some overt

39. *Ecclesiastical Records,* VI, 3890–91, 3908, 3999–4000, 4048, 4083–4; Mühlenberg, *Journals,* I, 665–6, 687; II, 50, 370; Perry, *Historical Collections, Pa.,* II, 367, 396–7, 411.

action to cause an upsurge of American sentiment. This the Parliament provided on March 22, 1765.[40]

The most momentous single fact about the stamp episode was the nearly unanimous revulsion of colonial opinion against the measure and those who promoted it, those who were to enforce it, and those in the colonies who openly supported it. Apart from royal officials, the one organized group to resist the popular trend was the missionary clergy. "In Newport," Ezra Stiles recorded, "was the greatest Body of Advocates for the Stamp Act of any Town in America. The Customs house Officers, officers of the three Men o'War, and about one hundred Gentlemen Episcopalians openly called the opposition Rebellion &c." In Massachusetts, John Adams noted that "the church people are, many of them favorers of the Stamp Act at present"; while on Long Island a missionary recognized his denomination as an alien element, and that *"we Europeans* are of the weak Side considering the Power of the People." [41]

Almost without exception, the Anglican clergy actively opposed any resistance to the Stamp Act by counseling passive obedience and branding any other conduct as disloyal. The Reverend Edward Winslow, stationed in John Adams's native Braintree, proudly claimed in January, 1766:

During this time of confusion among us I have endeavoured to urge upon the people of this Mission a special regard to the duties of loyalty to his Majesty, and deference and affection to the supreme Government of our Mother Country, together with a becoming confidence in the Wisdom of Justice of our superiors there, to alleviate or remove any burdens.

At Rye, the Reverend Ephraim Avery took "a great deal of Satisfaction" in having kept his people calm; while in New Jersey Thomas Chandler, though regretting the action of Parliament, worked heroically to hold his flock in line. The Reverend Charles Inglis of New York preached loyalty at the same time that he chided the

40. Noah Welles, *Patriotism Described and Recommended* (New London, 1764), 12, 16, 17.

41. Ezra Stiles, The Stamp Act, Stiles Papers; Adams, *Works,* II, 168; Reverend James Lyons of Brookhaven to Secy., Nov. 12, 1764, S.P.G. Correspondence, ser. B (Italics mine).

Government for its failure to anticipate trouble by denying the colonies bishops. "Even good policy dictates this Measure, were the Interest of Religion and our Church left out of the Question." Most missionaries feared that repeal of the Stamp Act would lead to further distress and possibly the extermination of the Church in the Northern Colonies. One thing above all is clear: the colonial clergy formed the core of the American Tories, who really date from this time.[42]

Clerical opinions and actions such as these were no secrets kept from those of the other side, nor was the attitude of the Anglican hierarchy unreported in America. Henry Cruger, Jr., wrote from Bristol to his father in New York, February 14, 1766, about the Stamp Act, to say that all of the king's immediate servants, among them nine bishops, "were for carrying Fire and Sword to America, with this Argument, that since you snarle and begin to shew your Teeth, they ought to be knocked out before you are able to bite." About the same time, a writer inquired in the *London Chronicle* whether American submission to the Stamp Act would not have meant "a further degree of humility, under the pastoral instruction of a Bishop?" News like this agitated the colonists, as did the uncontradicted report from London, March 6, that eleven of the thirteen bishops in the House of Lords opposed repeal of the obnoxious legislation.[43]

The Dissenters' response to the Stamp Act was immediate and unequivocal; that of the Anglican clergy made it irrevocable. The Nonconformists took due notice that the provisions of the new law requiring the affixing of stamps to all documents, including copies of wills, "in ecclesiastical matters in any court of probate, court of the ordinary, or other court exercising ecclesiastical jurisdiction within the said colonies," directly implied the Government's intention of erecting such church courts in the near future. They also noticed the £2 stamp required "for every skin . . . on which shall be engrossed . . . any donation, presentation, colla-

42. Perry, *Historical Collections, Mass.,* III, 521; Chandler to Secy., Jan. 18, 1766; Avery to Secy., Mar. 25, 1766; Inglis to Secy., Apr. 19, 1766, S.P.G. Correspondence, ser. B. II; Hawks and Perry, *Documentary History, Conn.,* II, 90.

43. *Commerce of Rhode Island,* I, 141; *London Chronicle,* Feb. 15, 1766; *Bos. Gaz.,* Apr. 28, 1766; *N.H. Gaz.,* May 1, 9, 1766.

tion, or institution to any benefice, or any writ or instrument for the like purpose, or . . . any degree taken in any . . . seminary of learning." While the "destructive" new law was being printed at New London, the *Providence Gazette* "hoped the PULPIT will take the contents thereof into consideration." Joseph Harrison, one of the best-informed men on America, gave his considered opinion in 1768 that "the dissenting clergy, were the chief Instruments in promoting and spiriting up the People to that Pitch of Madness, Tumult, and Disaffection which so generally prevailed . . . during the Stamp Act Times." [44]

In the eyes of the dissenting ministers, no distinction between religious and civil liberties any longer existed; LIBERTY itself faced extinction, and they rushed to its defense. Their willingness to fight was evident in Jonathan Mayhew's statement to Hollis as late as January, 1766, that the act "will never be received without much blood-shed." "The Presbyterians of New England have wrote to all their Brethren throughout the Continent, to Endeavour to stir up the Inhabitants of each Colony to act as they have done," Governor William Franklin reported to his father in London. Governor William Bull of South Carolina bore him out in this opinion. In Pennsylvania the ousted stamp agent, John Hughes, believed that the Stamp Act Congress was "indefatigably pushed forward by the Presbyterians principally." Through their connections with the dissenting printers of such "flagitious" newspapers as the *Boston Gazette* and its counterparts in the other seaboard towns, the ministers aroused what John Adams described as "the unconquerable rage of the People." "The people," said the lawyer, "even to the lowest ranks, have become more attentive to their liberties, more inquisitive about them, and more determined to defend them. . . . Our presses have groaned, our pulpits have thundered, our legislatures have resolved, our towns have voted." One of the New York triumvirate held that "this single Stroke has lost Great Britain the Affection of all her Colonies," and another boldly stated in a news-

44. A public meeting at New London resolved in December, 1765, "It is presumed no Person will publicly, in the Pulpit, or otherwise, inculcate the Doctrine of passive Obedience, or any other Doctrine to quiet the Minds of the People, in a tame Submission to any unjust Impositions." Clipping from a Boston newspaper in Sparks MSS, II, 3; Macdonald, *Select Charters*, 283; *Prov. Gaz.*, Aug. 24, *Extra.*, 1765; Harrison to Bishop Terrick, May 12, 1768, Fulham Palace MSS, Box II, No. 216.

paper article that, if no accommodation could be reached, "then the Connection between them ought to cease, and sooner or later it must inevitably cease, and perhaps end in the total Ruin of one or both of them." [45]

VI

Three crowded years had witnessed many disturbing events, which inexorably affected public opinion in the colonies. Through them ran the persistent theme of church and state, which reached a grand crescendo at the time of the Stamp Act. That a sinister Episcopalian influence was felt throughout the land, the Dissenters sincerely believed. They detected it in the rush of Anglican placemen to America and the news that the Church of England needed outlets for a surplus of young curates; they detected it in lay and clerical intrigues against the charter governments of New England; they detected it in the prelatical opposition to dissenting efforts to Christianize and educate the Indians; they detected it in the encouragement of Roman Catholicism in Canada; they detected it in the renewal of the old game of proselyting; they detected it in the curt denial of the legitimate requests of the New York Lutherans and Presbyterians for incorporation. In the London and American press they found confirmations, often lurid, always interesting, of their worst fears; and some of them fought hard with their pens in the spectacular pamphlet war.

By means of a superb intelligence service, the Dissenters came to know a great deal about the private sentiments and furtive activities of their adversaries in America and Britain. They were quickly and correctly informed about the schemes of the missionaries and the Archbishop of Canterbury to settle bishops in the colonies, forays which prompt use of the press and political conference forestalled by the creation of a powerful anti-Episcopalian public opinion on both sides of the ocean. Then, too, they resented the reluctance or incapacity of the government to silence Thomas Secker

45. Mass. Hist. Soc., *Proceedings,* LXIX, 183; William to Benjamin Franklin, Sept. 7, 1765, Morgans, *Stamp Act Crisis,* 157; J. Almon, *Collection of Papers Relating to the Public Dispute Between Great Britain and America* (London, 1777), 9, 46, 48, 49; *N.H. Gaz.,* Sept. 19, 1766; Adams, *Works,* II, 154; William Smith, *Historical Memoirs from 15 March 1763 to 9 July 1776* (New York, 1956), I, 29, 30; "Freeman" (attributed to John Morin Scott), *N.Y. Gaz.,* June 6, 1765.

and the clerics of the Venerable Society, whose intrigues had proved so untimely.

The Revenue Act of 1764 and the new methods of administering the Navigation Laws, the Currency Act, and the Stamp Act — political and financial measures all — oppressed a colonial public whose emotions, stimulated for over a half-century, had only recently been raised to the fever point.

This complex series of occurrences made the existence of a plot very real to the Americans, and should make it understandable to us today. The Grenville Acts turned the colonial protest into a nonsectarian channel for the first time. They were like the pieces of a mosaic suddenly falling into place. The colonial Dissenters could now see the threat of both mitre and sceptre; and their English brethren saw it too. An explosive situation such as this could never have resulted merely from the Parliamentary legislation of 1764–65, which did, however, add political fuel to the already smouldering fires of social and religious discontent.

Contemporaries on both sides perceived this truth. When he congratulated Samuel Langdon on "the Eminent Deliverance of Public LIBERTY," Ezra Stiles added, "Had a Parliamentary Revenue been established independent of the assemblies, both civil and religious Liberty had expired. £4000 or 5000 per ann. would soon have been appropriated for half a dozen Bishops on this Continent and a long string of &c. &c. &c. would have come in to throw the Ballance of Things in favor of Episcopacy and against our Denomination which compose three Quarters of the Inhabitants." And who can prove him wrong? Over at London the *St. James's Chronicle* had this to say: "The stamping and episcopizing our colonies were understood to be *only different branches of the same plan of power.*" Perhaps the soundest conclusion about politics and religion came from Francis Bernard: "The popular leaders have laboured so successfully, that the very principles of the common people have changed; and they now form to themselves pretensions and expectations which had never entered into their heads a year or two ago." [46]

We may recall here with this age, which knew its Greek, what Epictetus taught centuries before: that things in themselves are not nearly so important as the ideas people form of those things.

46. Stiles to Langdon, May 24, 1766, Stiles Papers; Bradford, *Mayhew,* 372; Bernard to Lords of Trade, Sparks MSS, II, 14.

X

THE GREAT FEAR

1766–1770

Religion and politics could never again be distinguished one from another after the uproar created in the colonies by the Stamp Act, and it would be idle to seek an understanding of the next series of political clashes between England and America without examining their ecclesiastical implications and the effect of the latter upon public opinion. The mounting Anglican militancy and political activity is best observed in the province of New York, to which the center of interest shifted after the middle of 1766. While comparing New York and Massachusetts as colonies of which he might like to be the royal governor, Francis Bernard asserted: "there is this Material Difference between the two Provinces": in New York "the Spirit of Jealousy and Opposition" to government "actuates Men of Rank and Ability, in Massachusetts it works only with Men of Middling or low Rank." This condition would, he believed, make New York the more difficult to govern; here Bernard referred to the Livingston or Presbyterian faction, whose leadership was furnished by the now notorious Triumvirate.[1]

No local issue gave rise to more sectarian bitterness than the decision of the Governor's Council, acting under the relentless prodding of the Episcopal clergy, to deny incorporation to the Presbyterian Church. When the Board of Trade and Plantations had referred the Presbyterian petition back to the Governor, Sir Henry Moore, for an opinion, Samuel Auchmuty, complaining and boasting at the same time, told Dr. Johnson how "Cooper and myself worked Day and Night to furnish our Friends [on the Council] with Reasons

1. Edward Channing and Archibald C. Coolidge, *The Barrington-Bernard Correspondence* (Cambridge, Mass., 1912), 142.

why the prayer" should not be answered. But the Archbishop of Canterbury had done nothing, despite his knowledge that Lord Dartmouth saw no impropriety in granting the request. However, Dr. Auchmuty had no doubt of success. Three days later the Presbyterian ministers offered additional information to the Governor, but they were ignored. On March 24, a committee of the Council, from which the one Presbyterian member, William Smith, Jr., was excluded, reported adversely to the Governor, and, as a result, on August 26 at the Court of St. James, the Privy Council dismissed the petition. About six months later, Ezra Stiles received a letter indicative of Presbyterian wrath over this Episcopalian in-fighting: "They retarded and threw cold Water upon the Application. The Bp. of London appeared [twice] openly at the Board of Trade in Opposition." The writer did not know, of course, that Thomas Secker, a former Nonconformist, had voted against it in the Privy Council.[2]

The Livingstonians attributed the delaying tactics of the New York Council and its refusal to allow the Presbyterians to see the committee report before it went off to London to the approaching dissolution of the Assembly and the election, in which James De Lancey, a leader of the Episcopalian faction, would be a candidate from Manhattan. Naturally the latter was reluctant to bring the matter into the open, but the irate Presbyterians made it a fundamental issue in the election of 1768. "An Old Whig" addressed the freeholders in a newspaper: he did not care a fig about a candidate's denomination, "but he *must* be an Opposer of every Measure repugnant to that Equality of Privileges, so essential to the Peace and Prosperity of a Country, planted by good and loyal Protestants of various Persuasions." Although John Livingston and John Morin Scott gained office, so did James De Lancey and three other Episcopalians. The Reverend Charles Inglis was jubilant about the victory over "the Independents," declaring: "It was the greatest Over-

---

2. Dr. Auchmuty inquired anxiously in October, 1767, about the fate of the Presbyterian application in London, because with "great trouble and difficulty we frustrated their attempt in this province." Auchmuty to Secy., Oct. 17, 1767, S.P.G. Correspondence, ser. B, II, pt. I, 115; *Ecclesiastical Records*, VI, 4067, 4081, 4083–4, 4098–9; Auchmuty to Johnson, Feb. 14, 1767, Hawks Papers, II, No. 11; Stiles, *Itineraries*, 253; Charles Chauncy, *A Reply to Dr. Chandler's Appeal Defended* (Boston, 1770), Appendix, iii–vi.

throw that Faction ever received here. They were outwrote as well as outvoted. This, with their late Disappointment in an Application to the King for a charter, has enraged them to a Degree of Phrenzy." [3]

The Rector of Trinity and his associates steadily pursued political interests. When, in July, 1768, a member of the Council lay dying, Dr. Auchmuty asked the Bishop of London to watch over the next appointment, "lest we have another presbyterian run upon us. The whole Council (except one) belong to the Church. That one came in, in a Clandestine Manner; another may do the same. . . . It is a vile policy to trust avowed Republicans with posts under the British Government." When writs for another election went out in January, 1769, he cautioned Sir William Johnson about an Albany assemblyman who had imprudently and warmly attached himself to "the L——n party; which you Sir know, are Enemies to Monarchy and the established Church. . . . The presbyterian party are determined . . . to try all their Strength at this Election. Scot and others here oppose the Delancey's, Crugers, and the Church Interest. . . . Every One that has any Loyalty, or regard for the Established Church of the Nation, must think himself in Duty bound to oppose the ambitious Scheme of a most restless and turbulent sect." [4]

Once again, the Anglicans carried "the Election all Hollow against the Miscreants," including the four city seats. When the Assembly next met, Colonel Lewis Morris, like his forebear, an Episcopalian, moved to exempt all denominations from taxes for the support of ministers of persuasions to which they did not belong. Skilled Anglican politicians converted this into a bill repealing the Ministry Act; they counted on it being lost in the Anglican Council. Upon its defeat, "a Majority" of the freeholders of Richmond County and 182 from Westchester requested a bill during the winter of 1769–70 such as Lewis Morris had proposed; again, after the Assembly had passed such a one, the Council allowed it to die after a second reading. In March the *New York Gazette* printed the pro-

3. Chauncy, *A Reply*, Appendix, v; *New York Journal*, Mar. 3, 1768; Inglis to Johnson, Mar. 22, 1768, Hawks Papers, II.

4. Auchmuty to Secy., July 9, 1768, S.P.G. Correspondence, ser. B, II, pt. I, 125; Auchmuty to Sir W. Johnson, Jan. 4, 1769, Gratz Collection, Box 21, Case 8.

ceedings relative to this affair, because, as the contributor said, "not above one Person in five Hundred" ever reads the Assembly's printed record.[5]

Sooner or later, any institution so enmeshed in provincial politics was bound to become involved in the great scramble for land between New York and New Hampshire over the region now known as Vermont. In the grants that Governor Benning Wentworth of New Hampshire made for 128 towns, he reserved in each of them a proprietary share for the S.P.G., one for a settled clergyman, and one for a glebe. When New York received jurisdiction over the area, William Samuel Johnson, son of President Johnson, filed a petition laying claim in the name of the Society for the Wentworth grants and charging that New York made grants without these for "public Uses," thus depriving the Society of the "greater and better part" of their rights. Notice of this petition disturbed Governor Moore, because it implied criticism of his land policy with respect to the Church. Mr. Auchmuty, in defense of the Governor, wrote the Secretary about Sir Henry's handsome gift of "a whole Township consisting of 2400 Acres" to Trinity Church and a large tract to King's College; these, the Rector asserted, equaled anything that Benning Wentworth had done. In a New York Council meeting of October, 1769, De Lancey insisted "that all our Grants in that Country [Vermont] ought to contain Reservations for the Society and Episcopalian Minister," but William Smith, Jr., opposed this measure on the grounds that the Council had no such orders and that the Society ought to make its own applications to the Crown for those "Reserved Parcels." Here was the basis for many openly expressed suspicions that the Church of England planned a big land grab in the western wilderness acquired from France.[6]

5. After the election of 1770, "Watchman No. 2" charged that the clergy spread a story about John Morin Scott that "if he got into the Assembly (the credulous were made to believe) the ruin of their church was inevitable; and it would prevent their getting a Bishop." *N.Y. Journal,* Apr. 12, 1770; James Sullivan & Alexander C. Flick, *The Papers of Sir William Johnson* (Albany, 1928), VI, 575; Smith, *Historical Memoirs,* I, 61, 66, 70; *N.Y. Mercury,* Jan. 9, Feb. 6, 1769; *N.Y. Gaz.,* Dec. 18, 1769; Jan. 8, Mar. 26, 1770; *Ecclesiastical Records,* VI, 4176–9.

6. In "The Exercise of a Spiritual Dominion not consistent with the Ends of Civil Government," a London writer gave the example of New York, where "Non-Episcopalians" were 10 to 1, but the latter engross power, and the Government

At the same time the Anglicans were carrying on a politico-ecclesiastical venture among the Indians. It revolved around Sir William Johnson, whose interest commenced in 1764, when he hoped for a bishopric in Canada to supply clergymen to replace the Jesuits among the Iroquois. In 1766 he was made a member of the Venerable Society and displayed almost as much zeal as the missionaries. The well-known failure of the Society to propagate the gospel among the natives, taken with the denial of the opportunity to the Massachusetts Congregationalists, pointed to a real need for some activity among the Six Nations. Samuel Auchmuty and Mr. Inglis agreed that more could be accomplished with them than by locating missions in settled communities and incurring the resentment of the Dissenters. For a time Sir William had seemed to favor Eleazar Wheelock's schemes for educating Indians, but he gradually transferred his support to the S.P.G. and tried to interest the Earl of Shelburne in the Society's proposals for conversion. Dr. Auchmuty had no time for Wheelock or his Indian henchman, the Reverend Samson Occom, who raised so much money in Britain, and he had nothing but contempt for "Wheelock's Cubs . . . Surely such Wretches ought not to be suffered to go among the Indians." The good doctor also expressed his fear to the Secretary that "Wheelock and his associates will engross the Indian Country, and lay the seeds of Schism so deep that it will hereafter be impossible to eradicate them." [7]

Thomas Chandler's *Appeal to the Public in Behalf of the Church of England in America* (1767) so impressed Sir William Johnson that in January, 1768, he offered 20,000 acres of land to support a bishop, provided the Society could get the Crown to grant an equal amount. This offer delighted the missionaries, and the Archbishop of Canterbury memorialized Lord Hillsborough for advice

---

grants them land at the same time it denies the majority a charter merely to hold private donations. *London Chronicle,* Dec. 9, 1769; Matt B. Jones, *Vermont in the Making* (Cambridge, Mass., 1939), 138–9, for petition of S.P.G. to Privy Council, Mar. 17, 1767 (P.R.O.:P.C., 1:53), Appendix B, 408; Auchmuty to Secy., June 12, 1767; Jan. 23, 1768, S.P.G. Correspondence, ser. B, pt. I, 105, 119; Smith, *Historical Memoirs,* I, 56.

7. *N.Y. Col. Docs.,* VII, 600, 1002; *Sir William Johnson Papers,* IV, 812; VI, 457; Perry, *Historical Collections, Pa.,* II, 400–401; Schneiders, *Johnson,* I, 372, 373; Auchmuty to Secy., July 9, 1768, S.P.G. Correspondence, ser. B, II, 126.

about approaching the King for the land, but the government did not wish to alienate any more colonial groups at this time. One would give much to learn just what went on in October at New London where Sir William spent "some weeks in quest of health" — Dr. Thomas Moffat and Duncan Stuart, customs collector, and, for two weeks, Joseph Harrison, forgathered and "planned and regulated all these Colonies into a system" which they dreamed of effecting. The baronet had encountered the most rabid Tory group in all America, and their promptings may explain his increasing aggressiveness in urging the authorities at home to support an American episcopate.[8]

The appointment by the British Government of a Roman Catholic missionary to the Nova Scotia Indians at a salary of £100 a year provoked suspicion and criticism in the colonial press. It gave the Reverend Mr. Inglis the idea that funds for the red men under Johnson's oversight ought also to be forthcoming, and he journeyed to the Mohawk country to discuss plans with the agent. Elated by the Indians' request for clergymen, Dr. Chandler notified the Society in June, 1771, that the two men had in preparation a memorial for the Lords of Trade: "The Motives that we urged in Favor of the Plan are chiefly of a Political Kind, as Considerations of a religious Nature, it is feared will have little Weight." [9]

II

The Society's missionaries fondly believed that their open display of loyalty during the late crisis now definitely entitled them to the episcopate they had always needed, only this time it would come as a reward. Charles Inglis led off from New York with an impassioned letter to Dr. Daniel Burton demonstrating that the prin-

8. *Sir William Johnson Papers,* V, 837–9; Schneiders, *Johnson,* I, 433, 435; Klingberg, *Anglican Humanitarianism,* 108–9; *N.Y. Mercury,* Nov. 6, 1769; *Bos. Gaz.,* July 5, 1773.

9. Inglis and Cooper to Secy., June 12, 1770; Chandler to Secy., June 24, 1771, S.P.G. Correspondence, ser. B, II, XXIV, 99; Inglis to S. Johnson, Oct. 10, 1770, Hawks Papers, II; and for the whole episode, Lydekker, *Inglis,* 48 ff. On the Nova Scotia incident, see Inglis to Secy., Mar. 8, 1770, S.P.G. Correspondence, ser. B, pt. 1, 234, 237; *N.H. Gaz.,* Nov. 9, 1770; *Bos. Gaz.,* Nov. 9, 1770; Mar. 18, 1771 (Letters of "Dick Vorrish" to "Jere O'Sullivan").

cipal value of an episcopate is as "a Means to securing the Affections and Dependance of the Colonies," and shortly thereafter he strengthened the false impression held at home by emphasizing that few Dissenters objected to bishops if they would not have to support them. Everywhere, from Maryland to New Hampshire, clergymen deluged the secretary of the S.P.G. with every imaginable argument for bishops. "The Dissenters very well know that the sending of a Bishop to America would contribute more to the increase of the Church here than all the money that has been raised by the Venerable Society," one insisted; another maintained that a bishop would win over to the Church of England the lads bred in the dissenting colleges who cannot at present afford to go to London for ordination. In a mood of self-deception, Thomas Chandler attempted to moderate the reluctance of the Bishop of London by telling him that "the disposition of this Country has been grossly misrepresented and that Bishops might be introduced even at this time without any considerable opposition, or clamor," because the Presbyterians and Independents, who are not one-half of the population, "are the only people who would be disobliged thereby." [10]

In their annual conventions, the Episcopal missionaries discovered a forum for the expression of their collective sentiments that enabled them to sway the Venerable Society and the Anglican hierarchy. At Shrewsbury, New Jersey, on October 1, 1766, Thomas Bradbury Chandler presided over the largest convention yet held, with delegates from five colonies present. After listening to the reading of a letter from the new Bishop of London, Richard Terrick, which explained that their Perth-Amboy address had reached London at a most inopportune moment and tended "to throw difficulties in the way of government," they heatedly resolved that "the only crime we are conscious of is, that we belong to the national church." Not only did they advise Bishop Terrick that "we hope . . . it is not unseasonable now, at this time of public tranquility, to renew our request," but they also agreed upon a program to bring about the much-desired American episcopate. Declaring that "Commissaries cannot be of any considerable service," they totally rejected

10. Inglis to Secy., Apr. 19, May 1, 1766, S.P.G. Correspondence, ser. B, II, Pt. I, 204, 209; Perry, *Historical Collections, Pa.,* II, 404–6; Clark, *History of St. John's Church,* 114–15; Schneiders, *Johnson,* I, 361.

Provost Smith's plan to unite New Jersey with Pennsylvania, and, though seriously divided by this alienation of Dr. Smith and Richard Peters, the majority of the convention accepted Chandler's vigorous bid for leadership. Nothing short of complete episcopacy suited this new Gideon, and by endorsing the Johnson-Chandler Plan to gain Bishop Butler's goal the Shrewsbury Convention committed the missionaries to a militant policy: (1) to quiet the fears of the American public that the presence of bishops would endanger religious liberty; (2) to enlist the Southern clergy in the crusade; and (3) to address Churchmen in England about their needs and difficulties. In a document of seven quarto pages drafted by the presiding officer, the Shrewsbury Convention dispatched the Plan to the Bishop of London. The American clergy were determined to take united action to secure bishops for the Church in America.[11]

All Anglicans, however, did not see eye to eye on the Johnson-Chandler Plan. The abrupt dismissal of Dr. Smith and his proposals produced a permanent coolness in Philadelphia. In telling Dr. Burton about the work of the convention, Dr. Auchmuty remarked: I was not there "but I find it high time to check their Career *a little* — they take too much upon them. . . . Doctor Smith is very angry with them . . . he has good reason to be so. . . ." He also conveyed to Dr. Johnson his misgivings that the warm and importunate proceedings of the Chandlerites "will hurt the cause," but "they are not to be put out of their way." The veteran of Stratford, in complete sympathy with the program and conduct of his Jersey lieutenant and unswayed by the New Yorker, urged the Archbishop of Canterbury to unite the English prelates in advocating that one or more bishops be sent to America, "even if they are refused or not permitted. If the Church must go into a state of open persecution, she must, and ought, rather than to let her bishops cease to be, or not to be, where it is necessary they should be, or dwindle into mere worldly political creatures. . . ."[12]

The year 1767 found the Episcopalians optimistic and eager to

11. Clark, *History of St. John's Church*, 118; Schneiders, *Johnson*, I, 389–91; "Seabury Minutes," 144–6.

12. Clark, *History of St. John's Church*, 124; Schneiders, *Johnson*, I, 370–71, 379, 382; Auchmuty to Secy., Dec. 20, 1766, S.P.G. Correspondence, ser. B, II, Pt. I, 92; Auchmuty to Johnson, Jan. 3, 1767, Hawks Papers, II, No. 10.

carry out their program. A "Special Convention" held at King's College in March strengthened their organization by combining the annual meetings of New York and New Jersey into one, to which delegates from other provinces would be invited. In May at the first "United Convention," also held in New York, the delegates took security precautions to ensure that in the future no copies of minutes or addresses should fall into the hands of unauthorized persons. Implementation of the Johnson-Chandler Plan began with the appointment of President Myles Cooper and the Reverend Robert McKean of Perth Amboy to solicit the support of Governor Horatio Sharpe and the parochial clergy of Maryland and to explain to the South the plan for an American episcopate. The first article of their program went into effect when a fall convention at Elizabeth Town unanimously endorsed a tract written by Mr. Chandler to explain episcopacy to Americans in general but to Southerners in particular. By December the Northern newspapers carried a full report of the doings at Elizabeth Town. They even mentioned the application to Britain for one or more bishops and Dr. Chandler's daring challenge that any objections should be placed before "the tribunal of the public." [13]

III

At Lambeth Palace, Archbishop Secker was very much aware of the temper of his inexperienced missionaries; yet he did everything in his power to get them what they — and he — wanted. In letters to Dr. Johnson and Provost Smith, written in July, 1766, he explained that he had sought permission to send out a colonial bishop, but it could not be done "when you and we were on fire about the Stamp Act." Therefore, too, the Perth-Amboy addresses were not presented, though the King was apprised of their contents. "Earnest and continued endeavours have been used with our successive ministers, but without obtaining more than promises to consider and confer about the matter." The King's attitude is most

13. "Seabury Minutes," 154–9; Chandler to Secy., Oct. 16, 1767, S.P.G. Correspondence, ser. B, XXIV, 91; Bos. News-Letter, Dec. 24, 1767; Prov. Gaz., Dec. 26, 1767; Newport Mercury, Dec. 28, 1767; New London Gaz., Jan. 15, 1768; Connecticut Journal, Jan. 8, 1768.

favorable, even to agreeing to the sending of a Protestant bishop to Quebec, where there are few Dissenters. Toward the end of the Grenville Ministry, there was a plan for an ecclesiastical establishment in Canada, "on which a bishop might easily have been grafted," but the Earl of Shelburne opposed it in committee as not favorable enough to the Papists. In his reply, Dr. Johnson urged making greater efforts with the hierarchy since the ministers seemed so indifferent; "I do know that the Dissenters plume themselves upon the weight they have with the ministry, and their zeal and venom against episcopacy." [14]

The Archbishop continued without letup to use every temporal means to procure bishops for America. In the winter of 1767 William Samuel Johnson arrived in England as the special agent of Connecticut and attorney for several colonial interests. Because of his father's eminence, as well as for his own legal talents, the English prelates received him warmly, and the S.P.G. appointed him its agent for the New Hampshire lands. Dr. Johnson warned him in June that Richard Stockton, a trustee of the College of New Jersey, was in Scotland, "I suppose as the synod's agent against bishops." He has been with Lord Shelburne who, "it is said here with triumph," has declared that "there is no manner of occasion for any bishops here." The clergyman suggested to his son that in his correspondence with his lordship he might "think it proper to endeavour that he may be convinced of the greatness of his mistake, and the great necessity of our being provided for." When Archbishops Secker and Drummond waited upon the Secretary of State in the fall to recommend "the appointment of Bishops in America," the former noted in his diary that they "could make no impression at all upon him." Apparently Richard Stockton and London Dissenters had met with a more sympathetic reception from "the Jesuit of Berkeley Square" than Lawyer Johnson or the prelates. [15]

Until his death on August 3, 1768, Thomas Secker kept up the fight for the colonial church, but without success. Thomas Hollis, who had known him many years, always insisted that it was the Archbishop who inspired the writing of Chandler's *Appeal* and

14. H. W. Smith, *Life of Smith*, I, 396; Schneiders, *Johnson*, I, 378; III, 286–8.

15. Schneiders, *Johnson*, I, 48, 405, 412; Secker, Memoirs, f. 74 (Lambeth Palace Library), quoted by Norman Sykes, *From Sheldon to Secker*, 210.

planned to allow copies of it to "run lurking among the ministry" and his London partisans. Hollis was also convinced that "these friends were above measure astonished at the industrious craft of Leviathan in procuring the *Address* of a Body of the Episcopal Clergy in N.A. at this nice juncture to second his operations at home."

The Archbishop's influence carried on after his death. His will created something of a sensation in both England and the colonies: he left £2000 to the Venerable Society, half of it to help establish a colonial bishop. He also left instructions that his letter to Horatio Walpole of 1751 be published. This news crossed the Atlantic at the time that the late Archbishop was under fire in the *London Chronicle* for attempting to episcopize America. "Phornia" held that Secker "could scarcely be ignorant that the passion and vehemence with which the project was espoused by some of the Church of England missionaries was one great ingredient of the jealousy entertained by the Colonies for some time of the designs of the Mother Country." He had, in his *Answer* to Jonathan Mayhew, misrepresented the Americans as barbarous and put his weight and authority behind the scheme. When Rivington published the letter to Walpole separately in 1769, it was widely reprinted by the colonial newspapers. The next year it provoked a rejoinder from Archdeacon Blackburne, republished in 1771 by Dunlap in Philadelphia. This searing critique reopened the whole controversy in England. By this time the late prelate appeared to many as more of a liability than an asset to the Episcopal cause in the New World.[16]

IV

The events of 1765–66 had convinced the Presbyterians that more than ever they must settle internal disputes and seek allies

16. Hollis to Eliot, May 25, 1768, Hollis Papers; *London Chronicle*, Aug. 13, Sept. 10, 1768; Sept. 16, 1769; June 29, 1769; *A Letter to the Right Honourable Horatio Walpole, Esq: Written Jan. 9, 1750–1, By the Right Reverend Thomas Secker, D.D., L.L.D. Lord Bishop of Oxford; Concerning Bishops in America* (London, 1769); Francis Blackburne, *A Critical Commentary on Archbishop Secker's Letter to Horace Walpole* [London, 1770] (Philadelphia, 1771). The copy of the last in the Library of Congress was sent by Jasper Mauduit to Ebenezer Hazard, Presbyterian bookseller of New York. *N.Y. Mercury*, Sept. 11, 1769.

if they were to stem the Anglican advance. At Philadelphia Francis Alison knew all about the Perth-Amboy addresses, as did the Reverend John Rodgers and William Livingston at New York. The Presbyterians in Pennsylvania also winced under the charges of the Tories that they were the principal inciters of the colonial opposition to the Stamp Act. Their attempt at settling their private difficulties having failed in 1764, they determined to try again inasmuch as the Stamp Act Congress had proved that intercolonial co-operation could be achieved. Their next move was truly a revelation of the new-found spirit of Americanism.

The union of the two Presbyterian synods in 1758 had been hailed by Ezra Stiles as a great step forward in a letter to Francis Alison in which he spoke of trying to bring all Protestants together. In the *Christian Union* he spread his plan before the public, and no individual was more impressed with it than the Philadelphia educator, who took a prominent part in the abortive organization of Pennsylvania Presbyterians in 1764. Two years later, however, his efforts brought lasting results.

May was the fateful month at Manhattan in 1766. The encouraging attendance of eighty ministers and elders at the annual meeting of the Synod of New York and Philadelphia outshone the display that a dozen or so clergymen made at the New York Episcopal Convention; and such news of the synod's meeting as they could get filled the Anglicans with agony and alarm. In truth, each party suspected and feared the worst from the machinations of the other.[17]

The Presbyterians from Philadelphia brought into the synod on May 30 an overture prepared by Francis Alison, who was absent because of illness, for obtaining some correspondence with the consociated churches of Connecticut, together with the draft of a letter to them. The synod enthusiastically approved and appointed the Reverend John Ewing and Dr. Alison's brother Patrick to present the letter and confer about it, and also a larger committee, headed by Dr. Alison, to handle any future negotiations with the Connecticut ministers. The General Association of Churches, meeting at Guilford, Connecticut, in June, agreed to meet with the Presbyterians; thereupon Patrick Alison and Ewing went on to Newport

17. *Journals of Captain John Montrésor* (N.-Y. Hist. Soc., *Collections*, 1881), 370; "Seabury Minutes," 141–2; Schneiders, *Johnson*, I, 378.

to consult with Ezra Stiles. Because the Presbyterians made no secret of their grand design, the news got to Lambeth Palace by August, and the Archbishop asked Provost Smith to provide him with more details.[18]

After listening to what Messrs. Ewing and Alison had to tell him, Ezra Stiles sent them off to Boston to talk with Charles Chauncy and Andrew Eliot; then, as might be expected, he dispatched a long letter to Francis Alison containing his ideas about union. Late that August, Samuel Purviance arrived from Philadelphia with a reply from Dr. Alison which requested an answer "by the first conveyance." In it the Vice Provost said:

I am greatly for an Union among all the anti-Episcopal Churches and I think it may be Effected without so much difficulty. . . . Let the Bottom to build on be broad: No authority be claimed by the body, but what is suasive. . . . The grand points to be kept in view, are the promoting religion and the good of the Societies, and a firm union against Episcopal Encroachments.

The Church of England are determined to introduce Bishops. I saw a Copy of an address sent to the two Archbishops, to the two universities, to the King, the bishop of London and the Society for Propagating the Christian Religion. In this the Clergy of the Provinces of New York and New Jersey assert that their Number is near a million; That it is unsafe for the King to neglect this part of the English Constitution; for Monarchy and Independence are inconsistent and they put them in mind of the times when the King and Episcopacy suffer'd the same enemies. . . . I could not get a copy from Dr. Smith, who favor'd me with a sight of it; but he told me in plain terms, that they were determined to have one, or more Bishops; and that the Lutherans would join with them and even the Quakers &c. We could not be uneasy had they fifty Bishops in America; tho' with that they would make the first Tryal in Jamaica and Antigua where there would be no opposition. What we dread is their political power, and their courts, of which [native-born] Americans can have no notion adequate to the mischiefs that they introduce.

18. *Records of the Presbyterian Church,* 351, 364; *Records of the General Assembly of the Colony of Connecticut* (Hartford, 1888), 57–9; H. W. Smith, *Life of Smith,* I, 397.

In a letter arriving a few weeks later, Alison declared that the Episcopalians "are unwearied in their applications from America, and their power is great in England; and every lawful method should be used to keep free from that yoke of Bondage." [19]

The arrangement of any accommodation between sectarian bodies is a most delicate matter, and no one realized this better than Stiles. He journeyed to the Commencement at Harvard College in July to sound out the Massachusetts ministers. The Reverend Ebenezer Pemberton, formerly of New York but now of Boston, thought that the most that could be accomplished at that time was the opening of a correspondence, "unless the plan was very acceptable indeed." "All are agreed to a Union in some form or other but I found none ripe to pronounce the plan," which Stiles knew "must take the nature of a social Confederacy between and among *three* distinct, separate, and independent Bodies." Chauncy Whittelsey and the Newporter's other Connecticut correspondents hesitated lest a union of American Dissenters be looked upon "with an evil Eye at Court . . . as a Twin Bro. of the civil Union of the Colonies" broached at Albany in 1754, "both begotten by a Commonwealth man" and intended for colonial independence. Might it not induce rather than prevent the sending of bishops? [20]

The extensive correspondence of the Rhode Island pastor at this stage indicates that Alison and the Presbyterians had turned to him as the one man whose ideas, knowledge, connections, residence at Newport, and capacity for negotiation, they could count on to work out a practical procedure for bringing the churches together. He accepted the responsibility and worked diligently and unobtrusively. He had collected the sense of the Congregational ministers and Connecticut Associations about union by October: they all agreed upon the expediency and necessity for it, but differed radically over the means for achieving it. Thereupon Stiles drew up some "Articles of Union," which he hoped would meet most objections: (1) There shall be held a meeting of the Congregational, Consociated, and Presbyterian pastors annually in September, to which each association or presbytery shall accredit two delegates. (2) The meeting shall "circulate" from New York to Philadelphia, New Haven, Hart-

19. Alison to Stiles, Aug. 7, 20, 1766, Stiles Papers.
20. Stiles to Alison, Aug. 26, Sept. 5, 1766, Stiles Papers; Stiles, *Itineraries,* 591.

ford, and Boston. (3) The delegates shall have no authority to exercise dominion or jurisdiction over any churches or ministers. (4) The "general Design" of the body shall be to gather and circulate information about "the Public State" of the cause and interest, to emphasize its loyalty to the King and submission to the law, and to publish a summary of its deliberations and resolves. This, the author thought, would preserve the liberties of individual churches which so concerned the New England Congregationalists, many of whom still opposed anything resembling the Heads of Agreement.[21]

About thirty representatives from the Presbyterian and Consociated churches gathered at Elizabeth Town, New Jersey, because of the presence of smallpox at New York. Considering the current fear of Roman bishops in Canada, it was symbolic rather than coincidental that the convention opened on the fifth of November. Delighted with Stiles's proposals, Francis Alison secured their adoption with few amendments as the "Plan of Union" — "the delegation from Connecticut behaved with great moderation and candor," he stated later. Copies of the Plan went out for approval by constituent bodies in New England with the request for them to send delegates to the next meeting at New Haven on September 10, 1767. "I had a most friendly letter from Dr. Chauncy," Alison told Stiles in reporting on the meeting, "and promising at their next [Boston] meeting in May to form a Plan of Union to comprehend all of the associated Congregational and Presbyterian Churches in North America and in Great Britain." Alison also mentioned that the "Congress" had agreed it would be advisable to publish "some remarks" on the plan in five cities "to shew that we are alarmed with just fears, lest the introduction of Bishops affect our civil and Religious liberties," and asked what Stiles's New England connections thought should be done.[22]

Next came a campaign of education to win reluctant New Eng-

21. Alison to Stiles, Aug. 7, Oct. 8, 1766; Chauncy to Stiles, Sept. 29, 1766; Stiles to Chauncy, Oct. 24, 1766, Stiles Papers.

22. Alison sent with his report a copy of the Butler Plan for bishops, taken from the *Annual Register* (1765), which William Allen had given to him. Alison to Stiles, Oct. 30, Dec. 4, 1766; Stiles to Chauncy, Nov. 3, 1768, Stiles Papers; the proceedings of this and succeeding meetings are in *Minutes of the Convention of Delegates from the Synod of New York and Philadelphia, and from the Associations of Connecticut; Held Annually from 1766 to 1775 Inclusive* (Hartford, 1843), 8-17.

landers for the union, and this Ezra Stiles undertook virtually by himself. The burden of the argument he used appears in a letter to Noah Welles:

I have for several years been of opinion that the public Litigation of the Episcopal Controversy will become necessary in America. The Situation and Exigencies of our Churches for this and the next succeeding Generations at least, I expect will require as vigilant and spirited a Defence as the first hundred years of the Reformation; tho' I am sensible I herein differ from some of my Brethren. The Episco[palians] are determined to have Bishops if possible — are intriguing the appropriation of one twentieth of the Lands this side Mississippi or 3 Rights out of 60 to the Churches, as a foundation of a future Revenue for the Episcopal Hierarchy.

As for the validity of Presbyterian ordination:

To convince our Adversaries is not to be expected as a Body — to confirm our Brethren and establish the rising Generation in Puritanism both in Polity, Doctrine and Holiness, is our Employment.

He begged Welles to devote his talents to the cause of union. "I am stationed in a very difficult part of the Lord's Vineyard," Stiles said, and must work silently among these Newport Episcopalians who want to change the charter. The squeeze was now on Welles, for three weeks later he received from his friend Livingston a copy of one of the Perth-Amboy addresses for a bishop: "a worse than useless Commodity in a New Country and a very expensive one in every Country." [23]

The great problem was to convince the Congregational ministers of Rhode Island, Massachusetts, and New Hampshire to join a body superior to the single church. To accomplish this, or as Stiles quaintly put it in Indian metaphor, "to brighten the Chain," the Newporter rode the "circuit." He succeeded in bringing over most of the New-Light Connecticut doubters, and, though the New Lights dominated the General Association, he saw to it that the Old Lights received ample protection under the plan. All of them had read

23. Stiles to Welles, Nov. 22, 1766, Stiles Papers; Livingston to Welles, Dec. 12, 1766, Johnson Family Papers, No. 84.

the *Christian Union,* and, moreover, the fact that he took no part in public activities stood him in good stead, for he had no real enemies. "It was well we did not set the press at work last fall, as the Brethren of the Synod proposed," he admitted to Ebenezer Devotion in August, "the End is answered without it." [24]

Swayed by the members of the Boston Association, the Congregational Churches turned out to be the stumbling blocks to complete union. They feared that British authorities might look upon the proposed Convention of Delegates as they had upon the Massachusetts Synod of 1725. Besides they thought such a meeting unnecessary; the same ends could be reached "by more silent Methods" of correspondence. Furthermore, the English Dissenters were reporting that an American episcopate "is laid aside for the present." But primarily they regarded the plan as not broad enough to prevent the exercise of spiritual dominion over individual churches; they did not fear absorption in a consociation or synod so much as "a new Police, which will subordinate Synods, G. Assembly and Convention to it." It would be an ecclesiastical equivalent of the Albany Plan for continental political union. Aware of this sentiment, Stiles prevailed upon Alison to make the Plan of Union more catholic by a provision forbidding the Convention from offering any advice about the internal workings of separate churches. Nevertheless, the Congregationalists declined to send delegates to New Haven. They did fraternally and sincerely declare their sympathy with the union and made it clear that they shared a common fear of episcopacy. The Convention assembled at New Haven on September 10, at the Yale Commencement. Francis Alison preached eloquently on religious liberty, and then the delegates proceeded to adopt the amended Plan of Union. The Convention also planned the next year's meeting and appointed committees to correspond with the association at Boston and brethren in New Hampshire, Rhode Island, Connecticut, New York, New Jersey, and Pennsylvania. To the most important committee, composed of Messrs. Alison, Ewing, and Treat, fell the duty of communicating with "our friends in Great

24. Stiles to Alison, Mar. 11, 1767; Alison to Stiles, June 19, 1767; Stiles to Devotion, Aug. 19, 1767; Stiles to Welles, Aug. 12, 1767, Stiles Papers; Isabel Calder, *Letters and Papers of Ezra Stiles* (New Haven, 1933), 15–16.

Britain," especially Dennys De Berdt and the merchant Samuel Smith.[25]

In spite of Ezra Stiles telling him that he considered the New Haven meeting as successful as could be expected, Francis Alison was pessimistic. Our Plan of Union, the Philadelphian wrote, is generous enough to hold the churches in union, "but this I fear is the reason that so many are afraid of it; it will not give importance to Shibboleths and nostrums, but will serve all in the dead Sea of forebearance and equality." But the optimistic Newport minister took the view that "the Embrio is formed." Later Ezra Stiles recorded that he aspired in time to accommodate "ten or a dozen different Controversies in our Churches from Virginia to New Hampshire." After all, in England, the Independents and the Presbyterians broke into two bodies when the Heads of Agreement failed, but on all common problems of Dissent they and the Baptists worked as one body.[26]

By the time that the Convention of Delegates met at Elizabeth Town in September, 1768, it was a going concern. Now fully organized, the union was a fact. At the first meeting at the Jersey community in 1766, Thomas Bradbury Chandler was out of town and such secrecy was preserved that he could find nothing out on his return. At New Haven in 1767, Dr. Johnson, who was there attending an Episcopal Convention, was chagrined that he could learn nothing about the Dissenters' meetings other than that there was a "grand design of coalescing or union" to report to Archbishop Secker. All the Anglican leaders knew, however, that silence on the part of the Dissenters did not mean retreat.[27]

The Anglicans did break through the mystery surrounding a lay organization formed at New York. Dr. Johnson learned of it from Samuel Auchmuty, who wrote him on July 22, 1769: "Doubtless you have heard of the New Solemn League and Covenant, that the

25. Chauncy to Stiles, Mar. 30, June 29, 1767; Stiles to Welles, Aug. 12, 1767; Stiles to Alison, Aug. 27, 1767; Stiles to Chauncy, Sept. 4, 1767; Stiles Papers; *Convention of Delegates*, 17–20; Schneiders, *Johnson*, I, 419.

26. Stiles to Alison, Oct. 3, 1766; Alison to Stiles, Dec. 12, 1767; Stiles to Welles, Jan. 15, 1768, Stiles Papers.

27. Schneiders, *Johnson*, I, 395–6, 419.

old [Reflector] leaven here have enter'd into, and the Methods (unlawful I will be bold to say) that they have pursued to draw in all the Dissenters, N: S: E: W: to join them." A dissenting minister, disapproving of the "Society of Dissenters," as they called themselves, confided the story to the rector, who immediately gave the news to Gaine's *Mercury*. The newspaper broke the story in the July 24 issue, printing the articles of organization, a circular letter distributed by the Society, and promising to give an account of "The Trades and Occupations of the Gentlemen" concerned in it, who were obscure men. The printer also struck off separate copies which Dr. Auchmuty sent off on the Falmouth packet for the Archbishop and the Bishop of London.[28]

Just how obscure William and Peter Van Brugh Livingston, John Morin Scott, Alexander MacDougall, Samuel Loudon, the printer, and the Presbyterian preachers of Manhattan were, only the Anglicans might say. The Dissenters had banded together in February, 1769, "for the preservation of their common and respective civil and religious Rights and Privileges, against all Oppressions and Encroachments by those of any Denomination whatsoever." Ultimately they aimed to create new societies which would send delegates to the parent organization (as to the Convention of Delegates). The articles provided for weekly meetings and a standing committee of correspondence. The circular letter set forth the "terrifying" prospect of losing religious liberty, and it also publicized the fact that several members had contributed to reprinting Thomas De Laune's *A Plea for Non-Conformists*, which Garrat Noel, bookseller, had for sale.[29]

In communicating his discovery to Samuel Johnson, Dr. Auchmuty exhibited a truculence matched only by his exultation: "we are ready for a newspaper war. . . . They are already beat out of their field"; and we are now superior. It is true that the Society was caught off guard, and the members tried to recover by candidly admitting in the next issue of the *Mercury* their open avowal of both the articles and the letter. The writer of the Society's reply

28. Auchmuty to Johnson, July 22, 1769, Hawks Papers, No. 17; Auchmuty to Secy., July 22, 1769, S.P.G. Correspondence, ser. B, II, 137.

29. Herbert L. Osgood, "The Society of Dissenters, founded at New York in 1769," *Amer. Hist. Review*, VI (1900–1901), 498–507.

charged that whoever published the first story had done so either to cause the members uneasiness or to deter them from their design, but that he would be disappointed in both. They welcomed the publicity; then the Dissenter took the offensive:

Wou'd that same Gentleman be kind enough to favour the Public with a Copy of the [Anglican] *Convention's* Petition for a Bishop to the University of Cambridge, the impartial World wou'd have an Opportunity to Judge, whose *Candour* and *Moderation* is the greatest.

The Society are not unfriendly to the religious Liberties of any Protestant Church whatever, tho' they openly profess themselves oppos'd to the Scheme of establishing Diocesan Episcopacy in America, and are determin'd to endeavour, by all lawful Ways and Means in their Power to prevent it. . . .

The priest and his Tory friends rejoined on August 7. They pointed out that the Society of Dissenters never had intended to publish the articles themselves and that not "even the *Standing Committee of Dissenters* in England (from whom it seems you expect singular Services)" can prevent this tale of disloyalty from reaching "the Royal Ear of Majesty itself . . . and then perhaps our gracious Sovereign may understand what his good Subjects the *American Whigs,* have long been driving at." For once, the Episcopalians seem to have silenced the Dissenters, since nothing further was heard of the Society after the *Mercury* ran an account in September of the Presbyterian "plots" of 1764 and 1766. It had been beat out of the field.[30]

Meanwhile, the Bostonians were not as ready to believe that the Episcopalians had failed and laid aside their designs for an American episcopate as they were when they refused to join with the consociated churches of Connecticut and the Presbyterians in a union against the Church of England. Andrew Eliot communicated the alarm felt to Dissenting friends in England, and he also hinted to some of the members of the General Court that they ought to state their position. In accord with, if not in answer to, Eliot's suggestion, the House of Representatives of Massachusetts Bay, in the

30. Auchmuty to Johnson, July 22, 1769, Hawks Papers, No. 17; *N.Y. Mercury,* July 31, Aug. 7, Sept. 25, 1769; *Pa. Chronicle,* Oct. 9, 1769.

course of framing instructions on January 12, 1768, to its colonial agent, Dennys De Berdt, gave expression to its collective fears:

The establishment of a Protestant Episcopate in America is also very zealously contended for: And it is very alarming to a people whose fathers, from the hardships they suffered under such an establishment, were obliged to fly their native country into a wilderness, in order peaceably to enjoy their privileges, civil and religious: Their being threatened with the loss of both at once, must throw them into a very disagreeable situation. We hope in God such an establishment will never take place in America, and we desire you would strenuously oppose it. The revenue raised in America, for ought we can tell, may be as constitutionally applied toward the support of Prelacy as of Soldiers and Pensioners: If the property of the subject is taken from him without his consent, it is immaterial, whether it is done by one man or five hundred; or whether it be applied for the support of ecclesiastick or military power, or both. It may be well worth the consideration of the best politician in Great-Britain or America, what the natural tendency is of a vigorous pursuit of these measures.

Both in the colonies and in England men such as Samuel Adams and Thomas Hollis saw to it that this extract appeared in the newspapers.[31]

Ezra Stiles summed up the year 1769 when he entered a notation in his diary under the heading "Trials and Difficulties" — "Concern for the Congr. Chhs., and prevalence of Episcy and Wickedness." Colonial Dissenters were striving to extend their connections with European Protestants. The Presbyterian Synod sent letters in May to sister synods in Scotland, North Ireland, Holland, Geneva, and Switzerland. It also made overtures to churches in South Carolina in an effort to bind Southern Presbyterianism to the cause. No wonder Stiles's cousin John Devotion sometimes wrote on the bottom of a letter: "To His Grace Bishop Newport, D.D." The great fear

31. Mass. Hist. Soc., *Collections*, 4 ser., IV, 421–2; *Journal of the Honourable House of Representatives of His Majesty's Province of the Massachusetts-Bay, in New England* (Boston, 1768), Appendix, 33. On the political repercussion of Anglicanism in Rhode Island, Connecticut, and Pennsylvania at this time, see Stiles to Alison, Apr. 23, 1768, Stiles Papers; *Trumbull Papers*, I, 288 (Mass. Hist. Soc., *Collections*, XLIX [1885]); Alexander Macraby to Sir Philip Francis, June 15, 1768, *Pennsylvania Magazine of History and Biography*, XI (1887), 284.

reached its summit when the Convention of Delegates assembled at the Yale Commencement of September, 1769. Convinced that a letter of October, 1768, had failed to reach the London Dissenters, John Rodgers complied with the request to send off another requesting English interposition in favor of the Convention. The contents focused upon the conviction that "no mutilated Bishop" would ever rest content without civil powers, Anglican professions notwithstanding.

We also know the Force of a british Act of Parliament; and have Reason to dread the Establishment of Bishops Courts among us. Should they claim the Right of holding these Courts, and of exercising the Powers belonging to their Office, by the common-law of England (which is esteemed the Birth-right of a British Subject) we could have no Counterballance to this enormous Power in our Colonies, when we have no Nobility or proper Courts to Check the dangerous Exertion of their Authority, and where Governors and Judges may be the needy Dependents of a prime Minister and therefore afraid to disoblige a Person who is sure of being supported by the whole Bench of Bishops in England. So that our civil Liberties appear to us to be in eminent Danger from such an Establishment. . . . We have so long tasted Sweets of civil and religious Liberty, that we cannot be easily prevailed upon to submit to a Yoke of Bondage, which neither we nor our Fathers were able to bear.[32]

When the members of the Elizabeth-Town assembly of October 3, 1770, analyzed the situation of Dissenters, they decided that the most important task was to enlarge the membership and in consequence the influence of their organization. They directed Dr. John Witherspoon, the distinguished president of the College of New Jersey, to take every opportunity during a journey eastward to persuade the preachers in Rhode Island and Massachusetts and in New Hampshire of "the importance of their uniting with us." The convention also considered the expediency of having an agent in London to look after the colonial dissenting interests, much as did the agents of the several provincial assemblies; they then appointed

32. Stiles, *Literary Diary*, I, 16; Stiles, *Itineraries*, 464; *Records of the Presbyterian Church*, 397, 399, 408, 413, 414, 416, 419; *Convention of Delegates*, 22-3, 25-6; Dissenting Deputies, Minutes, II, 70–73.

a committee of Messrs. Alison, Beatty, Ewing and Witherspoon to seek the proper person for the job. Colonial concern that the Londoners had not applied all possible pressure on the ministry and members of Parliament, and that they underestimated the seriousness of the threat, brings us to an examination of the actual state of affairs with the English Dissenters.[33]

V

The Nonconformist leaders in London, fully cognizant of the problem, used not only every available propaganda agency to whip up public opinion against the sending of bishops to America but also applied the power of the Dissenting Interest at points where it counted most. One must keep constantly in mind the significant fact that the view of Britain and of the Church of England held by Mayhew, Eliot, Chauncy, Livingston, Stiles, Welles, Rodgers, Alison, and their American followers was that reflected by the English Dissenters and their writings over a period of nearly a century. In the strictest sense it was, therefore, somewhat distorted. Thus the colonists never fully comprehended many things about the English society of the eighteenth century, signally, how latitudinarianism had transformed the outlook of many Anglicans. Likewise — and this is often completely passed over by English historians — Archbishop Secker, Bishops Osbaldeston and Terrick, and the rest of the hierarchy never had even a glimmer of the implications of the rapid growth of a dynamic society in a vastly greater environment and radically different intellectual climate across the water. All they really knew derived from the misinformation sent over to them by reactionary missionaries.

In a very real sense, Thomas Hollis directed, almost precepted, the extra-curricular reading of the Congregational and Presbyterian ministers of America as well as of English Nonconformists. When Edmund Quincy's letter of August 25, 1766, arrived reporting the death of Jonathan Mayhew, Hollis fixed upon the Reverend Andrew Eliot of New North Church as Mayhew's successor by sending him the customary introductory parcel of carefully chosen books and

33. *Convention of Delegates,* 28–9; *N.Y. Mercury,* Oct. 8, 1770; *N.H. Gaz.,* Nov. 4, 1768.

a batch of clippings from English newspapers. In an accompanying letter, Hollis referred to the danger posed by the settling of Roman Catholic bishops in Canada, and strongly advocated a greater use of the newspapers in the defense of the colonial cause. Eliot replied, agreeing on both of those points and making a generous acknowledgment of the great services of the English Dissenters:

The spirit of liberty would soon be lost, and the people would grow quite lethargic, if there were not some on watch, to awaken and arouse them. We, in America, are perhaps more obliged to our friends in Great Britain, who raised a Spirit among the people, than to the P_____t who repealed the [Stamp] Act which was calculated (I do not say designed) to enslave the Colonies.[34]

Andrew Eliot now took over Jonathan Mayhew's role of keeping Thomas Hollis abreast of all colonial developments, and the Englishman never slackened his efforts to present the Americans' case to the English public. He assured Eliot that everything that could be done in favor of liberty and support of the House of Hanover "in public prints, by private Individuals, *is done,* faithfully, and with Alacrity," and the clippings from the *St. James's Chronicle* and the *London Chronicle* bear him out. Hollis also commended the way that the American "public prints are watched over, vigilantly, to the same noble ends," but he warned that there had already been some "thwartings" of the press and that more would follow.[35]

Another staunch defender of the Dissenting Interest whom Thomas Hollis had recruited was Caleb Fleming, who wrote many unsigned pieces for the public prints. Young Sylas Neville learned from him that the Earl of Bute and George Grenville were "hatching a plan (to be executed after the meeting of the new Parliament) to send Bishops into America and absolutely enslave that country," but the Reverend Mr. Fleming believed that the people in America had been capable of leading them and hoped they "would die bravely

34. Quincy to Hollis, July 25, 1766, Hollis Papers; Mass. Hist. Soc., *Collections,* 4 ser., IV, 398, 400; Shipton, *Harvard Graduates,* X, 128–61.

35. Archbishop Secker had presented Harvard College with a set of his sermons. Eliot found the S.P.G. anniversary discourse of 1741 among them and was deeply provoked by it. His "Remarks," written late in 1767, were first published in Mass. Hist. Soc., *Collections,* 2 ser., II (1814), 190–210. Hollis to Eliot, Feb. 23, 1767, Hollis Papers.

with their swords in their hands rather than submit." He also dismissed the Anglican claims of strength, over one-third of all the inhabitants, by explaining that "many thousands of negroes" were included in the count and called such assertions "shameful falsehood and deception." His view was "that the first Bishop that goes there must be a bold fellow." [36]

Dr. William Gordon of Stepney acquired such an admiration for the colonies that he became an emigrant. In 1769, the year before he left England, Gordon advised Dr. Joseph Bellamy of Connecticut that there was no danger of bishops at that time, because of the unstable political situation resulting from the Townshend Acts. Also, some in the ministry believed a war to be imminent; "they will want troops from the colonies to act against the French and Spaniards in America." Later he reasoned with James Bowdoin of the Massachusetts Council about the necessity for making concessions to the New England Baptists in order to avoid "a clamour" against the Congregationalists in Court circles, where men "would gladly hearken to complaints of that kind. . . . I would wish that the colonies would allow full liberty of conscience." Once again, English pastors were giving the Americans sound advice about a touchy matter.[37]

A new face in the ranks of champions of the American fight against episcopacy was that of Archdeacon Francis Blackburne. The fact that he was a nephew of an archbishop and was himself in Holy Orders gave great weight to his pronouncements. In sending some prints and a letter from the cleric to Andrew Eliot in 1767, Thomas Hollis declared that the Bostonian and "Mr. Arch-Deacon Blackburne are the fittest of any two Persons in the several Countrys, to correspond together for public Benefit and private satisfaction. . . . The A. D. is a first rate man for eminency of active Virtue, and for Learning, Wit and Judgment; and in all Respects a Gentleman." He is, moreover, too able a man to rise "high in his own order." [38]

As Mr. Hollis had anticipated, Mr. Blackburne and the Boston

36. Hollis, Diary, 568, 588; Basil Cozens-Hardy, *The Diary of Sylas Neville, 1767–1788* (London, 1950), 31, 33, 69; *London Chronicle*, July 25, 1767.

37. Baird, "Civil Status of Presbyterians," 615; Mass. Hist. Soc., *Proceedings*, LXIII (1930), 303, 309, 311.

38. Hollis to Eliot, Feb. 23, Aug. 26, 1767, Hollis Papers.

minister proved to be congenial spirits. When Mr. Eliot wrote that those who were advocating an episcopacy for America had "other ends in view; to make a more pompous show, by which they hope to increase their faction; to add to the number of Lord Bishops; to extend their episcopal influence," he concluded, "as Dr. Blackburne judiciously observes in a letter I had from him — to prevent any reformation at home." And the Archdeacon reciprocated by taking over in full the New England version of its origins from Eliot's "Remarks on the Bishop of Oxford's Sermon," which the author had sent to Thomas Hollis.[39]

Archdeacon Blackburne's opposition to "the scheme of episcopizing" (Mayhew's term again) the colonies was based on the view that it would prevent any ecclesiastical reform in England itself. His attack on High-Church power in *The Confessional* won him popularity in America, and in his letters to Eliot he reiterated this theme when he charged that "Laudean Ecclesiastical Politics" were reviving. He paid his respects to Thomas Secker, whom he termed "the leading character of that Squadron," by saying that "No one, who is acquainted with the features of the master-workman in this Episcopal Fabric, can doubt, but that he intended by it to lock down upon us at home the Hierarchical Yoke, as well as to bend to it the Necks of our brethren the Colonists." [40]

The sermons preached before the S.P.G. prompted the unaffiliated Boston pastors, without prior consultation with the Convention of Delegates, to send off a letter reopening their ancient connection with the Dissenting Deputies on January 4, 1768. Recalling with gratitude the previous efforts of the Londoners to help them, the ministers rehearsed the grievances and predicted disaster if the Episcopalians succeeded in introducing diocesan bishops into their country. Because Jasper Mauduit and one other deputy were the

39. Mass. Hist. Soc., *Collections*, 4 ser., IV, 410–11, 421–2; 2 ser. II (1814), 190.

40. Dr. Myles Cooper procured a copy of *The Confessional* from England. Chandler wrote Johnson that it "makes more noise and will probably do more mischief than anything that has been published for ages past. . . . The design of it is to demolish all creeds, tests, and subscriptions; and the effect of it that thousands are coming over to it in great numbers." Thomas Hollis procured the publication of the tract. Blackburne, *Memoirs of Thomas Hollis*, I, 302; Schneiders, *Johnson*, I, 415; Blackburne to Eliot, Jan. 23, Aug. 18, 1767 (Harvard College Library), Autograph Letter File.

only ones remaining from the old Committee of Correspondence, a new one of ten members including Dennys De Berdt was appointed. The General Meeting of Deputies also assigned three members "to enquire of such Persons as they may think proper, in order to get the best information they can whether the design of introducing Bishops into America be dropt or not." Finding nothing to confirm the ministers' fears, the London Dissenters dispatched this news to Boston at once with the advice that they believed "the Government are so sensible of the confusion such a step would make," that, however warmly some prelates encourage it, they will never succeed. "However, Gentlemen, as you and we are engaged in one common cause," you may depend upon our constant endeavors and vigilance should the project be resumed.[41]

The Dissenting Deputies also convened a special meeting to discuss a letter of September 14, 1769, from Dr. John Rodgers for the Convention of Delegates at New Haven. As previously mentioned, this communication replaced one of October 5, 1768, which never reached the London body. Other letters on the same subject having arrived from Francis Alison and Nathaniel Taylor, the Committee directed Secretary Thomas Cotton to write to all three correspondents in the same vein as in the reply to the Bostonians. The Deputies also had this advice to offer to Alison regarding the idea of having a colonial ecclesiastical agent at London:

It is the opinion of the Committee, that a proper Person qualified to be your Agent in the manner specified in your Letter, would be very difficult to be found; and if such a one could be found, would not answer your end, as he would not have the weight with Administration as this Committee would; for whatever he might at any time say, they would look upon him as an Agent for the colonies and under their influence, whereas no such Bias could be imputed to this Committee.[42]

As so often happens when men have sought to influence government officials and political bodies, the direct evidence we should like to have does not exist; perhaps it never was committed to writing. At the New Haven Convention in 1767, Ezra Stiles told Ebenezer Devotion that he had reliable information that Lord

41. Dissenting Deputies, Minutes, II, 24–7, 28, 31.

42. Dissenting Deputies, Minutes, II, 70–73, 87, 89, 90, 92–4.

Shelburne and others concerned with American affairs totally opposed sending bishops to the colonies. Furthermore, some English prelates thought that spiritual bishops could be sent over at any time, but they preferred to wait until they could get some appointed "with Power." Relevant to this subject, Stiles also said that the many letters sent home intimating the alarm which bishops would create in America had "kept off those voracious Animals a few years longer. But none of these Things may go into our public prints — they are communicated to us from the Ministry under that Confidence." [43]

In the case of the American episcopate, there is every reason to conclude that it was the London Dissenters acting individually and through their organization who prevented any prelatical, ministerial, or parliamentary action from taking place, action which we have seen was seriously considered. Bishop William White (1748–1831), one of the principal organizers of the Protestant Episcopal Church of the United States of America, has left authoritative and certainly unbiased testimony on the subject:

Lest it be thought, that the dissenting interest in England has been magnified, it ought to be known, that the forces of the different denominations of dissenters — with the exception of the people called Quakers — was concentrated in a committee in London. The author was acquainted with a member of that committee in England, in 1771 and 1772, and knew that he had free access to the ministry. The impression then received, was its being an object of government to avoid any thing of a religious nature which might set the dissenters in a political opposition. They had great influence in elections to parliament.[44]

43. Stiles to Devotion, Aug. 19, 1767, Stiles Papers.

44. The Reverend William White was ordained deacon in London, December 23, 1770, and priest, April 25, 1772, and consecrated second American bishop, 1786. Rev. William White, D.D., *Memoirs of the Protestant Episcopal Church in the United States of America* (New York, 1880), 75.

XI

"NOISE AND CLAMOUR"

1767–1770

The Great Fear of Episcopacy reached its highest intensity during the years 1767–70 when Anglican missionaries, encouraged and assisted by prelates in England, persisted in their attempts to procure bishops for America at the same time that Charles Townshend and the ministry ventured for the second time to reorder the British Empire. Presbyterian and Congregational ministers and a few prominent laymen easily discerned their covert intentions, for, as Ezra Stiles said, "I have so thoroly studied the views and ultimate Designs of the American Episcopalians that I know I am not deceived." [1]

The problem facing the Dissenters was not an easy one, for, again quoting Ezra Stiles, "It is difficult to lay open and advance with *full force* the *objections* against Prelacy in America, peculiar to this *Age,* and to the present State of the Colonies. Our *peculiar Objections* are much founded in the *Anticipation of Futurity.*" The solution was the first concerted American press campaign — one that mobilized and focused intercolonial or American opinion directly on the threat to colonial liberty posed by such an ecclesiastical act and the serious eventualities it presaged. The Anglicans were soon conscious that an intensive campaign was being waged against them; Samuel Johnson wrote to his son in England that "there is some incendiary or other writer in the Boston papers in the spirit of Mayhew, that tries to blow up the colonies into a flame again." If, however, the press incensed some, it gave hope to others: "Providus," in an inflammatory article in the *Boston Gazette,* wrote:

1. Stiles feared the Townshend revenue scheme and "the Effect of an Alliance of Church and State here." Stiles to Chauncy, Apr. 22, Nov. 3, 1768, Stiles Papers.

"however little some may think of common Newspapers, to a wise Man they appear the Ark of God for the Safety of the People." Indeed, every "sluice of knowledge" was now opened, and the pastors and the printers began to develop and foster an incipient popular mood, at once nationalistic and revolutionary.[2]

II

From the time of his translation to Canterbury, Thomas Secker had pondered Samuel Johnson's suggestion that some effort should be made to quiet completely and finally colonial uneasiness as to what the Episcopalians intended to do and what they had no intentions of doing. The Reverend Charles Inglis maintained in 1766 that many principal Dissenters could be induced to abandon their objections to episcopacy if they were assured that they would not have to pay taxes to support colonial bishops, and that such prelates would not be vested with any civil powers. In fact the clergyman intended to compose such a piece himself but stood aside when "a better hand" offered.[3]

Just prior to the Episcopal Convention held at Shrewsbury, New Jersey, in the fall of 1766, Myles Cooper advised Thomas Bradbury Chandler of Samuel Johnson's recommendation that a judicious tract be written and distributed to allay the false fears of the Dissenters. The suggestion became the first item in the Johnson-Chandler Plan adopted at the meeting. After properly alleging his own inadequacy, Chandler agreed to prepare the piece, for, as he wrote Johnson, he was eager "to engage our Southern clergy heartily to join us, and to silence the clamors of the dissenters." So conscientiously did he devote what time he had to the task that in October, 1767, he was able to dispatch to the Secretary of the S.P.G. a copy of *An Appeal to the Public in Behalf of the Church of England in America.*[4]

Though dedicating his work to the Archbishop of Canterbury,

2. Stiles to Chauncy, Apr. 22, 1768, Stiles Papers; Schneiders, *Johnson,* I, 418; *Bos. Gaz.,* Dec. 7, 1767.

3. Inglis to Secy., May 1, 1766, S.P.G. Correspondence, ser. B, II, Pt. I, 209.

4. Schneiders, *Johnson,* I, 366; Chandler to Secy., Oct. 16, 1767, S.P.G. Correspondence, ser. B. XXIV, 91.

the author graciously acknowledged that the concept of the brochure had been Dr. Johnson's, and that he had merely undertaken it at the request of a voluntary convention of the clergy. Dr. Chandler came right into the open on the first page by stating that application had been made by the clergy of several colonies for one or more bishops; he also declared that there was no intention to keep this a secret but proposed to inform the public "candidly and explicitly" about the plan which was so reasonable because "no Invasion of the civil or religious Privileges of any, whether Churchmen or Dissenters, is thereby intended." [5]

For materials Dr. Chandler drew heavily from Secker's writings, especially the sermon of 1740/1 before the S.P.G. and the as yet unpublished letter to Horatio Walpole. First of all he presented the historical case for episcopacy to meet the Hobart-Welles argument; then he took up the serious need of the Church in America for a bishop to confirm and ordain. The requirement that candidates travel to England for ordination had produced genuine hardships and had actually cost the lives of several promising young men; the financial cost, £100, might be considered as a "Fee" for admission to the clergy and was prohibitive for many college students who otherwise would enter the Church. All that the missionaries really asked was to be on "an equal Footing with our Neighbours." Yet, three pages farther on, the doctor contradicted himself:

For as some Religion has ever been thought by the wisest Legislators, to be necessary for the Security of Civil Government, and accordingly has always been interwoven into the Constitution of it, so, in every Nation, that Religion which is thus distinguished, must be looked upon as, in the Opinion of the Legislature, the best fitted for its great Purpose.

The Episcopal clergy, said the rector, therefore consider themselves bound by sacred ties of principle and duty, as well as by inclination and interest, always to support the civil government. "Accordingly, no Trumpet of Sedition was ever heard to sound from our Pulpit — no seeds of Disaffection have been suffered more privately to be sown in our Houses." [6]

5. Thomas Bradbury Chandler, *An Appeal to the Public in Behalf of the Church of England in America* (New York, 1767), i, ix, 1–2.

6. After having seen a copy of the Secker letter, in June, 1770, Eliot remarked to Hollis: "I think it is very plain that the A-B-P set Dr. Chandler to work, and highly

Now is the proper time to complete episcopacy in America: there is peace with France, the late political troubles are settled, the Plan is so constructed that no group will suffer by it — those who are averse to Episcopal church government need have no bishops — and King George strongly favors the Church. From an "actual Survey" of 1762, Chandler deduced that out of a colonial population of three millions, the Church of England counted "near a Million of Members," and their necessities called aloud for an episcopate. Proceeding to explain in detail the revised Butler Plan, with emphasis on its reasonableness, the cleric also brought out "the commercial and political Advantages to be expected" from converting the heathen under it. Then, addressing himself to the Dissenters and reluctant Southern Anglicans, he insisted, in italic type:

That the Bishops to be sent to America, shall have no Authority, but purely of a Spiritual and Ecclesiastical Nature, such as is derived altogether from the Church and not from the State — That this Authority shall operate only upon the Clergy of the Church, and not upon the Laiety nor Dissenters of any Denomination — That the Bishops shall not interfere with the Property or Privileges, whether civil or religious of Churchmen or Dissenters — That, in particular, they shall have no Concern with the Probate of Wills, Letters of Guardianship and Administration, or Marriage-Licenses, nor be Judges of any cases relating thereto. . . . This, without any Reservation or Equivocation, is the exact Plan of an American Episcopate, which has been settled at Home.[7]

Though Dr. Chandler promised that every reasonable objection would be weighed, he declared that any opposition to the proposed plan would be sheer persecution and then proceeded to answer some of the standing criticisms of episcopacy. Certainly any uneasiness about bishops should vanish when Dissenters realized that no new laws would be made and no tithes collected. But here he weakened his defense by maintaining that a general tax to support three bishops would amount to only four pence in £100, which would be "no mighty Hardship." As for the idea that there might be "an Augmentation of their Powers, as soon as Circumstances

probable that he furnished him with a copy of his letter to Mr. Walpole, as the ground-work." Mass. Hist. Soc., *Collections*, 4 ser., IV, 443, 449; Chandler, *Appeal*, 18–25, 26–8, 39–46.

7. Chandler, *Appeal*, 54–60, 79.

will admit of it," the author impatiently brushed it aside by saying that "at this Rate there can be no End of objecting." [8]

A few days after the publication of the *Appeal,* the Reverend Mr. Chandler sent a copy to Bishop Terrick with a letter saying that it expressed the opinions of the clergy in most of the colonies and gave some of the bases upon which these judgments were founded. Then he went on to say: "There are some other Facts and Reasons, which could not be prudently mentioned in a Work of this Nature, as the least Intimation of them would be of ill Consequence in this irritable Age and Country; but were they known, they would have a far greater Tendency to engage such of our Superiors . . . as are governed altogether by political Motives, to espouse the Cause of the Church of England in America, than any contained in the Pamphlet." [9]

This admission of the ulterior political motives of the missionaries confirms the soundness of the Dissenters' suspicions as voiced by Ezra Stiles: "the fact is that they cannot be trusted." On a different score, Provost Smith took exception to the *Appeal:* he thought it was too long and tedious, and though he considered it rather well done on the whole, he wished it had not been published. He particularly decried the "extraordinary warmth" of it and also of the Perth-Amboy addresses, copies of which the Dissenters had already procured and published, raising "a great Flame." Of the few who saw the *Appeal* before it went to the printers, Dr. Auchmuty had predicted the consequences.[10]

Three months after publication, the author reported to Dr. Johnson that the *Appeal* was circulating but slowly and that it was very difficult to distribute copies southward. Some few had reached North Carolina through the instrumentality of the Reverend Charles Inglis, but Dr. Chandler thought that the Philadelphia clergy had been remiss in not assisting and defending him. One anonymous

8. Chandler, *Appeal,* 82, 105–9.

9. Chandler to Bishop of London, Oct. 21, 1767, Fulham Palace MSS, printed in Cross, *Anglican Episcopate,* 345–6.

10. Stiles to Chauncy, Nov. 3, 1768, Stiles to Chandler, "Not Sent," Apr. 9, 1768, Stiles Papers; Perry, *Historical Collections, Pa.,* II, 427, 429; Auchmuty to Peters, Aug. 16, 1768, Richard Peters Papers (Hist. Soc. Pa.), VI, 61; Auchmuty to Johnson, Mar. 21, 1769, Hawks Papers, II, No. 15.

writer from Lewes in the Delaware Counties issued an abusive reply which even charged Dr. Chandler with being without honor and attacked the plan for episcopacy by showing up the danger of spiritual courts and the projected attempts on the liberties of the people. The letter was reprinted in the *Pennsylvania Journal* of January 28, 1768, but no one had bothered to send a copy to Dr. Chandler.[11]

One reason for the apparent inattention of the Dissenters to Chandler's tract was their momentary concern with two other Episcopal writers. No Anglican prelate of the eighteenth century committed as great an indiscretion as did John Ewer, Bishop of Llandaff, when he preached the annual sermon before the S.P.G. on February 20, 1767. The Bishop discoursed with magnificent confidence on the reason for the absence of a standing ministry in the plantations: it was the "scandalous neglect" of the colonists:

Upon the adventurers what reproach could be cast, heavier than they deserved? Who, with their native soil, abandoned their native manners, and religion; and e'er long, were found in many parts living without remembrance or knowledge of God, without any divine worship, in dissolute wickedness, and the most brutal profligacy of manners. Instead of civilizing and converting barbarous Infidels, as they undertook to do, they became themselves Infidels and Barbarians. And is it not some aggravation of their shame, that this their neglect of religion was contrary to the pretences and conditions, under which they obtained royal grants and public authority to their adventures? The pretences and conditions were, that their design was, and that they should endeavour, the enlargement of commerce, and the propagation of Christian faith; the former they executed with sincerity and zeal, in the latter most notoriously failed. . . . In this way our Planters have excelled, having given double occasion of propagating Christianity among the native heathen of those regions, and among themselves also, who soon became heathen.[12]

11. Schneiders, *Johnson*, I, 433, 437; *Pa. Journal*, Jan. 28–May 26, 1768; *A Letter Concerning American Bishops &c., to Dr. Bradbury Chandler, Ruler of St. John's Church in Elizabeth-Town, In Answer to the Appendix of His Appeal to the Public &c.* (n.p. [Phila.] 1768), "By an Anti-Episcopalian."

12. It is barely possible that Bishop Ewer had seen at Fulham Palace some of the colorful communications from the Reverend Charles Woodmason about the "wild Scottish Presbyterians" of upcountry South Carolina. Richard J. Hooker, ed., *The*

The Bishop steered his account just one hundred eighty degrees off the true course set by the early settlers, particularly those of New England and Pennsylvania. The violence done to the legend of the fathers required no refutation; it needed only exposure before the people. But, punctuated by errors and misstatements of fact as it was, few quasi-official publications could have been better calculated to evoke high indignation in the colonies. Within a few months, William Warburton, Bishop of Gloucester, delivered a similar, though not as egregious, discourse to the same audience.[13]

Bishop Ewer's sermon met with harsh criticism in the *St. James's Chronicle* and the *London Chronicle* in April, and in July the *Boston Gazette* observed that Bishop Warburton's sermon "treats the whole Body of Dissenters in England and America, with the decent Name of Fanaticks" and "Presbyterian Faction &c." It was not until November that a copy of the Bishop of Llandaff's address, sent by Hollis, reached Andrew Eliot. He contemplated answering it himself, but Charles Chauncy, to whom he lent it, desired to "write an answer at large." For fifty-six pages, in a piece entitled *A Letter to a Friend,* the aging minister tore John Ewer's discourse to shreds. Dr. Chauncy expressed his contempt for S.P.G. anniversary sermons in general and the unreliable statistics offered in the annual abstracts, because he felt that his country deserved more just treatment. As for the sermon under review, the Bostonian had nothing but scorn. "Had the character you mention, as given the British Colonies, been contained in a discourse delivered by a common Clergy-man, before a common audience, it would, I believe, have given you no uneasiness," but for a Bishop to deliver it before the Venerable Society was incredible. With well-marshaled facts, he exposed the prelate's ignorance, and ended with a direct thrust:

The conduct of the Society has, for many years, given us reason to suspect their MAIN VIEW was to EPISCOPIZE the Colonies; but we were

---

South Carolina Backcountry . . . The Journal and other Writings of Charles Woodmason Anglican Itinerant (Chapel Hill, 1953). John Ewer, Bishop of Llandaff, *A Sermon Preached before the Incorporated Society for the Propagation of the Gospel in Foreign Parts* (London, 1767; reprinted, New York, 1768), 6–7, 8, 12.

13. Miscellaneous note in Eliot's handwriting in the Hollis Papers: "Dr. Warburton's Sermon is justly resented in America—He is G——r B——d's favorite Bishop."

never before, that I know of, told so in direct terms. . . . We prefer our own mode of worship and discipline to that of the Church of England; and we do it upon principle." [14]

Charles Chauncy's *Letter to a Friend* reached the New England public just as the "affair of a Colony Bishop" had people in a state of agitation. The Boston papers teemed with extracts from and communications about the *Letter,* most of them favorable. One enthusiast recommended distribution of free copies to the ministers and representatives of every town in Massachusetts to promote the interest of true religion. From ministerial associations came votes of thanks for the author's strictures on what John Devotion called "Llandaff's Whines and Scurrilous Reflections." None of the Society's annual sermons had ever pleased the Yankees, but John Ewer's had touched them in a tender spot. As Andrew Eliot noted:

The Fathers of New England are almost adored in the present Day, to intimate that they are ridiculed is abusive calumny — which a mitre ought not to cover.[15]

The Bishop of Llandaff was a "natural" for such a natural propagandist as William Livingston. The latter, believing that Dr. Chauncy had "treated that haughty prelate rather too tenderly and that he deserved a little severer correction," for Livingston thought he had never seen a pamphlet that "contained so many aberrations from the truth," proceeded to expose its many errors. Furthermore, the New Yorker argued that the Society's funds had been squandered, the Indians neglected, and that episcopizing was clearly its

14. Sometime during this year Francis Blackburne published at London some devastating *Observations on Dr. Ewer's, Lord Bishop of Llandaff, Sermon,* in which he used extracts from Andrew Eliot's manuscript "Remarks" on Bishop Secker's anniversary sermon of 1741. Mass. Hist. Soc., *Collections,* 2 ser., II (1814), 190; 4 ser., IV, 417–18; *London Chronicle,* July 11, 16, 1767; *Bos. Gaz.,* July 20, 1767; *Bos. News-Letter,* Oct. 8, 1767; Charles Chauncy, *A Letter to a Friend, Containing Remarks on Certain Passages in a Sermon Preached by the Right Reverend Father in God, John Ewer,* Bishop of Llandaff . . . (Boston, 1767), 5, 6, 8, 8n, 15, 20–21, 43–4, 51, 53.

15. Thomas Hollis had the Reverend Caleb Fleming prepare a reply to Chandler's *Appeal,* which was appended to the London printing of Chauncy's *Letter to a Friend.* Hollis, Diary, II, 656; *St. James's Chronicle,* June 2, 1768; *Bos. News-Letter,* Dec. 10, 24, 31, 1767; *Bos. Gaz.,* Feb. 1, Mar. 14, 1768; *New London Gaz.,* Jan. 15, 1768; Stiles, *Itineraries,* 470–71; Misc. note in Eliot's hand, 1767, Hollis Papers.

main objective. Most adroitly he interpreted Bishop Ewer's attack as directed principally against the New Englanders, of whom Livingston said: "I will venture to affirm, there is not a more virtuous, not a more religious people upon the face of the earth." Having presented his views in the manner of a lawyer, he expressed his contempt with a withering conclusion: "You cannot, my lord, require that we should transmit depositions from hence, to prove, that the sun shines in America as well as in Europe." [16]

Most readers liked the New Yorker's spirited defense of his country, which was published in May, 1768. Dr. John Rodgers sent copies to Stiles in Newport, who forwarded some to Messrs. Chauncy and Eliot, who had the tract reprinted at Boston, where it was much admired. At Manhattan, the Reverend Charles Inglis, realizing its effect, rushed into print to defend his superior from Livingston's "insolent, abusive, Letter," and he tried specifically to undo the lawyer's emphasis on New England: "I answer — that his Lordship's assertion, is absolutely true of all the colonies, those of *New-England* and part of *New-York* excepted. . . ." This pamphlet, *A Vindication,* was moderate in tone but lacked fire and controversial power; William Livingston, who was after much larger game than Mr. Inglis, completely ignored it.[17]

III

The real impact of Thomas Chandler's *Appeal* did not make itself felt until about six months after publication. Convinced that the pamphlet should be answered lest authorities in England as-

16. Livingston to Samuel Cooper, Mar. 26, 1768, Livingston Letterbook A; *Bos. News-Letter,* May 12, 1768; William Livingston, *A Letter to the Right Reverend Father in God, John, Lord Bishop of Llandaff, occasioned by his Sermon . . . in which the American Colonies are loaded with Reproach* (New York: the author, 1768), 1, 3, 5, 8, 9, 11–14, 15, 23–4; also original MS in Livingston Papers, Box 1, folder 1761–77.

17. Chauncy to Stiles, Mar. 16, May 9, 1768; Stiles to Rodgers, May 16, 1768, Stiles Papers; *Bos. Gaz.,* May 16, 1768; *Pa. Journal,* May 26, 1768; *N.Y. Journal,* July 9, 1768, *Sup.;* Inglis to Secy., Aug. 12, 1769, S.P.G. Correspondence, ser. B, II, Pt. I, 227, 229; Charles Inglis, *A Vindication of the Bishop of Llandaff's Sermon from the Gross Misrepresentations and Abusive Reflections contained in Mr. Livingston's Letter to His Lordship* (New York, 1768), 1, 3, 6, 55, 64, 71–81; *N.Y. Mercury,* Jan. 9, 1769.

sume colonial acquiescence in bishops, William Livingston once again consulted with his friend Noah Welles about what was on his mind. Tracts and sermons are useful to teach the lesson, but —

I conceive it would be of greater Advantage in *a weekly Paper,* inserted in one of our Public Prints; *which would be more generally read and constantly reprinted.* This would shew them on the other side of the water that even the apprehension of a Bishop's being sent, has raised a Flame here; and that appears the most probable way of deterring them from the Project. If they imagine the thing will go down without opposition (as Chandler roundly asserts) he will undoubtedly come. *Tis Noise and Clamour that is at present our best Policy.* I should therefore be glad to engage a few of the Friends of Liberty to furnish their Quota of such weekly Papers: and as soon as a competent Number is provided, to begin the Business. *By this means the Dissenters here, will be alarmed; and the Ministry intimidated.* By this means also the Paper will consist of greater variety; every man writing according to his own genius, and fall on such part of *the Appeal,* as is most adapted to it, or arguing against the Scheme [of Bishops] in General, without taking notice of the Appeal. I think we cannot answer it to Posterity, if we do not bear our Testimony against it. . . . The Design ought to be kept a profound secret.[18]

Within two weeks the project got under way, and the New Yorker persuaded James Parker, confirmed Anglican though he was, to print their essays in his *New York Gazette, or The Weekly Post Boy* for at least a year. Knowing that the printer was motivated solely by profit, Livingston urged his friends to support him by subscribing. On March 26, in explaining the policy of the clamor to the fiery Samuel Cooper, Samuel Adams's pastor at Boston, Livingston revealed the beginnings of the "American Whig" and went on to add:

A Number of Gentlemen will shortly open the Ball in Philadelphia. I should be glad the same Measure was pursued at Boston, and if it cannot be brought about, that at Least care be taken to reprint the Whig in one of your papers. Without some such opposition, I am apprehen-

18. Livingston to Welles, Feb. 2, 1768, Johnson Family Papers, No. 86. (Italics mine)

sive the ministry may be prevailed upon to gratify the lawn-sleeves by way of recompense for so often voting against their consciences for the court. . . . Pray, my dear Sir, bestir yourself at this critical Juncture, and help us to ward off this ecclesiastical stamp act, which, if submitted to will at length grind us to powder.

Dr. Cooper replied:

Your Plan and the Execution so far as I have seen is well adapted to rouse and awaken . . . and I hope will soon be universal. . . . The American Whig, could it be published in our Papers, considering what Dr. Chauncy has wrote, would render such a work among ourselves unnecessary. But this, though the Printers are ready to do it, and many eagerly desirous of it, cannot be obtain'd. Mr. Parker, who I am told has control of the Post-Office has given his Mandate against it, and threatened our Printers that if they presume to publish part of that Paper, they should have Nothing convey'd to them by the Post, without paying the Postage. This appears to me a very extraordinary Measure; and discovers with a witness, what our poor America is likely more and more to feel, the insolence of office. This has disgruntled people here, and will discredit his Design of enlarging the Numbers of his Subscribers among us.[19]

The New York public got its first look at the "American Whig" when it appeared on the front page of Parker's sheet, March 14, 1768. Once a week, until July 24, 1769, it titillated the colonial audience, a total of sixty-four numbers in all. Authors were Livingston, Scott, and Smith, the old Reflector Triumvirate, and Noah Welles, Dr. Chauncy of Boston, and possibly the Presbyterian ministers, John Rodgers, Joseph Treat, and Archibald Laidlie. Alexander MacDougall may also have been a member, but Noah Hobart declined to participate. William Livingston bore most of the burden, as he had thirteen years before. James Parker's threat notwithstanding, the Whigs appeared in other newspapers: Edes and Gill reprinted the first five in their *Boston Gazette,* and William Bradford ran sixteen numbers in the *Pennsylvania Journal.*[20]

19. Livingston to Welles, Feb. 16, 1768, Johnson Family Papers, No. 87; Livingston to S. Cooper, Mar. 26, 1768; Cooper to Livingston, Apr. 18, 1768, Livingston Letterbook A.

20. Schneiders, *Johnson,* I, 438. For a Tory view of the *American Whig,* see Judge Thomas Jones, *History of New York during the Revolutionary War,* I, 19, 21–3, 33.

It had been Livingston's hope in the beginning that alarm and clamor would be carried on in several places at once. With this in mind he suggested that Noah Welles induce Chauncy Whittelsey to promote a weekly paper at New Haven, and he hoped to prick the consciences of the Connecticut ministry and make them forget their internecine quarrels by intimating that a refusal to support this campaign would mean that, being safe behind their charter, they were indifferent to the woes of sister colonies. In this he failed, but certain parsons did help by distributing the *New York Gazette* in the colony.[21]

Farther south, at Philadelphia, William Livingston's scheme met with signal success. An amorphous society made up of Francis Alison, John Dickinson, "the Pennsylvania Farmer," and Judge George Bryan determined to "unmask" the Reverend Dr. Chandler and expose his false modesty and high claims. They "opened the Ball" with the first issue of their paper, "The Centinel," on March 24, ten days after the appearance of the "American Whig," in Bradford's paper, the *Pennsylvania Journal.* Efforts to engage Massachusetts, Rhode Island, and Connecticut may have failed, but the clamor issuing from New York and Philadelphia was enough to create "an universal alarm" and a good deal of noise in other parts of the country merely by reverberation.[22]

About two weeks before the publication of the first "American Whig," the New York–New Jersey Anglicans got wind of the plans for a general attack on the *Appeal,* but even so, they were not prepared for the force of the onslaught. On March 25, Dr. Chandler crossed to Manhattan to confer with his colleagues Cooper, Seabury, and Inglis. They decided to publish an answer, which they called "A Whip for the American Whig," by Timothy Tickle, Esq., in which they hoped to check the "overgrown, intolerable Insolence of these Factors in Dissention." Inglis wrote the first number, which appeared in Hugh Gaine's *New York Mercury* on April 4; then the Whip lashed at the Whig in sixty-four "weekly altercations" that did not stop until July 10, 1769. The authors of the "American Whig," having learned in the days of the *Independent Reflector* that the serious essay did not always permit the answering of abuse,

21. Livingston to Welles, Apr. 23, 1768, Johnson Family Papers, No. 85.

22. Alison to Stiles, Mar. 29, 1768, Stiles Papers; Richard J. Hooker, "John Dickinson on Church and State," *American Literature,* XVI (1944), 82–98.

or dealing it out, promptly met the Anglicans on their own terms by writing for Parker's paper under the pseudonym of Sir Isaac Foot on May 23, "A Kick for the Whipper," which outlasted all of the other newspaper series with sixty-eight numbers, ending January 29, 1770.[23]

An enterprising printer, who was also a High-Church Anglican, contributed in a new and different way to spreading the controversy. Several subscribers of John Holt's *New York Journal* asked him to reprint the "American Whig" in his paper; instead, he decided to print off in half-sheets all of the Whigs and Centinels, together with "the most pertinent of those that may be published in any other Paper, together with the Answers, that the Reader may have both sides of the Question fully before him." From April, 1768 to January, 1769, Holt carried out his promise, issuing gratis for subscribers and selling to others *A Collection of Tracts From the Late News Papers, &c. Containing Particularly The American Whig, A Whip for the American Whig, with Some other Pieces, on the Subject of the Residence of Protestant Bishops in the American Colonies, and in answer to the Writers who opposed it, &c.* He also sold the sheets in bound sets of two volumes each. Here was something novel, then and now, nearly an entire newspaper controversy in 837 pages of small print.[24]

It must not be thought that New York alone was witness to the spectacle of newspapers spawning all these curiously titled columns and of wrangling authors. True, in Philadelphia from March to June, the Alison clique enjoyed a virtual monopoly in their "Centinel," but on June 16 Provost Smith produced the first of two "Anti-Centinels." Although the Philadelphia clergy, and particularly Dr. Smith, had not been happy about the *Appeal* and its author, the Provost had said, in May, that "he shall not be left to stand alone, for the virulence of his antagonists is now not to be borne . . . I am determined now to contribute my mite for great openings are given to detect their shameful misrepresentations."

23. Schneiders, *Johnson*, I, 436; Chandler to Secy., June 24, 1768, S.P.G. Correspondence, ser. B, XXIV, 94; Inglis to Johnson, Mar. 22, 1768, Hawks Papers, No. 34; Livingston to Welles, Apr. 23, 1768, Johnson Family Papers, No. 85.

24. Jones, *History of New York*, I, 19; *N.Y. Journal*, Mar. 31, Apr. 14, Aug. 25, 1768; for John Holt, see *Dict. Amer. Biog.*, IX, 180.

By September, however, when Dr. Smith was preparing to issue "The Anatomist," which was to run in nineteen numbers of the *Pennsylvania Gazette,* he made it clear that he was not taking up his quill to defend Dr. Chandler; the first issue put it this way: "But is Dr. Chandler the Church of England . . . or had he any general commission from the Church of England? . . . and it is certain that no more than half a dozen . . . ever had an opportunity of seeing his pamphlet till in print, and of that number, it is confidently said, not one to the south of Delaware." Alison got out a number of issues of "The Remonstrant" to deal with "The Anatomist" but the wide circulation achieved by the latter — it was copied in the *Pennsylvania Journal, Pennsylvania Chronicle,* and the *New York Journal* — made it the more powerful contender in the newspaper war in that city.[25]

Ezra Stiles and others applauded the services of the Centinels and Whigs to the cause and asserted that, if ever episcopacy should be settled upon America, the columnists would "have the Effect at least to retrench the Episcopal Powers." Dr. Chandler, who was being "mauled from all Quarters," refused to answer the Centinel, for he explained to Samuel Johnson that "if the clergy in Pennsylvania will not interrupt him, let him go on to the end of the chapter." Uncertain as to how long the newspaper attacks on the *Appeal* were profitable, Francis Alison terminated his writing ventures on July 28, though two numbers of "The Centinel" were issued later, one on November 4, the other on December 8. The Vice Provost also believed that, because the Philadelphia Anglicans wanted to refrain from further embroilment in local politics, they might withdraw from the newspaper controversy, which they did, but not until February, 1769. When pressed by Stiles, Alison admitted that "our Centinel retired from his post, and fell asleep, as I think rather too soon, but, as our contests with the commons of England made Harmony in all the Colonies necessary, it was indeed to be of more importance to drop the debate and mind the main chance." [26]

25. Perry, *Historical Collections, Pa.,* II, 427, 429; *Pa. Gaz.,* Sept. 8, 1768; Alison to Stiles, Oct. 20, 1768, Stiles Papers.

26. Alison to Stiles, June 4, 1768, Oct. 20, 1768, Stiles Papers; Stiles, *Itineraries,* 435; Schneiders, *Johnson,* I, 443–4; in No. 19, "The Anatomist" announced in a "card" his closing down in the public interest.

The absence of support from Boston and Newport had greatly worried Francis Alison, and he inquired of Stiles whether or not there was any possibility of bishops coming, and, if so, if New England would be affected, or had they decided to leave everything up to the men of the Middle Colonies. It is probable that the New England attitude played a part in his premature decision of July to stop publishing the "Centinel." The failure of the New England Dissenters to use their public prints for extending the influence of the Whigs and Centinels was due to a complex of attitudes and reasons. Undoubtedly differences of opinion over the Convention of Delegates had something to do with their diffidence, and they also reacted against the concession in the "American Whig" No. 1 that Dr. Chandler's desire for bishops was reasonable. But probably the chief explanation lay in the weakness of the Anglican missionary group in New England: Dr. Chauncy reported that "profound silence" ruled over the Episcopalian quarters in Boston, and as for the Churchmen in Newport, Ezra Stiles wrote that they were

shocked and silent and nonplussed. . . . It mortifies them that there is such a terrible alarm on the most populous Tract of America. They curse the *Centinel,* they curse the *Whig,* they curse the *Bo. Gazette,* and finally they begin to curse themselves for making such a noise about Bps at this Time of Ferment and Zeal for Liby. They think it had been wiser to have deferr'd it till America had become cooler.[27]

Where consideration of general colonial harmony actuated the Pennsylvanians, the New York Dissenters refused to withdraw from the contest until their opponents did.

You will find that the Wig and Whip are still existing to the scandal of Religion and disgust of the public . . . I sincerely wish that my Advice concerning Chandler's Appeal had been followed, which was not to begin with a Nest of Hornets 'till we were assured of Success. We have, now we have lost the late good Archbishop less prospect for an American Bishop than ever; Ergo we shall become the butt of resentment and the Subject of Ridicule.

27. Stiles to Rodgers, Apr. 7, 1768; Stiles to Chauncy, May 5, 1768; Alison to Stiles, May 7, 1768, Stiles Papers.

This dirge by Dr. Auchmuty in March, 1769, was paralleled by a comment of the most conservative of the Connecticut Old-Light divines, William Hart: "The New York Whigg and Whipper, I think, do both disserve the cause of true religion, and tend to turn people aside to vain jangling, and inflame party zeal." Such, of course, was Livingston's aim.[28]

IV

As a general program for the "American Whig" and the "Centinel" had been carefully worked out in advance of publication, these essays exhibit a certain consistency and development, though on occasion their several authors made excursions into peripheral matters or digressed to answer their critics. Provost Smith's "Anatomist" papers also present a coherent point of view, but, aside from them, the Episcopalian writers left to their champion, Thomas Bradbury Chandler, the presentation of the case for bishops in several long tracts. In the meantime, they employed Timothy Tickle's "Whip" to beat the "American Whig" at every opportunity.

Though they had advance information of the Dissenters' intention to attack the *Appeal,* the New York Anglicans had not anticipated the coolly calculated fury and infinite variety of the assault, nor that they would be assailed from behind by the Philadelphia "Centinel." Their first reaction was one of astonishment; then it gave way to anger, as an account in a letter of William Livingston's to Noah Welles of an encounter little more than a month after hostilities began suggests:

I had an interview with Dr. Chandler at a Tavern in Elizabeth Town which had been invited by our mutual Friends. But he could not keep his Temper, throwing out a number of disrespectful Innuendoes against the Dissenters, of which Denomination I was the only one in Company — I would not take one of his hints, seeing him so greatly irritated. His passion increased to such a degree that he could not stay [to] Supper, but making a frivolous Excuse, left the Company. I really pitied his

28. Auchmuty to Johnson, Mar. 21, 1769, Hawks Papers, II, No. 15; Stiles, *Itineraries,* 497.

Travail, having a friendship for the Man, and knowing his person as a man of moral and unexceptionable Character, tho' I detest his bigotry and high-flying Notions.[29]

The incident occurred shortly after Timothy Tickle, Esq., had begun to swing his whip, and it probably helped to induce William Livingston to kick back as Sir Isaac Foot. Somewhat less agitated in July, Dr. Chandler confessed to his mentor:

The scene in New York of *whigging, whipping,* etc., is not pleasing to me; but yet I think that so long as there are Whigs, there ought to be Whips, however I wish some of them were applied with more judgment and discretion. But where so many people are in their turn to have a lick at the Whig, it is not to be expected that all will acquit themselves with equal prudence, dexterity and decency.[30]

The principal object of the Dissenters was to attack Chandler and his pamphlet, expose its "cautious ambiguity," refute it, and then proceed to an assault on the whole idea of instituting episcopacy in America. They stoutly asserted "the natural right of every man to choose his own religion." No "dry crust of unsavory controversy" was served in carrying out their plan; they spread before a hungry audience an assortment of eventualities when "the apostolic monarchs are come over" armed with "the sword of the Lord and of the Bishop" to chastise the colonists in a "torrent of episcopal vengeance." [31]

For more than a year the Whigs and Centinels covered every aspect of the controversy with episcopacy that had been adduced

29. Evidence of the influence of the "American Whig" was the formation at the College of New Jersey in 1769 of the American Whig Society in which James Madison had his anti-Episcopal bias strengthened. Dr. Auchmuty dreaded the success of the Presbyterians among the Dutch of New York, which would be "dangerous to Church and State." Auchmuty to Johnson, Mar. 21, 1769, Hawks Papers, II, No. 15; Livingston to Welles, Apr. 23, 1768, Johnson Family Papers, No. 85.

30. Schneiders, *Johnson,* I, 444; loose paper, *c.* Dec., Hollis to Eliot, Dec. 5, 1769, Hollis Papers.

31. Throughout this discussion citations are from the newspapers in which the essays originally appeared rather than the rare *Collection of Tracts.* "American Whig," *N.Y. Gaz.,* Mar. 14, Apr. 4, 1768.

since 1689. They brought wide reading to their historical argument, and forced their opponents to attempt an Anglican version of the origin of the colonies; from Hobart, Welles, and Chauncy, the dissenting scribblers drew materials for their defense of Presbyterian ordination. They questioned Chandler's "adulterated citations," which misled readers, and, levying on the statistical researches of Dr. Stiles, they pilloried the Jerseyman and the officials of the Venerable Society, who prepared the annual abstracts, for their false, or at least deceptive, use of figures. With satanic skill, both Centinels and Whigs pictured the missionaries as High-Church men and Jacobites, not always averse to alliances with the greatly feared Church of Rome. Francis Alison made canon law his concern, while Lawyer Livingston shrewdly tailored his argument for the victims of the current economic stringency and colonial concern over the Townshend Acts and drove home the high cost of episcopacy by printing a long itemized list of the articles needed for "his Lordship's palace, offices, &c.," coach and horses, cathedral edifice, elegant vestments, salaries for several episcopal officials, etc., etc., to the grand total of £21,740.0.0 annually! "If ever a bishop drives his gilded equipage in our streets, and shares in the public councils of the colony, and the missionaries are judges and justices in the counties, who, but the learned Doctor of Elizabeth-Town, cannot foresee the most tragical circumstances, from such a priestly mixture of power?" [32]

What strikes the modern reader of these papers is the variety of literary forms employed by both sides during this prolonged debate. There are essays, letters, sermons, legal briefs, anecdotes, imaginary pieces, verses, and jingles. High seriousness suffuses most of them; Alison and Livingston frequently battened down their essays with citations of authorities, but, when the writers thought it useful, they resorted to wit, satire, mockery, raillery, bitter sarcasm, and invective. They hurled charges, they slandered, they tried assaults, they indulged in character assassination. The "Whip"

32. "Nor are we prejudiced against any episcopalian for his religion," the Whig declared. "But it is the politics of the church, its domineering spirit, its perpetual strides towards universal dominion, its power and its thirst of domination, a thirst not to be satiated by our absolute destruction, that we are combined to oppose." *N.Y. Gaz.*, Aug. 22, Sept. 19, Dec. 5, 1768, Jan. 16, 1769; *Pa. Journal*, Mar. 24, 31, Apr. 14, 1768.

once accused Livingston of forgery and on another occasion of prevarication, and "Whigs" showed how the Episcopalians made figures lie. Neither party hesitated to quibble over words or inconsequential details as it sought to put the other side in the wrong. Many of these newspaper articles were unfair; others reeked of false sweetness and reasonableness.[33]

In handling all these weapons, the Dissenters had the great advantage. The initiative had been theirs, and they kept it. They had the largest audience, one whose already existing fears they had only to justify; they did not, like the Anglicans, have to convert men to new views. Above all, the Dissenters were rich in talents. The New York–New Jersey clergy, with only occasional assistance from their ablest penman, Provost Smith, really could not compete with Livingston, Alison, and their bench of able controversialists in literary competence, ecclesiastical learning, and forensic skill. The strongest point made against the Anglicans was the suspicion — which we have seen was not without foundation — of "some unavowed ecclesiastical machinations." The "American Whig" and the "Centinel" were contemporary with the "Letters of Junius" and compare most favorably with the papers of the undisclosed English journalist, but where the latter excelled in destructive talent, the colonial Dissenters surpassed him in constructive ideas. They were men contending for principles and ideals.[34]

We will miss the lasting significance of this torrid newspaper debate if we regard it solely as a display of journalistic fireworks or merely as un-Christian propaganda. Read carefully, these essays disclose men groping their way amid the heat of controversy toward certain fundamental principles now recognized as American. In the fifth number of the "American Whig," dated April 11, 1768,

33. Timothy Tickle charged in the 23rd "Whip" that the Dissenters openly boasted that if a bishop came over he would be assassinated. *N.Y. Mercury,* Sept. 12, 1768; *N.Y. Gaz.,* Apr. 17, 1769.

34. Livingston printed part of a letter from a missionary to one of the King's chaplains, with the dare that if the "Whip" demanded the author's name, he would print it. The italics are his. ". . . It is apprehended, that not only the church, but *even the well-being of the civil polity in America,* depends, in a great measure, *upon the settlement of episcopacy here; for republican principles in religion, naturally engender the same in civil* government, which of late have been avowedly very rife in those parts, and have appeared in open and alarming light, in many melancholy instances. . . ." *N.Y. Gaz.,* July 25, 1768.

Livingston offered his readers a glimpse of the future of their country:

The day dawns in which the foundation of this mighty empire is to be laid, by the establishment of a *regular American Constitution*. All that has hitherto been done, seems to be little besides the collection of materials for the construction of this glorious fabrick. 'Tis time to put them together. The transfer of the European part of the great family is so swift, and our growth is so vast, that before seven years roll over our heads [1775!] the first stone must be laid. — Peace or war; famine or plenty; poverty or affluence; in a word, no circumstance, whether prosperous or adverse, can happen to our parent; no, nay, no conduct of hers, whether wise or imprudent, no possible temper on her part, whether kind or cross-grained, will put a stop to this building. . . . What an aera is this to America! and how loud the call to vigilance and activity! As we conduct, so will it fare with us and our children.[35]

About this prophetic conception of a manifest destiny in or out of the British Empire, clustered a number of supporting ideas. Toleration was being, and for a half-century had been, slowly transformed into an ideal of religious freedom. Sectarianism in fact — the normal colonial ecclesiastical condition — was producing a new theory of complete separation of church and state suitable to the American environment and temper. American republicanism was emerging naturally in the politics of a society where religious republicanism had long prevailed. By inheritance and experience the colonists were anti-clerical, and they perceived the danger to their provinces of too intimate a connection between the clergy and politics. In the course of their exchanges, they fastened on the Episcopal missionaries once and for all the label of Tories, and they demonstrated to the public satisfaction that bishops represented incipient tyranny. Above all, these men sensed, if they did not openly proclaim it, that, despite many similarities, a really great difference was developing between England and America which necessitated a new solution satisfactory to the New World. This the neo-colonials of the opposite side did not grasp.[36]

35. *N.Y. Gaz.*, Apr. 11, 1768.

36. *N.Y. Gaz.*, Aug. 29, 1768.

V

During the novel newspaper attack on the Chandler tract and episcopacy for America in the years 1767–69, there was no letup in the familiar kind of pamphlet exchanges. The foremost controversial writers among the Dissenters of both America and England went after Dr. Chandler's scalp at the same time that the Whigs and Centinels picked up his trail. For the most part, however, the pamphleteers kept the discussion on a somewhat higher ecclesiastical level.

Shortly after the publication of the appeal, Noah Welles brought out at New Haven *A Vindication of the Validity and Divine Right of Presbyterian Ordination . . . in Answer to the Exceptions of Mr. Jeremiah Leaming,* and in April, 1768, "that learned Veteran, Dr. Chauncy," as one opponent dubbed him, issued *The Appeal to the Public Answered, In Behalf of the Non-Episcopal Churches in America.* Four hundred copies sold in one week, and the Boston newspapers took it right up, printing extracts and comments. The minister's main contention was that the Chandler party was deceiving the public when it said it desired anything less than "a COMPLETE CHURCH HIERARCHY after the pattern of that at home, with a like large revenue for their grand support, and with the allowance of no other privilege to dissenters but that of a bare toleration." If proof be needed, what about the denial of incorporation to the New York Presbyterians? The Boston minister ended on a note of unshaken faith: Episcopacy may be established south of Pennsylvania, but religious liberty must ever prevail to the northward, since it "was the great Errand of our fore-fathers coming over to this world. . . ." [37]

Comments on the *Appeal* by Micajah Towgood which appeared in the *London Chronicle* in June of 1768 disturbed the author by charging that he had recommended "that a tax is to be laid upon the Americans" for the support of a bishop; furthermore extracts from Dr. Chauncy's answer had been printed. Chandler had hoped that the Archbishop would see to it that the entire *Appeal* was reprinted, but no one had even defended him against Towgood.

37. *N.Y. Mercury,* Sept. 19, 1768; Chauncy to Stiles, May 23, 1768, Stiles Papers.

The following May Dr. Chandler issued his own reply: *The Appeal Defended: or the Proposed American Episcopate Vindicated. . . .* The Jerseyman fondly imagined he had delivered the last word, and for a time his optimism appeared to be justified by the slackening of the Dissenter's zeal in mid-summer of 1769. This led the impulsive Mr. Inglis to assure Secretary Burton that "our Paper War with the Dissenters is now over. They retired from the Field of Controversy with much Ignominy." Actually the New England divines had concluded that Dr. Chandler had not made any point which had not been anticipated in Archbishop Secker's early writings; Charles Chauncy's acid comment was that "the Dr's chief talent seems to lie in writing plausibly to no purpose," and Ezra Stiles bore out Francis Alison's assumption that the New Englanders were abandoning the burden to the Middle Colonies by saying: "I think the Whigs, Centinels, Foots and Spirit of Liberty in America will defeat this," and "I thank God, I fear none of their Enterprises. I have assurance of their Defeat." [38]

In spite of his expressed contempt for Chandler's abilities, Dr. Chauncy announced in October that he had a reply ready whenever American paper could be procured (the nonimportation agreement deterred the use of English paper; this same restriction delayed the printing of his long-awaited history of episcopacy). In January of 1770, the public received *A Reply to Dr. Chandler's Appeal Defended,* which devoted 180 pages to "mauling" the missionary; it reminded him that the Southern Anglicans "have neither complained for want of Bishops, or desired the mission of them." Only the provinces from Pennsylvania to Massachusetts "contain the complainers and petitioners," and the Venerable Society's aim has always been "to episcopize these colonies." The Boston pastor also taunted the Jersey rector about his use of terms: "he ought to have known, there are no *Dissenters* in any of the Colonies to the northward of Maryland, unless *episcopal* ones." All that the victim of this diatribe could say in his own defense was that Chauncy's pages were "filled with Blunders and Sophistry" and complain that the

---

38. *London Chronicle,* June 14, 27, 1768; Schneiders, *Johnson,* I, 447–8; *N.Y. Gaz.,* May 29, 1769; Mass. Hist. Soc., *Collections,* IV, 433; Inglis to Secy., Aug. 12, 1769, S.P.G. Correspondence, ser. B, II, Pt. I, 229–31; Chauncy to Stiles, July 25, 1769, Stiles Papers; Stiles to Rodgers, July 29, 1769, Stiles Papers.

Dissenter would not grant him a single point that he had established. His Anglican friends were urging him to rejoin, but "it is difficult to deal with such an Antagonist, supported by such a Party, who resolve that he shall have a public ovation, as often as he attacks the Author of the Appeal." [39]

At London, in the meantime, Archbishop Secker's letter to Walpole came out and elicited an able answer in Archdeacon Blackburne's *Critical Commentary*. A copy reached Boston through the offices of Thomas Hollis. Ezra Stiles was so delighted with it, for "he is so good a Friend to American Liberty," that he wished he might know him, saying of the Englishman, "he has opened the Cabinet, the Pandora's Box; and discovered the latent Intrigues of this Bsp." The New Englanders are obliged to the Archdeacon for "developing sundry Things, which tho' we believed before, yet were in the dark." [40]

In May, 1771, Charles Chauncy produced his *chef d'œuvre*, a volume which he had had in preparation for years, *A Complete View of Episcopacy, As exhibited from the Fathers of the Christian Church, until the Close of the Second Century: Containing an Impartial Account . . . of what they say concerning Bishops and Presbyters . . . Tending to shew, that they esteemed these ONE and the SAME ORDER of Ecclesiastical Officers*. The long title introduced a long book, whose 474 pages would have gone to the press early in 1769 if paper had been available. Read by subscribers from Georgia to New Hampshire, this treatise silenced the opposition. In fact, Samuel Seabury, who was tougher than most, confessed:

I am tired and beat out. Had I suspected there was so much Nonsense, so much trifling, so much Falsehood in the Way, I believe I never should have medled with him. Tis like suing a Beggar, or shearing a Hog or fighting a Skunk.

Still, the man whom his adversaries called "the velvet-mouth'd Dr. Chandler," seemingly under a compulsion to defend himself, came

39. Stiles, *Itineraries*, 449; *Bos. Gaz.,* Oct. 23, 1769; June 11, 1770; *Bos. News-Letter*, Jan. 25, 1770; Chandler to Secy., Jan. 5, July 5, 1770, S.P.G. Correspondence, ser. B, XXIV, 97–8.

40. Blackburne, *Memoirs of Thomas Hollis,* I, 435, 436; Stiles to Chauncy, Mar. 19, 1770 (Mass. Hist. Soc., MSS), 41F, 104.

back with a reply to the reply to the reply, or *The Appeal Farther Defended; in Answer to the Farther Misrepresentations of Dr. Chauncy,* in June, 1771, but his luck would not turn, for the Boston divine's *Complete View of Episcopacy* had beaten Chandler's piece to the book shops by a month.[41]

VI

The propaganda barrage laid down by the Dissenters greatly extended the amount of space the newspapers allotted to the question of an American episcopacy, and the momentum thus imparted to the public prints did not diminish noticeably with the disappearance of the Whigs, Centinels, and Kicks. In 1768 the Reverend Andrew Eliot wrote to Thomas Hollis, who was a firm believer in the value of the press in fighting any threat to liberty, that "the Episcopalian controversy at present engrosses the attention of the public. The papers at New York and Philadelphia are filled with it." Dr. Samuel Johnson testified that the "poor Church is frequently tantalized and insulted in the Boston newspapers," though no regular campaign was being waged there. In June, an English gentlewoman, sister of a customs official, remarked of the Yankees:

The poison of disaffection has been infused and spread by inflammatory writers over the Continent. . . . The Credulity of the Common people here is imposed upon by a number of Lies raised to irritate and inflame them. They believe that the Commissrs. [of Customs] have an unlimited power to tax even their Lands, and that its in order to raise a Revenue, for supportg a Number of Bishops that are coming over and they are inspired with an enthusiastic Rage for defending their Religion and liberties.[42]

Any one who even glances briefly through the newspaper files for the years 1767–70 can testify that hundreds upon hundreds of items of religious import appear in their columns. They vary in

41. Chauncy to Johnson, Apr. 21, 1770, Hawks Papers, II, No. 28; *N.Y. Gaz.,* Oct. 31, 1768; *Bos. Gaz.,* May 27, 1771; *Bos. News-Letter,* June 20, 1771. The pros and cons of the Chandler-Chauncy controversy are carefully analyzed in Cross, *Anglican Episcopate,* 161–94.

42. Eliot to Hollis, Apr. 18, 1768, Mass. Hist. Soc., *Collections,* 4 ser., IV, 425; Hulton, *Letters of a Loyalist Lady,* 13.

length from three-line squibs to long essays or letters to the printer, and they exhibit every form and device known to the journalists of the day. An astonishing number of them had their origin in one of four London papers — the *London Chronicle,* the *St. James's Chronicle, Lloyd's Evening Post,* and the *Public Advertiser* — inserted at the behest of Thomas Hollis and read and clipped by American printers three thousand miles distant.

Probably no single insertion gave a weightier demonstration of the meshing of religion and politics than "A Plan for the Better Government of British America," written in 1769 but not printed by *Lloyd's Evening Post* until August 29, 1770. Because it represented a sort of culmination of the official side of the debate, it was widely copied in New England, and two of the general propositions advanced evoked much discussion among those men of a republican turn:

That inequality of rank and fortune is not only requisite for the support of every government, but essentially necessary to the interests and the very existence of society.

and

That an established religion, or one prevailing sect, or mode of religion, is absolutely needful to the well-being and permanency of every government.

The author deduced from these propositions "that a political inequality, and a proper established religion, ought to take place in America without delay, which last can only be effected by the appointment of Bishops, a regular performance of the rites of the Church of England, and a due administration of its ordinances."

Though the author knew about the current revulsion against bishops in America, he declared that the good of the whole required the sending of one bishop immediately. Once in Boston (the best seat for him), the bishop would soon allay the fears of the Dissenters, and the majority of the inhabitants would grow used to his presence and accept him. In an appendix, the writer presented an elaborate plan for carrying out his scheme, which seemed to have an "official" quality to it. America would be erected into a second kingdom, and George III would be styled "King of North America and the Isles." Three dioceses would be created: the first would comprise Massachusetts, New Hampshire, Rhode Island, Nova Scotia, Canada, and Newfoundland; the second, with a cathedral in Philadelphia, would consist of Pennsylvania, New Jersey, New York, Maryland, Virginia, and Bermuda; while the provinces of North and South Carolina, Georgia, East and West Florida, and the Caribbean Islands would constitute the third. The plan was well conceived and plausible, even though it indicated that the author had no understanding of the colonial temper.

VII

For us of the twentieth century, it is very, very difficult to recover imaginatively a real understanding of the enormous effect of this controversy on the opinions and feelings of a pious, dissenting people grown accustomed to ecclesiastical self-government and currently engaged in a struggle to protect their liberties in the civil sphere. The bad news or threats they read about in every week's newspaper produced a final cumulative effect like the rising crescendo of a bolero. The agitation over an American episcopate reached its peak by 1770, and the public had grown almost frenzied in the course of it. Dr. John Rodgers issued a sort of final report for Dr. Eliot on April 12:

We think that the spirited opposition that has been made to an American Episcopate has if not entirely defeated the Measure, yet it has delayed its Execution and we hope for half a century at least, which is a great thing, and the future Friends of the Cause of Liberty will be under great advantages for its Defence against any future attempts on it of a like Nature.

Noise and clamor had indeed turned out to be the best policy, and they had exceeded the most optimistic expectations. Eight years before Lexington, when the ministers learned that "the Bishops are coming," they wrote and spread the alarm all over the colonies. The people were roused and kept the watch. Henceforth Ezra Stiles could rest, certain that "LIBERTY and CONGREGATIONALISM will be triumphant Sisters in America." Or, so he thought at the time.[43]

43. Rodgers to Eliot, Apr. 12, 1770 (Mass. Hist. Soc., MSS), 41F, 105; Stiles to Chauncy, Nov. 3, 1768, Stiles Papers.

XII

INDEPENDENCE FOR CHURCH AND STATE

1 7 7 1 – 1 7 7 5

Public opinion and emotions could not be maintained at a fever pitch indefinitely, and from the year 1770 through 1774 the agitation over ecclesiastical matters died down perceptibly. However, the latter-day assumption that the attempts to establish an episcopate ceased and that the colonials became apathetic about the issue are demonstrably incorrect. The public did not want, nor was it ever permitted, to forget the dangers episcopacy posed to religious freedom in America. Though the proportion of space given to political affairs increased after 1772, that accorded to ecclesiastical news was sizable and of a nature to remind the dissenting readers that religious as well as civil liberties were being threatened, and that, if one was lost, the other would go, too. Ambrose Serle, secretary to Admiral Lord Howe, was talking of this power of the public prints when he reported to Lord Dartmouth after hostilities with England began: "Among other Engines, which have raised the present Commotion next to indecent Harangues of the Preachers, none has had a more extensive or stronger Influence than the Newspapers of the respective Colonies." [1]

II

Though blocked for the time being in their plans to bring in bishops by the successful opposition of the English and American

1. A letter of Ambrose Serle to Lord Dartmouth, Nov. 8, 1776, contains the best brief statement of the religious causes of the American Revolution the author has seen; it also contains a shrewd assessment of the ecclesiastics of New York. Benjamin F. Stevens, *Facsimiles of Manuscripts in European Archives Relating to America, 1773–1783* (London, 1895), XXIV, Nos. 2045, 2046.

Dissenters, and severely handicapped by the loss of their great leader, Thomas Secker, the American missionaries nevertheless felt that eventually they would get what they were after. Admitting they had not succeeded in making their proposals for suffragan bishops palatable to any large number of Nonconformists, they turned hopefully to the second point in the Johnson-Chandler Plan and determined to bid for the support of the parish clergy of the Episcopal colonies south of Pennsylvania.

Samuel Johnson had frequently asserted that there could be no hope of obtaining an episcopate until the Southern Colonies joined the Northern Anglicans in petitioning for it. Upon returning from Maryland in 1767, Thomas Bradbury Chandler gave a discouraging report: aside from a few local clergymen like the fiery Jonathan Boucher, who ardently favored strengthening the Church, most of those he met were not only averse to bishops but they did not want the Northern Colonies to send men to fill vacancies down there or to add to their numbers.[2]

The Shrewsbury Convention sent President Myles Cooper of King's College and the Reverend Robert McKean on a mission to Maryland, the first official undertaking of its kind, and they found "the Inclinations" of their brethren more favorable to them and their project than they had been led to expect. On a second swing around the Southern circuit in 1770, Mr. Cooper was in Maryland when the clergy there drew up petitions to the King, two archbishops, Governor Eden, and the Proprietor asking for a bishop for their colony. Eight of the clergymen applied for membership in the Venerable Society, and, as Inglis wrote Samuel Johnson, the Northern members were so delighted with the news from the South that they were glad to recommend them. It was the hope of the Episcopalians that this action of petitioning would pave the way to get Virginia and the Carolinas to join Maryland in pleas for a bishop, and the Reverend Mr. Inglis was all set to frame a circular letter to be sent out to the clergy of the Old Dominion and the Carolinas to engage their concurrence.[3]

2. For the complicated situation in Lord Baltimore's province, see Charles A. Barker, *The Background of the Revolution in Maryland* (New Haven, 1940), 275–7, 358, 360–66; Schneiders, *Johnson*, I, 406, 408; Lydekker, *Inglis*, 117.

3. Myles Cooper to Secy., Nov. 19, 1767, S.P.G. Correspondence, ser. B, II; Perry, *Historical Collections, Maryland and Delaware*, IV, 342; Lydekker, *Inglis*, 117.

As usual, however, Mr. Inglis's optimism was greater than the facts warranted. William Eddis, an English layman, was puzzled by the situation but perceived it more realistically:

I cannot conceive on what principle the colonists are so strongly prejudiced against the introduction of the episcopal order . . . yet I am persuaded, any attempt to establish an hierarchy, would be resisted with as much acrimony as during the gloomy prevalence of puritanical zeal. . . . They have . . . conceived such rooted prejudices against the highest orders of the church, that they are positively persuaded the advantages to be acquired, by such an institution in the colonies, would by no means counter-balance the evils which might arise from it.

The governor also, as the Reverend Hugh Neil of Queen Anne's County advised Secretary Burton, received the petitioners very coldly and let them know "that the Livings in Maryland were Donatives and stood in no need of the aid of Episcopacy, &c. This casts a damp on many." [4]

The news of the Maryland petitions was immediately spread on the pages of practically every paper. It was known that Archbishop Secker had once declared that, if any American province ever asked for a bishop, one would be sent, and the dissenting leaders had appreciated that it was only a matter of time before such an event would take place; they were quite sure that some of the missionaries had had a hand in prompting the petitioning at this time. However, as Chauncy wrote to Stiles, there was no way to stop it, but he trusted that they would outlive and outgrow any inconvenience from it. [5]

In the Old Dominion, where the Church of England had been established for more than a century, the temper of the people was comparable to that of the Marylanders. For some years the Virginians had been reading the same news items in the gazettes printed by Purdie and Dixon, and by William Rind, that appeared

---

4. William Eddis, *Letters from America* (London, 1792), 49–51; Perry, *Historical Collections, Maryland and Delaware*, IV, 342–3.

5. Chauncy to Stiles, June 14, 1771, Stiles Papers; *N.Y. Gaz.*, Feb. 4, 1771; *Bos. News-Letter*, Feb. 14, 1771; *Essex Gazette*, Feb. 19, 1771; *N.H. Gaz.*, Feb. 22, 1771; *Providence Gaz.*, Feb. 23, 1771; *New London Gaz.*, Mar. 8, 1771; *N.Y. Mercury*, Mar. 11, 1771; Purdie and Dixon's *Virginia Gazette*, Mar. 28, 1771.

in the Northern press, and they must have gleaned considerable knowledge of the contest raging over episcopacy and reacted as the New Englanders did at a letter of Junius clipped from the *London Evening Post*, of December 19, 1769:

Divided as they are into a thousand forms of policy and religion, there is one point in which they all agree: They equally detest the pageantry of a K——g, and the supercilious hypocrisy of a Bishop.[6]

Dr. Samuel Johnson had made the initial approach to the Virginia Anglicans in the winter of 1766–67. John Holt, the New York printer, "a high-churchman, but a firm whig," came originally from Williamsburg. Having once served as mayor, Holt naturally knew all of the local celebrities, including the Reverend John Camm, Professor of Divinity at the College of William and Mary. In 1767, at Johnson's urging, Holt made an inquiry of Mr. Camm respecting the Virginia clergy's views on bishops and arranged a correspondence between the two divines; Dr. Johnson wrote directly to Camm on April 10. Frankly admitting he could never understand the Old Dominion's reticence on the religious issue, he said he had asked Holt to sound out Camm. Pleading that it was essential that the Southern provinces join in the applications to the government in England if they were to prevent the Presbyterians from gaining the ascendancy over the Church, Dr. Johnson urged the Virginian to whip up some Episcopalian spirit in "both the clergy and laity of your province, and if possible of all your southern provinces." [7]

Professor Camm evidently won his president, James Horrocks, a fellow Yorkshireman and Trinity College man, to the Johnson-Chandler Plan, and indirect evidence indicates that these two communicated the details of the scheme to conventions of the Virginia clergy long before Horrocks took his seat on the Governor's Council in May, 1770. There is some reason to think that Chandler's *Appeal* circulated in Virginia, and a "trusty Friend" of the Reverend Charles

6. Rind, *Virginia Gazette,* Mar. 8, 1770; Purdie and Dixon's *Va. Gaz.,* Aug. 8, 1767; Sept. 8, Oct. 27, 1768; Aug. 10, 1769; Jan. 18, Apr. 5, 1770; Jan. 2, 1772.

7. It is possible that Camm visited in Stratford in April, 1768, and gave Johnson a deplorable account of the clergy in Virginia. Schneiders, *Johnson,* I, 398–9, 402–3, 440.

Inglis set out in the winter of 1770 to carry copies of the "Circular Letter" to the principal clergymen; so, by various means, the Anglicans worked industriously to "prepare Matters for vigorous Operations" and were rewarded for their labors when a letter came from Mr. Horrocks in March, 1771, heartily endorsing the petitioning for bishops and promising to present the matter to the general meeting of the Virginia clergy in the late spring.[8]

Purdie and Dixon's sheet of May 9, 1771, carried Commissary Horrocks's call for a convention of the Virginia clergy on June 4, 1771, to discuss "the Expediency of an Application to proper Authority for an American Episcopate." Out of more than a hundred Episcopal divines in the colony, only eleven responded to the summons, but, nevertheless, Mr. Horrocks insisted on consideration of the question. The vote was eight (including the Commissary) for applying, four against petitioning; and two of the four non-signers, Professors Samuel Henley and Thomas Gwatkin of the College, protested that the convention was not representative of clerical opinion. They also deemed it ill-advised at the moment when strained relations with the Mother Country existed, and more importantly:

Because we cannot help considering it as extremely indecent for the Clergy to make such an Application without the Concurrence of the President, Council, and Representatives of this Province; an Usurpation directly repugnant to the Rights of Mankind.[9]

The enthusiasm and optimism nourished at Manhattan by Charles Inglis, who kept in touch with the Commissary, were not destined to last very long. Richard Bland, a leading member of the House of Burgesses, described to a London correspondent on August 1, 1771, what followed upon the meeting of the Episcopal Convention:

After much Jangle and Disputation, Formal Protests were published in the Gazettes by the four Protesters, against the legality as well as

8. P. & D. *Va. Gaz.*, Aug. 26, Sept. 14, 1769; June 6, 1771; Inglis to Johnson, Dec. 4, 1770; Mar. 28, 1771, Hawks Papers, II; Schneiders, *Johnson*, I, 477.

9. For an excellent account of the strictly internal course of the dispute, see George M. Brydon, *Virginia's Mother Church and the Political Conditions under which it Grew* (Philadelphia, 1952), II, 346–61; P. & D. *Va. Gaz.*, May 9, 16, June 6, 1771. The Henley-Gwatkin resolutions were printed verbatim in *London Chronicle*, Aug. 31, 1771.

regularity of the proceeding. This brought on a Severe Paper War. Mr. Camm . . . commenced Champion for a Bishop; and Messrs. Henley and Gwatkin . . . appeared in the Field of Battle against a Bishop. This War continued with much violence and personal abuse till the meeting of the Assembly, when the House of Burgesses put an end to it, at least Publickly by declaring unanimously against the expediency of an American Episcopate, and returned thanks to the four Clergymen for opposing a Measure by which much Disturbance, great anxiety and apprehension would certainly take place among his Majesty's Faithful subjects in America.

. . . If this scheme had been effected, it would have overturned all of the acts of Assembly relative to ecclesiastical jurisdiction, most of which acts have received the Royal assent, and have existed among us almost from the first establishment of the Colony.

. . . Our whole ecclesiastical constitution, which has been Fixed by the King's Assent, must be altered if a Bishop is appointed in America with any Jurisdiction at all, which will produce greater convulsions than anything that has as yet happened in this part of the Globe. For let me tell you, a Religious Dispute is the most Fierce and Destructive of all others to the Peace and Happiness of Government.

. . . I profess myself a sincere son of the established church, but I can embrace her Doctrines without approving of her Hierarchy, which I know to be a Relick of the Papal Incroachments upon the Common Law.[10]

Commissary Horrocks, having stirred up a hornet's nest, discovered that his health was failing and, abandoning John Camm to answer Gwatkin's and Henley's protests, sailed for England with his lady on June 20, 1771. The newspaper announced that he would also seek the appointment of a bishop, and, according to Bland, some gentlemen believed Horrocks expected to be "the First Right Reverend Father of the American Church." Now it was Anglican against Anglican in Virginia's newspapers. The Reverend Mr. Inglis procured copies of the petitions to the King and Bishop of London, together with the Henley-Gwatkin protests, for Inslee and Carr to insert in the *New York Gazette*. No doubt he imagined that he had

10. Richard Bland to Thomas Adams of London, *William and Mary Quarterly*, V (1896–97), 152–4.

made a great scoop, but he miscalculated, for the consequence was the spreading throughout the colonies of the story of the division in the Anglican ranks in Virginia and also of the extreme unpopularity of Commissary James Horrocks.[11]

To prop up the sagging Episcopal cause in the Old Dominion, Thomas Bradbury Chandler turned author again and wrote *An Address from the Clergy of New-York and New-Jersey, to the Episcopalians in Virginia; occasioned by some late Transactions in that Colony relative to an American Episcopate,* which appeared at New York in November, 1771. Basically it was a defense of the policy pursued by the American missionaries since 1767 (the Johnson-Chandler Plan), and an explanation of the Butler Plan for bishops without secular powers. The New Yorkers made the mistake of censuring the House of Burgesses for its endorsement of the actions of the four protesters, which immediately vitiated the claim that their object was solely "to promote the Cause of religious Liberty." [12]

Certain personal reflections on the protesters and the open disapproval of Virginia's revered lower house drew a prompt rejoinder from the Reverend Thomas Gwatkin in *A Letter to the Clergy of New-York and New-Jersey, occasioned by an Address to the Episcopalians of Virginia* (Williamsburg, 1772). The English-born cleric showed himself a strong Episcopalian but seriously questioned the wisdom, timing, and propriety of the application for bishops:

In the Name of Common Sense, who, or what, are the Reverend Gentlemen of New York and New Jersey, that, in this Protestant Country, this Land of Liberty, with such inquisitorial Solemnity presume to pass Sentence upon their Fellow Subjects!

For, said this colonial counterpart of Francis Blackburne, any future bishop would have to hold courts and exercise ecclesiastical

---

11. *Bos. News-Letter,* July 25, 1771; Bland to Adams, *William and Mary Quarterly,* V, 154; John P. Kennedy, ed., *Journal of the House of Burgesses of Virginia, 1770–72* (Richmond, 1906), 122; Inglis to Johnson, July 4, 1771, Hawks Papers, II; *N.Y. Gaz.,* June 24, 1771; *Bos. Evening Post,* July 1, 1771; for the Virginia debate, see both Purdie and Dixon's and Rind's newspapers, July–December, 1771.

12. Inglis to Johnson, Nov. 6, 1771, Hawks Papers, II; Chandler, *Address . . . to the Episcopalians in Virginia,* 6–8.

jurisdiction over the laity as well as the clergy, because the canon law so provided. Besides, their "new fangled Episcopate" would contravene the Virginia constitution by giving the bishops authority over the clergy that was now in the hands of the vestries:

Numberless Passages in your Pamphlet, the Petition, &c. show that your Intention is to apply not merely to the *Spiritual,* for the *Consecration,* but to the *Civil Powers,* for the *Establishment of an American Episcopate.* But this must meet with perpetual Opposition from the Dissenters. . . . In Fact, there never was a Controversy carried on where Religion had so little Concern.

In closing, Professor Gwatkin delivered two slashing remarks, according his Northern brethren "a Distinguished Place in the Catalogue of those turbulent Ecclesiastics who have been the Pest and Scandal of holy Religion," and branding their plan for an episcopate a "simple Matter for Ridicule." No Dissenter ever hit them harder than Gwatkin.[13]

In March, 1772, Purdie and Dixon stated in their *Gazette:* "Many of our Readers, for some time have complained of their being tired of the Dispute about an American Episcopate, and we must acknowledge that we begin to be sick of it likewise, seeing that there is no prospect of its Termination." Still, the show went on, for it had a compelling fascination for the bulk of the people of the Old Dominion to whom open debate on a public question was a novelty, dating only as far back as the founding of the second *Virginia Gazette* by William Rind in 1766. Every point made for and against bishops in the Northern press during the past sixty years was repeated over and over, along with discussion of certain specific provincial questions, notably the constitutional problem and the power of vestries. When the debate broadened after March, 1772, into an examination of toleration in general, the question raised was whether Protestant Dissenters such as the growing Presbyterian and Baptist bodies should be required to maintain the Church of England by the payment of tithes. Virginia's conservative

13. Bishop William White, commenting on the Virginia petition, agreed with Gwatkin's protest: "It was not unlikely, that the British government, had they sanctioned an Episcopacy in the colonies, would have endeavored to render it subservient to the support of a party, on the plan of the newly projected domination." White, *Memoirs,* 78.

treasurer, Robert Carter Nicholas, opposed the appointment of Henley to his parish because of his stand on bishops, and kept up a running argument with the clergyman in the papers from 1772 to the eve of the revolt. In the course of these exchanges the whole question of establishment in Virginia came under review. The question of episcopacy merged with problems of toleration and establishment and led without a break to James Madison's religious clause in the celebrated Bill of Rights of 1776, to the bill for disestablishment of the same year, and the final statute for religious freedom passed in 1786.[14]

South of Virginia the efforts of the United Convention to win support for an Anglican episcopate fared even less satisfactorily. One of the grievances of the North Carolina Regulators was a recent law establishing the Church of England in their province, and they bitterly resented Governor William Tryon's characterization of them as "a faction of Quakers and Baptists, who aimed to overset the Church of England," when most of their leaders were Episcopalians. In this colony, overwhelmingly composed of Nonconformists, the Church really amounted to very little. Professor Henley and other Virginia writers held up the violence of the Regulators as a horrible example of the kind of civil strife that might ensue if bishops were sent where Dissenters predominated, while Dr. Chandler insisted the rebellion "could never have happened, but in a Part of the Country where the Principles of the Church of England were but little known, and never properly taught." Disallowance by the Privy Council in 1773 of the charter for Queen's College in Mecklenburg County because of its Presbyterian management did not endear the Church to the Tar Heels. From Charles Town in South Carolina in 1774, the Reverend William Tennent wrote to Ezra Stiles that "the Episcopalians here are highly enraged at your Tory Clergy who are desirous of episcopal principalities, and many of the first in the province do declare to

14. Carl Bridenbaugh, *Seat of Empire: The Political Role of Eighteenth-Century Williamsburg* (Williamsburg, 1958), 68; see both Virginia newspapers for January, 1772 to June, 1774, especially Jan. 21, Mar. 12, June 4, 1772 of P. & D.'s *Virginia Gazette,* and Rind's *Va. Gaz.,* May 12, May 27, June 10, Dec. 2, 1773; and for Northern interest, the Philadelphia, New York, New London, Boston, and Portsmouth papers, 1771–72, particularly *N.Y. Journal,* Aug. 22, 29, Sept. 5, 1771.

me that they will turn Dissenters in a Body if the parliament offers to send Bishops over." [15]

Far from advancing the cause, the attempt of Dr. Chandler and his New York associates to gain Southern backing for their Episcopal scheme turned out miserably. They succeeded only in increasing the fear of prelacy throughout the South and in inspiring fierce opposition not merely among the body of the laity, who saw the threat to the power of their vestries, but also in a majority of the clergy of the Old Dominion, who did not aspire to be governed and disciplined by bishops or deprived of the livings to which local vestrymen had appointed them. It would be a mistake to assume, as has so often been done, that prior to 1774 colonial Dissenters and Anglicans shared no anti-Episcopal sentiment, for, as we have seen, the Southern Anglicans, especially in Virginia, enjoyed through their vestries a virtually congregational form of church polity, which neither they nor the majority of their parish clergy had any remote desire to change. Republicanism in religion existed in all of the colonies, not just in New England. When, in 1771, the S.P.G.'s missionaries attempted to bring the Southerners into line, it took less than a year to weld them in sentiment to the Northern Dissenters and the Nonconformists at home. At no time after 1771 did religious differences stand in the way of political union in the face of British misrule. The men of the cloth and their printer allies had set them all to singing in the mood of "Blest be the tie that binds."

III

During the missionary venture in the South, the New Yorkers implemented the third feature of the Johnson-Chandler Plan, pressing their superiors in Britain for action. The news from London augured well; a "Person of Eminence" was quoted as predicting that the issue of bishops for America would be taken up soon, now that "our late Party Rage" was over, for some judicious men, some

---

15. *Pa. Chronicle*, Aug. 12, 1771; P. & D. *Va. Gaz.*, June 20, 1771; Chandler to Secy., June 24, 1771, S.P.G. Correspondence, ser. B, XXIV, 99; Carl Bridenbaugh, *Myths and Realities: Societies of the Colonial South* (Baton Rouge, 1952), 188–9; Stiles, *Itineraries*, 576.

in the Ministry and those connected with them, thought it would be "good Policy, as well as of Justice and Piety" to send them over.[16]

As soon as the indefatigable Reverend Thomas Bradbury Chandler gave the press his *Address to the Virginia Clergy,* he set about drawing up a number of petitions to be sent home with President Myles Cooper, who sailed for London on the mast ship, October 13, 1771:

He goes partly as a missionary from us, in order to convert the guardians of the Church from the error of their ways. I think our sending missionaries among them is almost as necessary as their sending missionaries to America. But I fear the difficulty of proselyting such a nation will be found greater than that of converting the American savages.

This intelligence circulated with extraordinary rapidity in the colonial newspapers. The old apprehensions and animosities which it awakened were soon increased by the reports that Messrs. Cooper and Horrocks had joined forces in the business of petitioning for American bishops and were "moving every spring to support this pious institution." With their English informant, Americans agreed that "something should certainly be done." [17]

The death of Dr. Samuel Johnson on January 6, 1772, proved to be as great a loss to the Anglican cause in America as that of Archbishop Secker four years before. Now only Thomas Bradbury Chandler remained to lead the Episcopal forces. In 1774 he produced a long tract defending Secker's letter to Walpole and criticizing Archdeacon Blackburne's *Critical Commentary* upon it. In this last blast of the trumpet in the religious conflict, he displayed less acerbity and less poise than in previous publications, but he continued to claim for his side that "they aim at no more than they pretend." This was much like shouting "Wolf" in the Dissenters' ears.[18]

16. *N.Y. Mercury,* Dec. 9, 1771; *Massachusetts Spy,* Dec. 19, 1771.

17. *N.Y. Mercury,* Oct. 14, 1771; Schneiders, *Johnson,* I, 483; Rev. John Preston to Secy., Mar. 10, 1772, S.P.G. Correspondence, ser. B, XXIV, 282; *Mass. Spy,* Jan. 30, 1772; *New London Gaz.,* May 22, 1772; *Providence Gaz.,* May 23, 1772.

18. This was the first time that Bishop Sherlock's memorial for bishops (1749/50) was published in England or America. Dr. William Smith owned the manuscript copy. Thomas Bradbury Chandler, *A Free Examination of the Critical Commentary*

In the critical year 1774, the most ardent missionaries turned directly to political writing. Dr. Chandler's *American Querist* propounded one hundred questions to the patriots; the fourth one branded the Americans' bigotry in politics as bad as their bigotry in religion and naturally productive of intolerance. The tract proved the cleric an unequivocal Tory. A letter from the Reverend Samuel Peters to Dr. Auchmuty at the time of the meeting of the First Continental Congress, urging him and his friends to close ranks against the rebels, riled the populace when it was printed in the *Boston Evening Post*. Inaccurately as well as indiscreetly, Peters related that one Episcopal minister was threatened by a Connecticut mob that shouted:

Down with the Church, the Rags of Popery, &c. Their Rebellion is obvious, and Treason is common, and Robbery is the daily Devotion.

Though the Connecticut clergy published a letter repudiating Mr. Peters's statements, and by implication Dr. Auchmuty's, the propaganda damage could not be repaired.[19]

The high Toryism of Dr. Samuel Auchmuty had been part of his birthright, and he could never refrain from giving it vent. On April 19, 1775, he wrote a letter to Captain John Montrésor of the British Army which fell into patriot hands and was published as a broadside. He quoted a London communication of March 4 praising the New York clergy under the Doctor's leadership for their fine behavior in the crisis, and then added:

I must own I was born among the saints and rebels, but it was my misfortune. Where are your Congresses now: What say Hancock, Adams, and all their rebellious followers? Are they still bold? I trow not. We have

on *Archbishop Secker's Letter to Mr. Walpole, to which is added, by Way of an Appendix, A Copy of Bishop Sherlock's Memorial* (New York, 1774), iv, 34, 103–22. Hugh Gaine bound this pamphlet with Beilby Porteus, *A Review of the Life and Character of Archbishop Secker*, which he reprinted from the London edition of 1773.

19. Thomas Bradbury Chandler, *The American Querist: or, Some Questions Proposed Relative to the Present Disputes Between Great Britain and her American Colonies* (New York, 1774), 2; *Bos. Eve. Post*, Oct. 24, Nov. 14, 1774. Writing as "A. W. Farmer," Samuel Seabury turned out to be one of the most effective pamphleteers and less vitriolic than in his ecclesiastical pieces. Moses C. Tyler, *Literary History of the American Revolution* (New York, 1941), I, 334–5.

lately been plagued with a rascally Whig Mob here, but they have effected nothing. . . .

As Dr. Auchmuty wrote these words, Hancock and Adams were safe; the embattled farmers had fired the shot at Concord bridge. Worst of all for the Anglican clergy, Isaiah Thomas soon ran this letter in the *Massachusetts Spy* and a broadside in reply from "C. J." was hawked about New York. It purported to be from an Episcopalian who declared that many persons believed that the Church of England, because of its close connection with the state, was inimical to liberty in America. Otherwise, why did Dr. Chandler, Dr. Cooper, and Mr. Seabury, "those zealous Advocates for Episcopacy, abscond as soon as they found copies of some Letters sent hence to England. . . . It appears too from Auchmuty's Correspondent's Letter, that the Clergy have interested themselves warmly against us." [20]

IV

Up to the outbreak of the War for Independence, organized Dissent preserved and strengthened its transocean communications, but the energies of the English Nonconformists were principally absorbed in efforts to procure a relaxation of the requirement that the Protestant Dissenting ministers subscribe to certain of the Thirty-Nine Articles of the Church of England. A group of liberal Anglicans, with headquarters at the Feathers Tavern in London, appealed to Parliament to end subscription, but the House of Commons refused to receive the Feathers Petition by a vote of 217 to 71; still, the experience encouraged the Protestant Dissenting ministers to approach Parliament once more, as they had in the days of Sir Robert Walpole. Sir George Saville eloquently argued their case before the Commons, which passed a Relief Bill in 1772 and another (somewhat different) in 1773, but in each instance high Tory and prelatical influence brought about defeat of the bills in the House of Lords.[21]

20. *Dr. Samuel Auchmuty to Capt. J. Montrésor; Chief Engineer, at Boston* (Broadside: Library of Congress); *Mass. Spy,* May 24, 1775.

21. Three Denominations, Minute Book, II, 105, 109–10, 113, 116, 148–52, 153–9; Dissenting Deputies, Minutes, II, 126.

This attempt at ecclesiastical reform in the Mother Country produced a furious literary activity among the Dissenters. The Reverend Philip Furneaux successfully challenged the great Blackstone's interpretation of the Toleration Act, for which he received the thanks of the Body of the Three Denominations. Of greater interest to the colonists was *A Calm and Plain Answer to the Enquiry, Why are you a Dissenter from the Church of England?* by the Reverend Micajah Towgood, the veteran Presbyterian apologist, the fourth edition of which was reprinted at Boston in 1773.[22]

Pressing as were their own immediate concerns, the London Nonconformists habitually found time to inform and assist their brethren overseas. Taking advice from London, the Convention of Delegates meeting at Norwalk in Connecticut, September, 1771, voted unanimously not to appoint an agent in London, but to correspond with the Dissenting Deputies. Accordingly, Dr. John Rodgers informed Jasper Mauduit of the proposed Maryland addresses and the crossing of Commissary Horrocks with the Virginia petition for bishops, and declared that the assemblies of Connecticut and Massachusetts had instructed their agents to oppose any such Episcopalian moves. A second letter, informing Mr. Mauduit of President Cooper's mission, revealed that the Americans were gravely alarmed about this new threat to their liberties. In fact the letter from the Convention of Delegates wasted no words in declaring that, if bishops were to be established in America, it was highly probable that the happy connection between Great Britain and her colonies might be broken. In view of this, they again asked the Dissenting Deputies to use their utmost skill to prevent any such measures.[23]

Thomas Cotton of Guy's Hospital, secretary of the Dissenting Deputies, told his Committee of Correspondence in February, 1772, that, though the petitions had been presented, "he was well assured nothing would come of it." Letters sent to Messrs. Alison and Rodgers indicated that the Deputies were watching the situation

22. Philip Furneaux, *Letters to the Honourable Mr. Justice Blackstone, concerning the Exposition of the Act of Toleration, and Some Positions relative to Religious Liberty in his Celebrated Commentaries on the Laws of England* (2nd ed., London, 1771); Three Denominations, Minute Book, II, 89; *London Chronicle,* June 1771–Aug. 1773, and for the same dates, *Bos. Gaz.; Bos. News-Letter; Providence Gaz.; N.H. Gaz., passim.*

23. *Convention of Delegates,* 30–35; Dissenting Deputies, Minutes, II, 118, 119–21.

but that the men in power did not seem to be in favor of granting any such petitions at present; the Committee did advise, however, that the colonials send over counter-petitions as soon as possible.[24]

After considering these messages, the Elizabeth-Town Convention of September, 1772, directed Cotton Mather Smith to thank the Deputies for their information and promises of "constant attention" to their interests, and also to reaffirm the Convention's belief that the American missionaries had by no means dropped the project. Inasmuch as the Cooper-Horrocks mission had failed, the Delegates did not send any counter-petitions but informed the Dissenting Deputies that they were collecting reliable statistics on their vast superiority in numbers and importance for their colleagues to hold up to the public view in Britain. "If the intelligence we propose to send you should be communicated to the public through the channel of some of your newspapers or magazines, which circulate farthest through the kingdom, we presume it might give more just ideas of the true state of things on this continent, that it is probable many at present have." [25]

No answer came from the Londoners before the next convention, which met at Stamford, Connecticut, in September, 1773, with delegates from as far away as South Carolina. The members ordered Dr. John Witherspoon to inquire about the existing state of affairs in England and report to the Dissenting Deputies that Dr. Rodgers and others had calculated that the ratio of Dissenters to Episcopalians in the province of New York was 20 to 1; in Connecticut about the same; in New Jersey and Pennsylvania somewhat greater; and in New Hampshire, Massachusetts, and Rhode Island, still greater. In the "Episcopal Colonies" of the South, "the non-Episcopalians are in some of them a majority, and in the rest a large and growing population." As a further service, the Convention had ordered the gathering of information about "the state of religious liberty" in the several colonies for use "in the grand struggle we or posterity may be called to make in this glorious cause." At the next annual meeting, the Convention judged it inexpedient

24. Dissenting Deputies, Minutes, II, 124, 129–31; *Convention of Delegates*, 36–7; *Records of the General Association of . . . Connecticut*, 71–2.

25. *Convention of Delegates*, 38–9.

to write to its London associates, because it had received no answer to Dr. Witherspoon's communication.[26]

For some reason, not until October 29, 1774, did Chairman Lucas (who had succeeded Jasper Mauduit) read the Witherspoon letter to his Committee; an answer was directed, but no mention is made of it in the minutes of the Convention of Delegates. This, so far as the records show, was the last transatlantic communication from the Dissenting Deputies to their colonial brethren. They had performed their tasks nobly and well. That no bishop ever went out to America was largely due to the Londoners' prompt actions before any movement could gain headway. No contemporary understood more clearly the impulse behind their remarkably effective work than the Anglican, Francis Blackburne:

It was their concern for, and their desire to preserve to the Americans of their own Antiepiscopal persuasion, the *full exercise of their civil and religious rights* (which they apprehended upon good grounds, might be encroached upon, by the admission of Bishops into any of the American Provinces) that occasioned their vigilance. . . . They knew the hardship of those legal disabilities under which they themselves lay at home. They had good reason to believe, that the influence of the established Hierarchy contributed to continue this grievance. Their brethren in America were as yet free from it, and if Bishops were let in among them, and particularly, under the notion of presiding in *established* Episcopal Churches, there was the highest probability, they would take their precedents of Government and Discipline from the Establishment in the mother country, and would probably never be at rest, till they had established it on the basis of an exclusive Test. They knew their American brethren thought on this subject, just as they themselves did. They knew how *cautiously* the projectors of the plan covered their march from all the Colonies, but their own confidants. They knew that, without their interposition, the arrival of a Bishop in America would probably be the first notice the Colonists would have of his appointment at home. They were aware of the alarm this would give them, and of the dis-

26. On its own, the Presbyterian Synod had opened a correspondence on religious liberty with Geneva, North Holland, and Scotland. *Records of the Presbyterian Church,* 413–16, 426, 453; Dissenting Deputies, Minutes, II, 148–9, 179–81, 182; *Convention of Delegates,* 41–2.

agreeable consequences of their opposition, with respect to the Government. They wisely, therefore, and like good patriots, signified their apprehensions to the Government, and strengthened them with such proofs, as entirely convinced the Ministry, how much the public peace and welfare depended upon the suppression of this pernicious project.[27]

V

The *Boston News-Letter* reported from Purdie and Dixon's *Virginia Gazette* for June 11, 1772, the heartening news from London that the petition lately presented to the King had been rejected, "it being considered, in its true light, as the desire of a few meddling Priests, and not of the People!" This was the last time the Episcopalians approached the throne or the government on the subject, but of course the colonists, while rejoicing over this particular item, had no way of foreseeing that. They could call to mind many previous occasions when they had been buoyed up by glad tidings only to learn a few weeks or months later that the Episcopalians were moving in force again.[28]

As in the past, the colonial printers continued to play a large part in keeping the specter of episcopacy before the public. In 1773 an anonymous pamphlet entitled *The Case of the Scotch-Presbyterians of the City of New-York* appeared at Manhattan. It was evident even then that it was the work of Dr. John Rodgers, who had been preparing data on the history of the oppression of the Presbyterians for some time and, just lately, for the Convention of Delegates. Sparing no words, the author stated that "the malice and insolence of the stratagem to defeat the petition of the Presbyterian Church of New-York, may stand in the place of a thousand arguments, for the immediate appointment of such an agent." The Dutch Reformed Church of Albany experienced similar frustrations.

27. Thomas Hollis wrote to Andrew Eliot in 1771: "I think it is possible that the Confusions which are likely to break out soon here att home, will put an End to American Episcopation, and that if those Confusions should not break out, and that the E[arl] of B[ute] should reign Favorite, that Scheme will then be driven into Execution at all Events." Hollis had retired in 1770 to Dorset, where he died four years later. Hollis to Eliot, Aug. 28, 1771, Hollis Papers; Dissenting Deputies, Minutes, II, 148–9, 179–2; Blackburne, *Critical Commentary*, 48–9.

28. *Bos. News-Letter*, July 2, 1772.

In 1774 a petition for their incorporation was turned down again when James De Lancey and John Watts called for a rejection. Fifteen days after the fight at Lexington, however, Lord Dartmouth instructed Governor Tryon that, even though the applications of the Dutch Reformed and Presbyterians for incorporation involved "constitutional questions of great difficulty," the King had authorized him to grant charters, if the legal officers and Council of the province agree that they "are free from any difficulty of such a nature." This reluctant display of the royal grace and favor came some eighty years too late. Fighting had begun in what, as far as New York was concerned, Ambrose Serle properly termed a religious war.[29]

In Massachusetts, the attention of the ministers had been turned to the changing attitude of Thomas Hutchinson toward the church of his fathers. One of the saving graces of Acting Governor Thomas Hutchinson was the fact that he was a native-born Congregationalist and a regular attendant at Dr. Pemberton's church. By 1771, however, he began to drift toward the Anglican shore, and he confided to Sir Francis Bernard that the only reason he did not go all the way over to the Church of England was that the Episcopal clergy were of the opinion that he could do them more service by staying where he was. The Governor did not go to any lengths to conceal his new preference: the papers notified the public that he had stood up with two customs officers at a christening held in Cambridge at Apthorp House; when he received his commission as governor, and the several denominations sent the customary addresses to him, the Congregationalists did not receive the encouraging answer he accorded the Episcopalians. The denouement occurred with the Governor's Thanksgiving Proclamation for 1771, which recommended to the ministers and the people "to return thanks to Almighty God, that he has been pleased to continue to them their civil and religious privileges." Only a few country parsons and Dr. Pemberton read the proclamation. It was news thought worth printing in Pennsylvania that Massachusetts "Clergymen who could not conscientiously read" it said the congregations should

29. Dr. Rodgers also supplied ten key documents in an appendix. *The Case of the Scotch Presbyterians of the City of New-York* (New York, 1773), 3–8; appendix, 10–36; Smith, *Historical Memoirs*, 169; *N.Y. Col. Docs.*, VIII, 572–4.

"praise God for the mercies we *really* enjoy, not forgetting to bewail the loss of those privileges of which we are deprived by our fellow men." [30]

Late in 1772 the Boston Town Meeting voted favorably on Samuel Adams's motion to create a Committee of Correspondence to state "the Rights of the Colonists . . . as Men, as Christians, and as Subjects," and to communicate the same to the other towns of the province "and to the World"; this was the sort of thing Jonathan Mayhew had advocated to James Otis in 1766. On November 20, the Town Meeting approved a statement of rights and enumerations of the violations of these rights by British authorities, and ordered 600 copies printed for distribution. Locke was quoted on the right of "mutual toleration"; a strong anti-Roman spirit appeared in the assertion that never in the civil compact did men yield up to a government their essential and natural religious rights; and of course there was a striking, though concise, statement about "our Ancestors." Small wonder, then, that in writing his satire in 1775–76, John Trumbull knew that his readers would appreciate the reminiscences of the town-meeting orator, "great Squire M'Fingal":

> Did not the deeds of England's Primate
> First drive your fathers to this climate
> Whom jails and fines and every ill
> Forced to their good against their will?
>
> *   *   *
>
> Say, at what period did they grudge
> To send you Governor or Judge,
> With all their Missionary crew,
> To teach you law and gospel too?
> They brought all felons in the nation
> To help you on in population;
> Proposed their Bishops to surrender,
> And made their priests a legal tender,

---

30. Hutchinson to Bernard, Dec. 24, 1771, printed by Edes and Gill, *Bos. Gaz.*, Nov. 6, 1775; Jan. 21, Feb. 25, 1771; Stiles, *Literary Diary*, I, 85, 110; *Essex Gazette*, Oct. 29, 1771; *Pa. Chronicle*, Nov. 18, Dec. 2, 1771; Thomas Hutchinson's version is in his *History of Massachusetts-Bay*, II, 249–50.

Who only asked, in surplice clad,
The simple tithe of all you had.

* * *

In wide-sleeve pomp of godly guise,
What solemn rows of Bishops rise!
Aloft a Cardinal's hat is spread
O'er punster Cooper's reverend head.
In Vardell, that poetic zealot,
I view a lawn-bedizen'd Prelate;
While mitres fall, as 'tis their duty,
On heads of Chandler and Auchmuty.[31]

Closely related to the issue of episcopacy in the colonial mind
was the hereditary fear of Rome, which the colonists shared with
the English, especially the Nonconformists. Genuine, if misplaced,
concern arose over the religious problems in the territories ceded
by France in 1763, which seemed borne out when orders were
twice issued to Governor Robert Melville of Grenada to admit
Roman Catholics to all offices in the island in preference to the
Protestants living there. To the northward in Canada and Nova
Scotia, the introduction of a Roman Catholic bishop was news that
was read in papers all up and down the coast, but it was the passage by Parliament of the Quebec Act in 1774 that seemed to confirm the worst fears about Roman Catholicism, not only of the
New Englanders but of all colonists. It was a silversmith and en-
graver, Paul Revere, however, who blended episcopacy and Ro-

31. Space does not permit discussion of the New England Baptists, who detested
episcopacy at the same time that they resented Congregational establishment. In
1769 the Reverend Morgan Edwards went to London to complain about persecution. To Thomas Hollis, a Baptist himself, "The Baptists of N.E. seem to have
been off their guard and duped by the Episcopalians." Stiles pointed out that the
denomination had been invited to join the Convention of Delegates, but had declined, in part because of Episcopal persuasion. Stiles, *Literary Diary*, I, 78, 169;
Smith, *Historical Memoirs*, I, 107, 172; Mass. Hist. Soc., *Collections*, 4 ser., IV,
455–6; Hollis to Eliot, Aug. 28, 1771, Hollis Papers; *Pa. Chronicle*, Jan. 21, 28,
Feb. 4, 1771. For the Committee of Correspondence, "Boston Town Records,
1770 through 1777," Record Commissioners of the City of Boston, *Eighteenth
Report* (Boston, 1887), 93, 94–7, 105; *Bos. News-Letter*, Dec. 17, 1772; *London
Chronicle*, July 1, 3, 1773; John Trumbull, "M'Fingal," Cantos I, II, The Town-
Meeting A.M. and P.M., in Vernon L. Parrington, *The Connecticut Wits* (New York,
1926), 60, 73, 74, 92.

manism indelibly in a vivid graphic form that even a child could understand, "The Mitred Minuet," produced for Joseph Greenleaf's *Royal American Magazine*. Proof that the children were aware of the issues of that day can be found in the diary of a twelve-year-old girl:

Dr. Pemberton and Dr. Cooper had on gowns, in the form of the Episcopal cassock we hear, the Docts. design to distinguish themselves from the inferior clergy by these strange habits (at a time too, when the good people of N.E. are threaten'd with, and dreading of an episcopal bishop). . . . Unkle says, they have all popes in their bellys.[32]

Many individuals from all the colonies and all classes gave a hand in fighting back the march of the Episcopalians, but the leadership came from the ministers. In 1781, the former Chief Justice Peter Oliver, a vitriolic arch-Tory, was not intending to compliment the pastors when he said it might not be amiss "to reconnoitre Mr. *Otis's* Black Regiment, *the dissenting Clergy,* who took so active a Part in the Rebellion"; Dr. Chauncy was "the Head Master of the School of Prophets" and Andrew Eliot his usher, and Oliver was not far from wrong. The Episcopalian menace had driven many Congregational ministers into politics, but if they could take "Fervidus" who wrote for the *Boston Gazette* as their guide, such action was "a most laudable, because a most necessary employment." [33]

The Convention of Delegates had been meeting regularly for some years; after 1773 the members had been concentrating on gathering materials for the history of religious liberty ordered by the convention for use as propaganda. The plan was a monumental one, for the ministers hoped to cover every continental colony including Nova Scotia and the two Floridas. In conjunction with this, they undertook to collect data for a history of the colonial colleges

32. Mass. Hist. Soc., *Collections,* 4 ser., IV, 448; *N.H. Gaz.,* May 10, 1771; *Bos. Eve. Post,* Feb. 3, 1772; *Mass. Spy,* June 6, 1771; Mar. 26, June 4, 1772; Jan. 14, 21, 1773; *Pennsylvania Packet,* Oct. 31, 1774; Henry C. Lodge, *The Works of Alexander Hamilton* (New York, 1904), I, 181, 187–96; *N.Y. Journal,* Mar. 30, 1775; Alice M. Earle, *Diary of Anna Green Winslow* (Boston, 1894), 14–15; *Royal American Magazine* (October, 1774), facing p. 126.

33. Peter Oliver, The Origin and Progress of the American Rebellion (Egerton MSS, 2671, Br. Museum: L.C. Transcript), 45; *Bos. Gaz.,* May 18, 1772.

and seminaries of learning. Some progress was reported when the convention met at Greenfield, Connecticut, in 1775, and it was voted to obtain in addition some accounts of the several religious sects in addition to histories already under way; then the meeting was adjourned to convene again the next year at Elizabeth Town. But the histories were never completed and the meeting was not held; the essential need for them no longer existed after July 4, 1776. The Christian Union had been achieved, and so the memorable experiment came to an end.[34]

VI

John Adams never tired of emphasizing the important distinction between the American Revolution and the War for Independence. "The revolution was in the minds and hearts of the people, and in the union of the colonies; both of which were substantially effected before hostilities commenced." This "great intellectual, moral, and political change" occurred when the designs of the British Government dawned upon the colonists during the fifteen years before the Battle of Lexington. "The rise and progress of this knowledge, the gradual expansion and diffusion of the change in the minds of the people and the growing hopes of a union . . . cannot be traced but by a diligent perusal of the pamphlets, newspapers, and handbills of both parties, and the proceedings of the legislatures from 1761 to 1774, when the union of the colonies was formed." [35]

The issue of mitre and sceptre had been a *constant*, to use a mathematical term, in Anglo-American relations ever since 1630, even in the Episcopal colonies, where congregational polity existed in fact, whatever the theory, in the parish vestries. Specifically, for eighty-six years after 1689, Episcopal pressure increased intermittently but inexorably. This was a very long time, during which the minds and emotions of three — occasionally four — generations of dissenting colonists were unconsciously conditioned for revolt.

The Dissenters of England and America, allied in defense of what they conceived to be their natural religious liberties, worked out

34. *Convention of Delegates,* 40, 45, 46, 47, 48; *Records of the Presbyterian Church,* 473.

35. Adams, *Works,* X, 172–3, 180, 182, 184, 185–6, 188, 288, 313.

the first great voluntary transatlantic organization of the English-speaking peoples. On the Western shore, the dissenting ministry achieved the first effective intercolonial arrangement, one which adumbrated political union and contributed a useful device to it. Herein American dissent provides the spectacle of a genuine addition to the political organization of the emerging American people suited to the requirements of a great continental area.

In part the suspicions of the sincerity and true motives of the leaders of the Church of England grew out of the open and unabashed attempts of the Anglican missionaries to dominate America in the sphere of religion. They were constantly trying to proselyte among the Nonconformists of the thickly settled areas, to improve their own social position at the expense of humiliation of the Dissenters, or to secure political power in order to attain ultimately complete establishment (though of course this was unvoiced in America). These pursuits made an indelible impression on the American mind.

Organized Dissent in Britain and America employed the press with a thoroughness and success unknown elsewhere in that age. The Nonconformist ministers belonged to the fourth quite as much as to the first estate of the old British Empire. With some help from the laity, they built a propaganda machine with which they fixed in the minds of the English Nonconformists and almost the entire American public, once and for all, the idea of the identity of religious and civil liberty. And in the colonial mind, the members of Otis's Black Regiment firmly implanted the thought that the British Government's designs had evil potentials for religion quite as much as for politics.

Anglican intrigues in the Middle Colonies forced the Dissenting pastors into politics; in New England they were already there. Out of the frequently unseemly contests between curate and minister grew the characteristically American notion that the clergy have no place in the doings of legislative assemblies. Furthermore, the colonial Episcopal clergy, by their preaching of nonresistance, passive submission, and above all, by their almost unanimous support of the Stamp Act, became the nucleus around which the Tory Party formed. This legacy led the patriots to link those "inimical" to their cause with Episcopacy.

There appears to be little doubt that if the American rebellion had been suppressed, not only the dispatch of bishops but the establishment of the Church of England in the colonies would have ensued. As late as 1774, one who had long resided in the New World sent a scheme to Lord North and followed it up with a letter to the *Gazetteer* proposing a gradual increase in the strength of the Church in America, because the colonial troubles were caused by "the fanatics, chiefly . . . few or none of the Church of England . . . being among the refractory." Ambrose Serle encountered the Reverend Charles Inglis in 1777, and the two:

Passed an agreeable hour in Conversation . . . relative to the ecclesiastical Establishment in these Colonies [after their defeat], on the necessity and Manner of which we agreed.[36]

One striking aspect of this history of church and state in England and her colonies was the political ineptitude of a politically minded clergy. However reasonable the pleas for bishops without political authority might be — and frequently this was conceded — they did not convince the Nonconformists that the framers had no ulterior motives, and, as we know, good reason for such doubts existed. Furthermore the Venerable Society seemed to excel in making ill-timed moves. A large majority of the episodes with which we have concerned ourselves in this volume and which engendered so much bitterness on both sides originated in the conclaves of the Anglican clergy in America. We cannot, of course, place the entire blame for the ecclesiastical strife of eighteenth-century America solely on the missionaries; they were, after all, merely understrappers.

It was the hierarchy of the Church of England, managing an ecclesiastical empire without the knowledge of the most vital facts, for they displayed an ignorance of religious conditions and systems in the colonies, that made such blunders possible. No High-Church

36. Leslie M. Broughton, *Edmund Burke Selections* (New York, 1925), 149, 150, 152; Harry H. Clark, *Thomas Paine: Representative Selections* (New York, 1944), 21, 41; Joseph Priestly, *An Address to the Protestant Dissenters of all Denominations on the Approaching Election of Members of Parliament. . . .* (London, 1774); Edward H. Tatum, Jr., *The American Journal of Ambrose Serle* (San Marino, 1940), 89–90, 115–16, 131, 196, 209, 277; Joseph Galloway, *Historical and Political Reflections on the Rise and Progress of the American Revolution* (London, 1780), 11–12; David Ramsay, *History of the American Revolution* (Philadephia, 1789), I, 26, 27, 28, 29, 31; *Gazetteer, and New Daily Advertiser,* Apr. 6, 1774.

official ever crossed to investigate the situation in America; only one person, an unknown and inconsequential layman, was ever authorized to do so. The Church of England must, therefore, share with the English political system, Parliament, and the Crown the responsibility for the loss of the colonies.

The great controversy over church and state profoundly stimulated the growth, after 1740, of a sense of American nationality. The most "American" fact about the English colonies, aside from the huge natural environment, was their varied religious composition and ecclesiastical organization, which figured far more in the lives of most of the inhabitants than government and politics, even of the local variety. One thing the missionaries did accomplish: their activities caused colonial Dissenters and most of the Southern clergy, and Anglican laity, to draw together years before the program of British politicians created a similar reaction. Republicanism in church quite as much as in state was the form of polity congenial to these people. To buttress their belief in their religious and civil institutions, they availed themselves of their historical tradition which, because of almost universal literacy, was more widely shared by the "public" than in any European country. Indubitably religion provided the foundation for early American nationalism.

VII

The protestations of the colonial Dissenters that they had no quarrel with the Church of England or its members but only with the hierarchy turned out to be true. Bishop White made a strong point about this in his *Memoirs*. The fundamental conviction emerging from the long war of words was that in America there should be no union of church and state effected by bishops and the accompaniments of a complete establishment. This was a *universal colonial belief,* one held by Anglicans as well as Dissenters. In the remarkable series of state constitutions — the first such written documents of history — framed between 1776 and 1784, provisions were inserted providing for disestablishing the Church of England from Maryland to Georgia (Virginia's celebrated statute was passed in January, 1786). As the North Carolina instrument tersely stated: "There shall be no establishment of any one religious church or denomination in this State, in preference to any other." Delaware and New York also eliminated the preferred position of the Anglican Church. In the latter state, where the bitterest colonial conflict took place, the Constitution of 1777 provided that all parts of the common law and statutes "as may be construed to establish or maintain any particular denomination of Christians or their ministers . . . hereby are, abrogated and rejected." Thus ended the Ministry Act of 1693! On the positive side, the New York constitution guaranteed "the free exercise and enjoyment of religious profession and worship," and thereafter incorporation by the Presbyterians met no obstacle. Only New Hampshire, Massachusetts, and Connecticut, where the Congregationalists made up the overwhelming majority of the population, retained a quasi-established church, but even there all sects enjoyed a much improved position.[37]

In commenting upon a recent stamp tax levied by the Massachusetts legislature and the appointment of Samuel Seabury as the first Episcopal bishop for the United States, the *Boston Gazette* in March, 1785, exclaimed:

TWO WONDERS OF THE WORLD — a Stamp Act in Boston and a Bishop in Connecticut.[38]

Religious freedom, seeds of which had been transplanted from England, germinated in the rich and varied American soils. No longer could the Dissenters be called dissenters. They no longer had need of the firm support their English brethren always accorded them in former years; nor could they return anything more than fraternal sympathy to those who still labored under religious disabilities. Although the declared fact of religious liberty had not

37. For the religious provisions of the several state constitutions, see Francis N. Thorpe, ed., *The Federal and State Constitutions, Colonial Charters, and other Organic Laws of the States, Territories, and Colonies . . . now . . . Forming in the United States of America* (Washington, 1909), I, 566; II, 779, 784, 785; III, 1689–90, 1697, 1700, 1889, 1890, 1900, 1903, 1906, 1908, 1909; IV, 2451; V, 2597–8, 2636–7, 2788, 2793, 3082; VI, 3253, 3740, 3741; VII, 3814, 3817. For the Articles of Confederation, Samuel E. Morison, *Sources and Documents illustrating the American Revolution* (Oxford, 1951), 178.

38. *Bos. Gaz.*, May 30, 1785.

yet been achieved everywhere, when the English Nonconformists published an impressive four-volume history in 1812, they recorded with evident pride the rapid religious recovery of the former colonies after the Peace of 1783:

It has been asserted, indeed, that there scarcely ever was a body of men collected for war so humane and moral, and who returned to their farms so little corrupted, as those who composed the American army; and the religious liberty which the new republic established, was so complete, that the dearest rights and interests of men were eminently promoted by the revolution.[39]

39. Bogue and Bennett, *History of the Dissenters,* IV, 494.

Short-Title List of Manuscripts

It has not been thought necessary to append any formal bibliography to this study. The footnotes indicate the newspapers, pamphlets, printed sources, and the few secondary authorities used. These will be already familiar to most scholars; the full reference has been given the first time a source is cited. Below is a short-title and finding list of the principal manuscripts cited.

DISSENTING DEPUTIES, MINUTES. The Protestant Dissenting Deputies, Minutes, Volumes I, II (Nov. 9, 1732—May 20, 1791). City of London Library, Guildhall. Dr. Williams's Library has a negative microfilm, from which, through the good offices of Dr. J. R. Pole, Mr. Roger Thomas kindly supplied a positive copy.

FULHAM PALACE MSS. Archives of the Bishop of London, Fulham Palace. Transcripts in the Library of Congress, Washington, D.C.

HOLLIS, DIARY. Thomas Hollis, Diary, 1759–1770. Original privately owned in London. There is a two-volume typed transcript, paged continuously, in the Institute of Early American History and Culture, Williamsburg, Va. Loaned by the courtesy of Dr. Lester J. Cappon.

HOLLIS, PAPERS. Thomas Hollis Papers, one volume, Massachusetts Historical Society, Boston.

HAWKS PAPERS. Letters of Samuel Johnson, Hawks MSS, II, New-York Historical Society, New York City.

JOHNSON FAMILY PAPERS. A Collection of [81] Letters from my good Friend & Ingenious Correspondent Mr. Wm. Livingston, 1742–1773. Johnson Family Papers, Sterling Memorial Library, Yale University, New Haven, Conn. Used by permission of the Librarian, James T. Babb.

LIVINGSTON PAPERS. William Livingston Papers, Box 1; Folder 1761–1777; Letter Book A. Mass. Hist. Soc.

MAYHEW PAPERS. Reverend Jonathan Mayhew Papers, Mark Bortman Collection, Boston University. Used through the courtesy of Professor Robert E. Moody.

THREE DENOMINATIONS, MINUTE BOOK. Minute Books of the Body of Protestant Ministers of the Three Denominations in and about the City of London. Volumes I, II (1727–1797), Dr. Williams's Library, Gordon Square, London. Film kindly supplied by the librarian, Roger Thomas.

S.P.G. CORRESPONDENCE. Society for the Propagation of the Gospel in Foreign Parts, Correspondence. Series B. Transcripts and films in Library of Congress.

STILES PAPERS. Ezra Stiles Papers. Sterling Memorial Library, Yale University, New Haven, Conn. Used by permission of the Librarian, James T. Babb.

Index